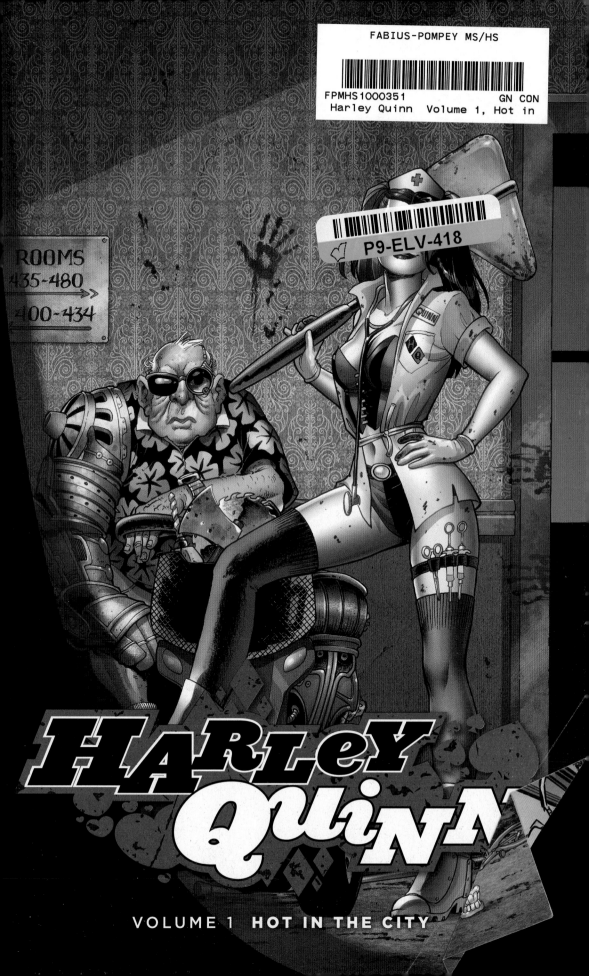

ROOMS
435-480 ▸▸
400-434

# HARLEY QUINN

VOLUME 1  HOT IN THE CITY

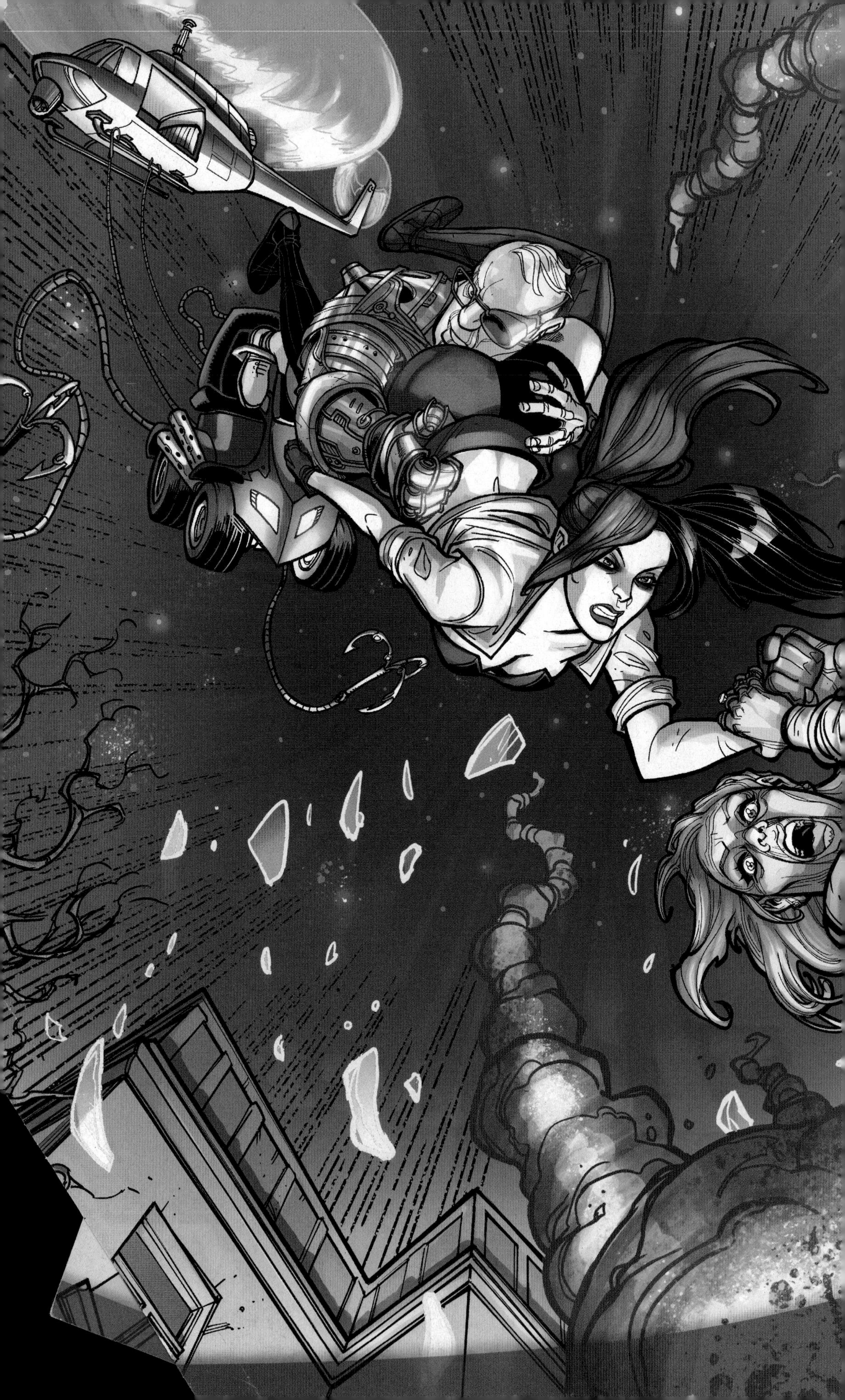

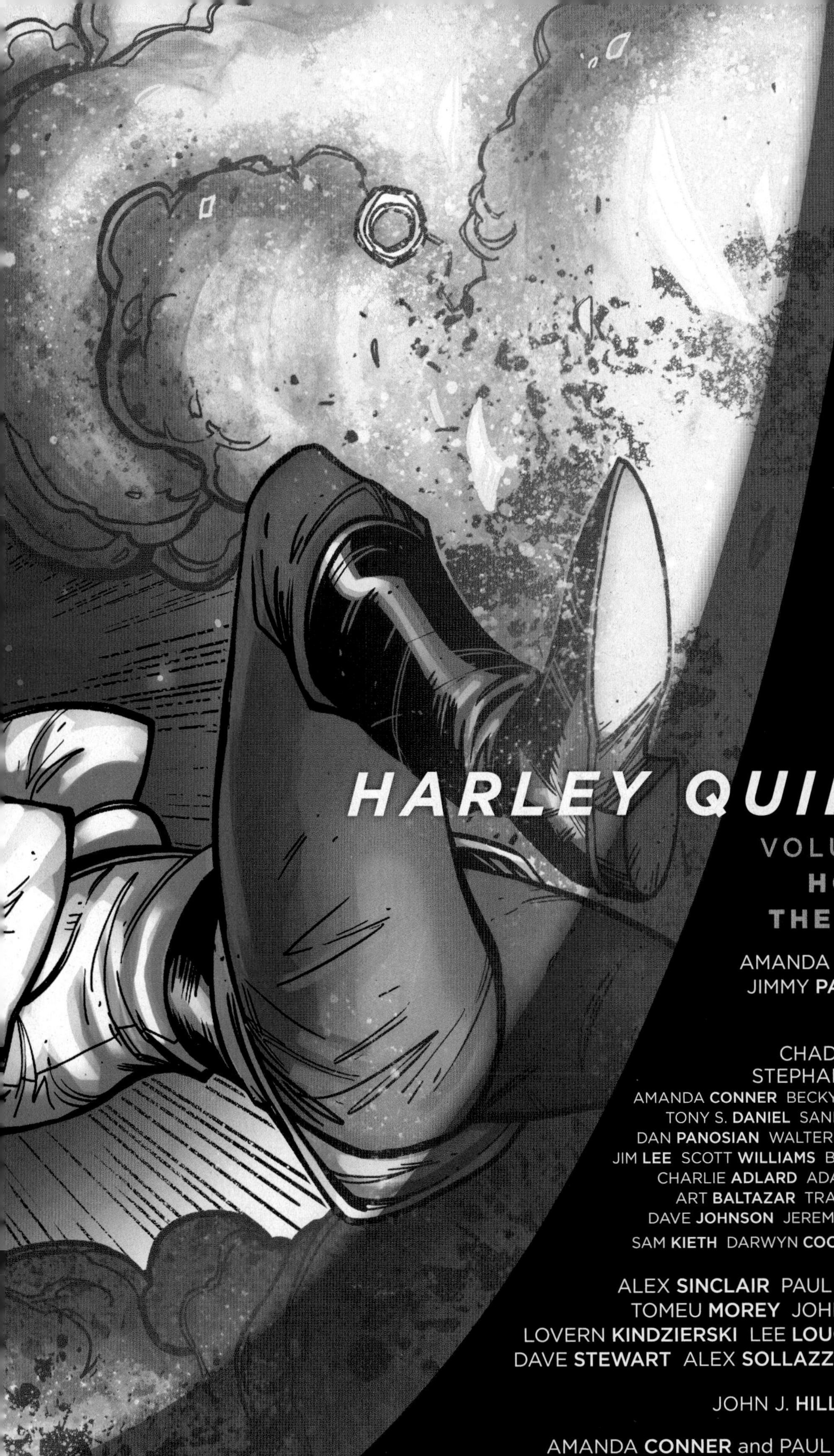

# HARLEY QUINN

## VOLUME 1

## HOT IN THE CITY


AMANDA **CONNER**
JIMMY **PALMIOTTI**
writers

CHAD **HARDIN**
STEPHANE **ROUX**
AMANDA **CONNER** BECKY **CLOONAN**
TONY S. **DANIEL** SANDU **FLOREA**
DAN **PANOSIAN** WALTER **SIMONSON**
JIM **LEE** SCOTT **WILLIAMS** BRUCE **TIMM**
CHARLIE **ADLARD** ADAM **HUGHES**
ART **BALTAZAR** TRADD **MOORE**
DAVE **JOHNSON** JEREMY **ROBERTS**
SAM **KIETH** DARWYN **COOKE** artists

ALEX **SINCLAIR** PAUL **MOUNTS**
TOMEU **MOREY** JOHN **KALISZ**
LOVERN **KINDZIERSKI** LEE **LOUGHRIDGE**
DAVE **STEWART** ALEX **SOLLAZZO** colorist

JOHN J. **HILL** letterers

AMANDA **CONNER** and PAUL **MOUNTS**
collection cover artists


**HARLEY QUINN** created by PAUL **DINI** & BRUCE **TIMM**

KATIE KUBERT  CHRIS CONROY Editors – Original Series  MATT HUMPHREYS Assistant Editor – Original Series
JEB WOODARD Group Editor – Collected Editions  PETER HAMBOUSSI Editor – Collected Edition  ROBBIE BIEDERMAN Publication Design

BOB HARRAS Senior VP – Editor-in-Chief, DC Comics

DIANE NELSON President  DAN DIDIO and JIM LEE Co-Publishers
GEOFF JOHNS Chief Creative Officer  AMIT DESAI Senior VP – Marketing & Global Franchise Management
NAIRI GARDINER Senior VP – Finance  SAM ADES VP – Digital Marketing  BOBBIE CHASE VP – Talent Development
MARK CHIARELLO Senior VP – Art, Design & Collected Editions  JOHN CUNNINGHAM VP – Content Strategy
ANNE DEPIES VP – Strategy Planning & Reporting  DON FALLETTI VP – Manufacturing Operations
LAWRENCE GANEM VP – Editorial Administration & Talent Relations  ALISON GILL Senior VP – Manufacturing & Operations
HANK KANALZ Senior VP – Editorial Strategy & Administration  JAY KOGAN VP – Legal Affairs
DEREK MADDALENA Senior VP – Sales & Business Development  JACK MAHAN VP – Business Affairs
DAN MIRON VP – Sales Planning & Trade Development  NICK NAPOLITANO VP – Manufacturing Administration
CAROL ROEDER VP – Marketing  EDDIE SCANNELL VP – Mass Account & Digital Sales
COURTNEY SIMMONS Senior VP – Publicity & Communications  JIM (SKI) SOKOLOWSKI VP – Comic Book Specialty & Newsstand Sales
SANDY YI Senior VP – Global Franchise Management

HARLEY QUINN VOLUME 1: HOT IN THE CITY

DC Comics, 2900 W. Alameda Avenue, Burbank, CA 91505
Printed by Transcontinental Interglobe Beauceville, Canada. 4/22/16. Third Printing.
ISBN: 978-1-4012-5415-5

Library of Congress Cataloging-in-Publication Data

Palmiotti, Jimmy, author.
Harley Quinn. Volume 1, Hot in the city / Jimmy Palmiotti, Amanda Conner.
pages cm. — (The New 52!)
Includes bibliographical references and index.
ISBN 978-1-4012-4892-5 (hardback)
1. Graphic novels.  I. Conner, Amanda, illustrator. II. Title. III. Title: Hot in the city.

PN6728.H367P35 2014
741.5'973—dc23

2014034093

PEFC Certified
Printed on paper from
sustainably managed
forests and controlled
sources
PEFC/01-31-106   www.pefc.org

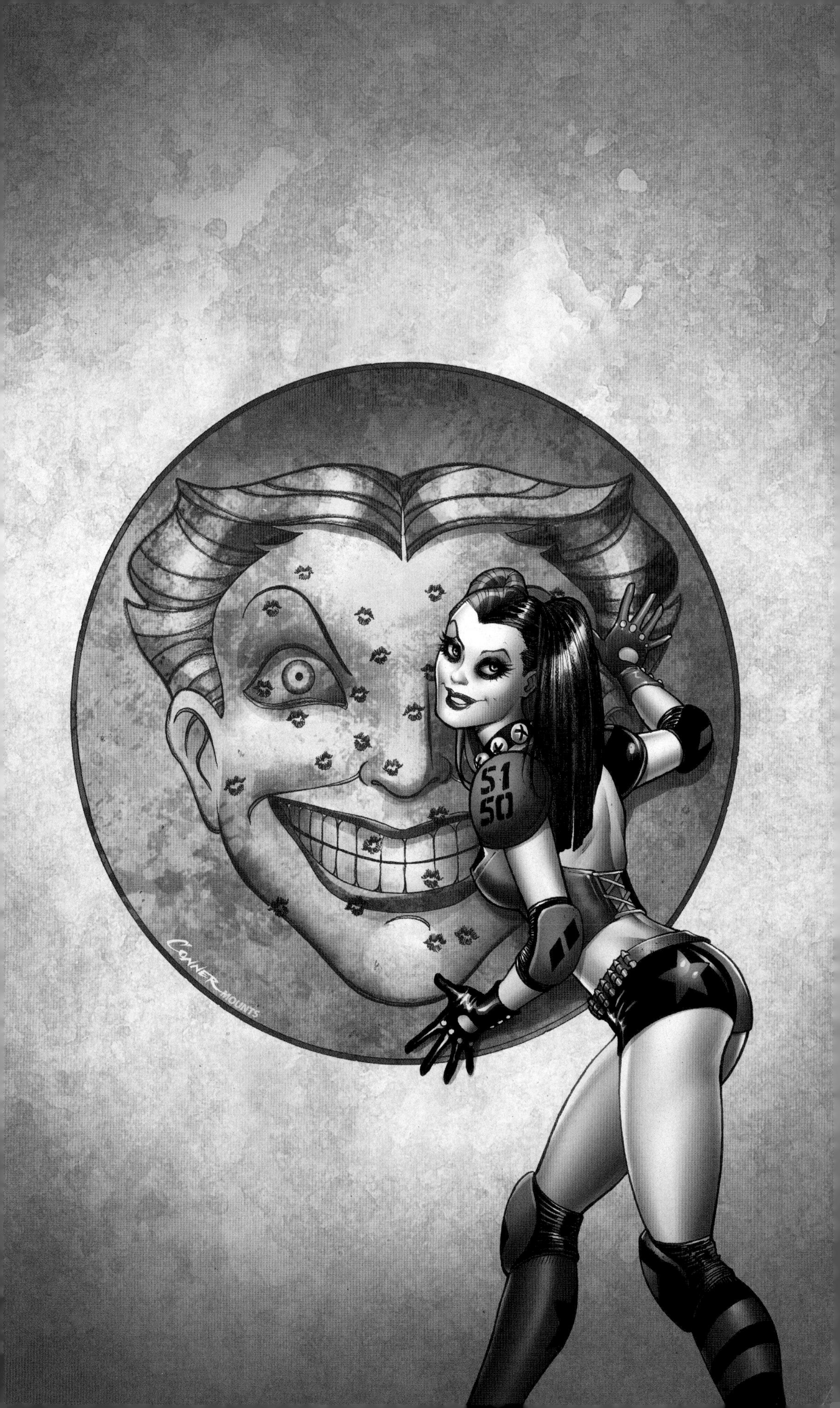
51
50
CONNER
MOUNTS

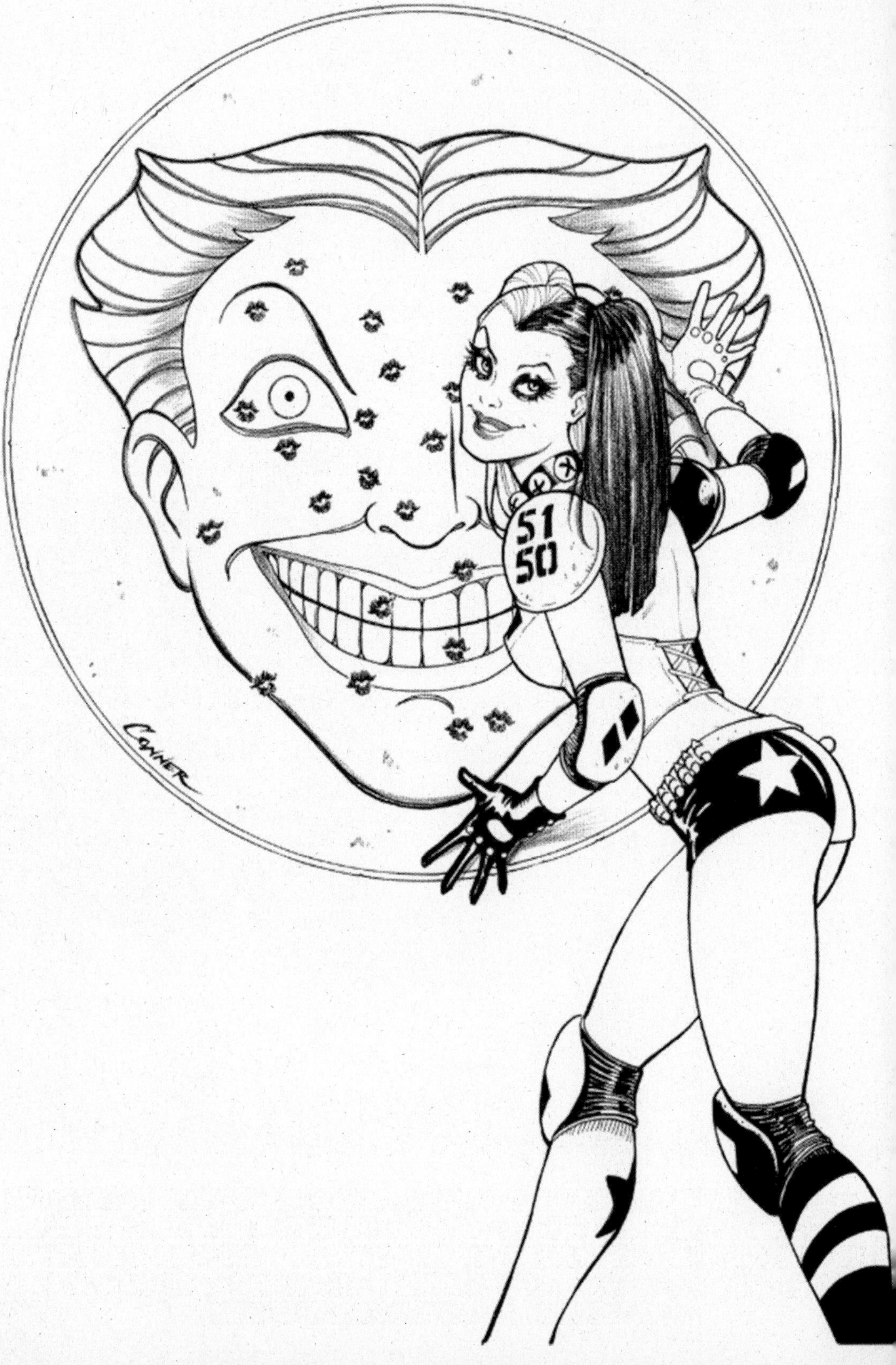
51
50
CONNER

I DON'T KNOW WHAT I'D DO WITHOUT THESE WONDERFUL *DISTRACTIONS* IN MY LIFE.

OH, FRUITCAKES.
YOU'RE SO *FULL* OF IT.
DAN JACKALS SOUR MASH WHISKEY
YEAH... YOU'RE RIGHT.

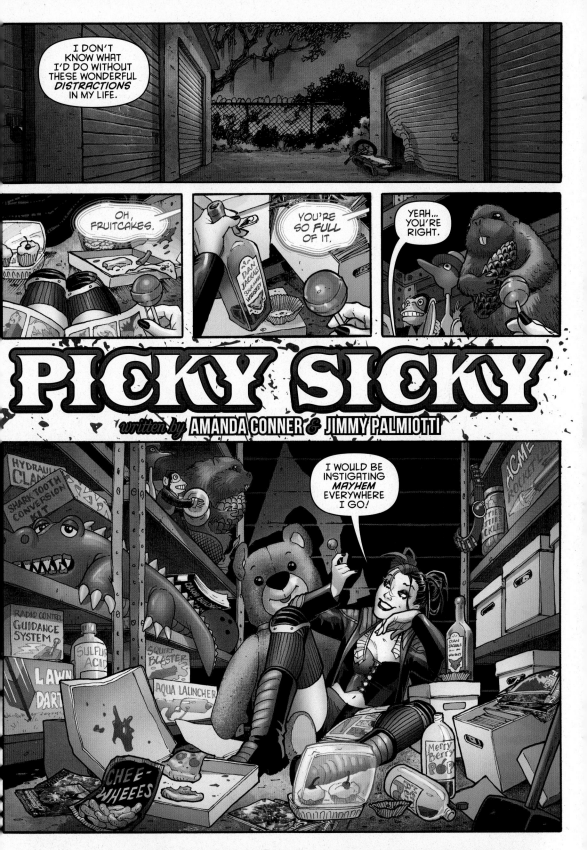

# PICKY SICKY

*written by* AMANDA CONNER & JIMMY PALMIOTTI

I WOULD BE INSTIGATING *MAYHEM* EVERYWHERE I GO!
SHARK TOOTH CONVERSION KIT
GUIDANCE SYSTEM
SQUIRT BLASTER
AQUA LAUNCHER
CHEE-WHEEES
Merry Berry POP

*art by* AMANDA CONNER • BECKY CLOONAN • TONY S. DANIEL & SANDU FLOREA • STEPHANE ROUX • DAN PANOSIAN
WALTER SIMONSON • JIM LEE & SCOTT WILLIAMS • BRUCE TIMM • CHARLIE ADLARD • ADAM HUGHES • ART BALTAZAR
TRADD MOORE • DAVE JOHNSON • JEREMY ROBERTS • SAM KIETH • DARWYN COOKE • CHAD HARDIN *colors by* PAUL MOUNTS
TOMEU MOREY • JOHN KALISZ • LOVERN KINDZIERSKI • ALEX SINCLAIR • LEE LOUGHRIDGE • DAVE STEWART • ALEX SOLLAZZO
*letters by* JOHN J. HILL *cover by* AMANDA CONNER & PAUL MOUNTS

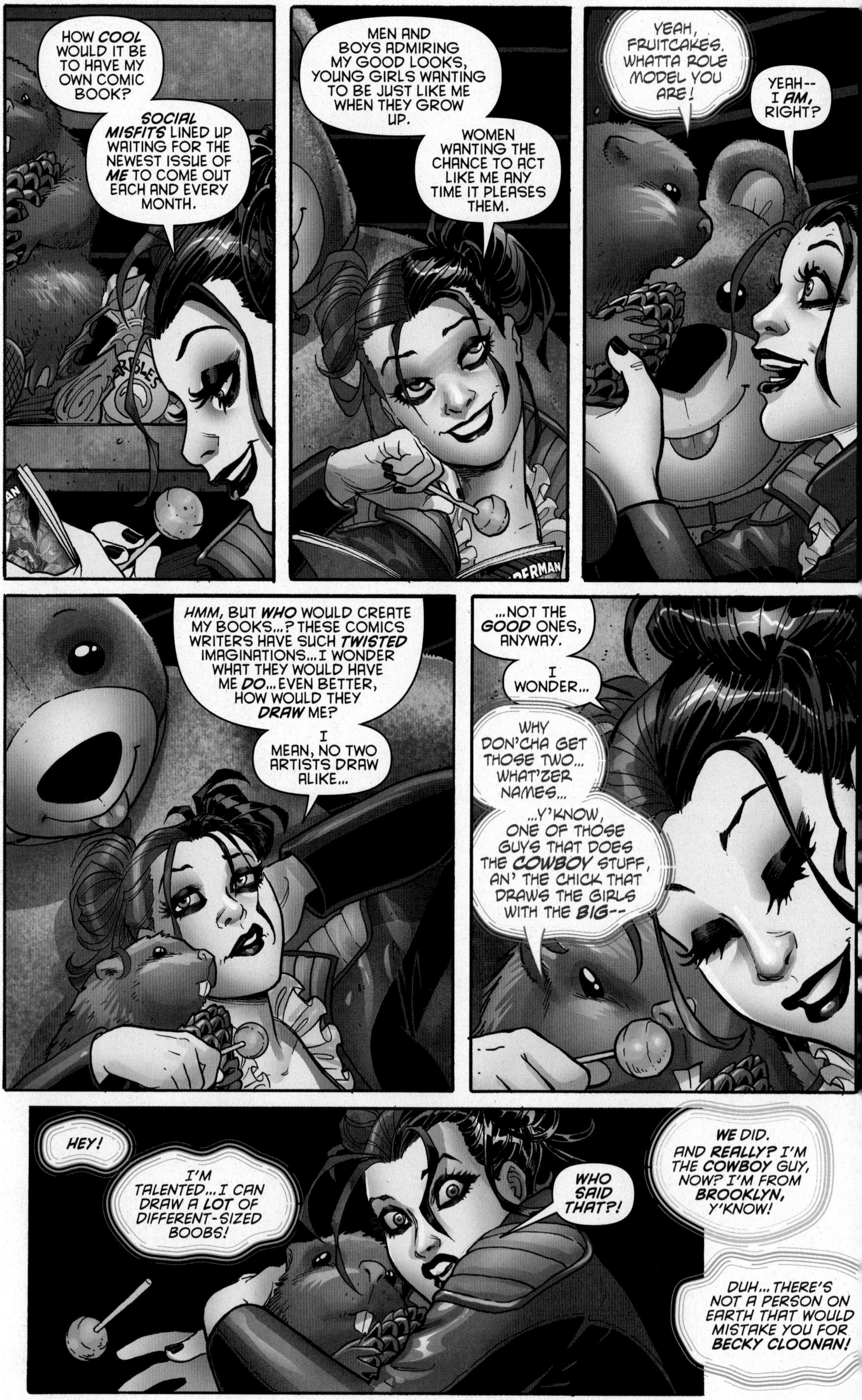

HOW COOL WOULD IT BE TO HAVE MY OWN COMIC BOOK?
SOCIAL MISFITS LINED UP WAITING FOR THE NEWEST ISSUE OF ME TO COME OUT EACH AND EVERY MONTH.
MEN AND BOYS ADMIRING MY GOOD LOOKS, YOUNG GIRLS WANTING TO BE JUST LIKE ME WHEN THEY GROW UP.
WOMEN WANTING THE CHANCE TO ACT LIKE ME ANY TIME IT PLEASES THEM.
YEAH, FRUITCAKES. WHATTA ROLE MODEL YOU ARE!
YEAH-- I AM, RIGHT?
HMM, BUT WHO WOULD CREATE MY BOOKS...? THESE COMICS WRITERS HAVE SUCH TWISTED IMAGINATIONS...I WONDER WHAT THEY WOULD HAVE ME DO...EVEN BETTER, HOW WOULD THEY DRAW ME?
I MEAN, NO TWO ARTISTS DRAW ALIKE...
...NOT THE GOOD ONES, ANYWAY.
I WONDER...
WHY DON'CHA GET THOSE TWO... WHAT'ZER NAMES...
...Y'KNOW, ONE OF THOSE GUYS THAT DOES THE COWBOY STUFF, AN' THE CHICK THAT DRAWS THE GIRLS WITH THE BIG--
HEY!
I'M TALENTED...I CAN DRAW A LOT OF DIFFERENT-SIZED BOOBS!
WHO SAID THAT?!
WE DID. AND REALLY? I'M THE COWBOY GUY, NOW? I'M FROM BROOKLYN, Y'KNOW!
DUH...THERE'S NOT A PERSON ON EARTH THAT WOULD MISTAKE YOU FOR BECKY CLOONAN!

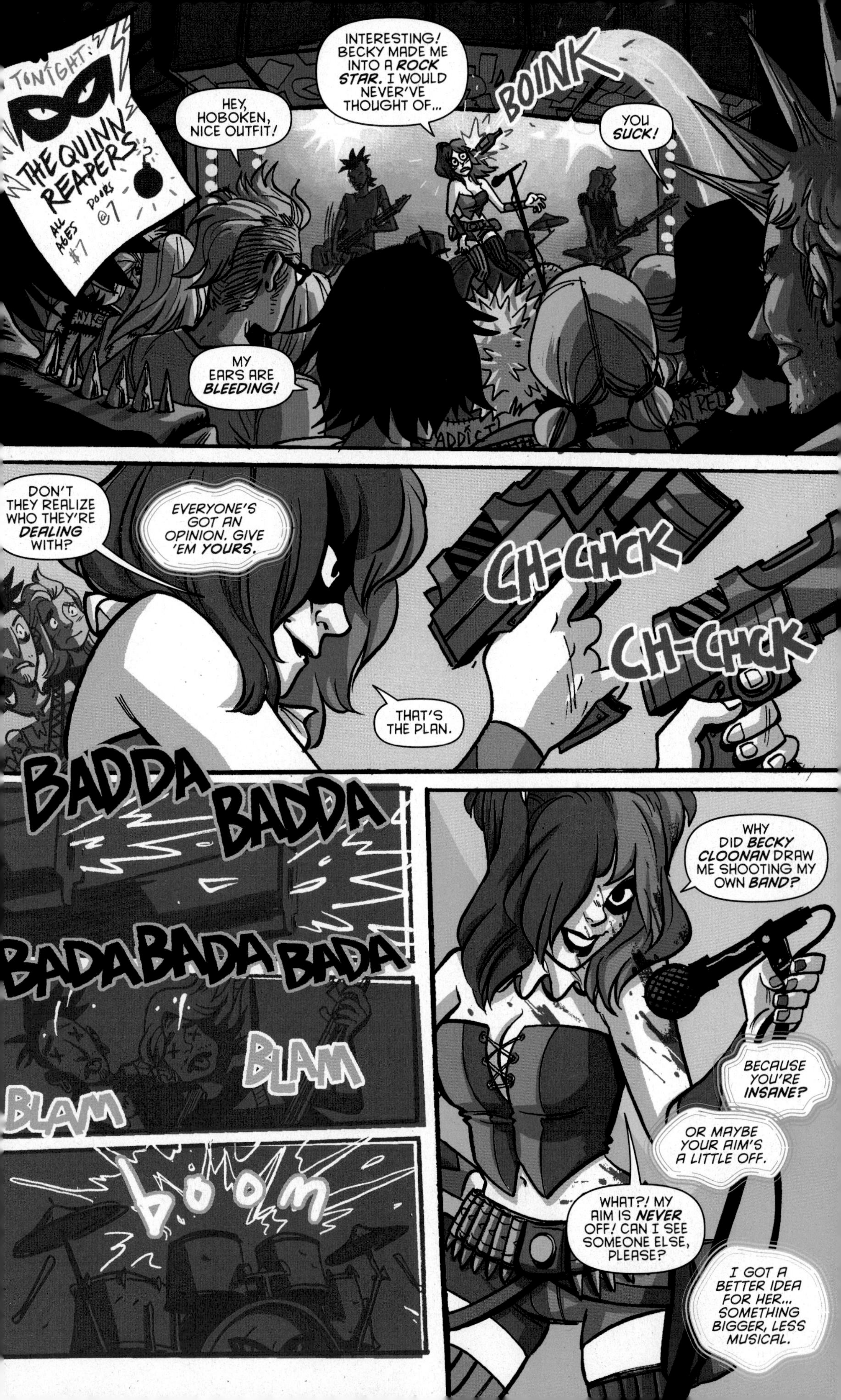

TONIGHT: THE QUINN REAPERS
ALL AGES $7
DOORS @7
HEY, HOBOKEN, NICE OUTFIT!
INTERESTING! BECKY MADE ME INTO A ROCK STAR. I WOULD NEVER'VE THOUGHT OF...
BOINK
YOU SUCK!
MY EARS ARE BLEEDING!
DON'T THEY REALIZE WHO THEY'RE DEALING WITH?
EVERYONE'S GOT AN OPINION. GIVE 'EM YOURS.
CH-CHCK
CH-CHCK
THAT'S THE PLAN.
BADDA BADDA
BADA BADA BADA
BLAM
BLAM
b o o m
WHY DID BECKY CLOONAN DRAW ME SHOOTING MY OWN BAND?
BECAUSE YOU'RE INSANE?
OR MAYBE YOUR AIM'S A LITTLE OFF.
WHAT?! MY AIM IS NEVER OFF! CAN I SEE SOMEONE ELSE, PLEASE?
I GOT A BETTER IDEA FOR HER... SOMETHING BIGGER, LESS MUSICAL.

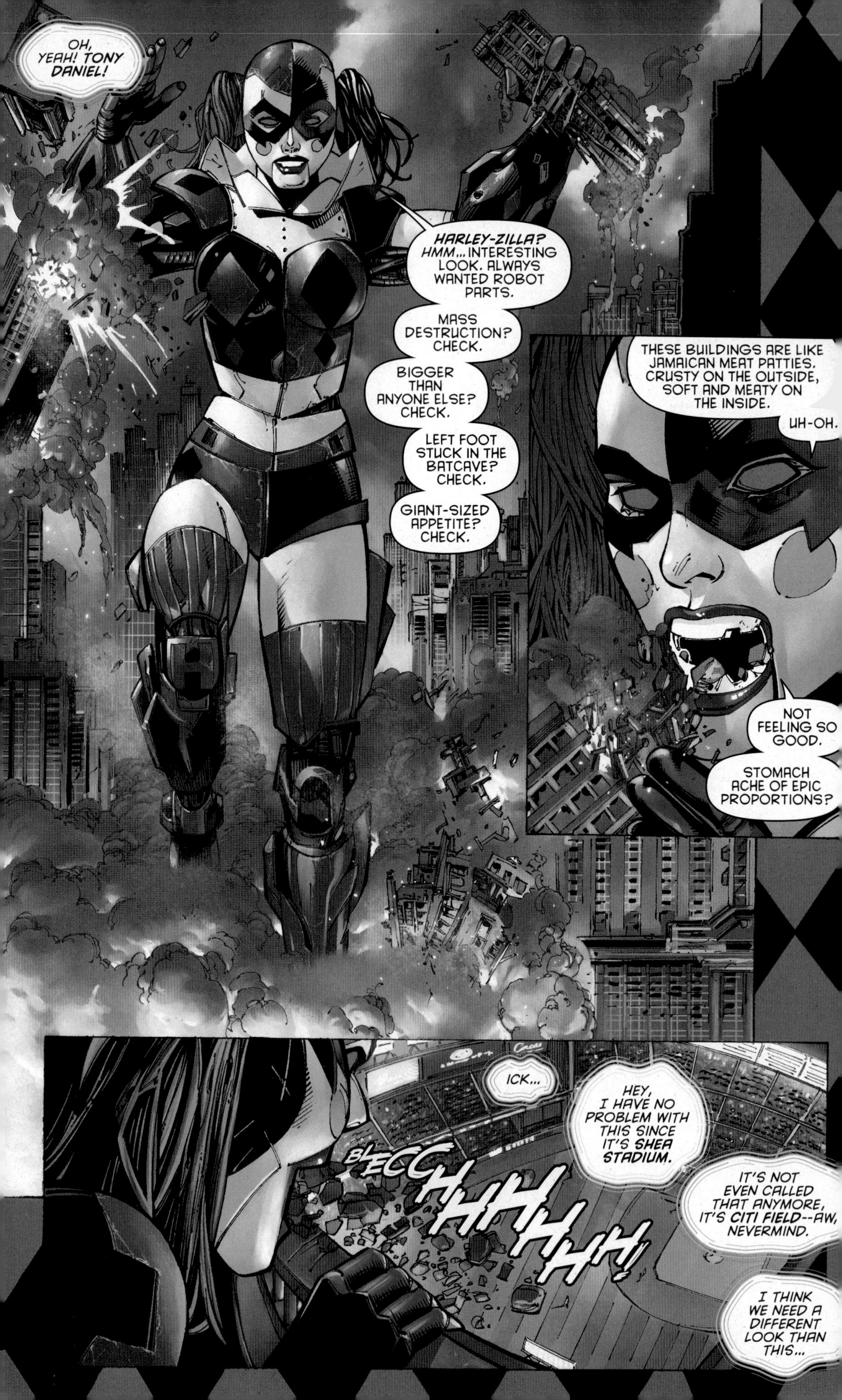
OH, YEAH! TONY DANIEL!
HARLEY-ZILLA? HMM... INTERESTING LOOK. ALWAYS WANTED ROBOT PARTS.
MASS DESTRUCTION? CHECK.
BIGGER THAN ANYONE ELSE? CHECK.
LEFT FOOT STUCK IN THE BATCAVE? CHECK.
GIANT-SIZED APPETITE? CHECK.
THESE BUILDINGS ARE LIKE JAMAICAN MEAT PATTIES. CRUSTY ON THE OUTSIDE, SOFT AND MEATY ON THE INSIDE.
UH-OH.
NOT FEELING SO GOOD.
STOMACH ACHE OF EPIC PROPORTIONS?
ICK...
BLECCHHHHHHH!
HEY, I HAVE NO PROBLEM WITH THIS SINCE IT'S SHEA STADIUM.
IT'S NOT EVEN CALLED THAT ANYMORE, IT'S CITI FIELD--AW, NEVERMIND.
I THINK WE NEED A DIFFERENT LOOK THAN THIS...

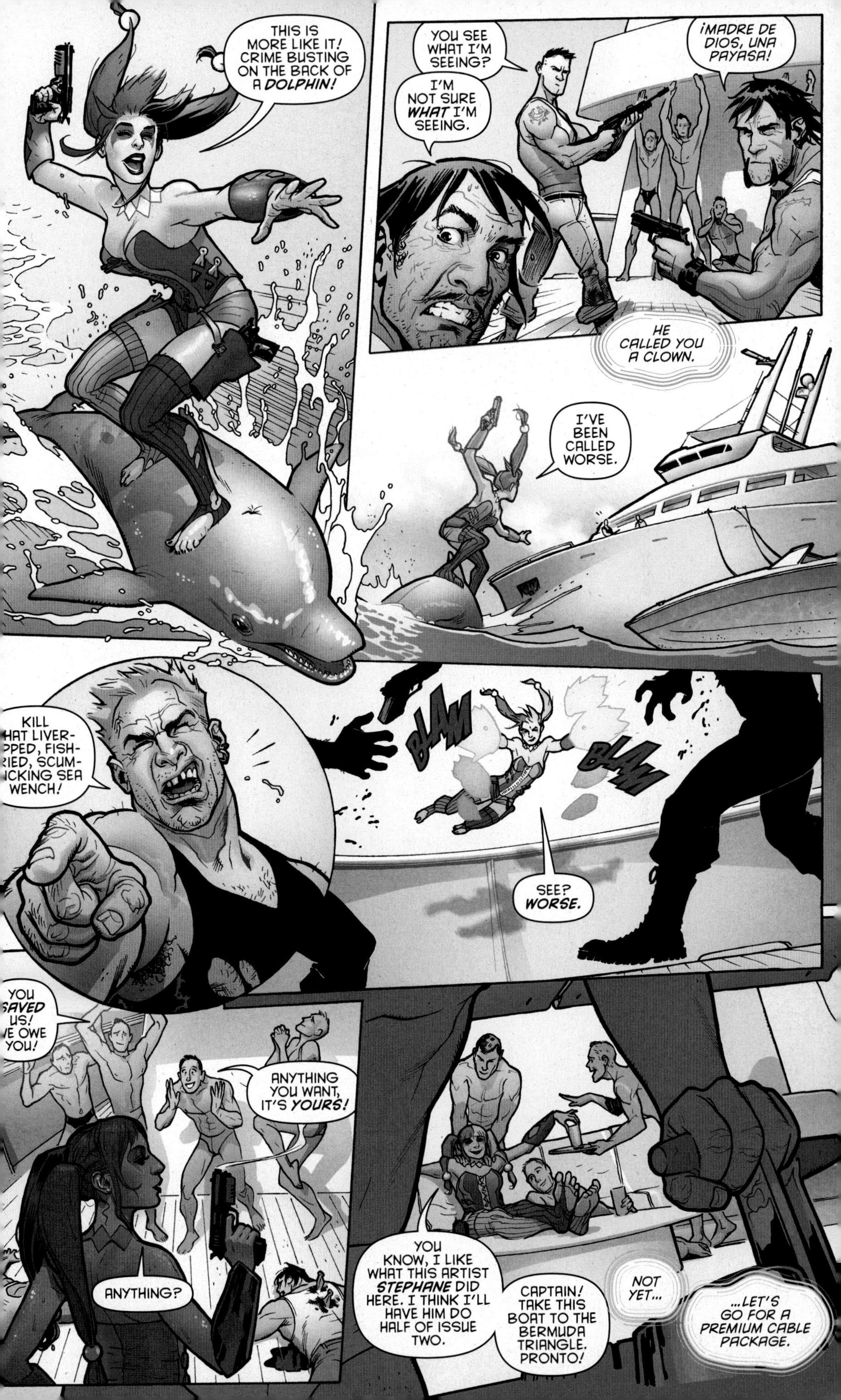
THIS IS MORE LIKE IT! CRIME BUSTING ON THE BACK OF A DOLPHIN!
YOU SEE WHAT I'M SEEING?
I'M NOT SURE WHAT I'M SEEING.
¡MADRE DE DIOS, UNA PAYASA!
HE CALLED YOU A CLOWN.
I'VE BEEN CALLED WORSE.
KILL HAT LIVER-PPED, FISH-RIED, SCUM-ICKING SEA WENCH!
BLAM
BLAM
SEE? WORSE.
YOU SAVED US! E OWE YOU!
ANYTHING YOU WANT, IT'S YOURS!
ANYTHING?
YOU KNOW, I LIKE WHAT THIS ARTIST STEPHANE DID HERE. I THINK I'LL HAVE HIM DO HALF OF ISSUE TWO.
CAPTAIN! TAKE THIS BOAT TO THE BERMUDA TRIANGLE. PRONTO!
NOT YET...
...LET'S GO FOR A PREMIUM CABLE PACKAGE.

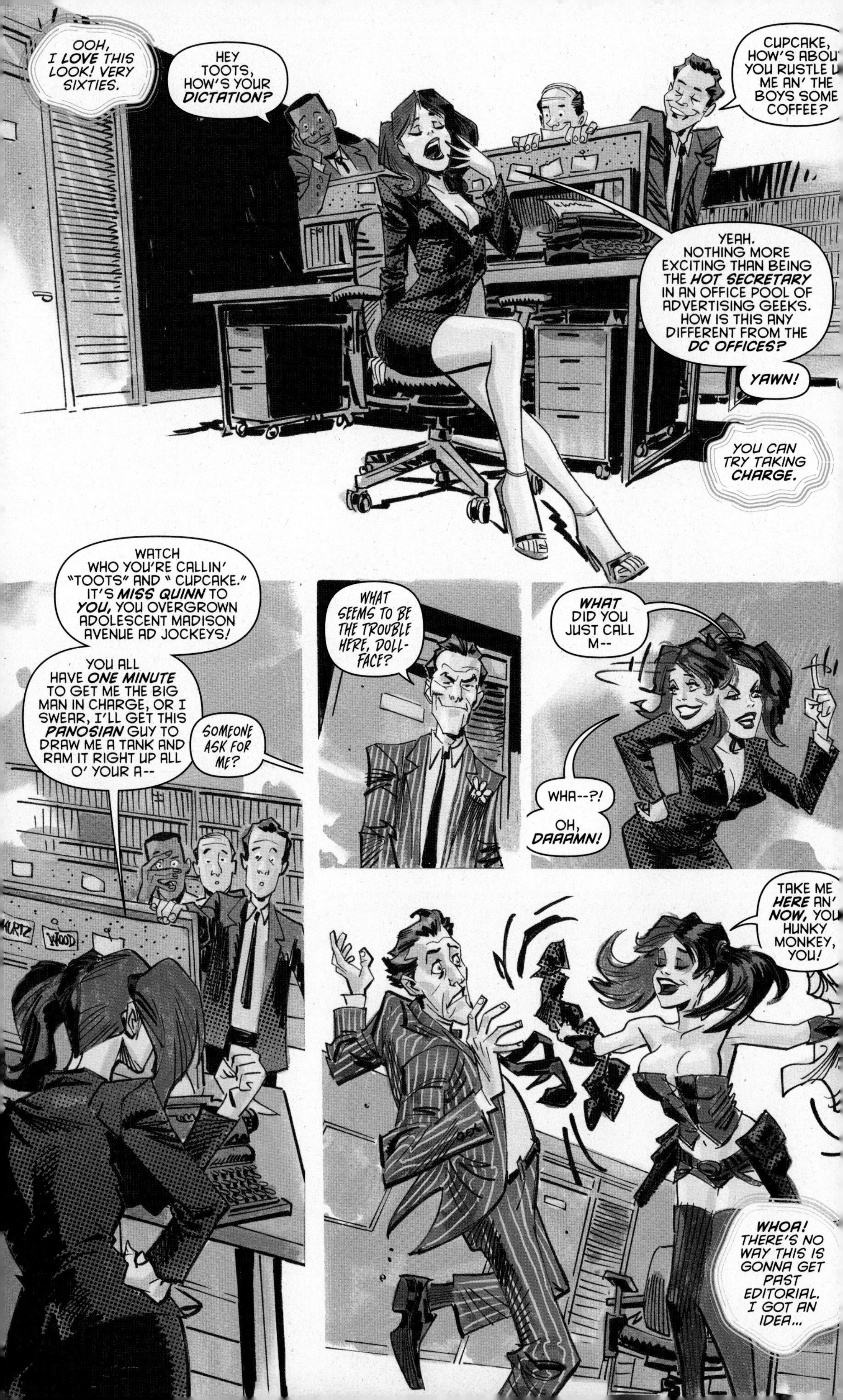

OOH, I LOVE THIS LOOK! VERY SIXTIES.
HEY TOOTS, HOW'S YOUR DICTATION?
CUPCAKE, HOW'S ABOUT YOU RUSTLE U ME AN' THE BOYS SOME COFFEE?
YEAH. NOTHING MORE EXCITING THAN BEING THE HOT SECRETARY IN AN OFFICE POOL OF ADVERTISING GEEKS. HOW IS THIS ANY DIFFERENT FROM THE DC OFFICES?
YAWN!
YOU CAN TRY TAKING CHARGE.
WATCH WHO YOU'RE CALLIN' "TOOTS" AND " CUPCAKE." IT'S MISS QUINN TO YOU, YOU OVERGROWN ADOLESCENT MADISON AVENUE AD JOCKEYS!
YOU ALL HAVE ONE MINUTE TO GET ME THE BIG MAN IN CHARGE, OR I SWEAR, I'LL GET THIS PANOSIAN GUY TO DRAW ME A TANK AND RAM IT RIGHT UP ALL O' YOUR A--
SOMEONE ASK FOR ME?
KURTZ
WOOD
WHAT SEEMS TO BE THE TROUBLE HERE, DOLL-FACE?
WHAT DID YOU JUST CALL M--
WHA--?!
OH, DAAAMN!
TAKE ME HERE AN' NOW, YOU HUNKY MONKEY, YOU!
WHOA! THERE'S NO WAY THIS IS GONNA GET PAST EDITORIAL. I GOT AN IDEA...

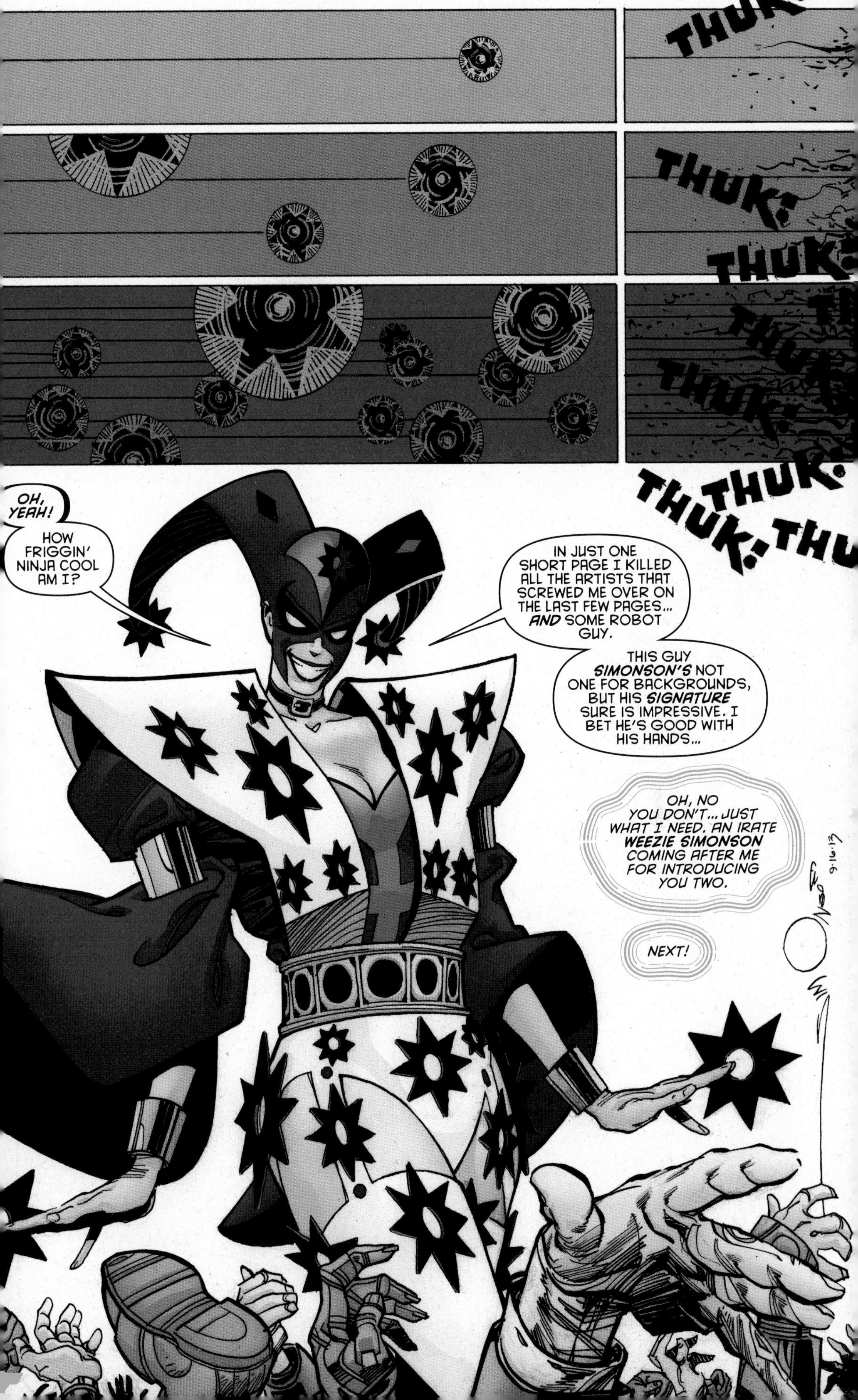
THUK!
THUK!
THUK!
THUK!
THUK!
THUK!
THUK!
OH, YEAH!
HOW FRIGGIN' NINJA COOL AM I?
IN JUST ONE SHORT PAGE I KILLED ALL THE ARTISTS THAT SCREWED ME OVER ON THE LAST FEW PAGES... AND SOME ROBOT GUY.
THIS GUY SIMONSON'S NOT ONE FOR BACKGROUNDS, BUT HIS SIGNATURE SURE IS IMPRESSIVE. I BET HE'S GOOD WITH HIS HANDS...
OH, NO YOU DON'T... JUST WHAT I NEED. AN IRATE WEEZIE SIMONSON COMING AFTER ME FOR INTRODUCING YOU TWO.
NEXT!
9·16·13

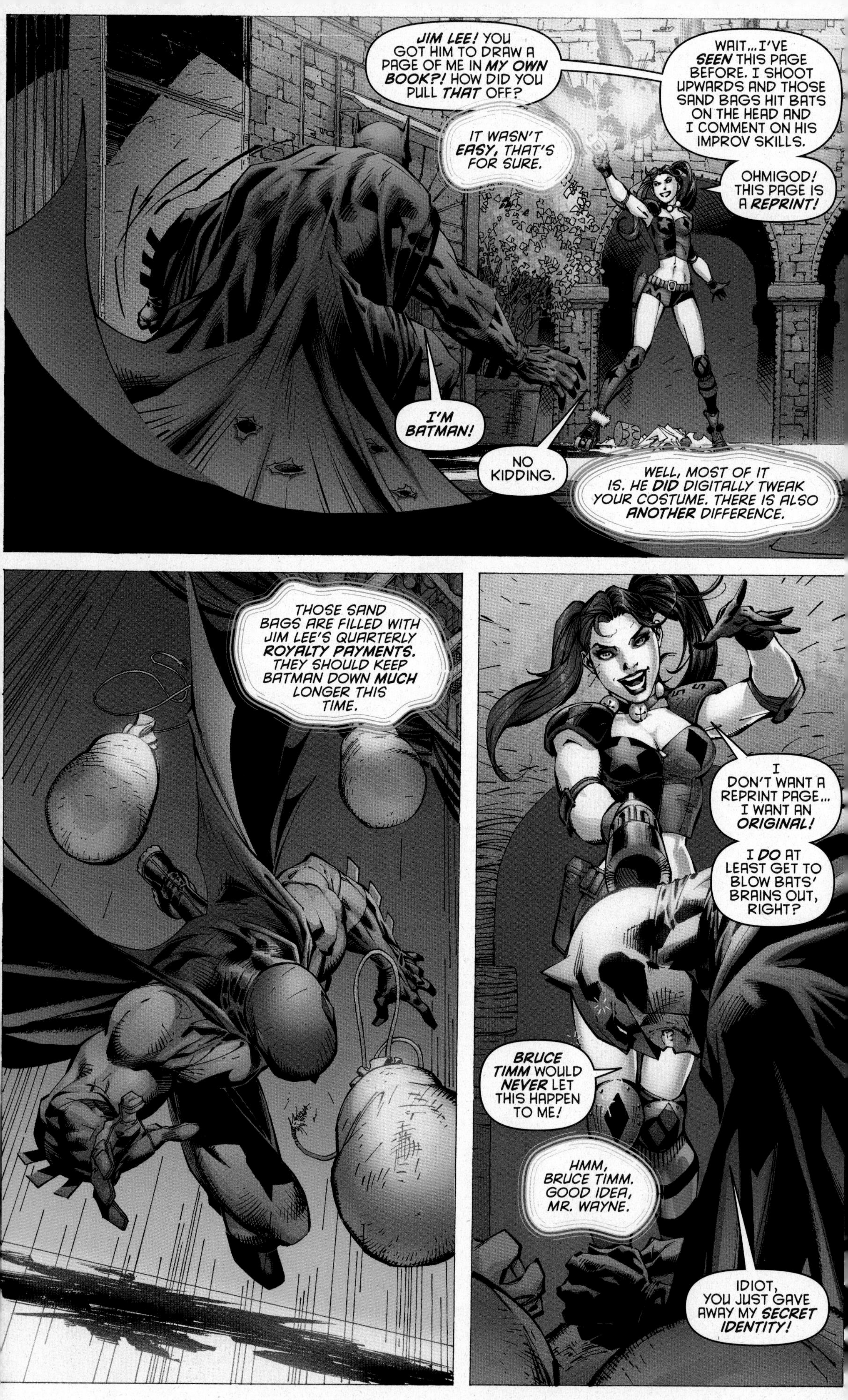

JIM LEE! YOU GOT HIM TO DRAW A PAGE OF ME IN MY OWN BOOK?! HOW DID YOU PULL THAT OFF?
IT WASN'T EASY, THAT'S FOR SURE.
WAIT...I'VE SEEN THIS PAGE BEFORE. I SHOOT UPWARDS AND THOSE SAND BAGS HIT BATS ON THE HEAD AND I COMMENT ON HIS IMPROV SKILLS.
OHMIGOD! THIS PAGE IS A REPRINT!
I'M BATMAN!
NO KIDDING.
WELL, MOST OF IT IS. HE DID DIGITALLY TWEAK YOUR COSTUME. THERE IS ALSO ANOTHER DIFFERENCE.
THOSE SAND BAGS ARE FILLED WITH JIM LEE'S QUARTERLY ROYALTY PAYMENTS. THEY SHOULD KEEP BATMAN DOWN MUCH LONGER THIS TIME.
I DON'T WANT A REPRINT PAGE... I WANT AN ORIGINAL!
I DO AT LEAST GET TO BLOW BATS' BRAINS OUT, RIGHT?
BRUCE TIMM WOULD NEVER LET THIS HAPPEN TO ME!
HMM, BRUCE TIMM. GOOD IDEA, MR. WAYNE.
IDIOT, YOU JUST GAVE AWAY MY SECRET IDENTITY!

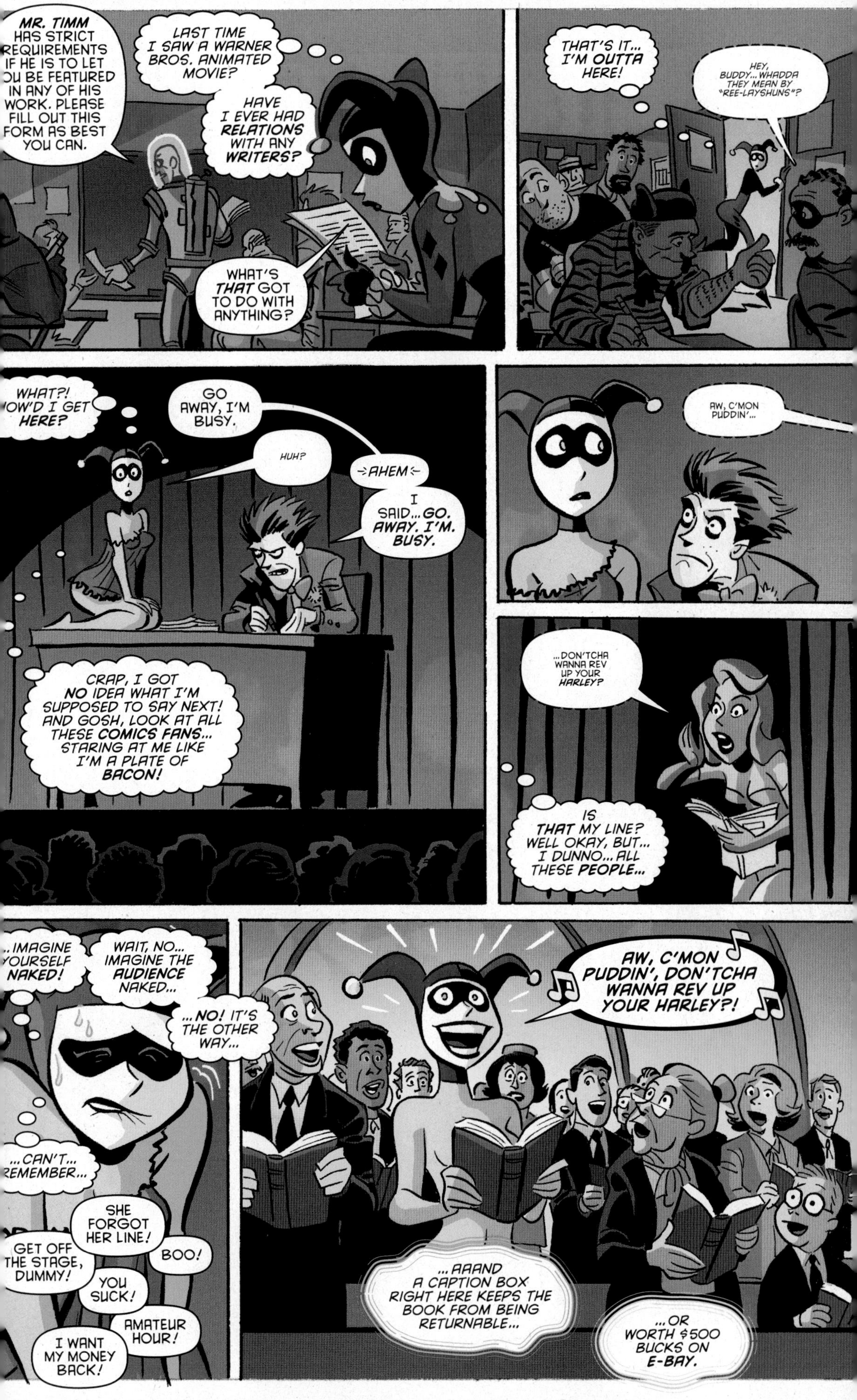
MR. TIMM HAS STRICT REQUIREMENTS IF HE IS TO LET YOU BE FEATURED IN ANY OF HIS WORK. PLEASE FILL OUT THIS FORM AS BEST YOU CAN.
LAST TIME I SAW A WARNER BROS. ANIMATED MOVIE?
HAVE I EVER HAD RELATIONS WITH ANY WRITERS?
WHAT'S THAT GOT TO DO WITH ANYTHING?
THAT'S IT... I'M OUTTA HERE!
HEY, BUDDY... WHADDA THEY MEAN BY "REE-LAYSHUNS"?
WHAT?! HOW'D I GET HERE?
GO AWAY, I'M BUSY.
HUH?
AHEM
I SAID... GO. AWAY. I'M. BUSY.
CRAP, I GOT NO IDEA WHAT I'M SUPPOSED TO SAY NEXT! AND GOSH, LOOK AT ALL THESE COMICS FANS... STARING AT ME LIKE I'M A PLATE OF BACON!
AW, C'MON PUDDIN'...
...DON'TCHA WANNA REV UP YOUR HARLEY?
IS THAT MY LINE? WELL OKAY, BUT... I DUNNO... ALL THESE PEOPLE...
...IMAGINE YOURSELF NAKED!
WAIT, NO... IMAGINE THE AUDIENCE NAKED...
...NO! IT'S THE OTHER WAY...
...CAN'T... REMEMBER...
SHE FORGOT HER LINE!
GET OFF THE STAGE, DUMMY!
BOO!
YOU SUCK!
AMATEUR HOUR!
I WANT MY MONEY BACK!
AW, C'MON PUDDIN', DON'TCHA WANNA REV UP YOUR HARLEY?!
...AAAND A CAPTION BOX RIGHT HERE KEEPS THE BOOK FROM BEING RETURNABLE...
...OR WORTH $500 BUCKS ON E-BAY.

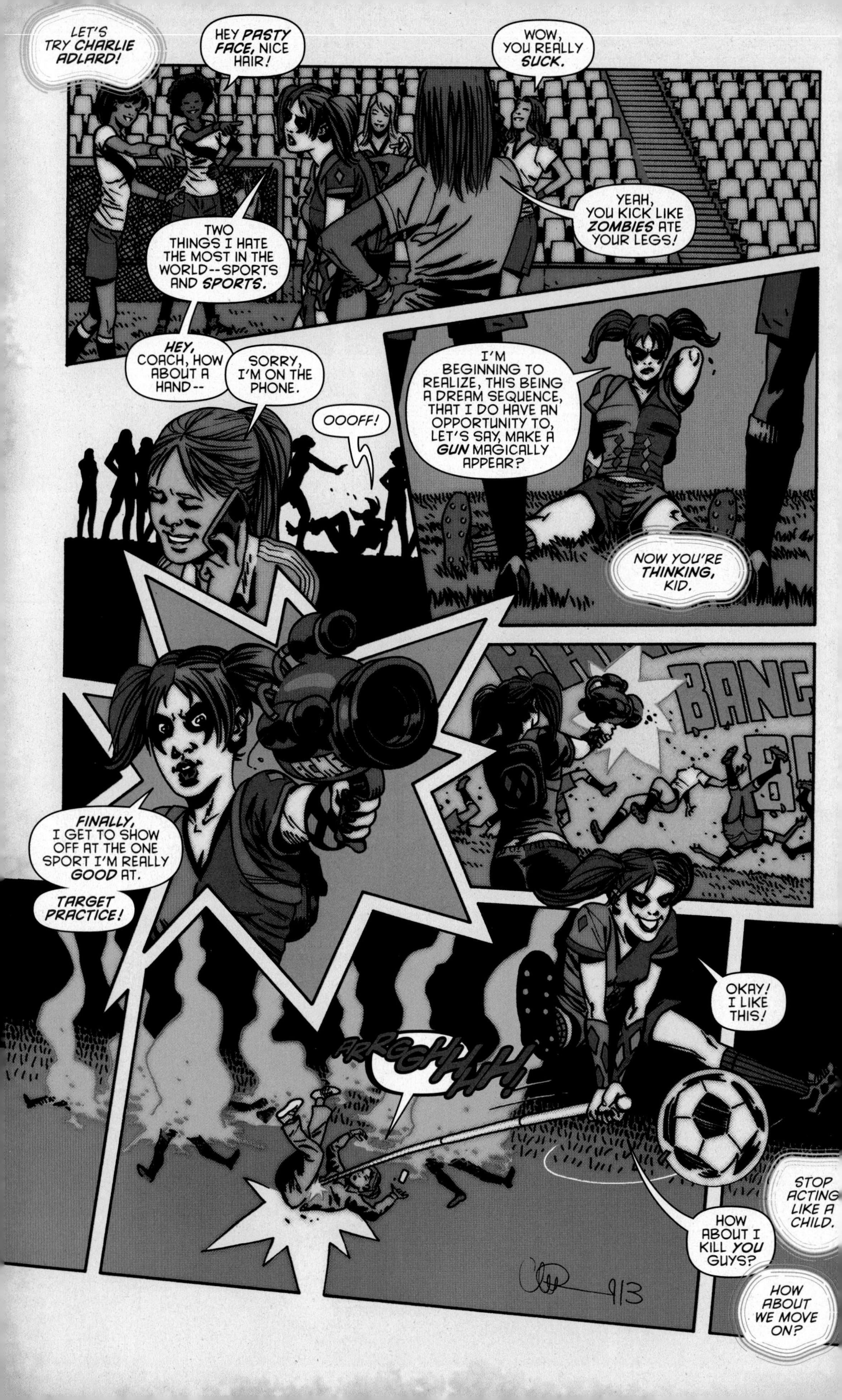
LET'S TRY CHARLIE ADLARD!
HEY PASTY FACE, NICE HAIR!
WOW, YOU REALLY SUCK.
TWO THINGS I HATE THE MOST IN THE WORLD--SPORTS AND SPORTS.
YEAH, YOU KICK LIKE ZOMBIES ATE YOUR LEGS!
HEY, COACH, HOW ABOUT A HAND--
SORRY, I'M ON THE PHONE.
OOOFF!
I'M BEGINNING TO REALIZE, THIS BEING A DREAM SEQUENCE, THAT I DO HAVE AN OPPORTUNITY TO, LET'S SAY, MAKE A GUN MAGICALLY APPEAR?
NOW YOU'RE THINKING, KID.
BANG
FINALLY, I GET TO SHOW OFF AT THE ONE SPORT I'M REALLY GOOD AT.
TARGET PRACTICE!
OKAY! I LIKE THIS!
ARRRGGHHHHH!
HOW ABOUT I KILL YOU GUYS?
STOP ACTING LIKE A CHILD.
HOW ABOUT WE MOVE ON?

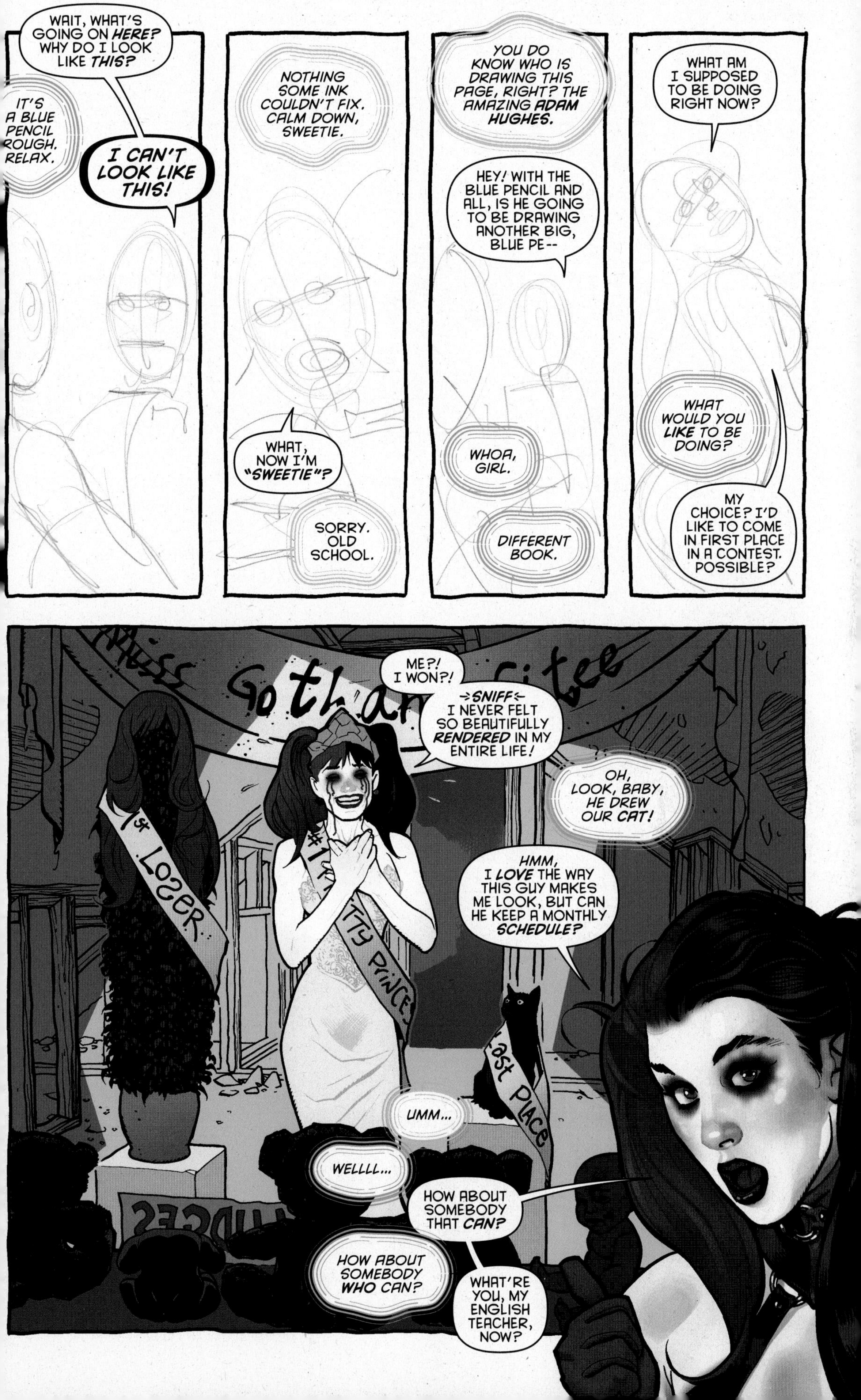

WAIT, WHAT'S GOING ON *HERE*? WHY DO I LOOK LIKE *THIS*?
IT'S A BLUE PENCIL ROUGH. RELAX.
I CAN'T LOOK LIKE THIS!
NOTHING SOME INK COULDN'T FIX. CALM DOWN, SWEETIE.
WHAT, NOW I'M *"SWEETIE"*?
SORRY. OLD SCHOOL.
YOU DO KNOW WHO IS DRAWING THIS PAGE, RIGHT? THE AMAZING **ADAM HUGHES**.
HEY! WITH THE BLUE PENCIL AND ALL, IS HE GOING TO BE DRAWING ANOTHER BIG, BLUE PE--
WHOA, GIRL.
DIFFERENT BOOK.
WHAT AM I SUPPOSED TO BE DOING RIGHT NOW?
WHAT WOULD YOU *LIKE* TO BE DOING?
MY CHOICE? I'D LIKE TO COME IN FIRST PLACE IN A CONTEST. POSSIBLE?
ME?! I WON?!
*SNIFF* I NEVER FELT SO BEAUTIFULLY *RENDERED* IN MY ENTIRE LIFE!
OH, LOOK, BABY, HE DREW OUR *CAT*!
HMM, I *LOVE* THE WAY THIS GUY MAKES ME LOOK, BUT CAN HE KEEP A MONTHLY *SCHEDULE*?
1st Lozer
Last Place
UMM...
WELLLL...
HOW ABOUT SOMEBODY THAT *CAN*?
HOW ABOUT SOMEBODY *WHO* CAN?
WHAT'RE YOU, MY ENGLISH TEACHER, NOW?

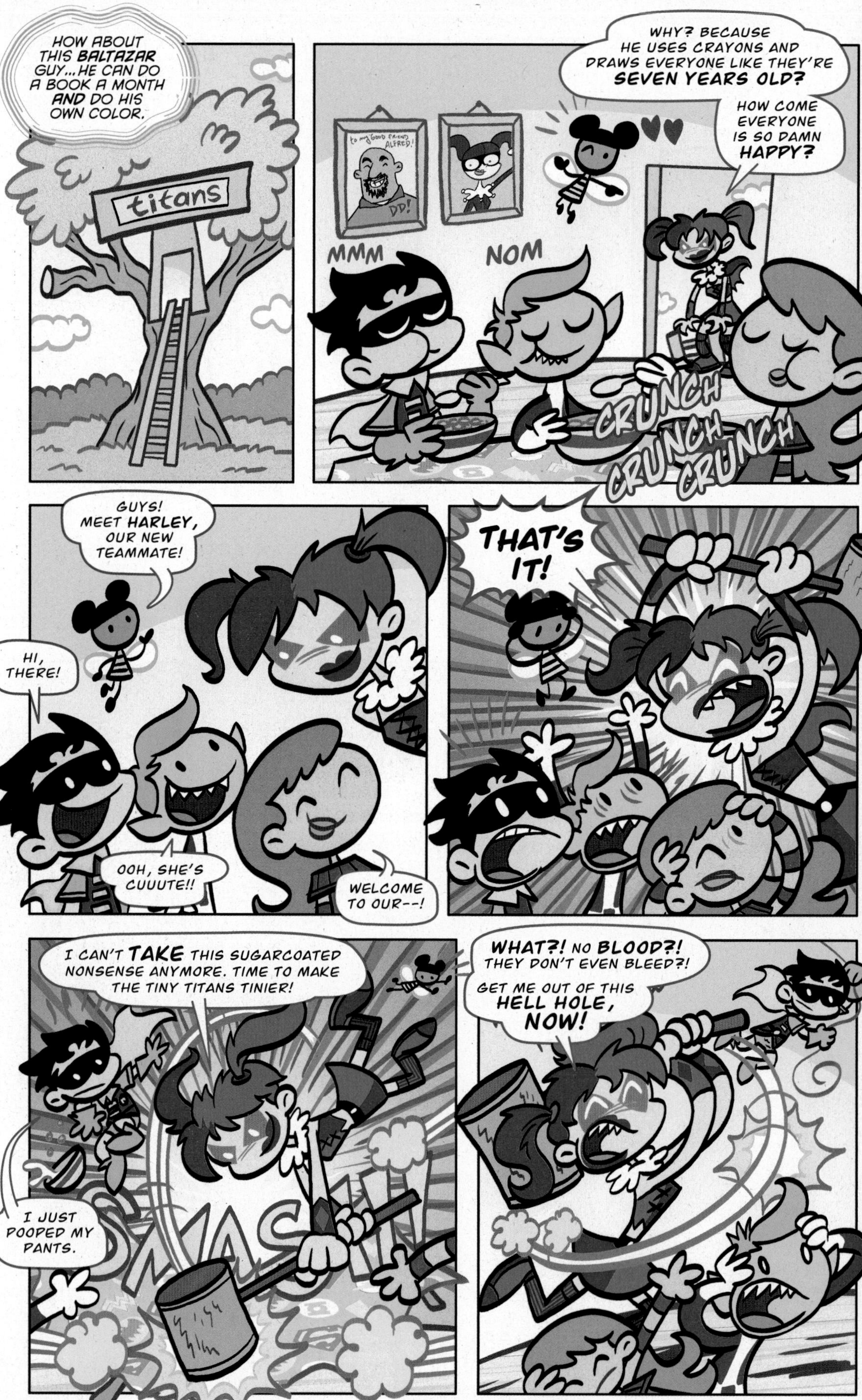

HOW ABOUT THIS BALTAZAR GUY... HE CAN DO A BOOK A MONTH AND DO HIS OWN COLOR.
titans
WHY? BECAUSE HE USES CRAYONS AND DRAWS EVERYONE LIKE THEY'RE SEVEN YEARS OLD?
HOW COME EVERYONE IS SO DAMN HAPPY?
to my good friend ALFRED! DD!
MMM
NOM
CRUNCH CRUNCH CRUNCH
GUYS! MEET HARLEY, OUR NEW TEAMMATE!
HI, THERE!
OOH, SHE'S CUUUTE!!
WELCOME TO OUR--!
THAT'S IT!
I CAN'T TAKE THIS SUGARCOATED NONSENSE ANYMORE. TIME TO MAKE THE TINY TITANS TINIER!
I JUST POOPED MY PANTS.
WHAT?! NO BLOOD?! THEY DON'T EVEN BLEED?!
GET ME OUT OF THIS HELL HOLE, NOW!

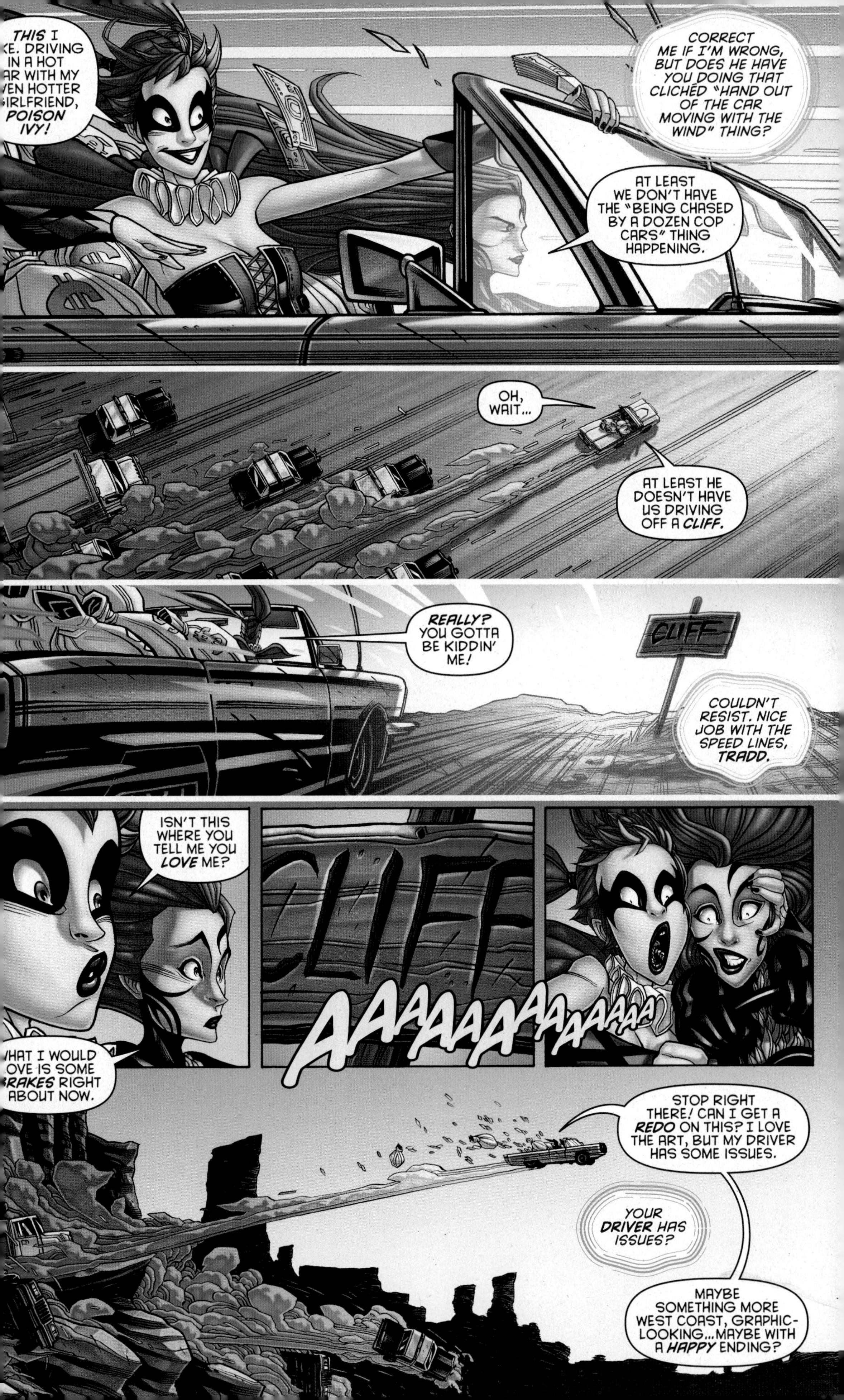
THIS I
KE. DRIVING IN A HOT AR WITH MY VEN HOTTER IRLFRIEND, POISON IVY!
CORRECT ME IF I'M WRONG, BUT DOES HE HAVE YOU DOING THAT CLICHÉD "HAND OUT OF THE CAR MOVING WITH THE WIND" THING?
AT LEAST WE DON'T HAVE THE "BEING CHASED BY A DOZEN COP CARS" THING HAPPENING.
OH, WAIT...
AT LEAST HE DOESN'T HAVE US DRIVING OFF A CLIFF.
REALLY? YOU GOTTA BE KIDDIN' ME!
CLIFF
COULDN'T RESIST. NICE JOB WITH THE SPEED LINES, TRADD.
ISN'T THIS WHERE YOU TELL ME YOU LOVE ME?
HAT I WOULD OVE IS SOME RAKES RIGHT ABOUT NOW.
CLIFF
AAAAAAAAAAAAAA
STOP RIGHT THERE! CAN I GET A REDO ON THIS? I LOVE THE ART, BUT MY DRIVER HAS SOME ISSUES.
YOUR DRIVER HAS ISSUES?
MAYBE SOMETHING MORE WEST COAST, GRAPHIC-LOOKING...MAYBE WITH A HAPPY ENDING?

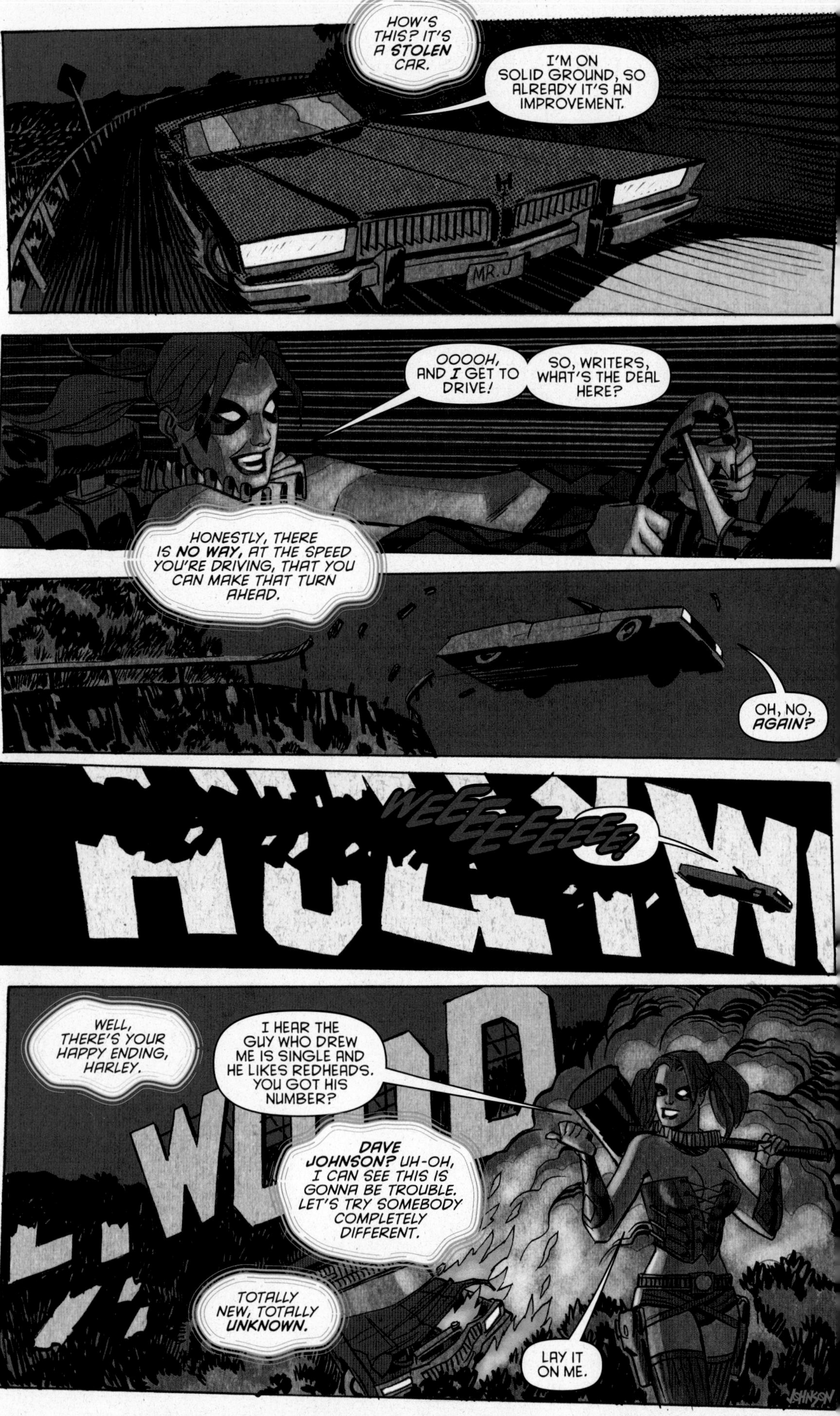
HOW'S THIS? IT'S A **STOLEN** CAR.
I'M ON SOLID GROUND, SO ALREADY IT'S AN IMPROVEMENT.
MR. J
OOOOH, AND *I* GET TO DRIVE!
SO, WRITERS, WHAT'S THE DEAL HERE?
HONESTLY, THERE IS **NO WAY,** AT THE SPEED YOU'RE DRIVING, THAT YOU CAN MAKE THAT TURN AHEAD.
OH, NO, *AGAIN?*
WEEEEEEEEEE!
WELL, THERE'S YOUR HAPPY ENDING, HARLEY.
I HEAR THE GUY WHO DREW ME IS SINGLE AND HE LIKES REDHEADS. YOU GOT HIS NUMBER?
**DAVE JOHNSON?** UH-OH, I CAN SEE THIS IS GONNA BE TROUBLE. LET'S TRY SOMEBODY COMPLETELY DIFFERENT.
TOTALLY NEW, TOTALLY **UNKNOWN.**
LAY IT ON ME.
JOHNSON

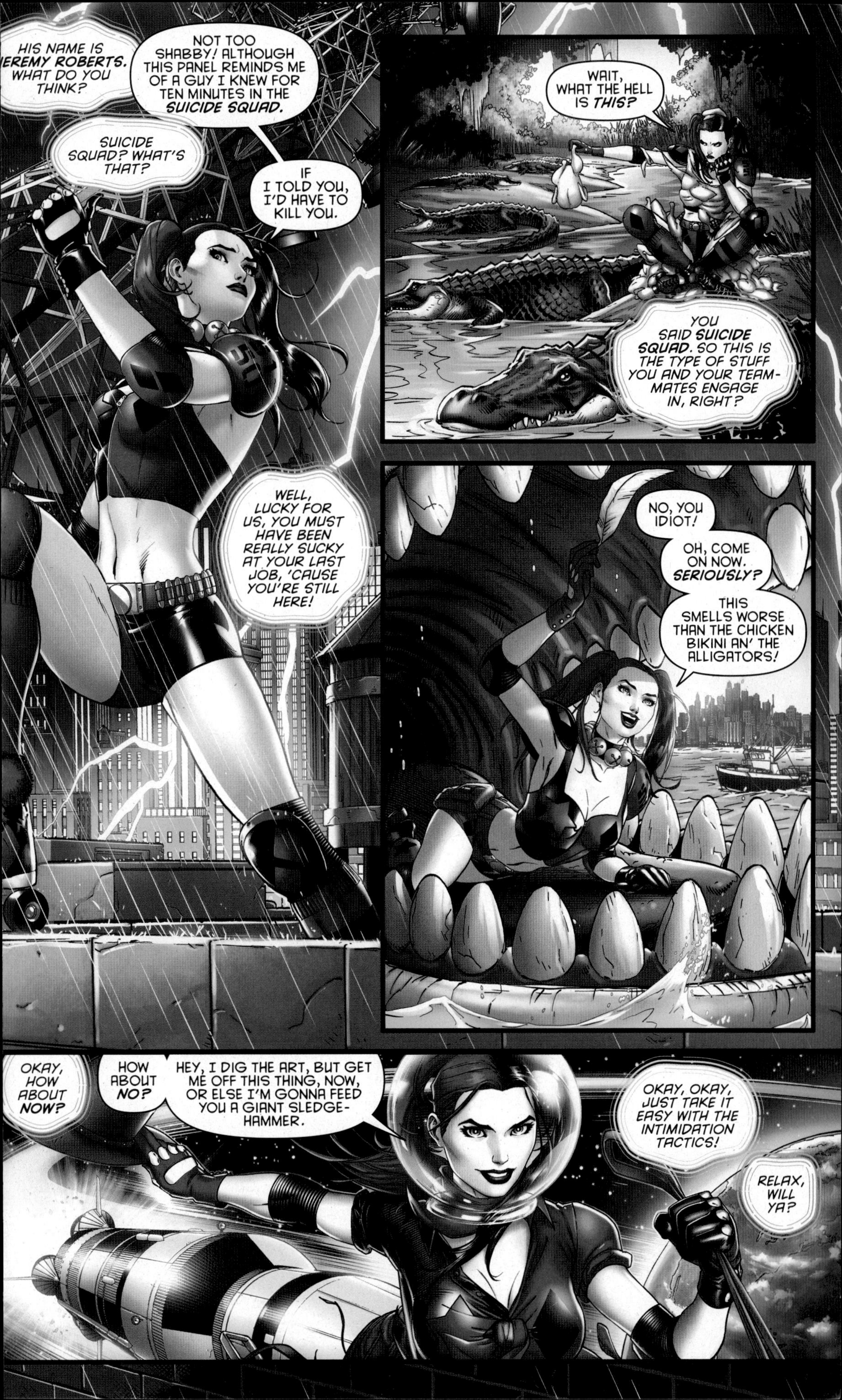

HIS NAME IS JEREMY ROBERTS. WHAT DO YOU THINK?
NOT TOO SHABBY! ALTHOUGH THIS PANEL REMINDS ME OF A GUY I KNEW FOR TEN MINUTES IN THE SUICIDE SQUAD.
SUICIDE SQUAD? WHAT'S THAT?
IF I TOLD YOU, I'D HAVE TO KILL YOU.
WELL, LUCKY FOR US, YOU MUST HAVE BEEN REALLY SUCKY AT YOUR LAST JOB, 'CAUSE YOU'RE STILL HERE!
WAIT, WHAT THE HELL IS THIS?
YOU SAID SUICIDE SQUAD. SO THIS IS THE TYPE OF STUFF YOU AND YOUR TEAM-MATES ENGAGE IN, RIGHT?
NO, YOU IDIOT!
OH, COME ON NOW. SERIOUSLY?
THIS SMELLS WORSE THAN THE CHICKEN BIKINI AN' THE ALLIGATORS!
OKAY, HOW ABOUT NOW?
HOW ABOUT NO?
HEY, I DIG THE ART, BUT GET ME OFF THIS THING, NOW, OR ELSE I'M GONNA FEED YOU A GIANT SLEDGE-HAMMER.
OKAY, OKAY, JUST TAKE IT EASY WITH THE INTIMIDATION TACTICS!
RELAX, WILL YA?

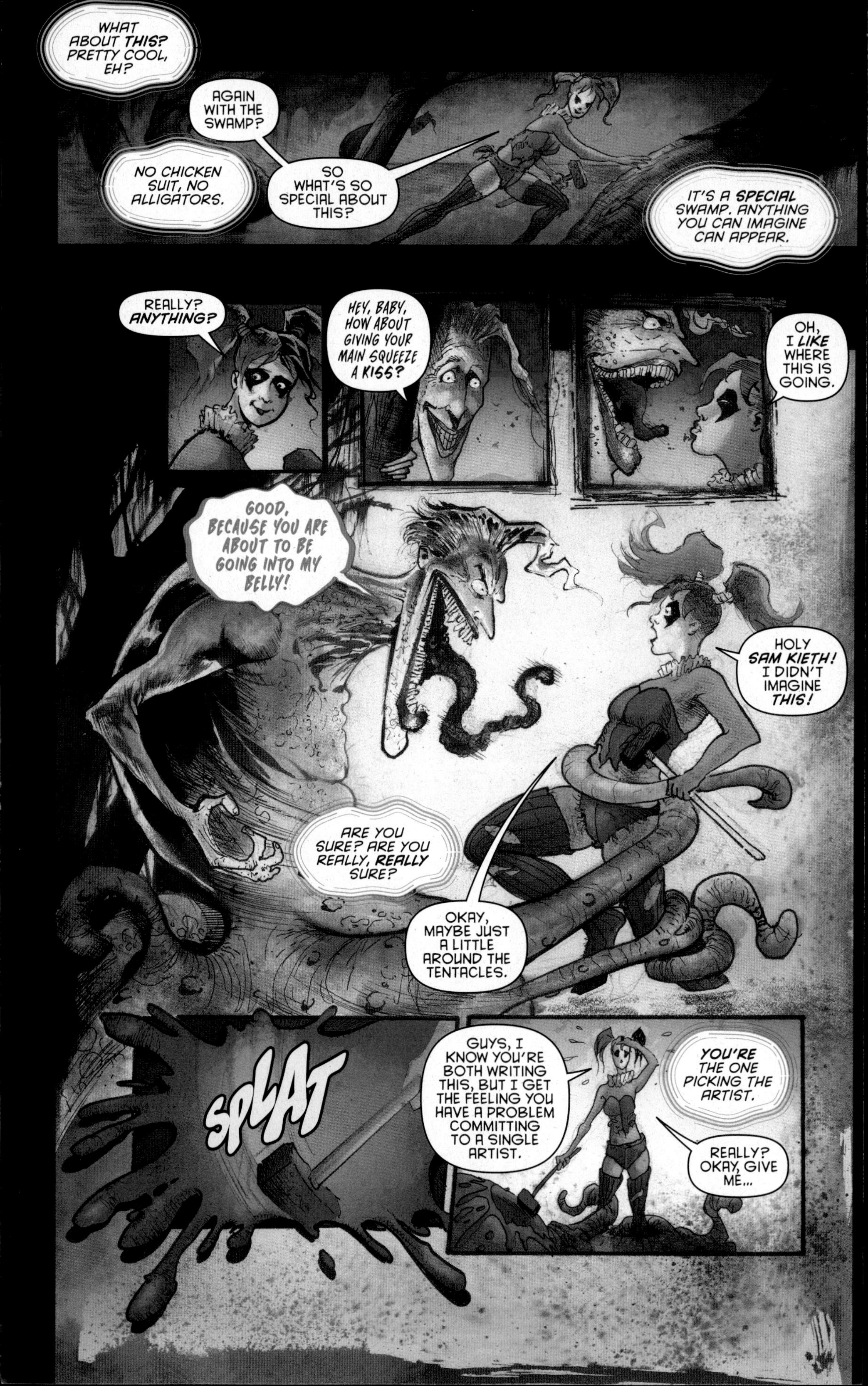

WHAT ABOUT **THIS?** PRETTY COOL, EH?
AGAIN WITH THE SWAMP?
NO CHICKEN SUIT, NO ALLIGATORS.
SO WHAT'S SO SPECIAL ABOUT THIS?
IT'S A **SPECIAL** SWAMP. ANYTHING YOU CAN IMAGINE CAN APPEAR.
REALLY? ***ANYTHING?***
HEY, BABY, HOW ABOUT GIVING YOUR MAIN SQUEEZE A **KISS?**
OH, I **LIKE** WHERE THIS IS GOING.
GOOD, BECAUSE YOU ARE ABOUT TO BE GOING INTO MY BELLY!
HOLY ***SAM KIETH!*** I DIDN'T IMAGINE ***THIS!***
ARE YOU SURE? ARE YOU REALLY, ***REALLY*** SURE?
OKAY, MAYBE JUST A LITTLE AROUND THE TENTACLES.
SPLAT
GUYS, I KNOW YOU'RE BOTH WRITING THIS, BUT I GET THE FEELING YOU HAVE A PROBLEM COMMITTING TO A SINGLE ARTIST.
***YOU'RE*** THE ONE PICKING THE ARTIST.
REALLY? OKAY, GIVE ME...

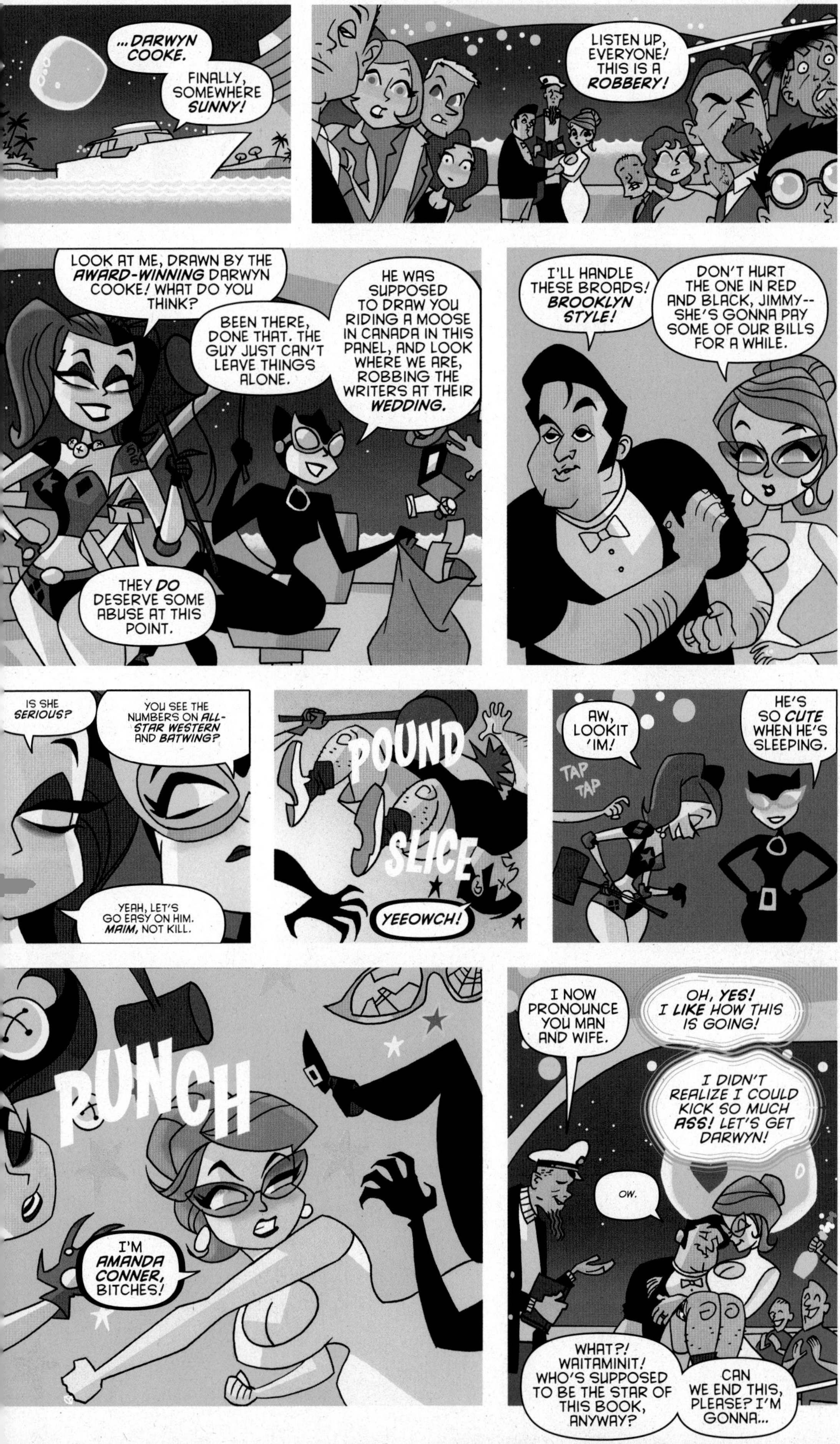
...DARWYN COOKE.
FINALLY, SOMEWHERE SUNNY!
LISTEN UP, EVERYONE! THIS IS A ROBBERY!
LOOK AT ME, DRAWN BY THE AWARD-WINNING DARWYN COOKE! WHAT DO YOU THINK?
BEEN THERE, DONE THAT. THE GUY JUST CAN'T LEAVE THINGS ALONE.
HE WAS SUPPOSED TO DRAW YOU RIDING A MOOSE IN CANADA IN THIS PANEL, AND LOOK WHERE WE ARE, ROBBING THE WRITERS AT THEIR WEDDING.
THEY DO DESERVE SOME ABUSE AT THIS POINT.
I'LL HANDLE THESE BROADS! BROOKLYN STYLE!
DON'T HURT THE ONE IN RED AND BLACK, JIMMY-- SHE'S GONNA PAY SOME OF OUR BILLS FOR A WHILE.
IS SHE SERIOUS?
YOU SEE THE NUMBERS ON ALL-STAR WESTERN AND BATWING?
YEAH, LET'S GO EASY ON HIM. MAIM, NOT KILL.
POUND
SLICE
YEEOWCH!
AW, LOOKIT 'IM!
TAP TAP
HE'S SO CUTE WHEN HE'S SLEEPING.
PUNCH
I'M AMANDA CONNER, BITCHES!
I NOW PRONOUNCE YOU MAN AND WIFE.
OH, YES! I LIKE HOW THIS IS GOING!
I DIDN'T REALIZE I COULD KICK SO MUCH ASS! LET'S GET DARWYN!
OW.
WHAT?! WAITAMINIT! WHO'S SUPPOSED TO BE THE STAR OF THIS BOOK, ANYWAY?
CAN WE END THIS, PLEASE? I'M GONNA...

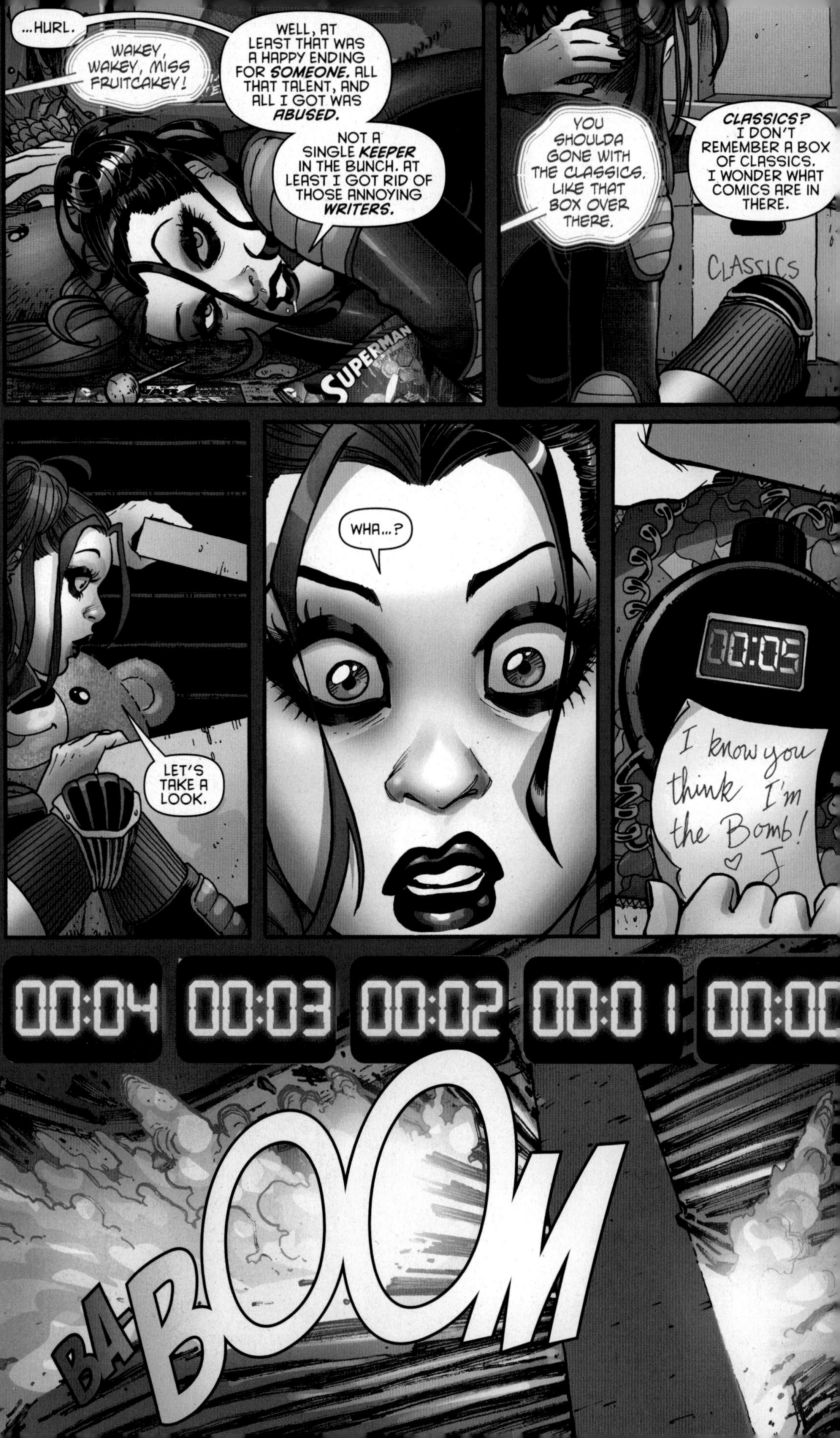
...HURL.
WAKEY, WAKEY, MISS FRUITCAKEY!
WELL, AT LEAST THAT WAS A HAPPY ENDING FOR *SOMEONE.* ALL THAT TALENT, AND ALL I GOT WAS *ABUSED.*
NOT A SINGLE *KEEPER* IN THE BUNCH. AT LEAST I GOT RID OF THOSE ANNOYING *WRITERS.*
SUPERMAN
YOU SHOULDA GONE WITH THE CLASSICS. LIKE THAT BOX OVER THERE.
*CLASSICS?* I DON'T REMEMBER A BOX OF CLASSICS. I WONDER WHAT COMICS ARE IN THERE.
CLASSICS
LET'S TAKE A LOOK.
WHA...?
00:05
I know you think I'm the Bomb! ♡ J
00:04
00:03
00:02
00:01
00:00
BA-BOOM

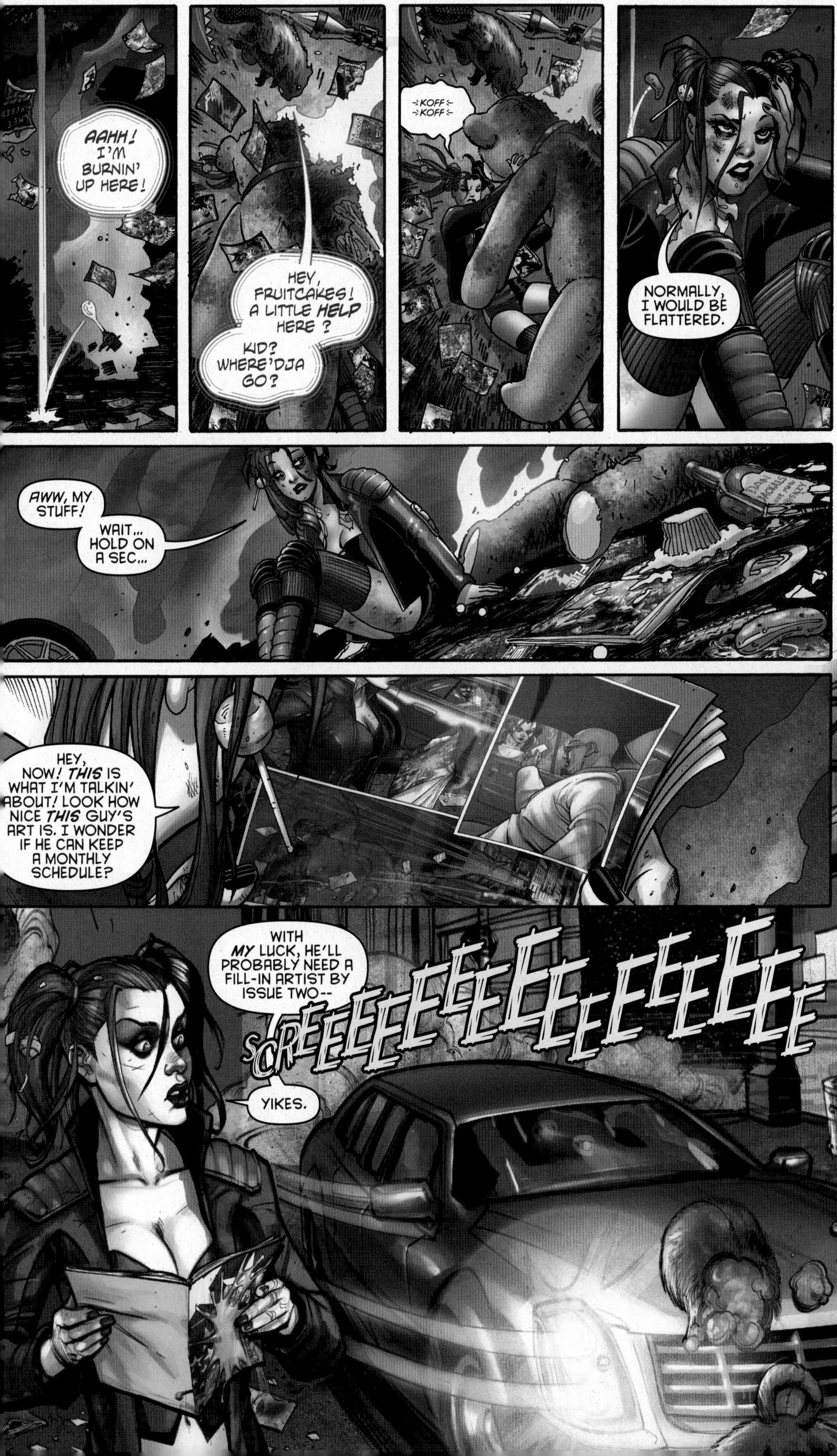
AAHH! I'M BURNIN' UP HERE!
HEY, FRUITCAKES! A LITTLE HELP HERE?
KID? WHERE'DJA GO?
KOFF KOFF
NORMALLY, I WOULD BE FLATTERED.
AWW, MY STUFF!
WAIT... HOLD ON A SEC...
HEY, NOW! THIS IS WHAT I'M TALKIN' ABOUT! LOOK HOW NICE THIS GUY'S ART IS. I WONDER IF HE CAN KEEP A MONTHLY SCHEDULE?
WITH MY LUCK, HE'LL PROBABLY NEED A FILL-IN ARTIST BY ISSUE TWO--
SCREEEEEEEEEEEEEEEE
YIKES.

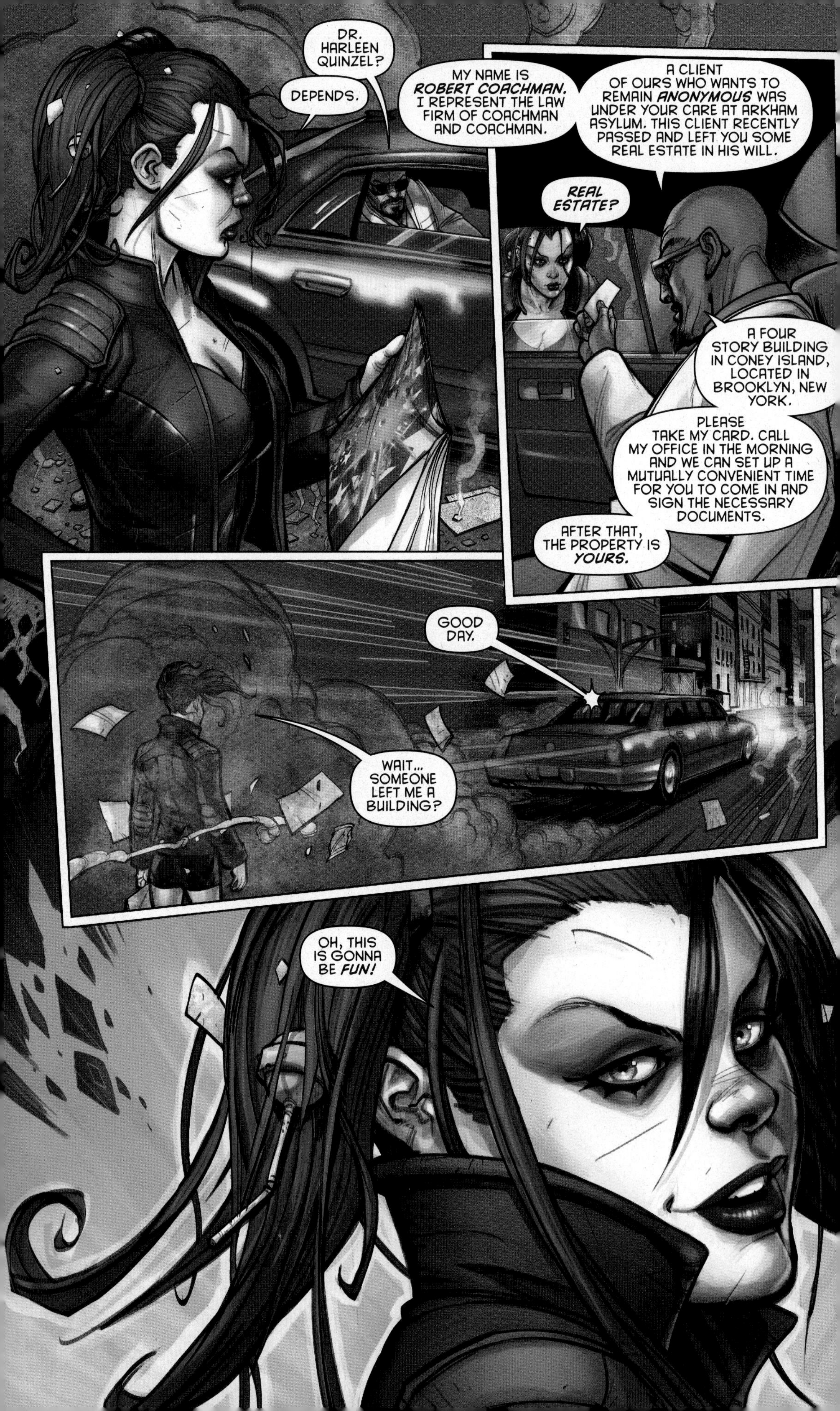
DR. HARLEEN QUINZEL?
DEPENDS.
MY NAME IS *ROBERT COACHMAN.* I REPRESENT THE LAW FIRM OF COACHMAN AND COACHMAN.
A CLIENT OF OURS WHO WANTS TO REMAIN *ANONYMOUS* WAS UNDER YOUR CARE AT ARKHAM ASYLUM. THIS CLIENT RECENTLY PASSED AND LEFT YOU SOME REAL ESTATE IN HIS WILL.
*REAL ESTATE?*
A FOUR STORY BUILDING IN CONEY ISLAND, LOCATED IN BROOKLYN, NEW YORK.
PLEASE TAKE MY CARD. CALL MY OFFICE IN THE MORNING AND WE CAN SET UP A MUTUALLY CONVENIENT TIME FOR YOU TO COME IN AND SIGN THE NECESSARY DOCUMENTS.
AFTER THAT, THE PROPERTY IS *YOURS.*
GOOD DAY.
WAIT... SOMEONE LEFT ME A BUILDING?
OH, THIS IS GONNA BE *FUN!*

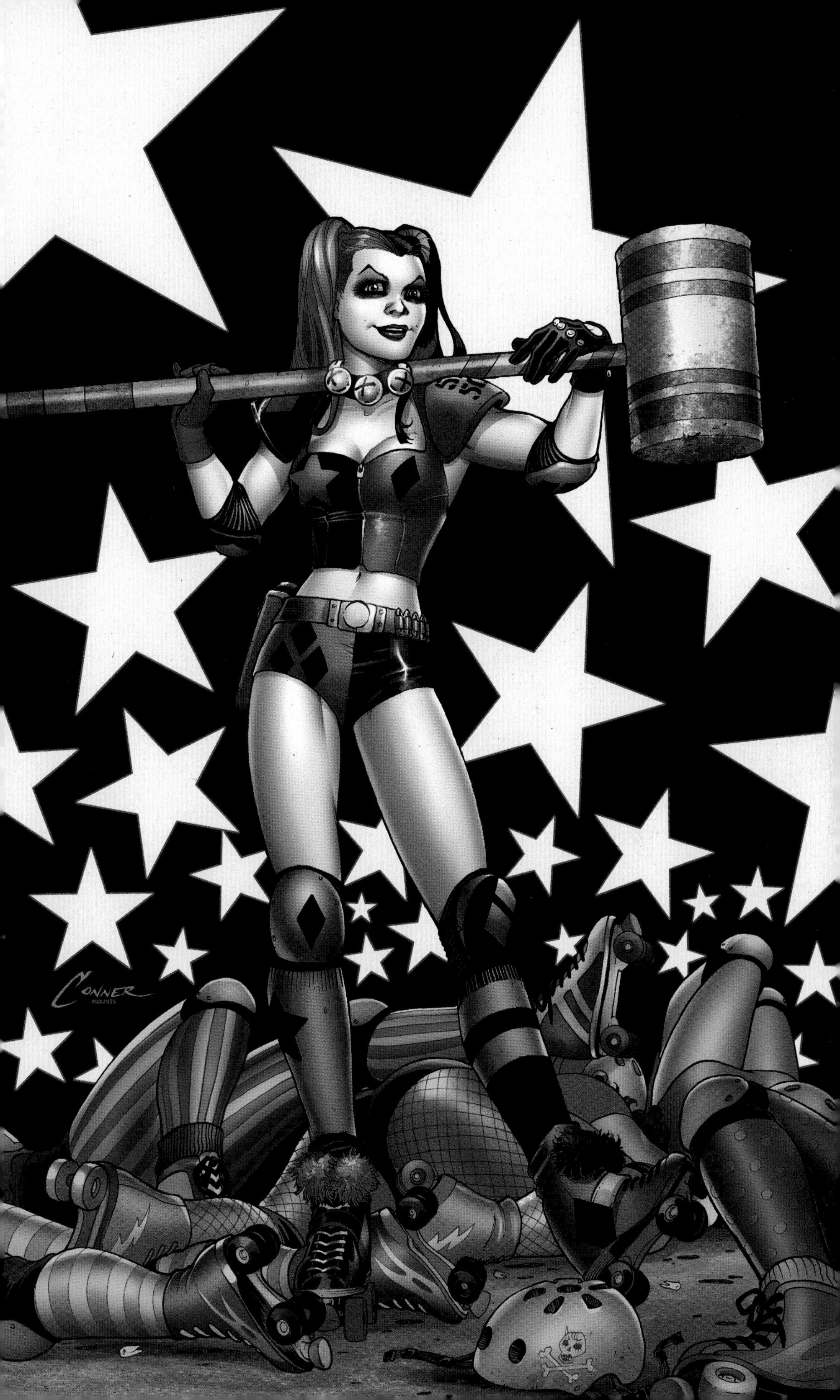
CONNER
MOUNTS

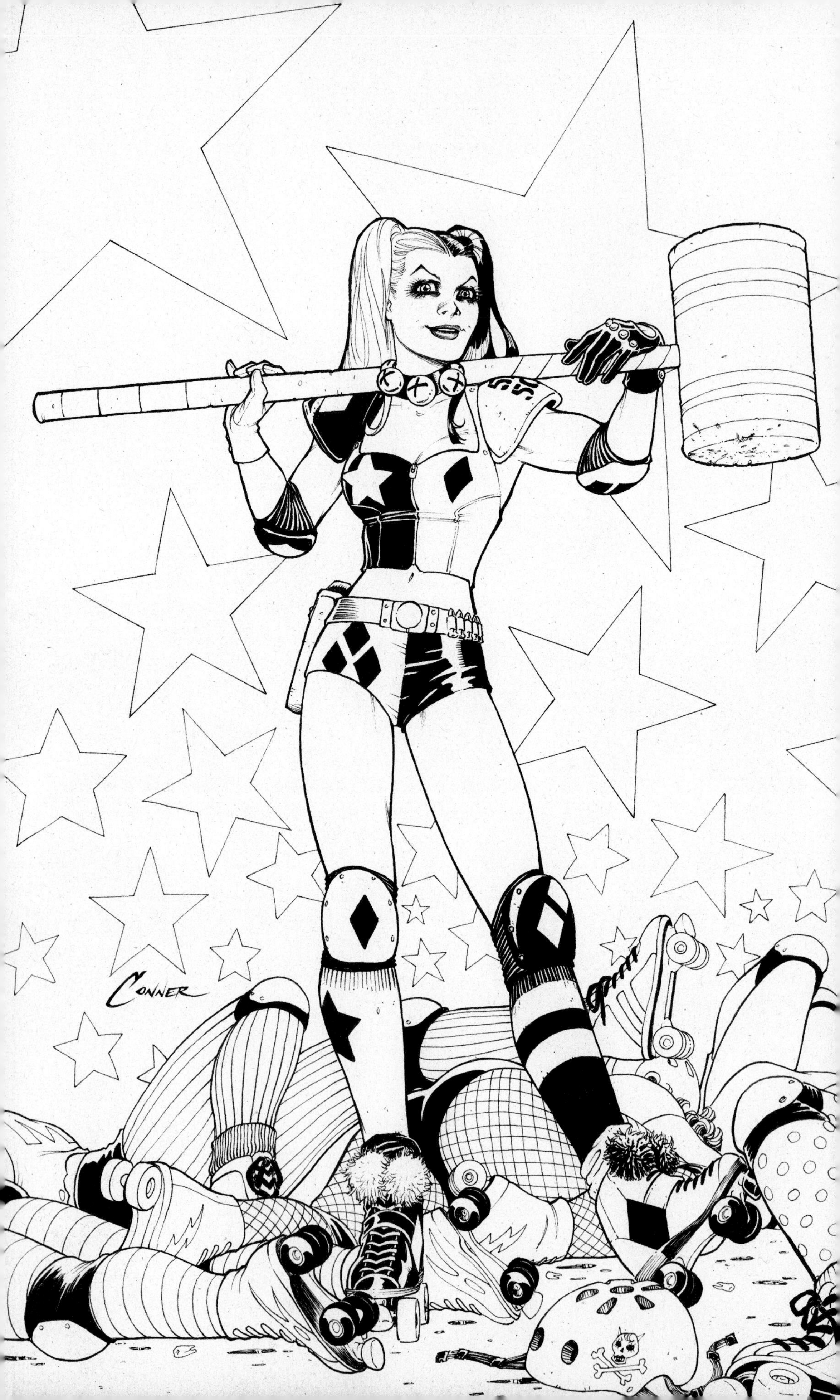
CONNER

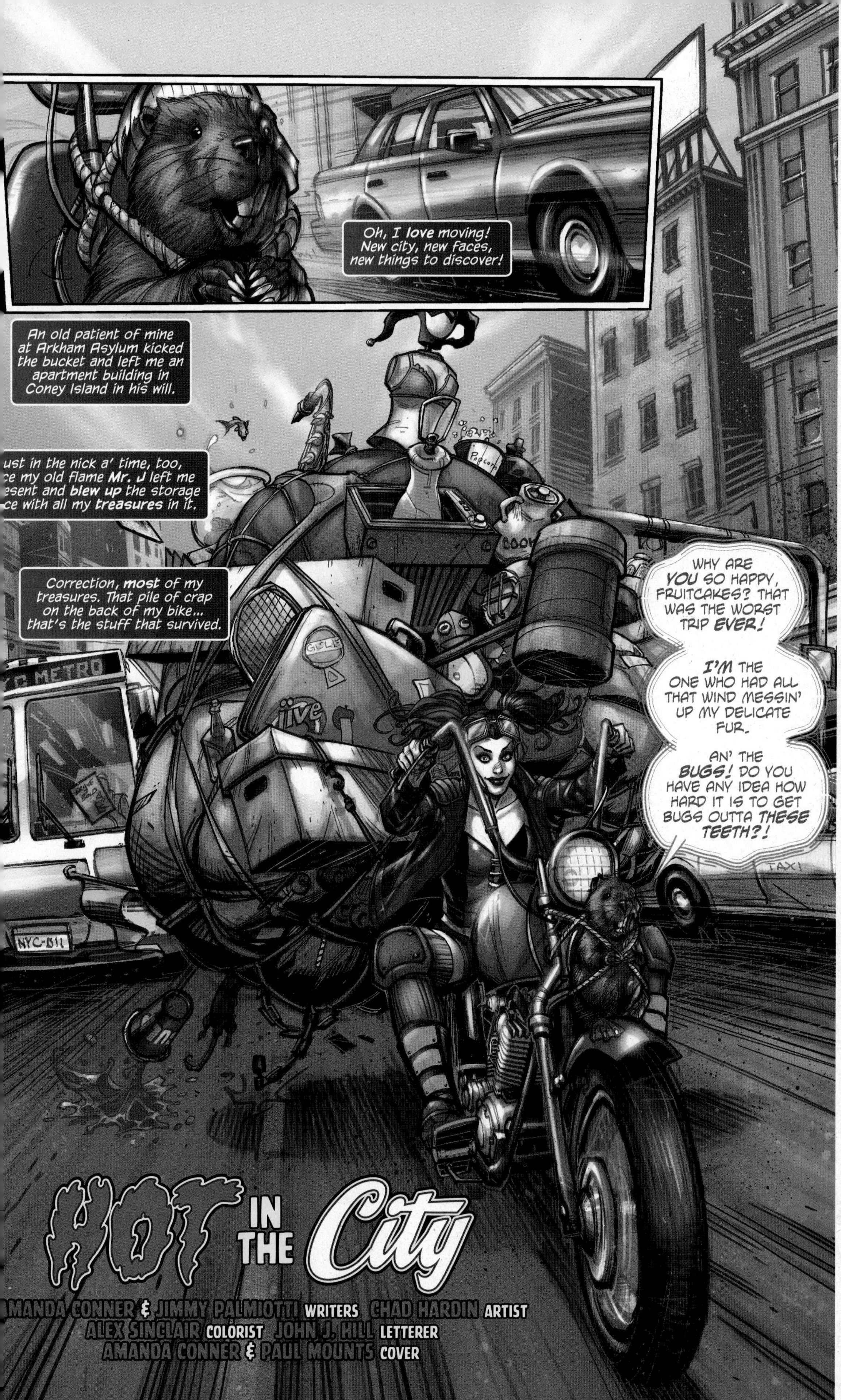

Oh, I **love** moving! New city, new faces, new things to discover!
An old patient of mine at Arkham Asylum kicked the bucket and left me an apartment building in Coney Island in his will.
ust in the nick a' time, too, ce my old flame **Mr. J** left me esent and **blew up** the storage ce with all my **treasures** in it.
Correction, **most** of my treasures. That pile of crap on the back of my bike... that's the stuff that survived.
WHY ARE **YOU** SO HAPPY, FRUITCAKES? THAT WAS THE WORST TRIP **EVER!**
**I'M** THE ONE WHO HAD ALL THAT WIND MESSIN' UP MY DELICATE FUR.
AN' THE **BUGS!** DO YOU HAVE ANY IDEA HOW HARD IT IS TO GET BUGS OUTTA **THESE TEETH?!**
METRO
TAXI
HOT IN THE City
AMANDA CONNER & JIMMY PALMIOTTI WRITERS CHAD HARDIN ARTIST
ALEX SINCLAIR COLORIST JOHN J. HILL LETTERER
AMANDA CONNER & PAUL MOUNTS COVER

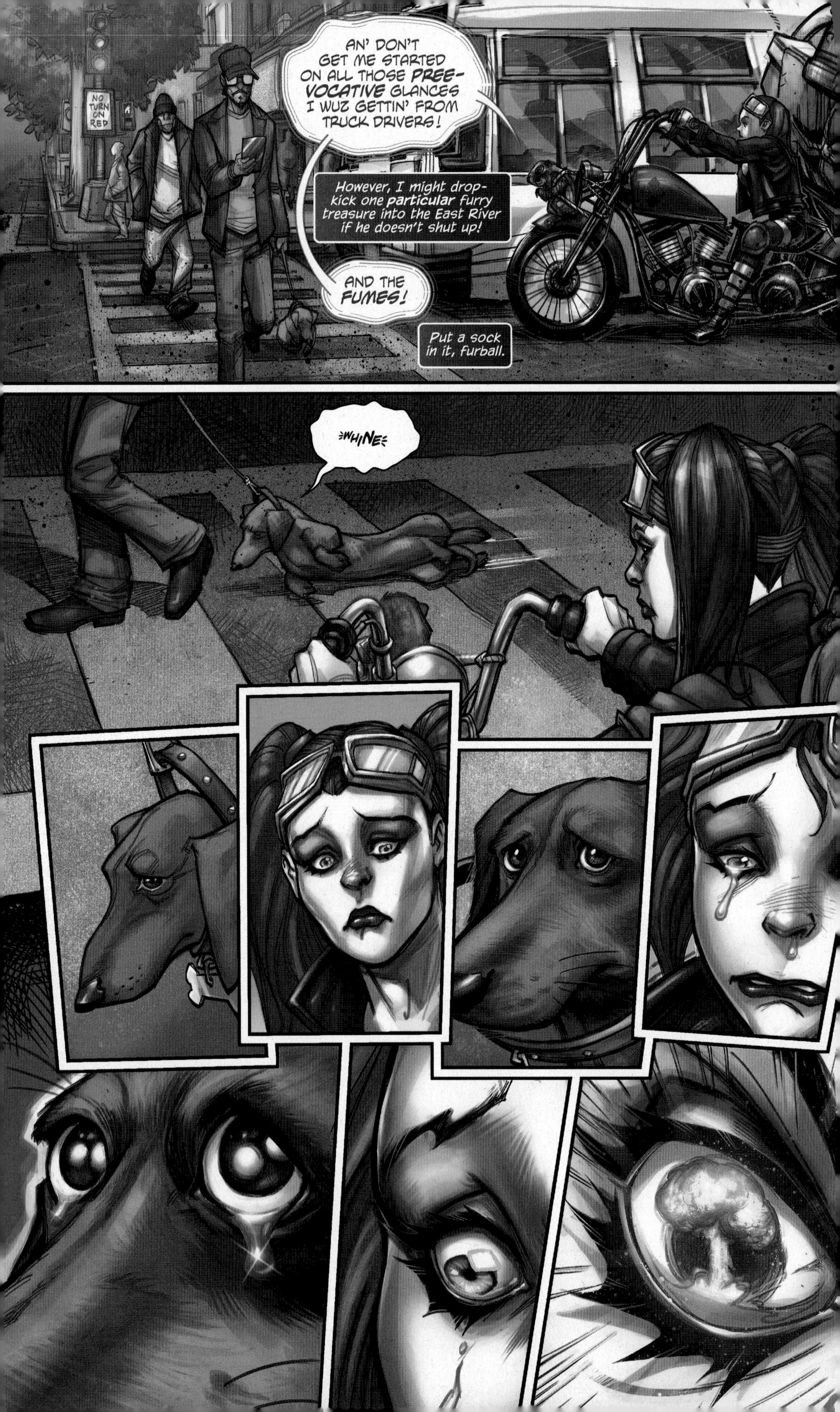
NO TURN ON RED
AN' DON'T GET ME STARTED ON ALL THOSE PREE-VOCATIVE GLANCES I WUZ GETTIN' FROM TRUCK DRIVERS!
However, I might drop-kick one particular furry treasure into the East River if he doesn't shut up!
AND THE FUMES!
Put a sock in it, furball.
WHINE

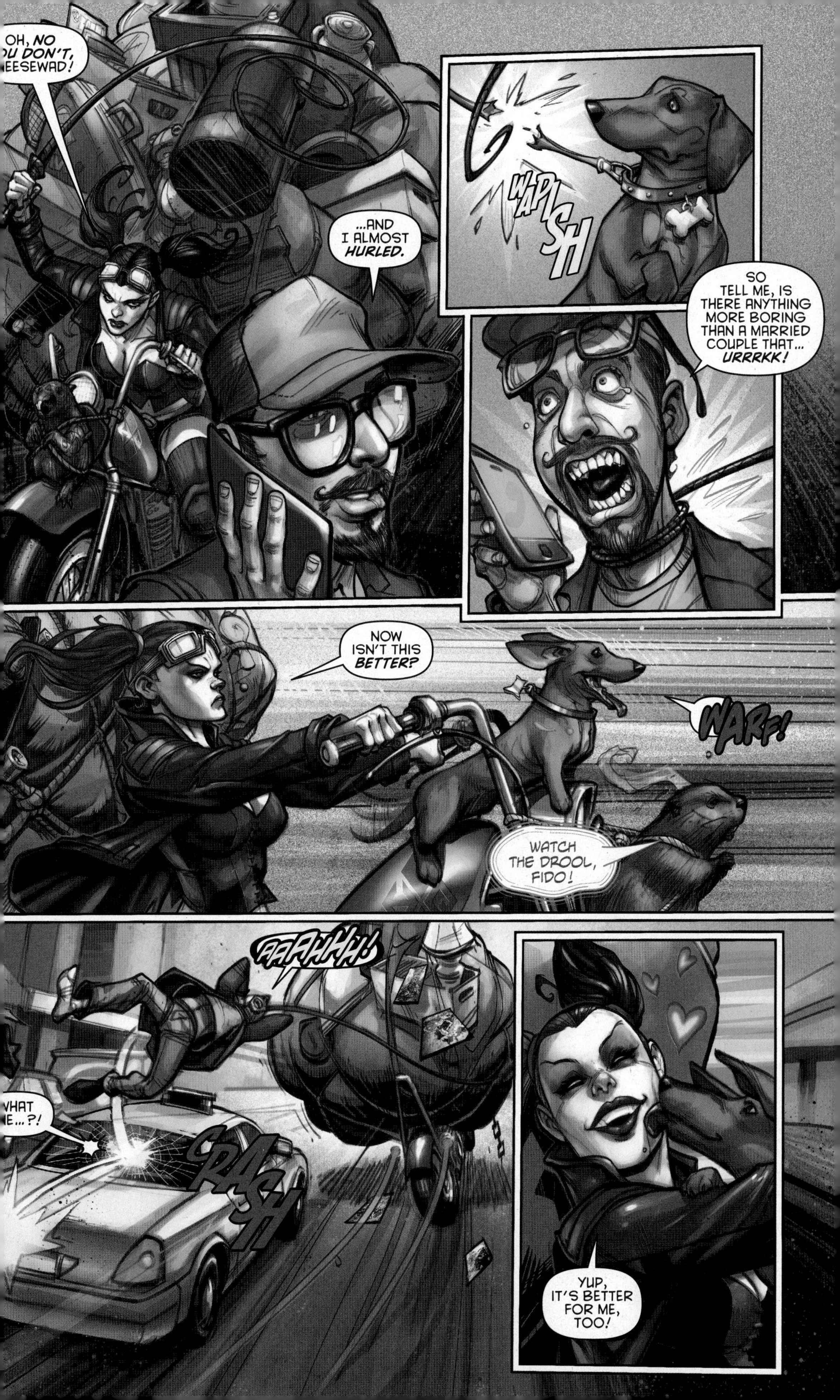
OH, NO
OU DON'T,
EESEWAD!
...AND
I ALMOST
HURLED.
WAPISH
SO TELL ME, IS THERE ANYTHING MORE BORING THAN A MARRIED COUPLE THAT... URRRKK!
NOW ISN'T THIS BETTER?
WARF!
WATCH THE DROOL, FIDO!
AAAHHH!
WHAT
E...?!
CRASH
YUP, IT'S BETTER FOR ME, TOO!

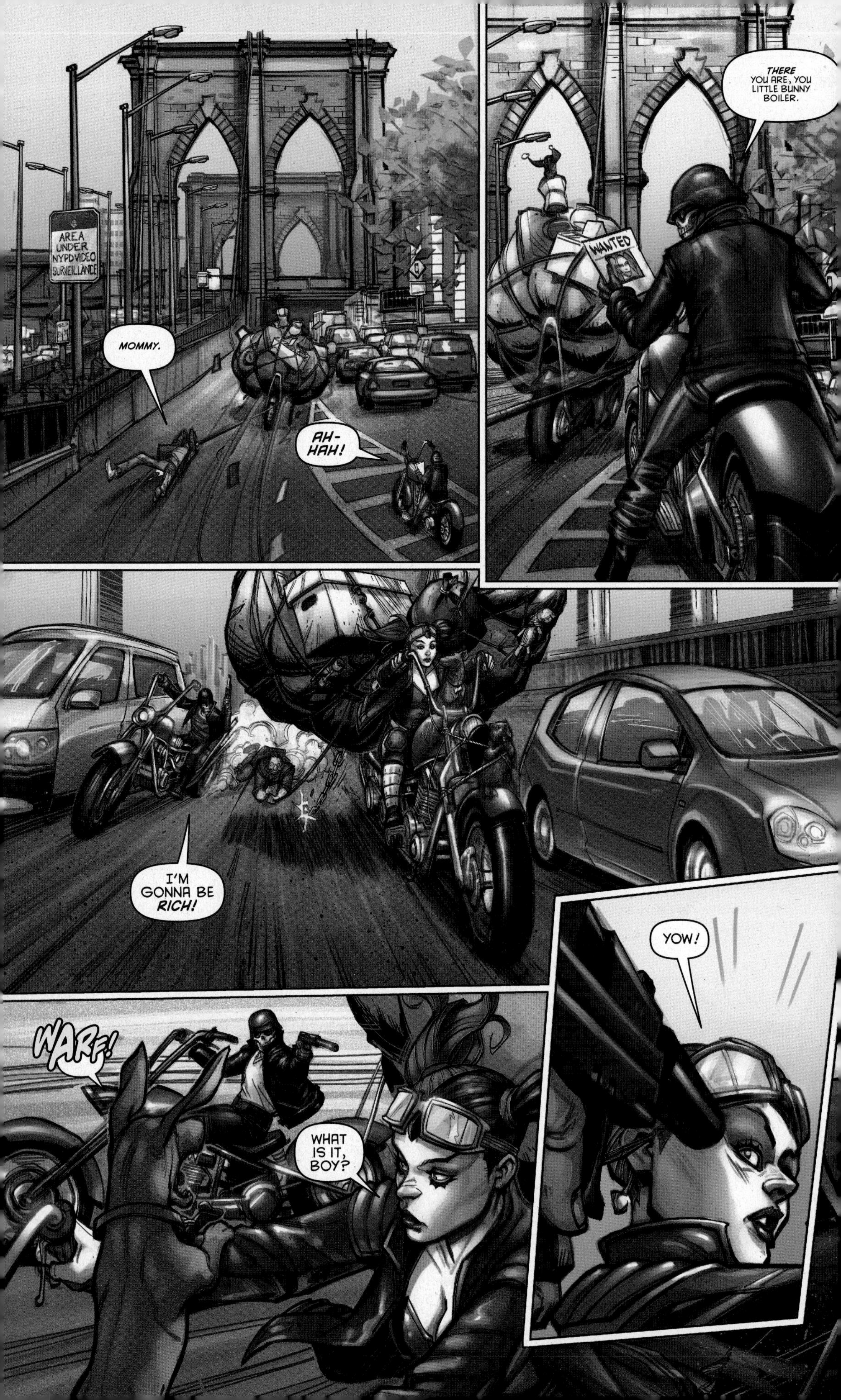

AREA UNDER NYPD VIDEO SURVEILLANCE
MOMMY.
AH-HAH!
THERE YOU ARE, YOU LITTLE BUNNY BOILER.
WANTED
I'M GONNA BE RICH!
WARF!
WHAT IS IT, BOY?
YOW!

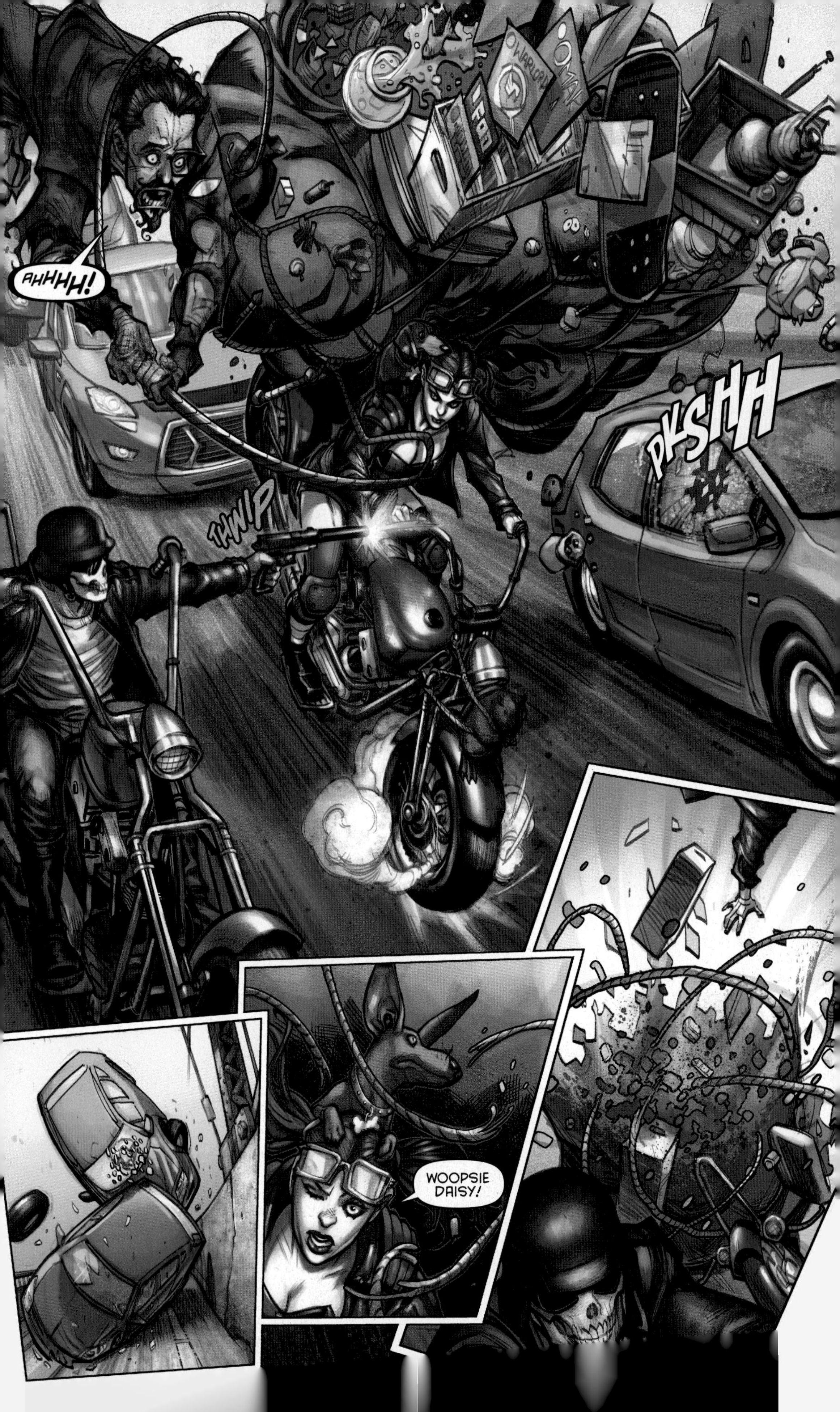
AHHHH!
PKSHH
THWIP
WOOPSIE DAISY!

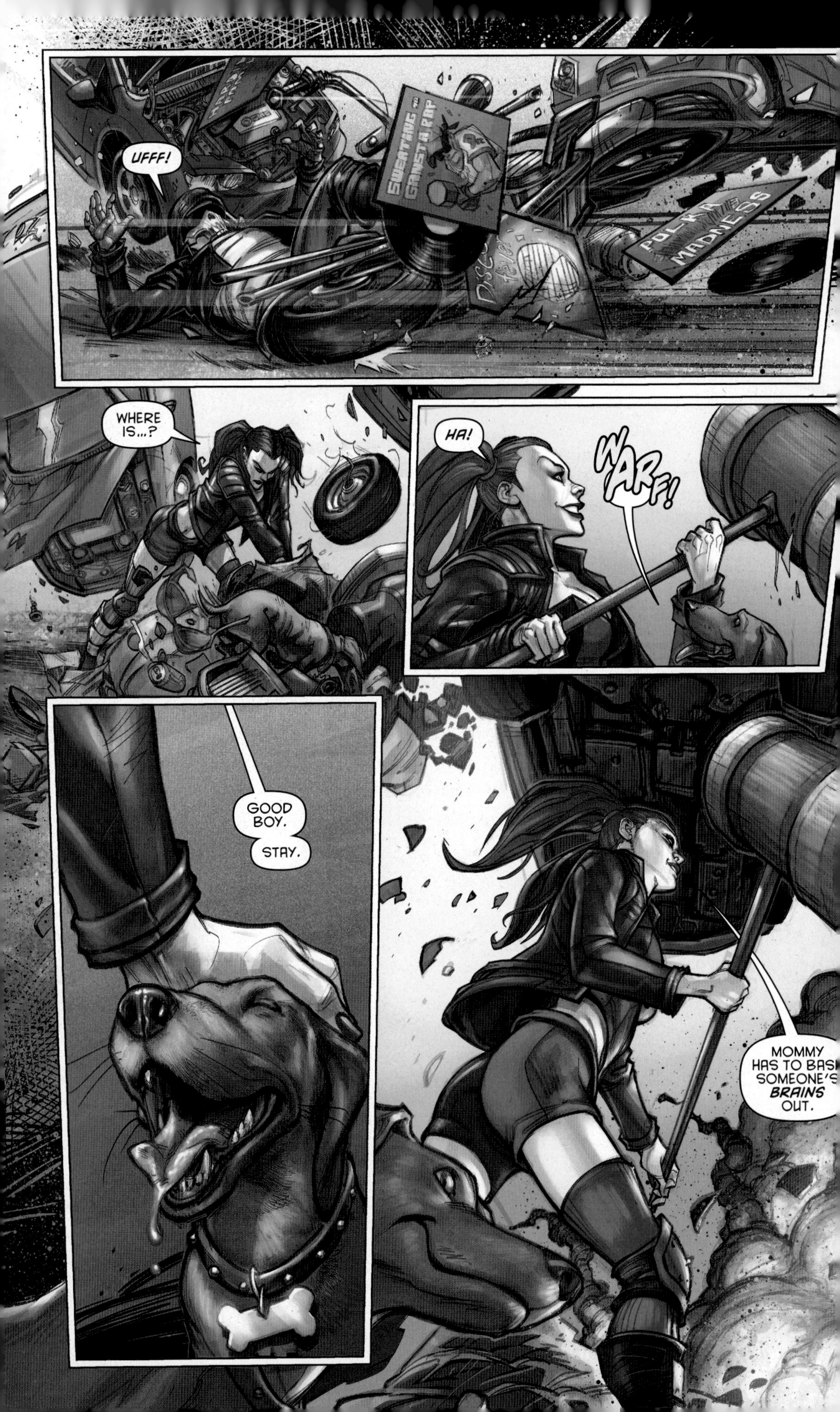
UFFF!
SWEATING TO GANSTA RAP
POLKA MADNESS
WHERE IS...?
HA!
WARF!
GOOD BOY.
STAY.
MOMMY HAS TO BAS SOMEONE'S *BRAINS* OUT.

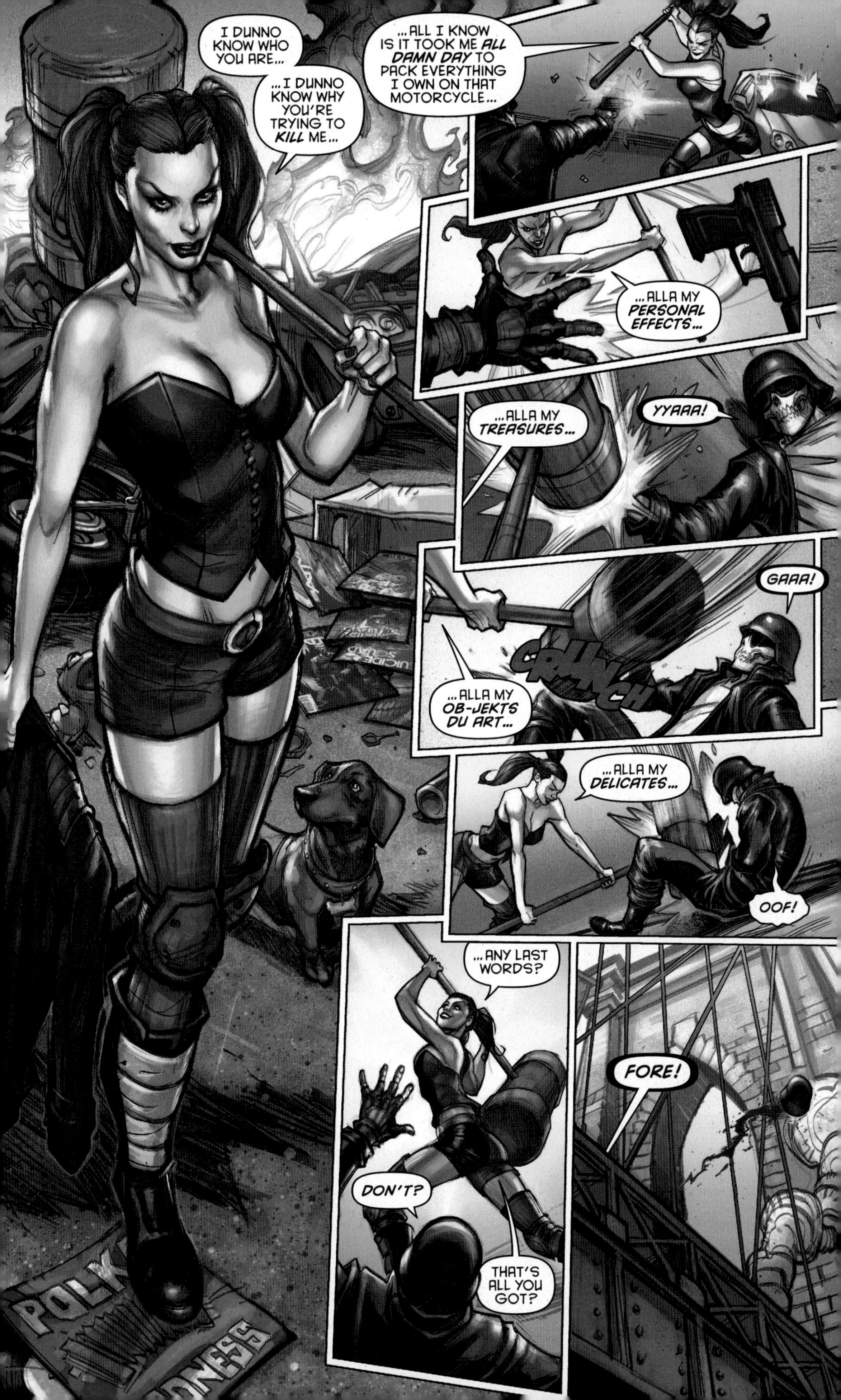
I DUNNO KNOW WHO YOU ARE...
...I DUNNO KNOW WHY YOU'RE TRYING TO KILL ME...
...ALL I KNOW IS IT TOOK ME ALL DAMN DAY TO PACK EVERYTHING I OWN ON THAT MOTORCYCLE...
...ALLA MY PERSONAL EFFECTS...
...ALLA MY TREASURES...
YYAAA!
GAAA!
CRUNCH
...ALLA MY OB-JEKTS DU ART...
...ALLA MY DELICATES...
OOF!
...ANY LAST WORDS?
DON'T?
THAT'S ALL YOU GOT?
FORE!

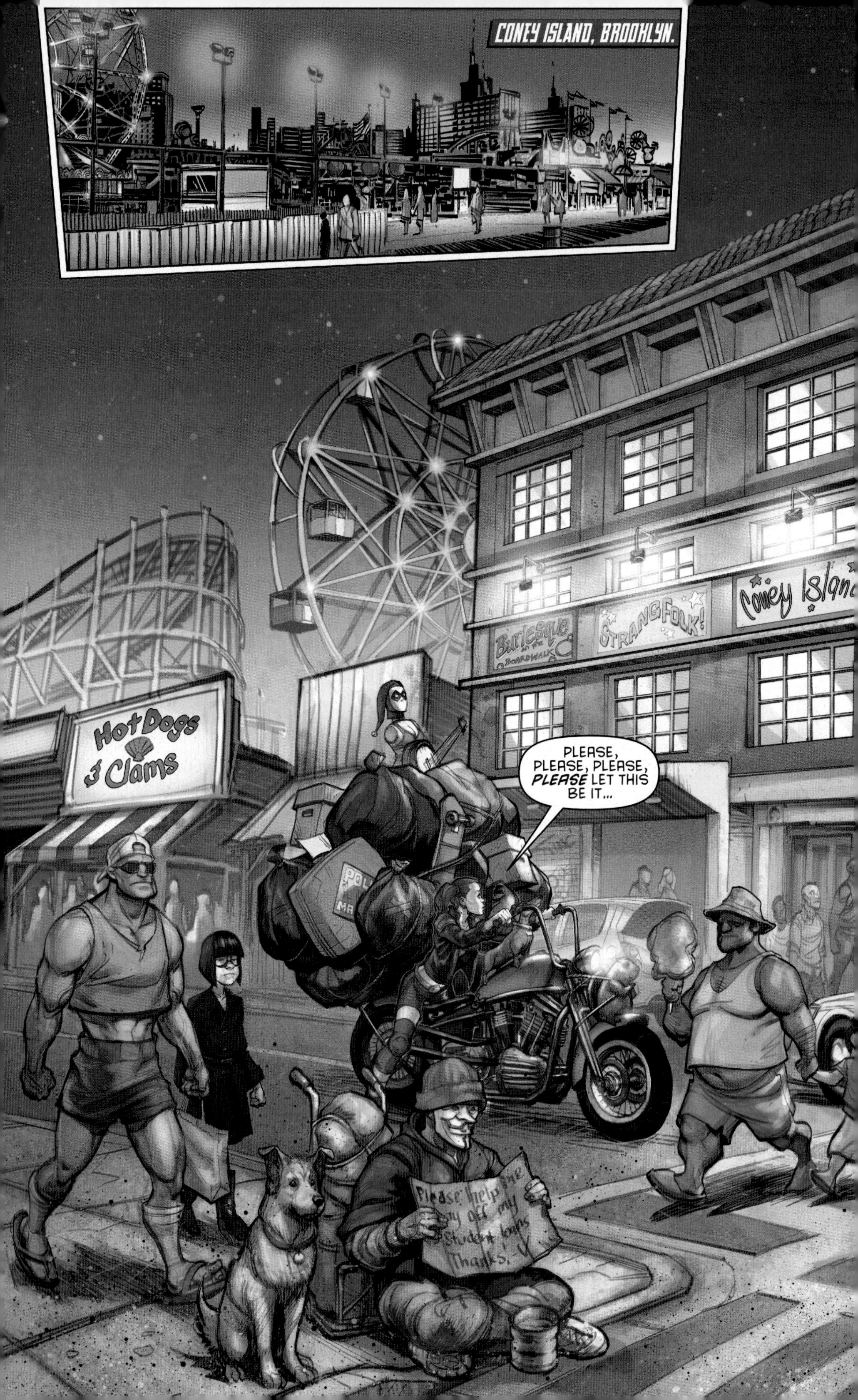
CONEY ISLAND, BROOKLYN.
Hot Dogs
Clams
Burlesque
BOARDWALK
STRANGFOLK!
Coney Islan
PLEASE, PLEASE, PLEASE, *PLEASE* LET THIS BE IT...
Please help
off my
Student loans
Thanks!

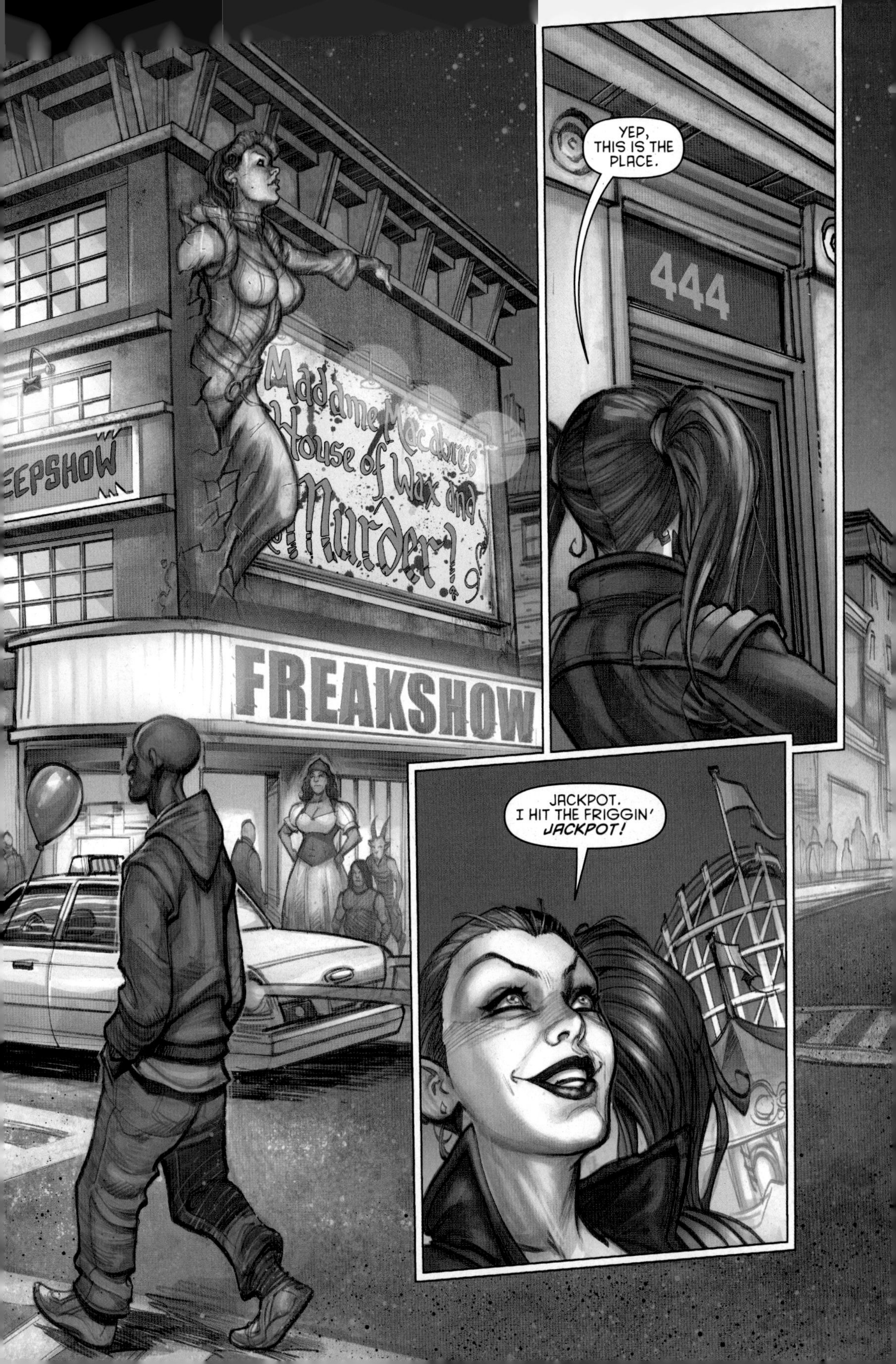
EEPSHOW
Maddame Macabre's House of Wax and Murder?
FREAKSHOW
YEP, THIS IS THE PLACE.
444
JACKPOT. I HIT THE FRIGGIN' *JACKPOT!*

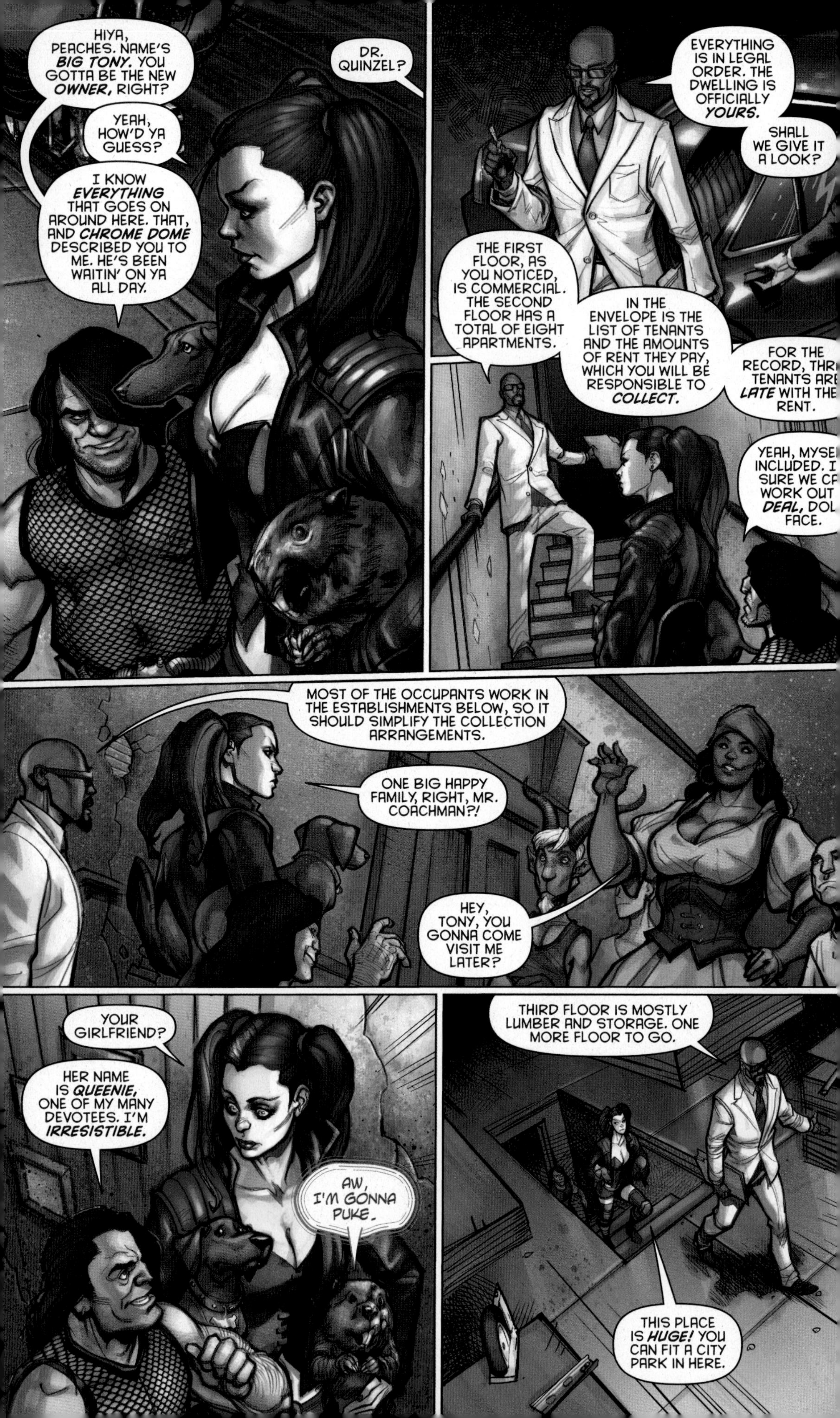
HIYA, PEACHES. NAME'S BIG TONY. YOU GOTTA BE THE NEW OWNER, RIGHT?
DR. QUINZEL?
YEAH, HOW'D YA GUESS?
I KNOW EVERYTHING THAT GOES ON AROUND HERE. THAT, AND CHROME DOME DESCRIBED YOU TO ME. HE'S BEEN WAITIN' ON YA ALL DAY.
EVERYTHING IS IN LEGAL ORDER. THE DWELLING IS OFFICIALLY YOURS.
SHALL WE GIVE IT A LOOK?
THE FIRST FLOOR, AS YOU NOTICED, IS COMMERCIAL. THE SECOND FLOOR HAS A TOTAL OF EIGHT APARTMENTS.
IN THE ENVELOPE IS THE LIST OF TENANTS AND THE AMOUNTS OF RENT THEY PAY, WHICH YOU WILL BE RESPONSIBLE TO COLLECT.
FOR THE RECORD, THR TENANTS ARE LATE WITH THE RENT.
YEAH, MYSE INCLUDED. I SURE WE CA WORK OUT DEAL, DOL FACE.
MOST OF THE OCCUPANTS WORK IN THE ESTABLISHMENTS BELOW, SO IT SHOULD SIMPLIFY THE COLLECTION ARRANGEMENTS.
ONE BIG HAPPY FAMILY, RIGHT, MR. COACHMAN?!
HEY, TONY, YOU GONNA COME VISIT ME LATER?
YOUR GIRLFRIEND?
HER NAME IS QUEENIE, ONE OF MY MANY DEVOTEES. I'M IRRESISTIBLE.
AW, I'M GONNA PUKE.
THIRD FLOOR IS MOSTLY LUMBER AND STORAGE. ONE MORE FLOOR TO GO.
THIS PLACE IS HUGE! YOU CAN FIT A CITY PARK IN HERE.

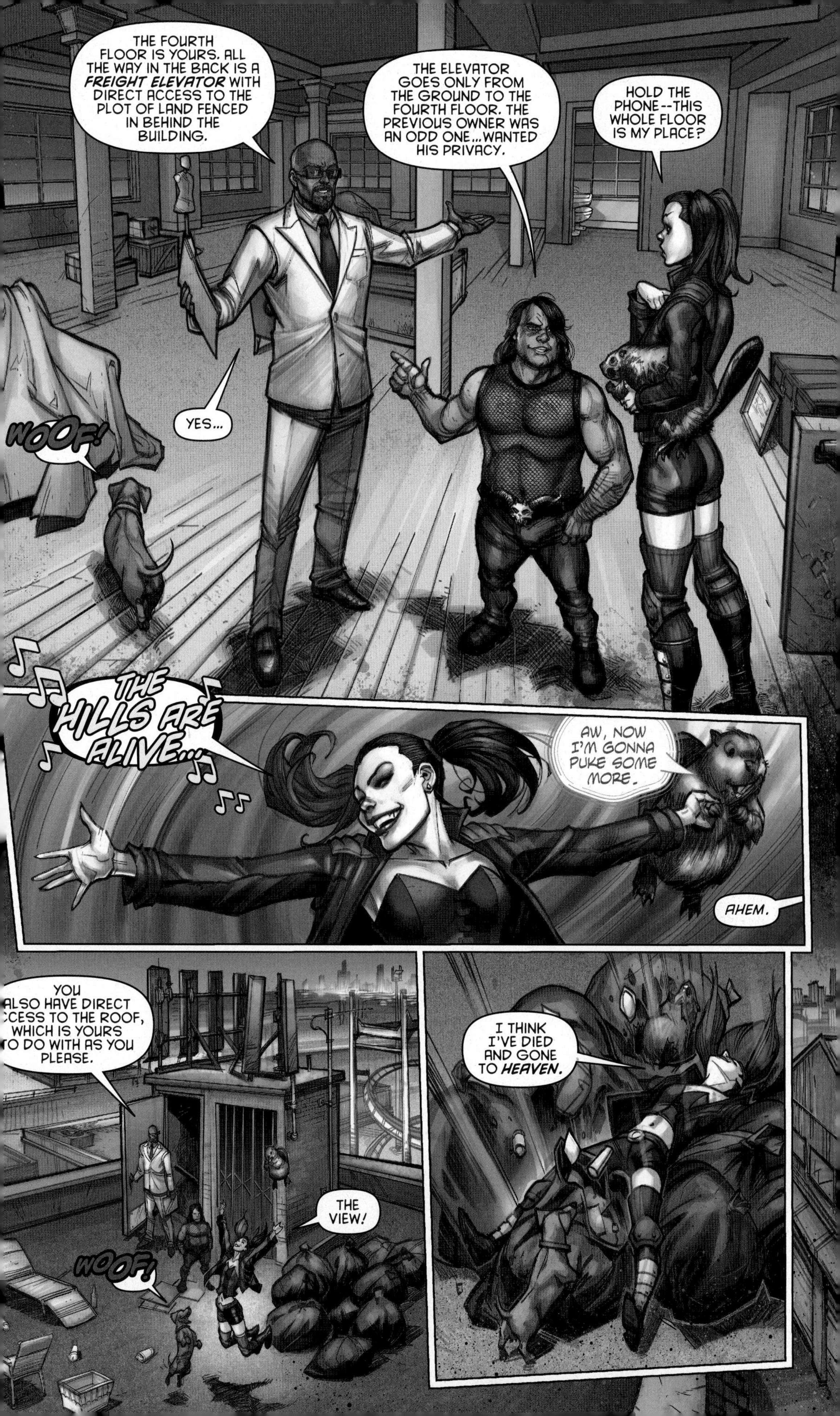
THE FOURTH FLOOR IS YOURS. ALL THE WAY IN THE BACK IS A FREIGHT ELEVATOR WITH DIRECT ACCESS TO THE PLOT OF LAND FENCED IN BEHIND THE BUILDING.
THE ELEVATOR GOES ONLY FROM THE GROUND TO THE FOURTH FLOOR. THE PREVIOUS OWNER WAS AN ODD ONE... WANTED HIS PRIVACY.
HOLD THE PHONE--THIS WHOLE FLOOR IS MY PLACE?
YES...
WOOF!
THE HILLS ARE ALIVE...
AW, NOW I'M GONNA PUKE SOME MORE.
AHEM.
YOU ALSO HAVE DIRECT ACCESS TO THE ROOF, WHICH IS YOURS TO DO WITH AS YOU PLEASE.
THE VIEW!
WOOF!
I THINK I'VE DIED AND GONE TO HEAVEN.

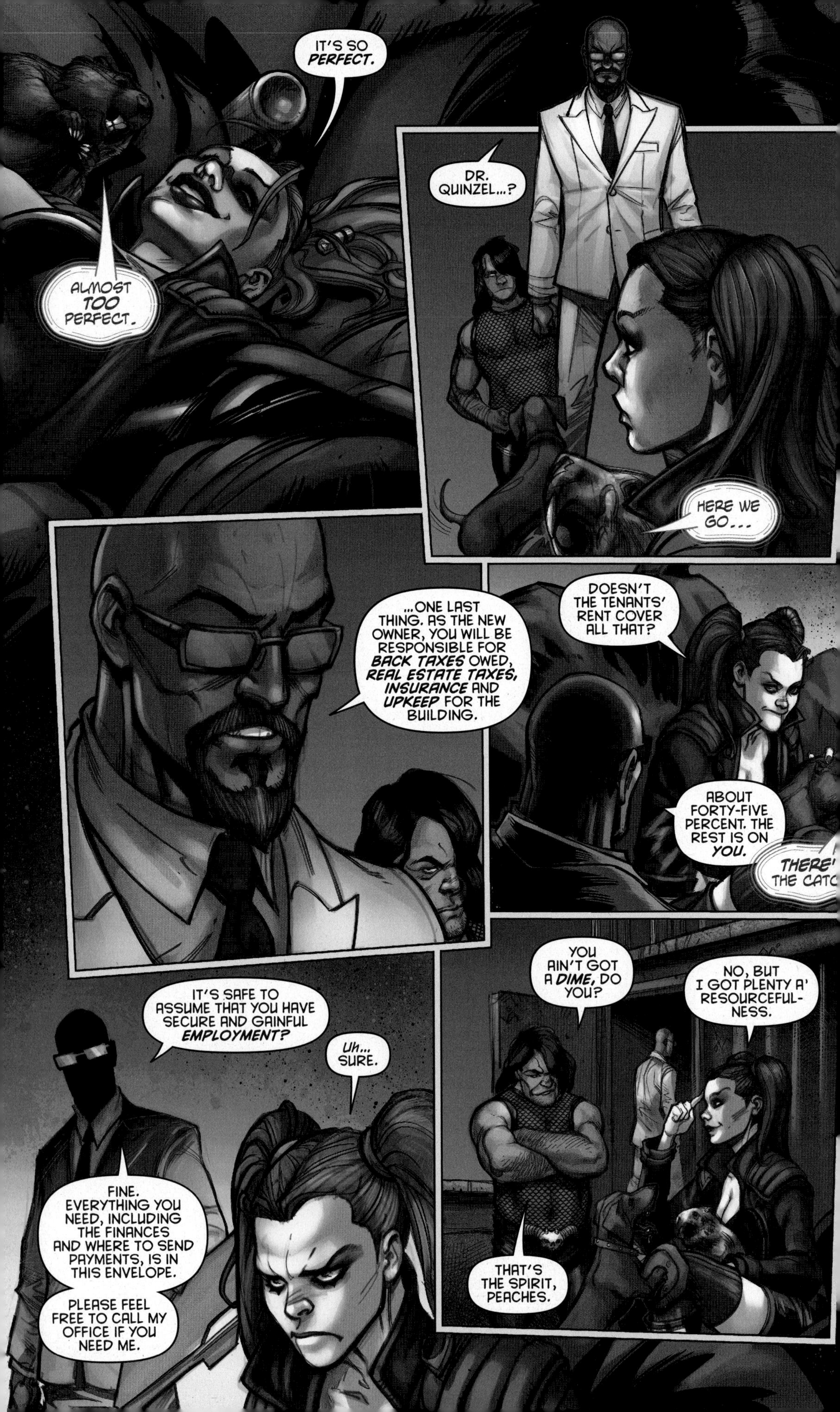

IT'S SO *PERFECT.*
ALMOST *TOO* PERFECT.
DR. QUINZEL...?
HERE WE GO...
...ONE LAST THING. AS THE NEW OWNER, YOU WILL BE RESPONSIBLE FOR *BACK TAXES* OWED, *REAL ESTATE TAXES, INSURANCE* AND *UPKEEP* FOR THE BUILDING.
DOESN'T THE TENANTS' RENT COVER ALL THAT?
ABOUT FORTY-FIVE PERCENT. THE REST IS ON *YOU.*
*THERE'* THE CATC
IT'S SAFE TO ASSUME THAT YOU HAVE SECURE AND GAINFUL *EMPLOYMENT?*
Uh... SURE.
FINE. EVERYTHING YOU NEED, INCLUDING THE FINANCES AND WHERE TO SEND PAYMENTS, IS IN THIS ENVELOPE.
PLEASE FEEL FREE TO CALL MY OFFICE IF YOU NEED ME.
YOU AIN'T GOT A *DIME,* DO YOU?
NO, BUT I GOT PLENTY A' RESOURCEFUL-NESS.
THAT'S THE SPIRIT, PEACHES.

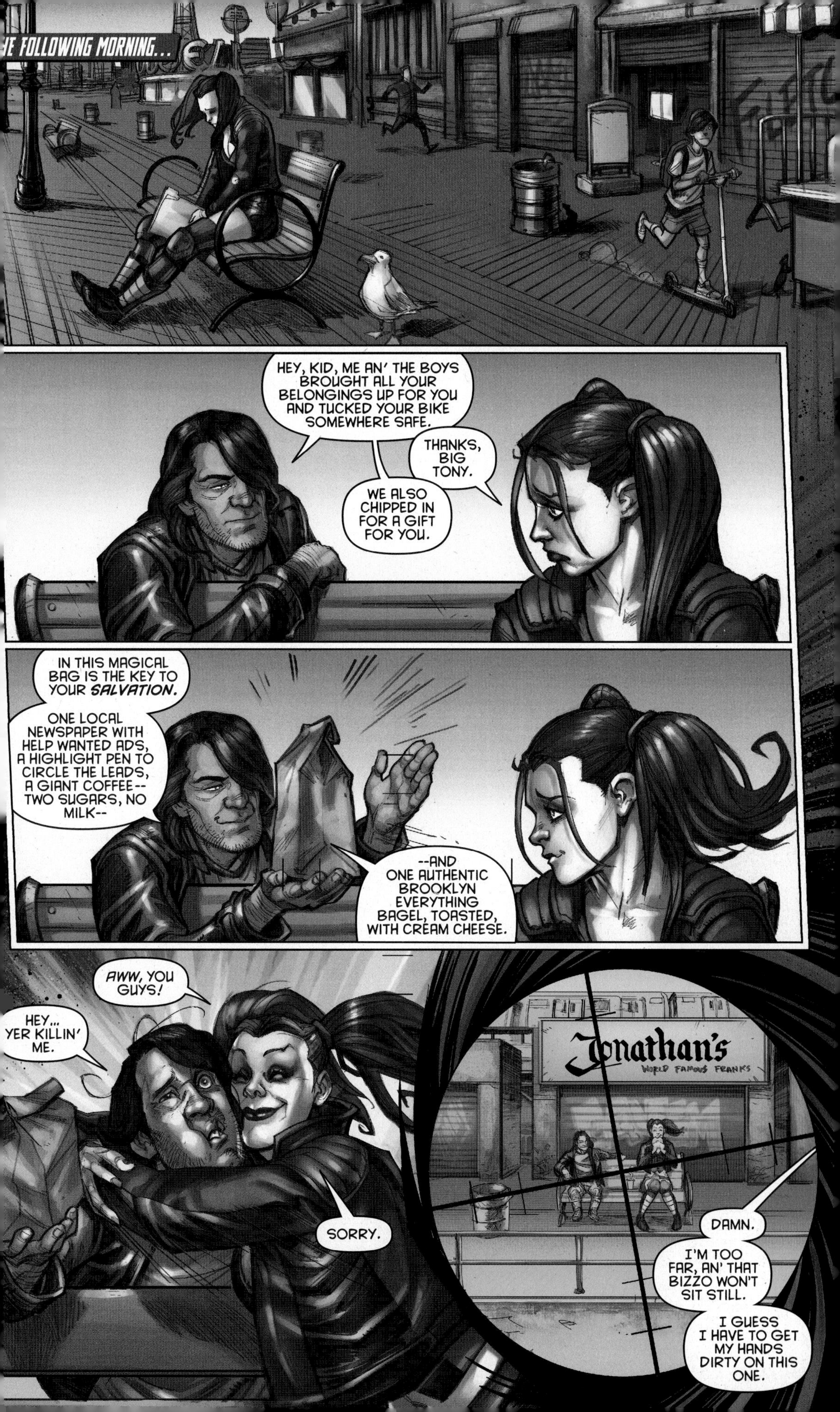

THE FOLLOWING MORNING...
HEY, KID, ME AN' THE BOYS BROUGHT ALL YOUR BELONGINGS UP FOR YOU AND TUCKED YOUR BIKE SOMEWHERE SAFE.
THANKS, BIG TONY.
WE ALSO CHIPPED IN FOR A GIFT FOR YOU.
IN THIS MAGICAL BAG IS THE KEY TO YOUR *SALVATION.*
ONE LOCAL NEWSPAPER WITH HELP WANTED ADS, A HIGHLIGHT PEN TO CIRCLE THE LEADS, A GIANT COFFEE-- TWO SUGARS, NO MILK--
--AND ONE AUTHENTIC BROOKLYN EVERYTHING BAGEL, TOASTED, WITH CREAM CHEESE.
*AWW, YOU GUYS!*
HEY... YER KILLIN' ME.
SORRY.
Jonathan's
WORLD FAMOU$ FRANKS
DAMN.
I'M TOO FAR, AN' THAT BIZZO WON'T SIT STILL.
I GUESS I HAVE TO GET MY HANDS DIRTY ON THIS ONE.

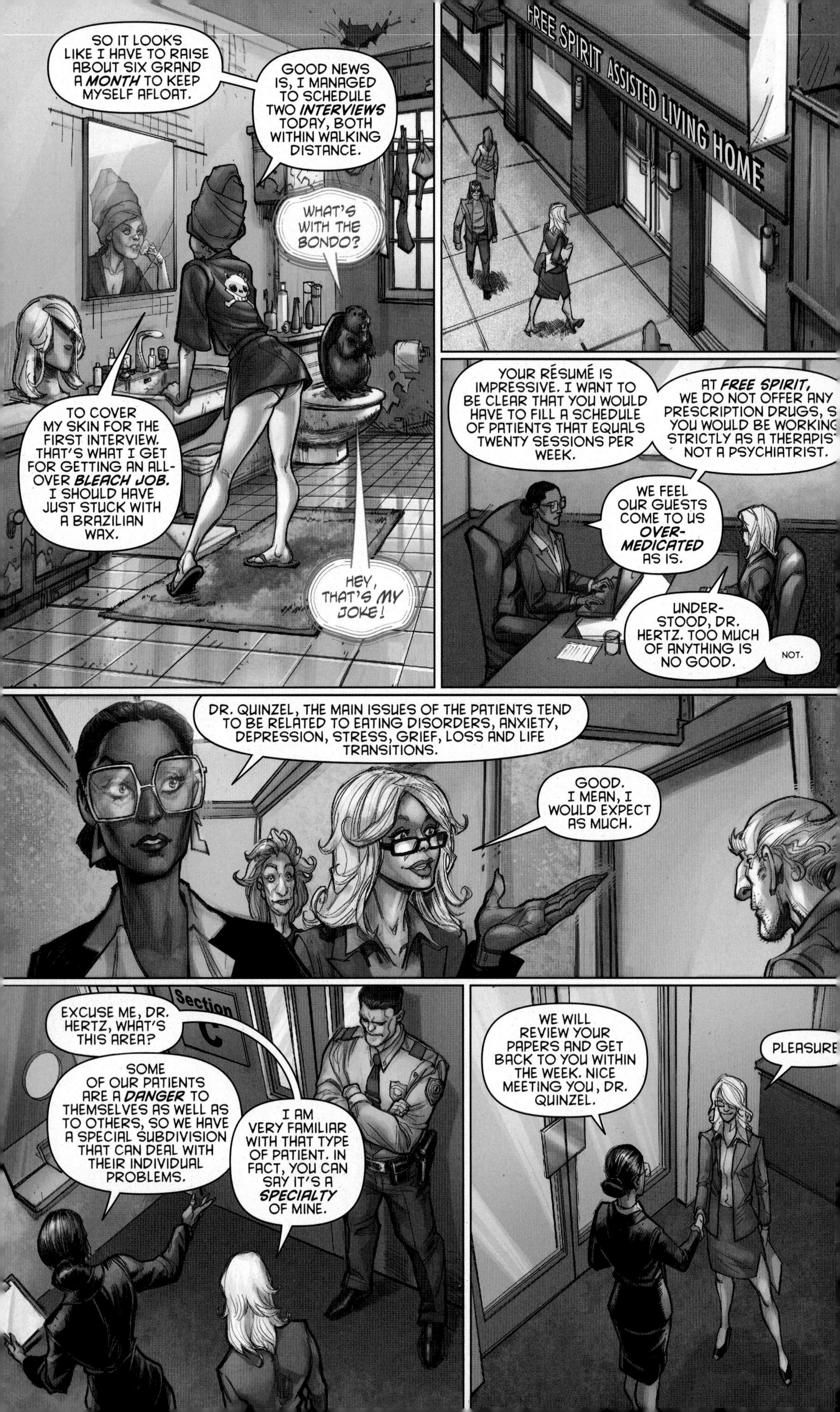
SO IT LOOKS LIKE I HAVE TO RAISE ABOUT SIX GRAND A *MONTH* TO KEEP MYSELF AFLOAT.
GOOD NEWS IS, I MANAGED TO SCHEDULE TWO *INTERVIEWS* TODAY, BOTH WITHIN WALKING DISTANCE.
WHAT'S WITH THE BONDO?
TO COVER MY SKIN FOR THE FIRST INTERVIEW. THAT'S WHAT I GET FOR GETTING AN ALL-OVER *BLEACH JOB.* I SHOULD HAVE JUST STUCK WITH A BRAZILIAN WAX.
HEY, THAT'S *MY* JOKE!
FREE SPIRIT ASSISTED LIVING HOME
YOUR RÉSUMÉ IS IMPRESSIVE. I WANT TO BE CLEAR THAT YOU WOULD HAVE TO FILL A SCHEDULE OF PATIENTS THAT EQUALS TWENTY SESSIONS PER WEEK.
AT *FREE SPIRIT,* WE DO NOT OFFER ANY PRESCRIPTION DRUGS, S YOU WOULD BE WORKING STRICTLY AS A THERAPIS NOT A PSYCHIATRIST.
WE FEEL OUR GUESTS COME TO US *OVER-MEDICATED* AS IS.
UNDER-STOOD, DR. HERTZ. TOO MUCH OF ANYTHING IS NO GOOD.
NOT.
DR. QUINZEL, THE MAIN ISSUES OF THE PATIENTS TEND TO BE RELATED TO EATING DISORDERS, ANXIETY, DEPRESSION, STRESS, GRIEF, LOSS AND LIFE TRANSITIONS.
GOOD. I MEAN, I WOULD EXPECT AS MUCH.
Section C
EXCUSE ME, DR. HERTZ, WHAT'S THIS AREA?
SOME OF OUR PATIENTS ARE A *DANGER* TO THEMSELVES AS WELL AS TO OTHERS, SO WE HAVE A SPECIAL SUBDIVISION THAT CAN DEAL WITH THEIR INDIVIDUAL PROBLEMS.
I AM VERY FAMILIAR WITH THAT TYPE OF PATIENT. IN FACT, YOU CAN SAY IT'S A *SPECIALTY* OF MINE.
WE WILL REVIEW YOUR PAPERS AND GET BACK TO YOU WITHIN THE WEEK. NICE MEETING YOU, DR. QUINZEL.
PLEASURE

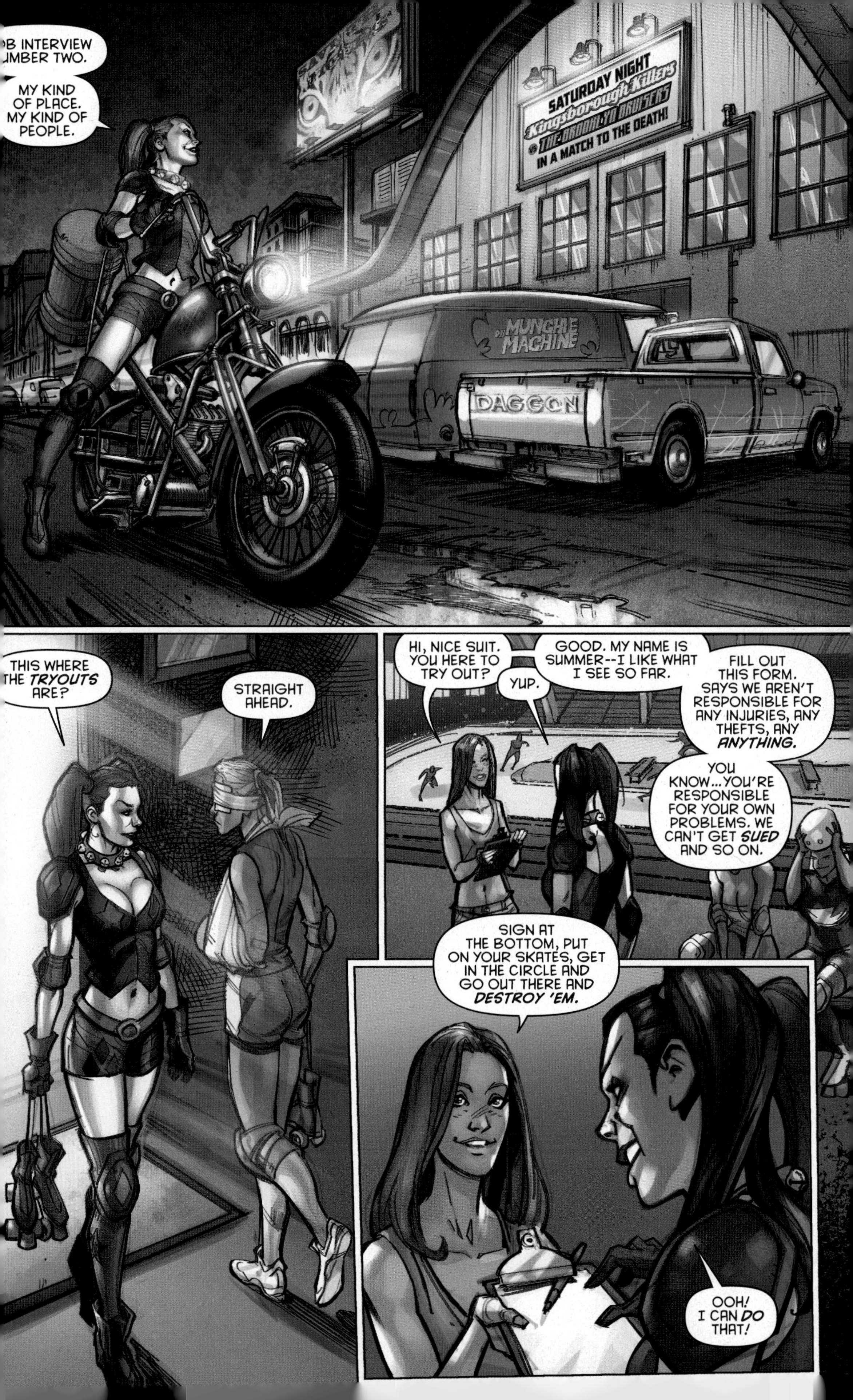

B INTERVIEW UMBER TWO.
MY KIND OF PLACE. MY KIND OF PEOPLE.
SATURDAY NIGHT
Kingsborough Killers
vs THE BROOKLYN BRUISERS
IN A MATCH TO THE DEATH!
MUNCHIE MACHINE
DAGGON
THIS WHERE THE *TRYOUTS* ARE?
STRAIGHT AHEAD.
HI, NICE SUIT. YOU HERE TO TRY OUT?
YUP.
GOOD. MY NAME IS SUMMER--I LIKE WHAT I SEE SO FAR.
FILL OUT THIS FORM. SAYS WE AREN'T RESPONSIBLE FOR ANY INJURIES, ANY THEFTS, ANY *ANYTHING.*
YOU KNOW...YOU'RE RESPONSIBLE FOR YOUR OWN PROBLEMS. WE CAN'T GET *SUED* AND SO ON.
SIGN AT THE BOTTOM, PUT ON YOUR SKATES, GET IN THE CIRCLE AND GO OUT THERE AND *DESTROY 'EM.*
OOH! I CAN *DO* THAT!

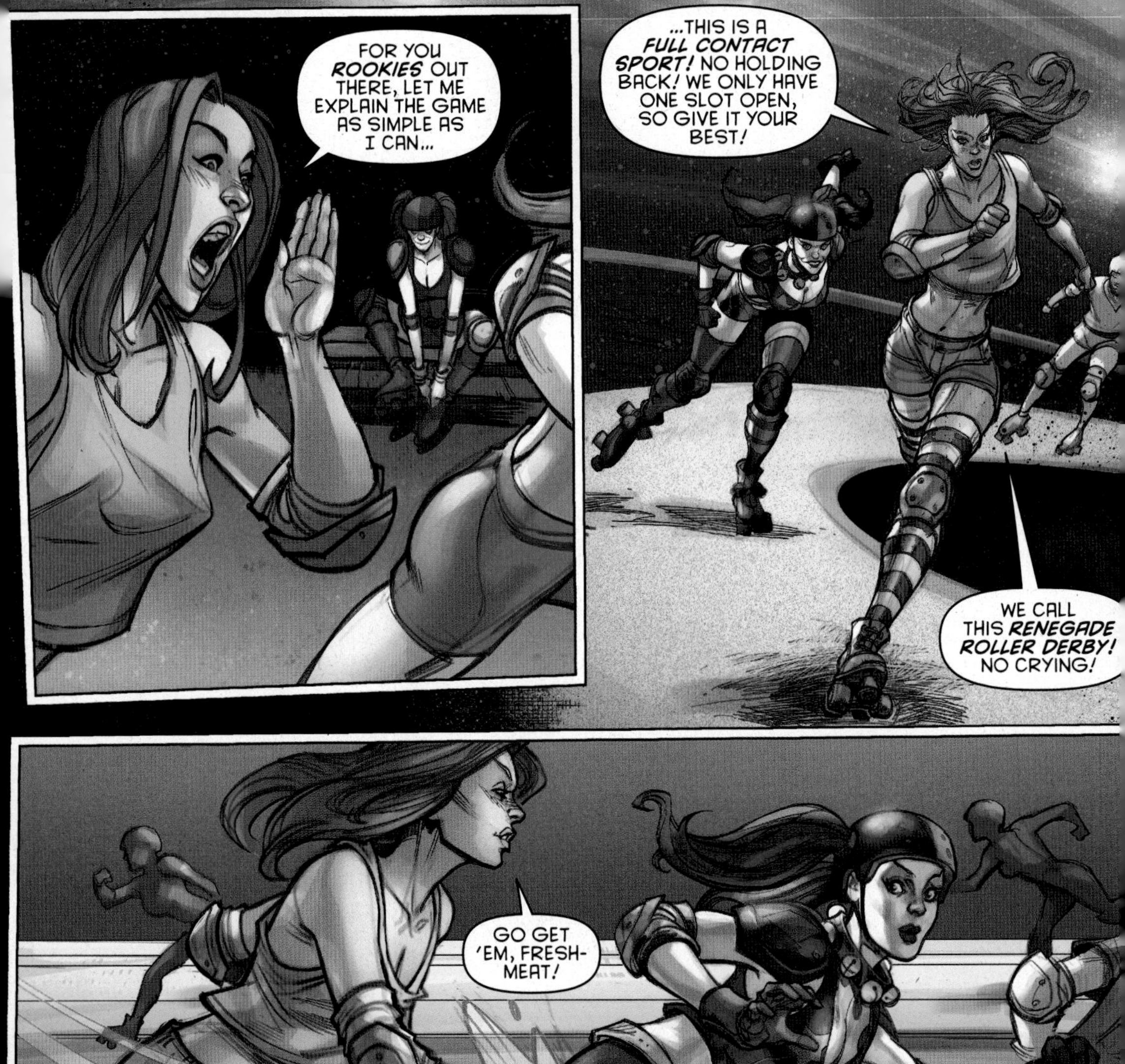

FOR YOU ROOKIES OUT THERE, LET ME EXPLAIN THE GAME AS SIMPLE AS I CAN...
...THIS IS A FULL CONTACT SPORT! NO HOLDING BACK! WE ONLY HAVE ONE SLOT OPEN, SO GIVE IT YOUR BEST!
WE CALL THIS RENEGADE ROLLER DERBY! NO CRYING!
GO GET 'EM, FRESH-MEAT!
EACH TEAM DESIGNATES A "JAMMER"--THE PERSON WHO SCORES BY LAPPING MEMBERS OF THE OTHER TEAM!
EACH TEAM ASSISTS THEIR OWN JAMMER, WHILE HINDERING THE OPPOSING JAMMER!
SO I'M CLEAR, BOTH TEAMS PLAY OFFENSE AND DEFENSE AT THE SAME TIME.
FOR THIS TRYOUT, WE'RE GOING TO HIRE THE LAST MAN STANDING...SO GO TO IT, LADIES! SHOW ME WHAT YOU GOT!

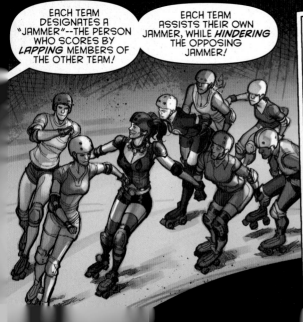

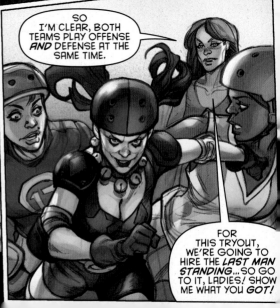

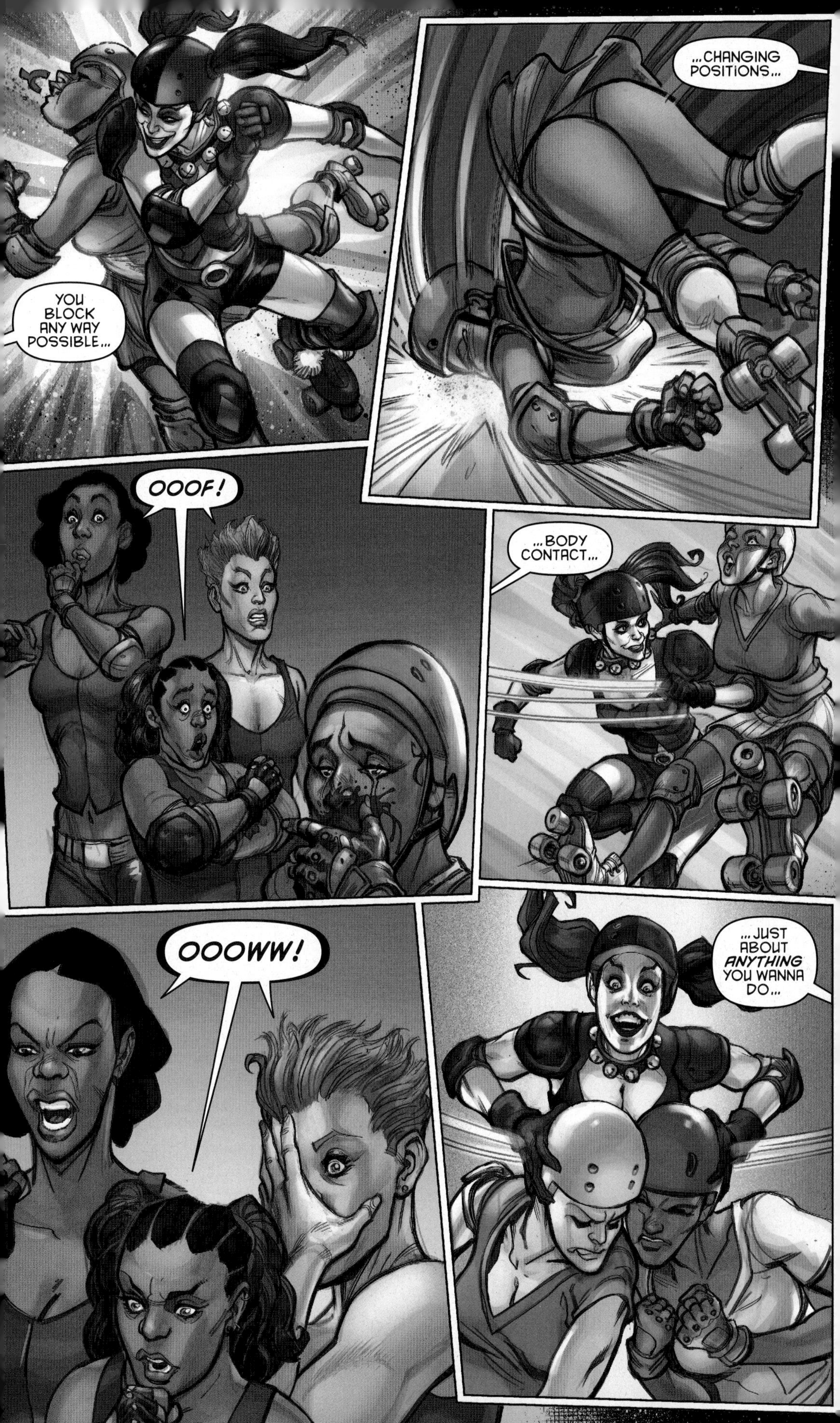
YOU BLOCK ANY WAY POSSIBLE...
...CHANGING POSITIONS...
OOOF!
...BODY CONTACT...
OOOWW!
...JUST ABOUT *ANYTHING* YOU WANNA DO...

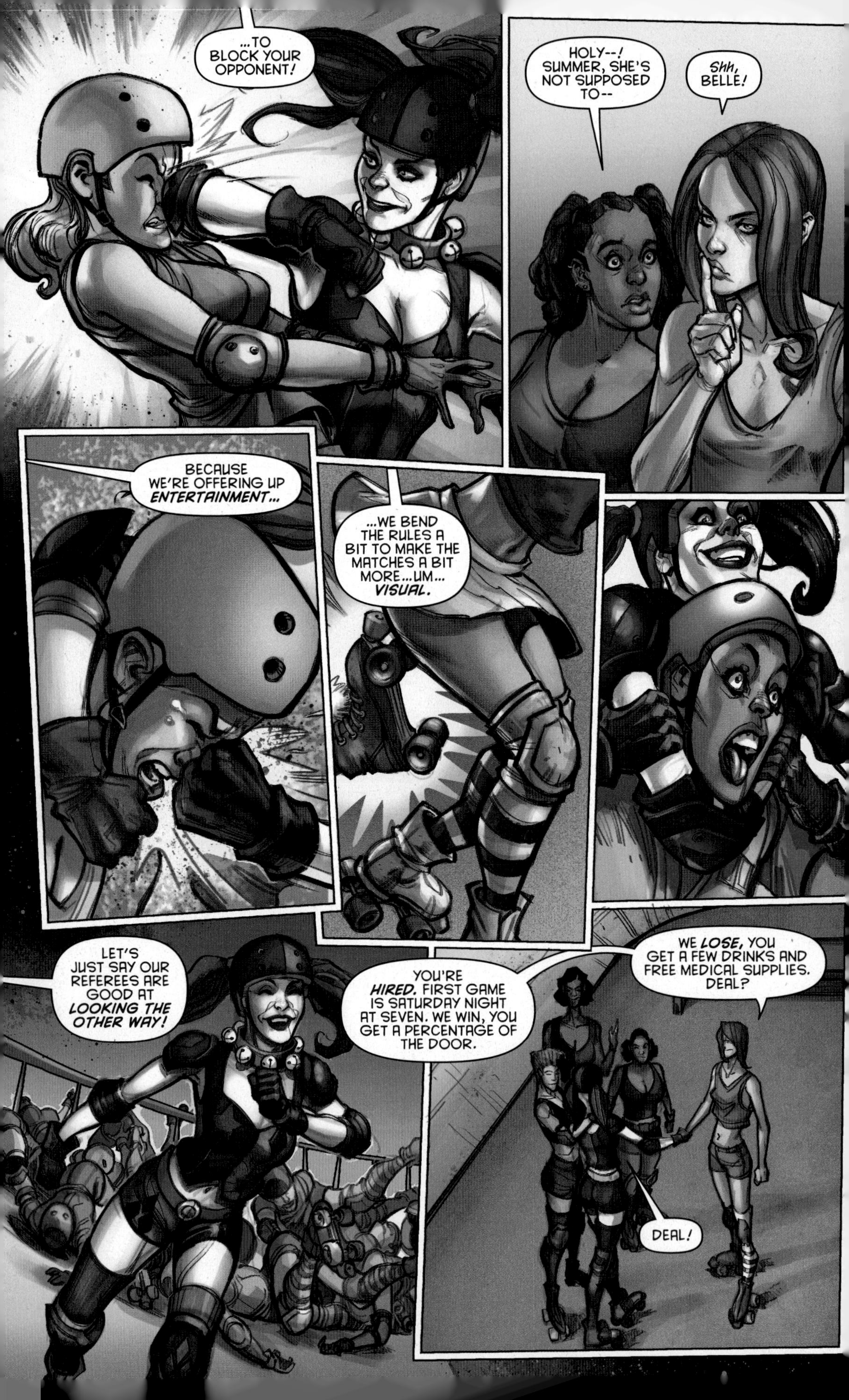
...TO
BLOCK YOUR
OPPONENT!
HOLY--! SUMMER, SHE'S NOT SUPPOSED TO--
Shh, BELLE!
BECAUSE WE'RE OFFERING UP ENTERTAINMENT...
...WE BEND THE RULES A BIT TO MAKE THE MATCHES A BIT MORE...UM... VISUAL.
LET'S JUST SAY OUR REFEREES ARE GOOD AT LOOKING THE OTHER WAY!
YOU'RE HIRED. FIRST GAME IS SATURDAY NIGHT AT SEVEN. WE WIN, YOU GET A PERCENTAGE OF THE DOOR.
WE LOSE, YOU GET A FEW DRINKS AND FREE MEDICAL SUPPLIES. DEAL?
DEAL!

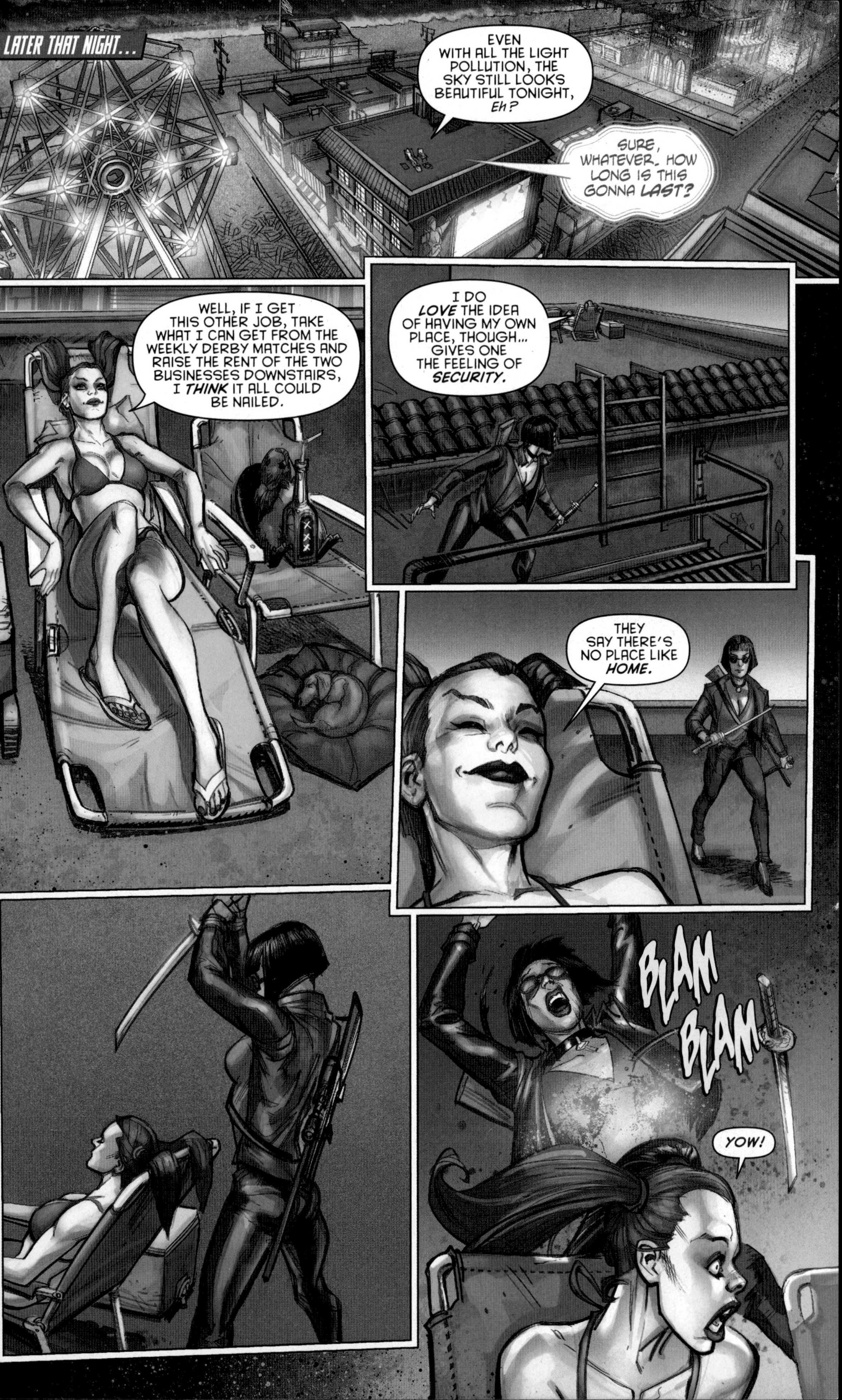
LATER THAT NIGHT...
EVEN WITH ALL THE LIGHT POLLUTION, THE SKY STILL LOOKS BEAUTIFUL TONIGHT, Eh?
SURE, WHATEVER. HOW LONG IS THIS GONNA LAST?
WELL, IF I GET THIS OTHER JOB, TAKE WHAT I CAN GET FROM THE WEEKLY DERBY MATCHES AND RAISE THE RENT OF THE TWO BUSINESSES DOWNSTAIRS, I THINK IT ALL COULD BE NAILED.
I DO LOVE THE IDEA OF HAVING MY OWN PLACE, THOUGH... GIVES ONE THE FEELING OF SECURITY.
THEY SAY THERE'S NO PLACE LIKE HOME.
BLAM BLAM
YOW!

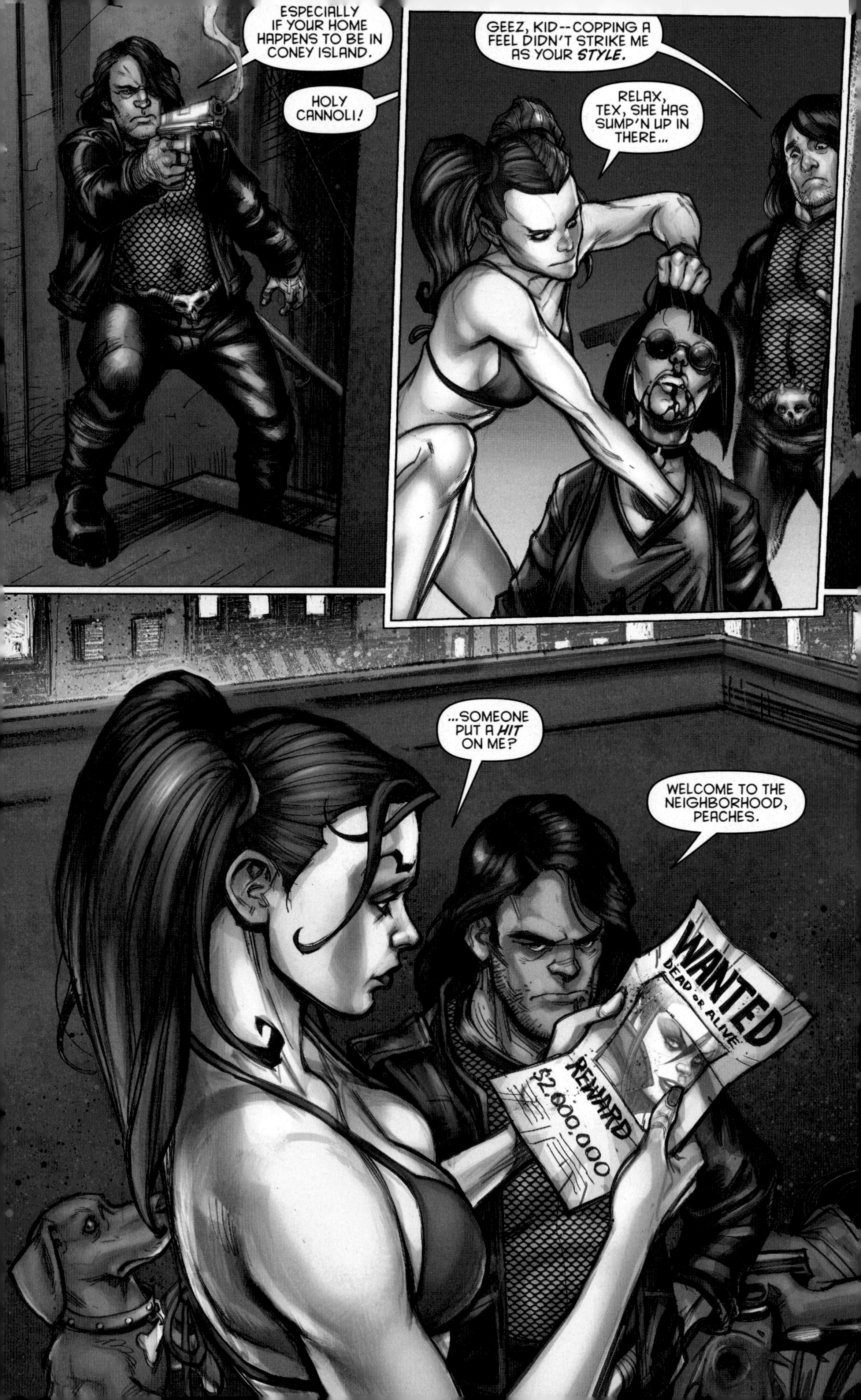
ESPECIALLY IF YOUR HOME HAPPENS TO BE IN CONEY ISLAND.
HOLY CANNOLI!
GEEZ, KID--COPPING A FEEL DIDN'T STRIKE ME AS YOUR STYLE.
RELAX, TEX, SHE HAS SUMP'N UP IN THERE...
...SOMEONE PUT A HIT ON ME?
WELCOME TO THE NEIGHBORHOOD, PEACHES.
WANTED
DEAD OR ALIVE
REWARD
$2,000,000

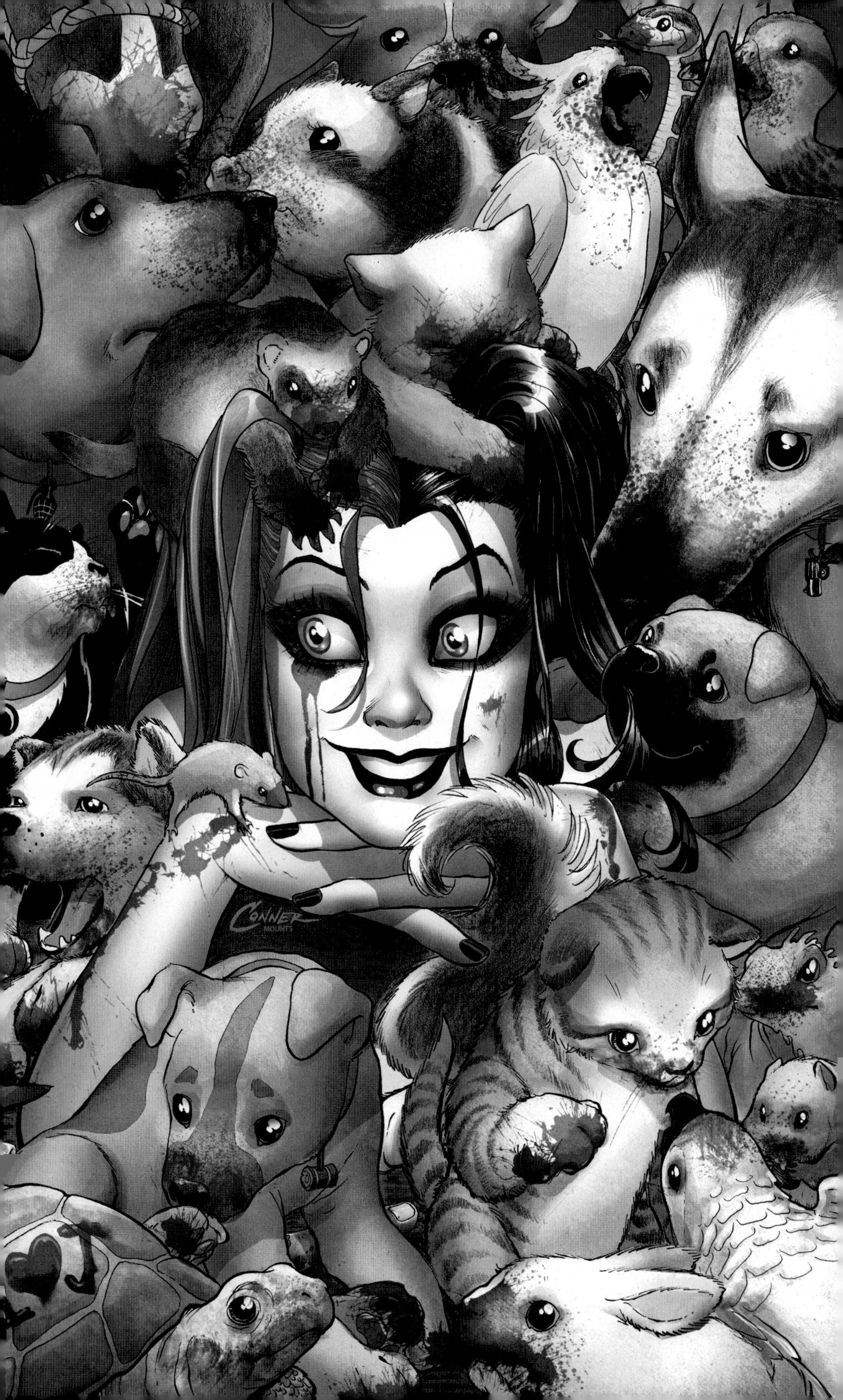
CONNER
MOUNTS

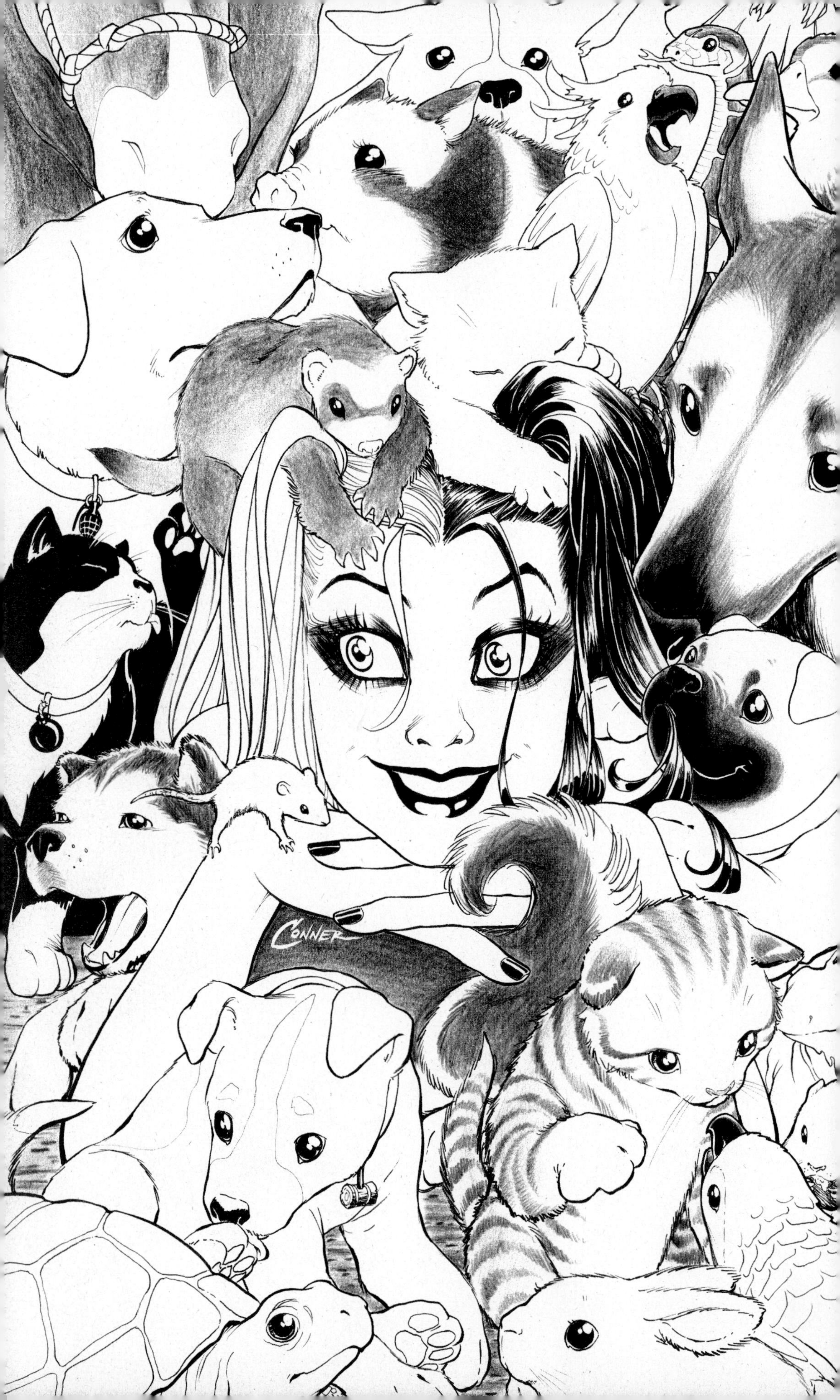
CONNER

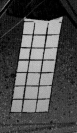

# HELTER SHELTER

AMANDA CONNER &
JIMMY PALMIOTTI WRITERS
CHAD HARDIN &
STEPHANE ROUX ARTISTS
ALEX SINCLAIR COLORIST
JOHN J. HILL LETTERER
AMANDA CONNER &
PAUL MOUNTS COVER

MISS ME, SUGAR? I SURE MISSED *YOU*, PUDDIN' POP!

AHEM...

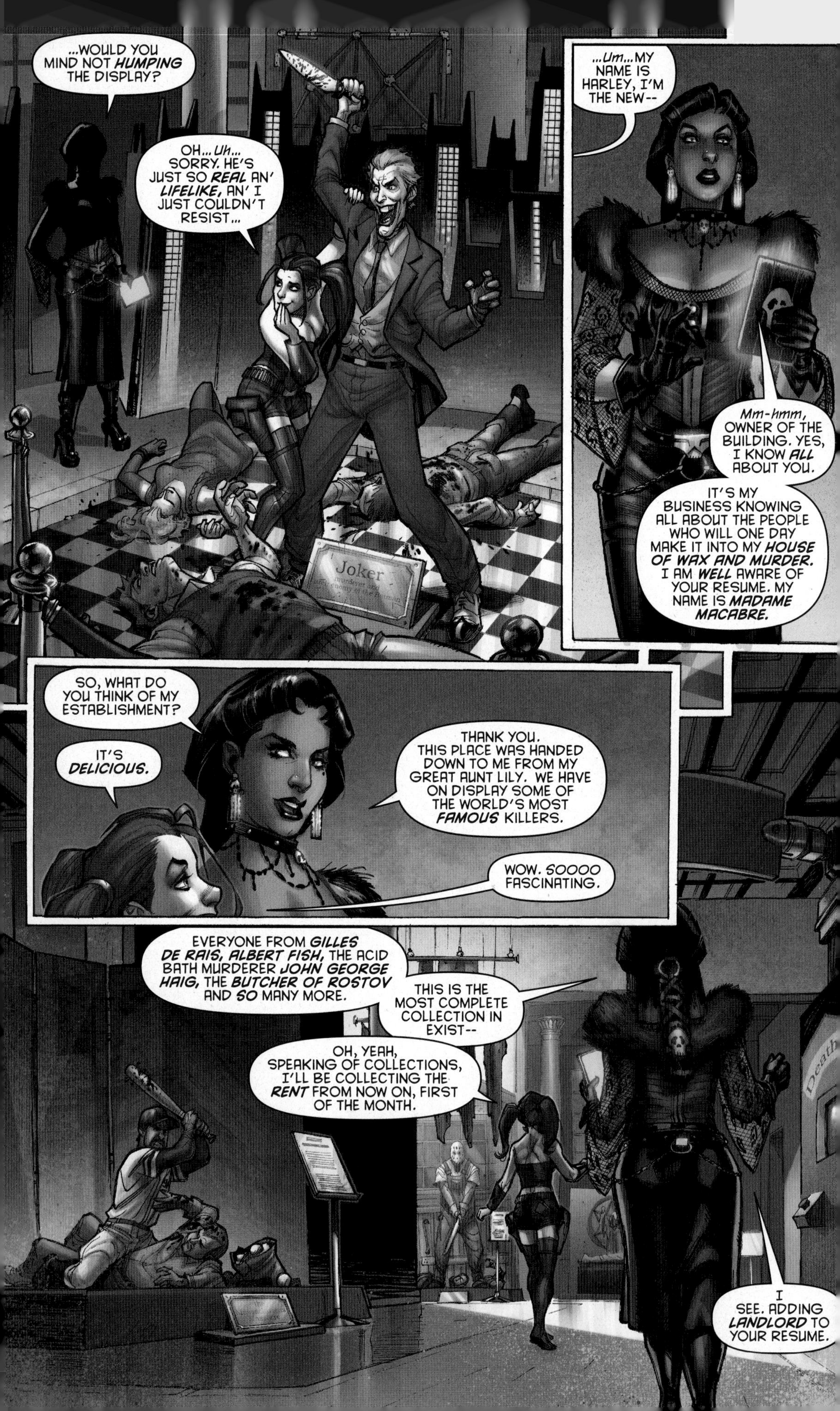

...WOULD YOU MIND NOT *HUMPING* THE DISPLAY?
OH... *Uh*... SORRY. HE'S JUST SO *REAL* AN' *LIFELIKE,* AN' I JUST COULDN'T RESIST...
Joker
...*Um*... MY NAME IS HARLEY, I'M THE NEW--
*Mm-hmm,* OWNER OF THE BUILDING. YES, I KNOW *ALL* ABOUT YOU.
IT'S MY BUSINESS KNOWING ALL ABOUT THE PEOPLE WHO WILL ONE DAY MAKE IT INTO MY *HOUSE OF WAX AND MURDER.* I AM *WELL* AWARE OF YOUR RESUME. MY NAME IS *MADAME MACABRE.*
SO, WHAT DO YOU THINK OF MY ESTABLISHMENT?
IT'S *DELICIOUS.*
THANK YOU. THIS PLACE WAS HANDED DOWN TO ME FROM MY GREAT AUNT LILY. WE HAVE ON DISPLAY SOME OF THE WORLD'S MOST *FAMOUS* KILLERS.
WOW. *SOOOO* FASCINATING.
EVERYONE FROM *GILLES DE RAIS, ALBERT FISH,* THE ACID BATH MURDERER *JOHN GEORGE HAIG,* THE *BUTCHER OF ROSTOV* AND *SO* MANY MORE.
THIS IS THE MOST COMPLETE COLLECTION IN EXIST--
OH, YEAH, SPEAKING OF COLLECTIONS, I'LL BE COLLECTING THE *RENT* FROM NOW ON, FIRST OF THE MONTH.
I SEE. ADDING *LANDLORD* TO YOUR RESUME.

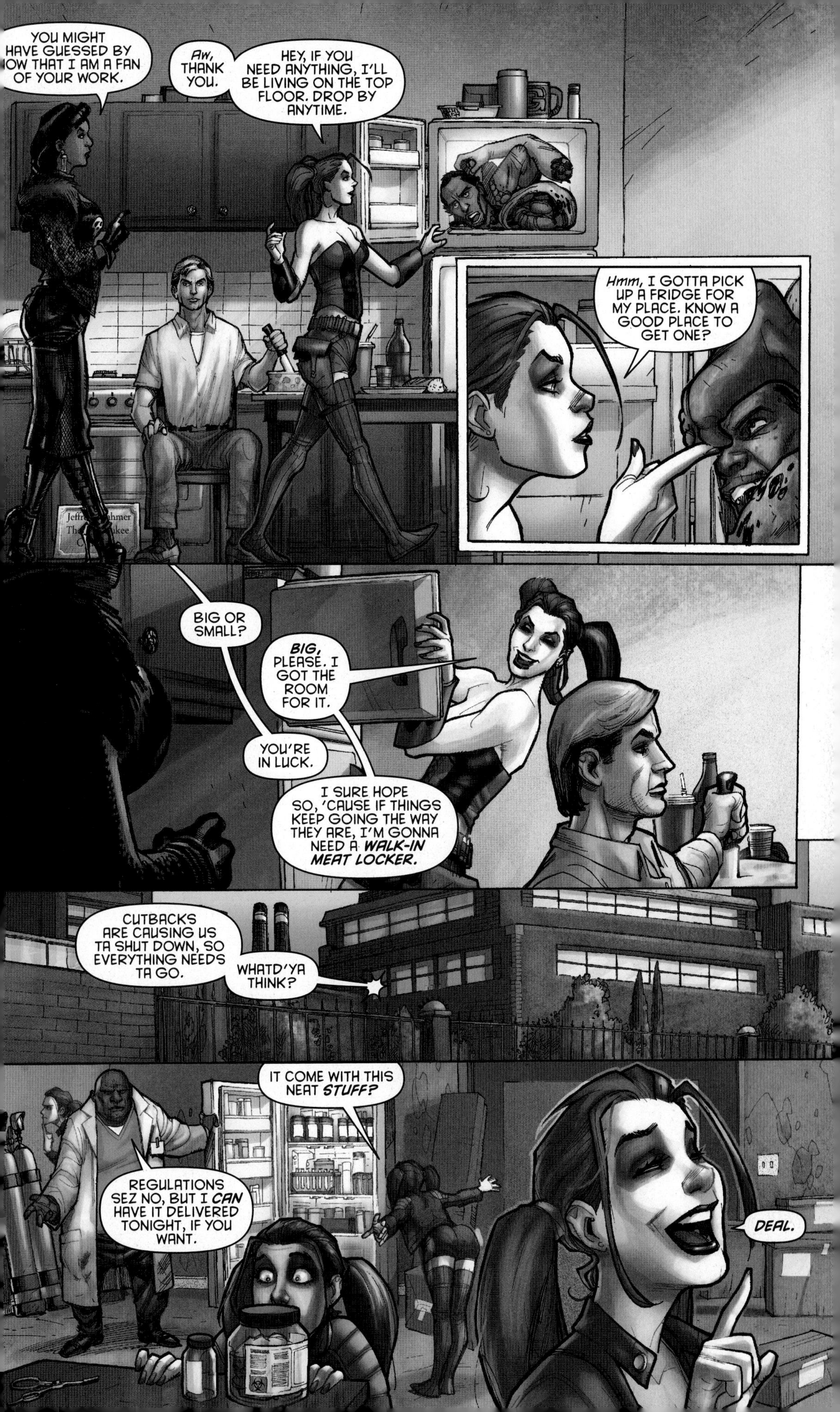
YOU MIGHT HAVE GUESSED BY NOW THAT I AM A FAN OF YOUR WORK.
Aw, THANK YOU.
HEY, IF YOU NEED ANYTHING, I'LL BE LIVING ON THE TOP FLOOR. DROP BY ANYTIME.
Hmm, I GOTTA PICK UP A FRIDGE FOR MY PLACE. KNOW A GOOD PLACE TO GET ONE?
BIG OR SMALL?
BIG, PLEASE. I GOT THE ROOM FOR IT.
YOU'RE IN LUCK.
I SURE HOPE SO, 'CAUSE IF THINGS KEEP GOING THE WAY THEY ARE, I'M GONNA NEED A WALK-IN MEAT LOCKER.
CUTBACKS ARE CAUSING US TA SHUT DOWN, SO EVERYTHING NEEDS TA GO.
WHATD'YA THINK?
IT COME WITH THIS NEAT STUFF?
REGULATIONS SEZ NO, BUT I CAN HAVE IT DELIVERED TONIGHT, IF YOU WANT.
DEAL.

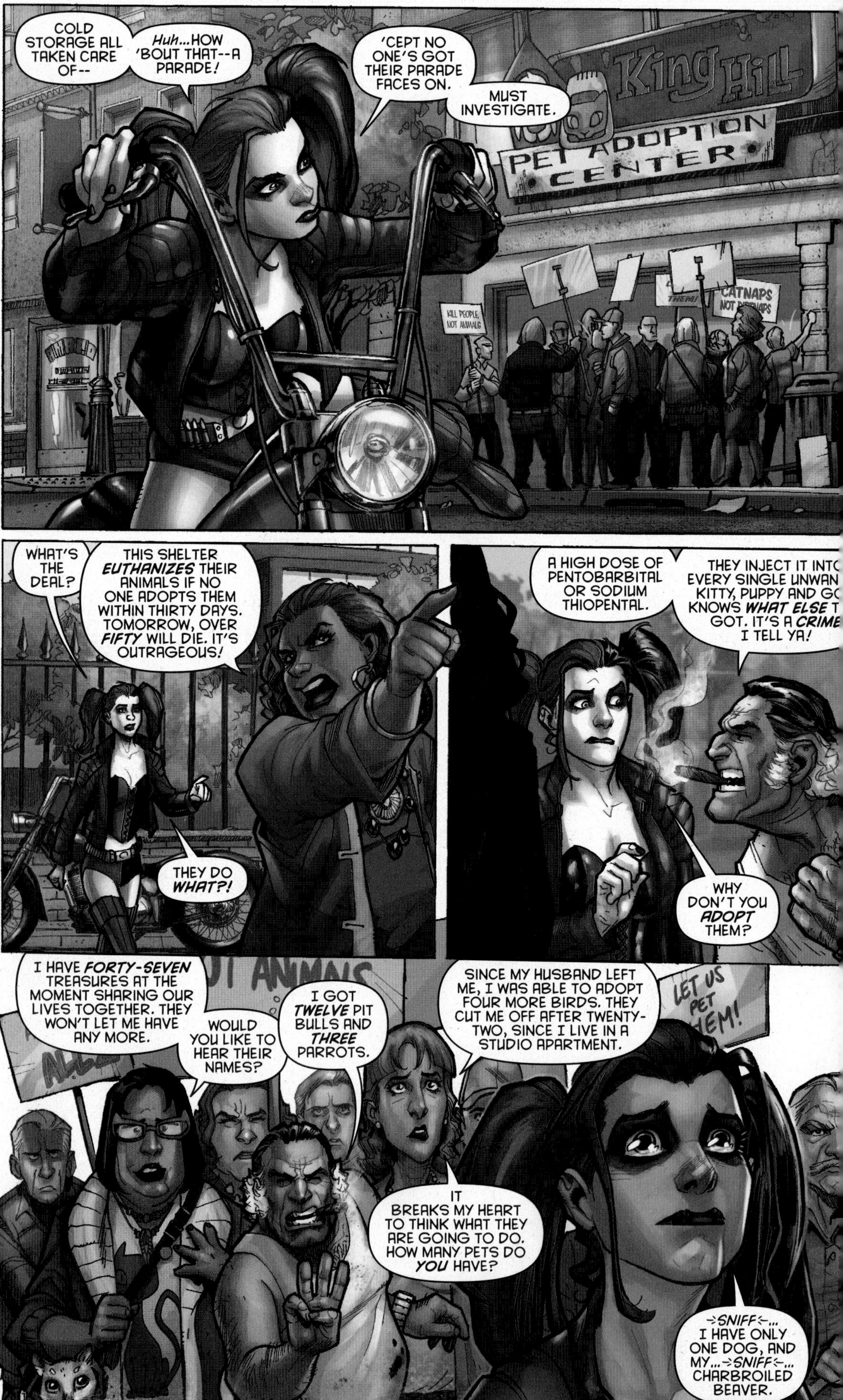
COLD STORAGE ALL TAKEN CARE OF--
*Huh*...HOW 'BOUT THAT--A PARADE!
'CEPT NO ONE'S GOT THEIR PARADE FACES ON.
MUST INVESTIGATE.
King Hill
PET ADOPTION CENTER
KILL PEOPLE, NOT ANIMALS
CATNAPS
WHAT'S THE DEAL?
THIS SHELTER ***EUTHANIZES*** THEIR ANIMALS IF NO ONE ADOPTS THEM WITHIN THIRTY DAYS. TOMORROW, OVER ***FIFTY*** WILL DIE. IT'S OUTRAGEOUS!
THEY DO ***WHAT?!***
A HIGH DOSE OF PENTOBARBITAL OR SODIUM THIOPENTAL.
THEY INJECT IT INTC EVERY SINGLE UNWAN KITTY, PUPPY AND GO KNOWS ***WHAT ELSE*** T GOT. IT'S A ***CRIME*** I TELL YA!
WHY DON'T YOU ***ADOPT*** THEM?
I HAVE ***FORTY-SEVEN*** TREASURES AT THE MOMENT SHARING OUR LIVES TOGETHER. THEY WON'T LET ME HAVE ANY MORE.
WOULD YOU LIKE TO HEAR THEIR NAMES?
I GOT ***TWELVE*** PIT BULLS AND ***THREE*** PARROTS.
SINCE MY HUSBAND LEFT ME, I WAS ABLE TO ADOPT FOUR MORE BIRDS. THEY CUT ME OFF AFTER TWENTY-TWO, SINCE I LIVE IN A STUDIO APARTMENT.
LET US PET
IT BREAKS MY HEART TO THINK WHAT THEY ARE GOING TO DO. HOW MANY PETS DO ***YOU*** HAVE?
*SNIFF*... I HAVE ONLY ONE DOG, AND MY...*SNIFF*... CHARBROILED BEAVER.

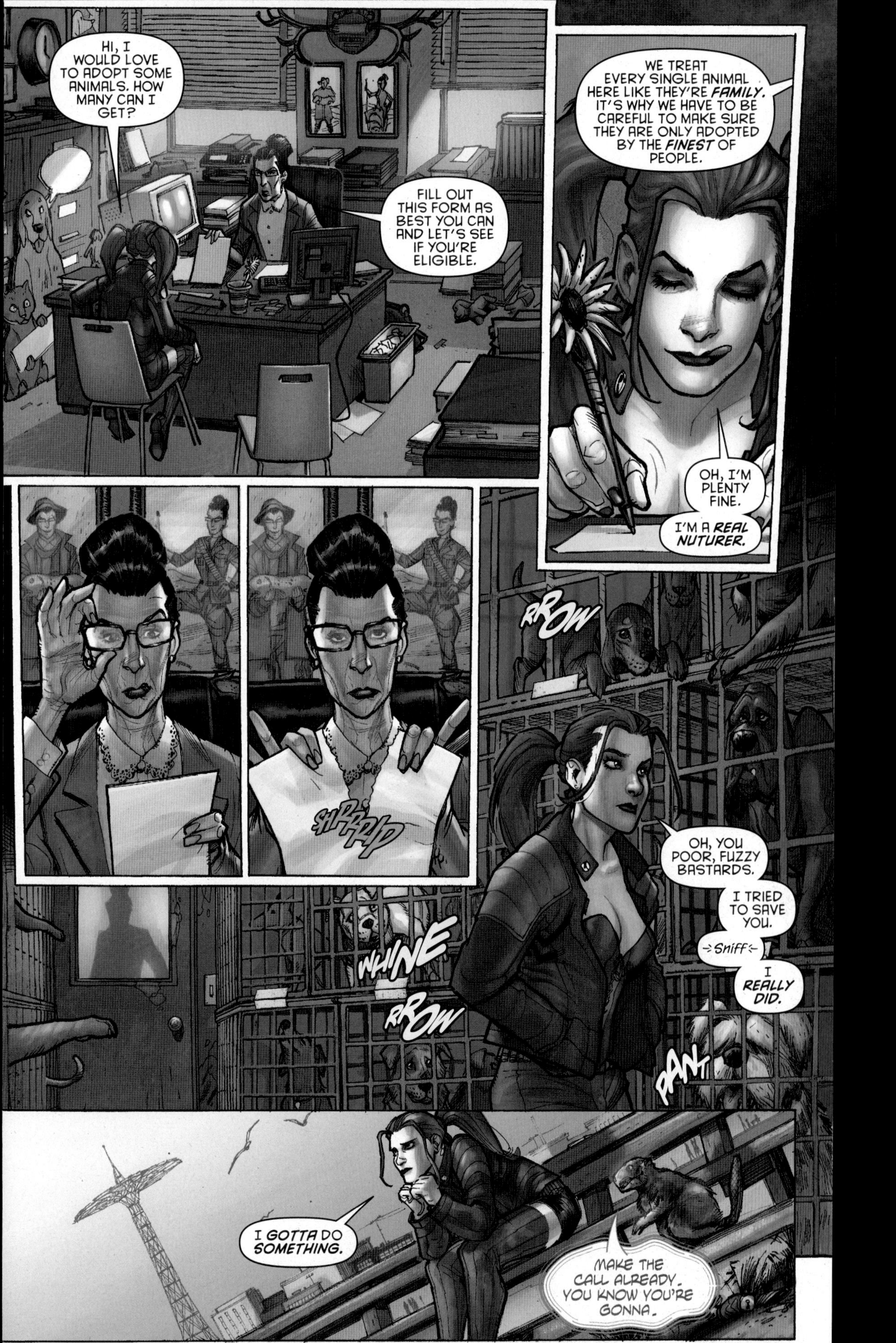
HI, I WOULD LOVE TO ADOPT SOME ANIMALS. HOW MANY CAN I GET?
FILL OUT THIS FORM AS BEST YOU CAN AND LET'S SEE IF YOU'RE ELIGIBLE.
WE TREAT EVERY SINGLE ANIMAL HERE LIKE THEY'RE FAMILY. IT'S WHY WE HAVE TO BE CAREFUL TO MAKE SURE THEY ARE ONLY ADOPTED BY THE FINEST OF PEOPLE.
OH, I'M PLENTY FINE.
I'M A REAL NUTURER.
SHRRRIP
RROW
OH, YOU POOR, FUZZY BASTARDS.
I TRIED TO SAVE YOU.
Sniff
I REALLY DID.
WHINE
RROW
PANT
I GOTTA DO SOMETHING.
MAKE THE CALL ALREADY. YOU KNOW YOU'RE GONNA.

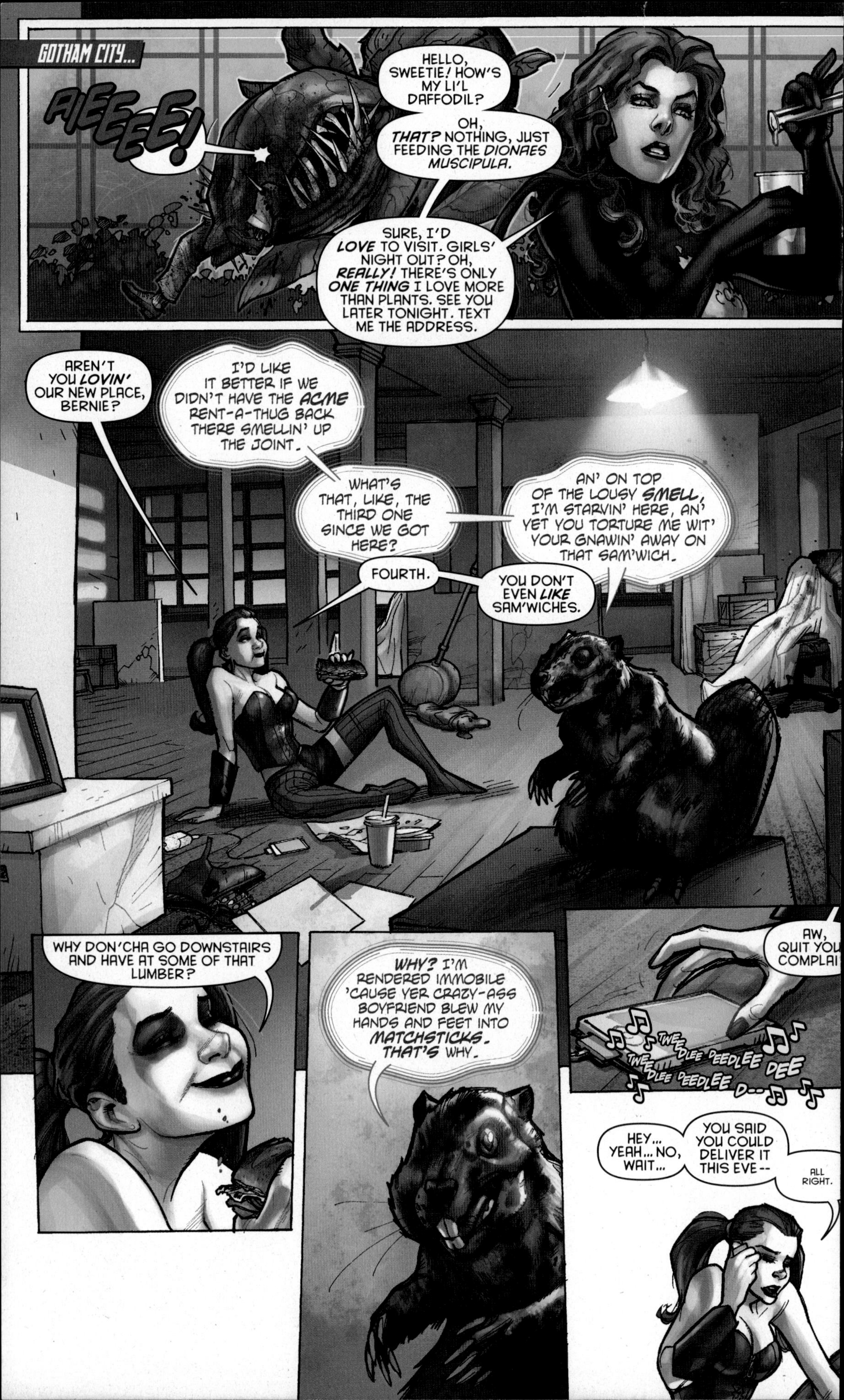
GOTHAM CITY...
AIEEEEE!
HELLO, SWEETIE! HOW'S MY LI'L DAFFODIL?
OH, THAT? NOTHING, JUST FEEDING THE DIONAES MUSCIPULA.
SURE, I'D LOVE TO VISIT. GIRLS' NIGHT OUT? OH, REALLY! THERE'S ONLY ONE THING I LOVE MORE THAN PLANTS. SEE YOU LATER TONIGHT. TEXT ME THE ADDRESS.
AREN'T YOU LOVIN' OUR NEW PLACE, BERNIE?
I'D LIKE IT BETTER IF WE DIDN'T HAVE THE ACME RENT-A-THUG BACK THERE SMELLIN' UP THE JOINT.
WHAT'S THAT, LIKE, THE THIRD ONE SINCE WE GOT HERE?
FOURTH.
AN' ON TOP OF THE LOUSY SMELL, I'M STARVIN' HERE, AN' YET YOU TORTURE ME WIT' YOUR GNAWIN' AWAY ON THAT SAM'WICH.
YOU DON'T EVEN LIKE SAM'WICHES.
WHY DON'CHA GO DOWNSTAIRS AND HAVE AT SOME OF THAT LUMBER?
WHY? I'M RENDERED IMMOBILE 'CAUSE YER CRAZY-ASS BOYFRIEND BLEW MY HANDS AND FEET INTO MATCHSTICKS. THAT'S WHY.
AW, QUIT YOU COMPLAI
TWEEDLEE DEEDLEE DEE TWEEDLEE DEEDLEE D--
HEY... YEAH... NO, WAIT...
YOU SAID YOU COULD DELIVER IT THIS EVE--
ALL RIGHT.

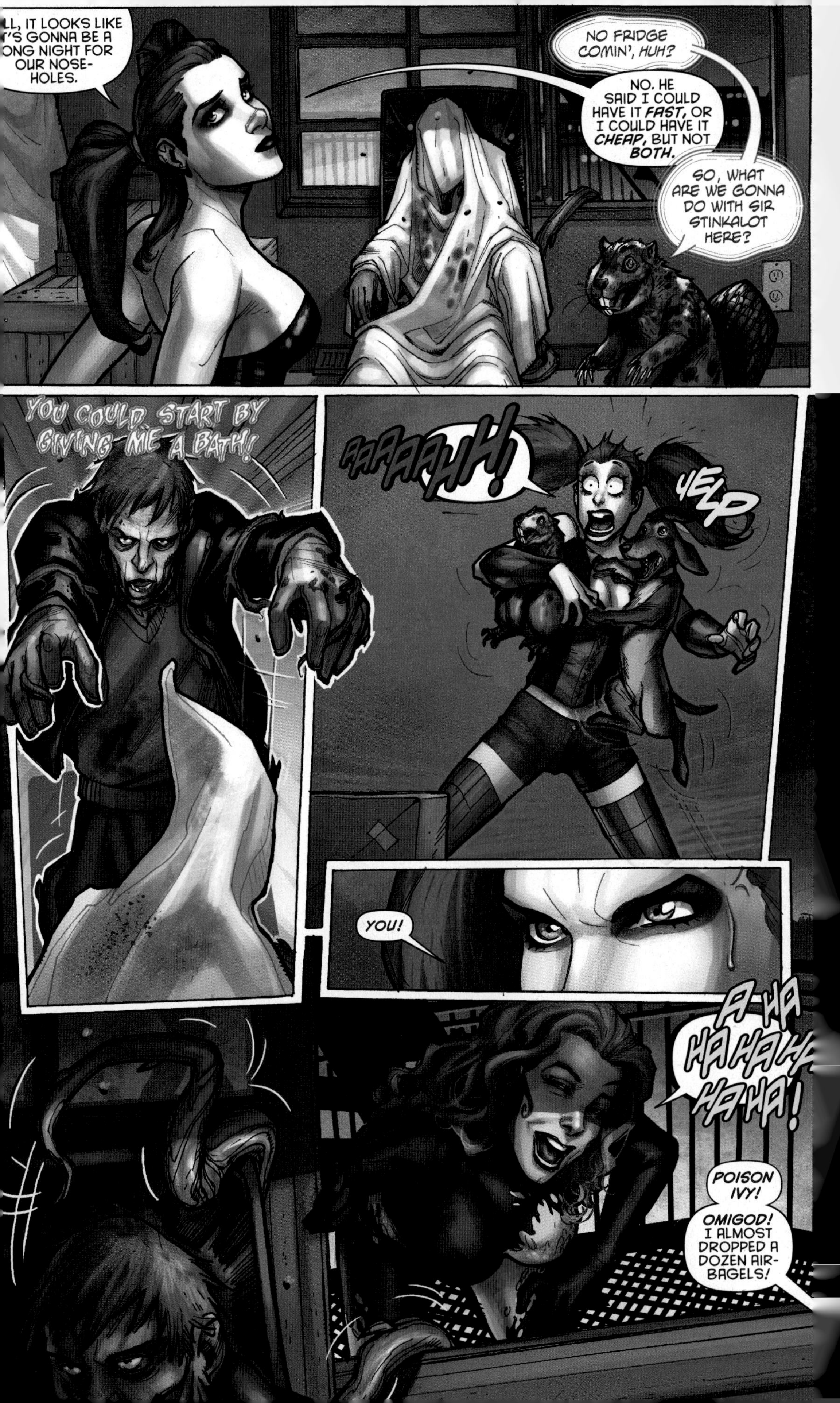
LL, IT LOOKS LIKE
T'S GONNA BE A
ONG NIGHT FOR
OUR NOSE-
HOLES.
NO FRIDGE COMIN', HUH?
NO. HE SAID I COULD HAVE IT FAST, OR I COULD HAVE IT CHEAP, BUT NOT BOTH.
SO, WHAT ARE WE GONNA DO WITH SIR STINKALOT HERE?
YOU COULD START BY GIVING ME A BATH!
AAAAAAUH!
YELP
YOU!
A HA HA HA HA HA HA!
POISON IVY!
OMIGOD! I ALMOST DROPPED A DOZEN AIR-BAGELS!

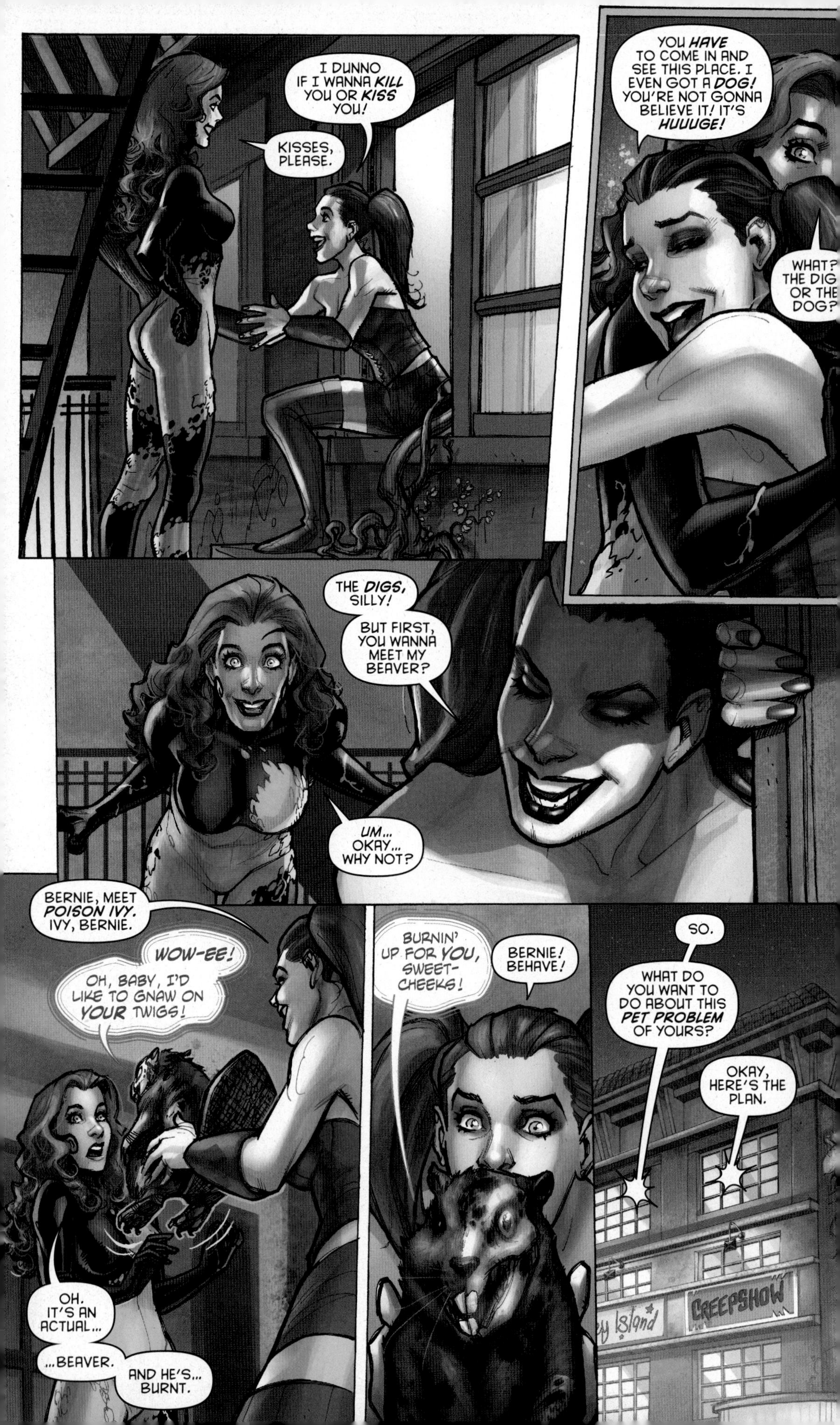
I DUNNO IF I WANNA KILL YOU OR KISS YOU!
KISSES, PLEASE.
YOU HAVE TO COME IN AND SEE THIS PLACE. I EVEN GOT A DOG! YOU'RE NOT GONNA BELIEVE IT! IT'S HUUUGE!
WHAT? THE DIG OR THE DOG?
THE DIGS, SILLY!
BUT FIRST, YOU WANNA MEET MY BEAVER?
UM... OKAY... WHY NOT?
BERNIE, MEET POISON IVY. IVY, BERNIE.
WOW-EE!
OH, BABY, I'D LIKE TO GNAW ON YOUR TWIGS!
OH. IT'S AN ACTUAL...
...BEAVER.
AND HE'S... BURNT.
BURNIN' UP FOR YOU, SWEET-CHEEKS!
BERNIE! BEHAVE!
SO.
WHAT DO YOU WANT TO DO ABOUT THIS PET PROBLEM OF YOURS?
OKAY, HERE'S THE PLAN.
CREEPSHOW

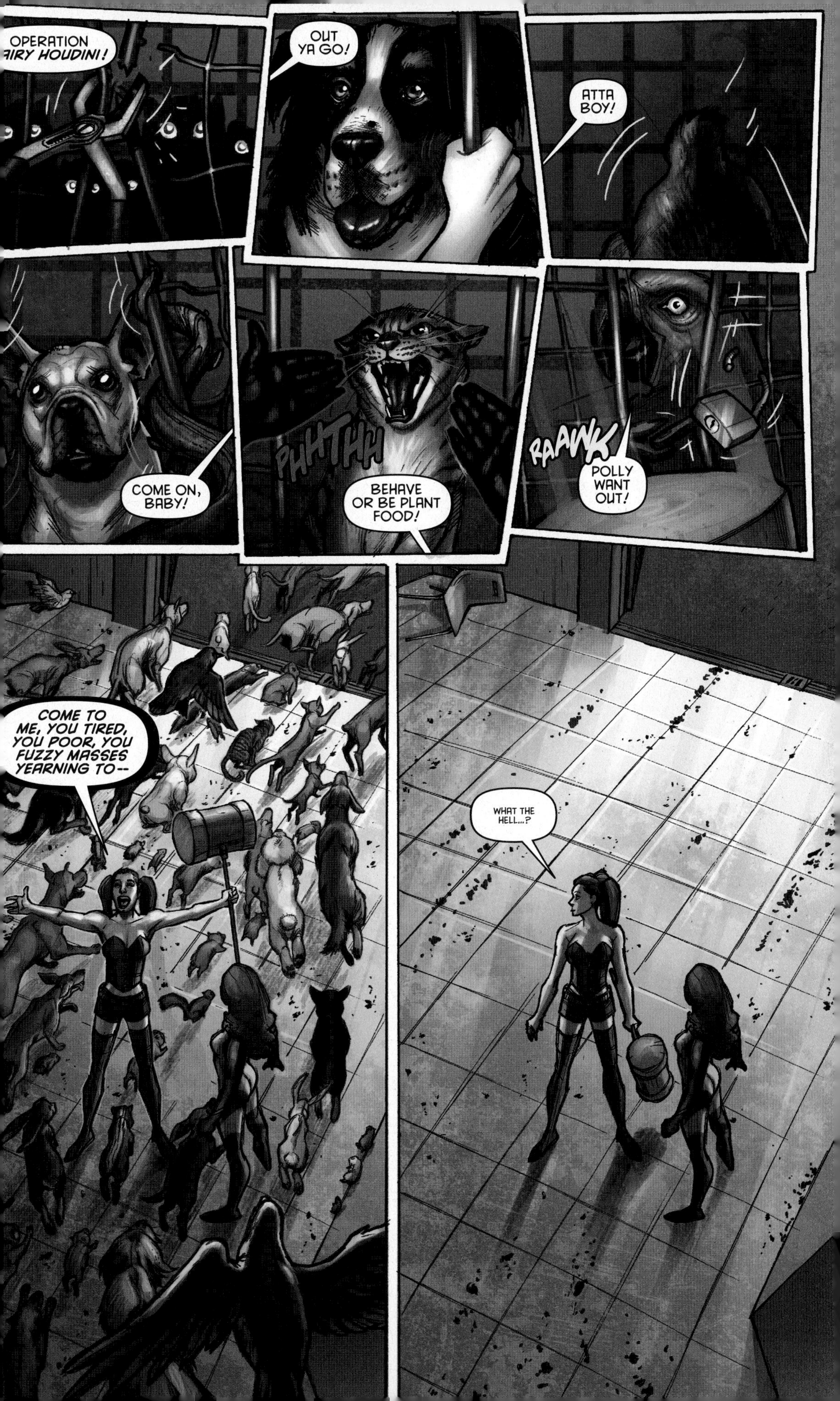

OPERATION HAIRY HOUDINI!
OUT YA GO!
ATTA BOY!
COME ON, BABY!
PHHTHH
BEHAVE OR BE PLANT FOOD!
RAAWK
POLLY WANT OUT!
COME TO ME, YOU TIRED, YOU POOR, YOU FUZZY MASSES YEARNING TO--
WHAT THE HELL...?

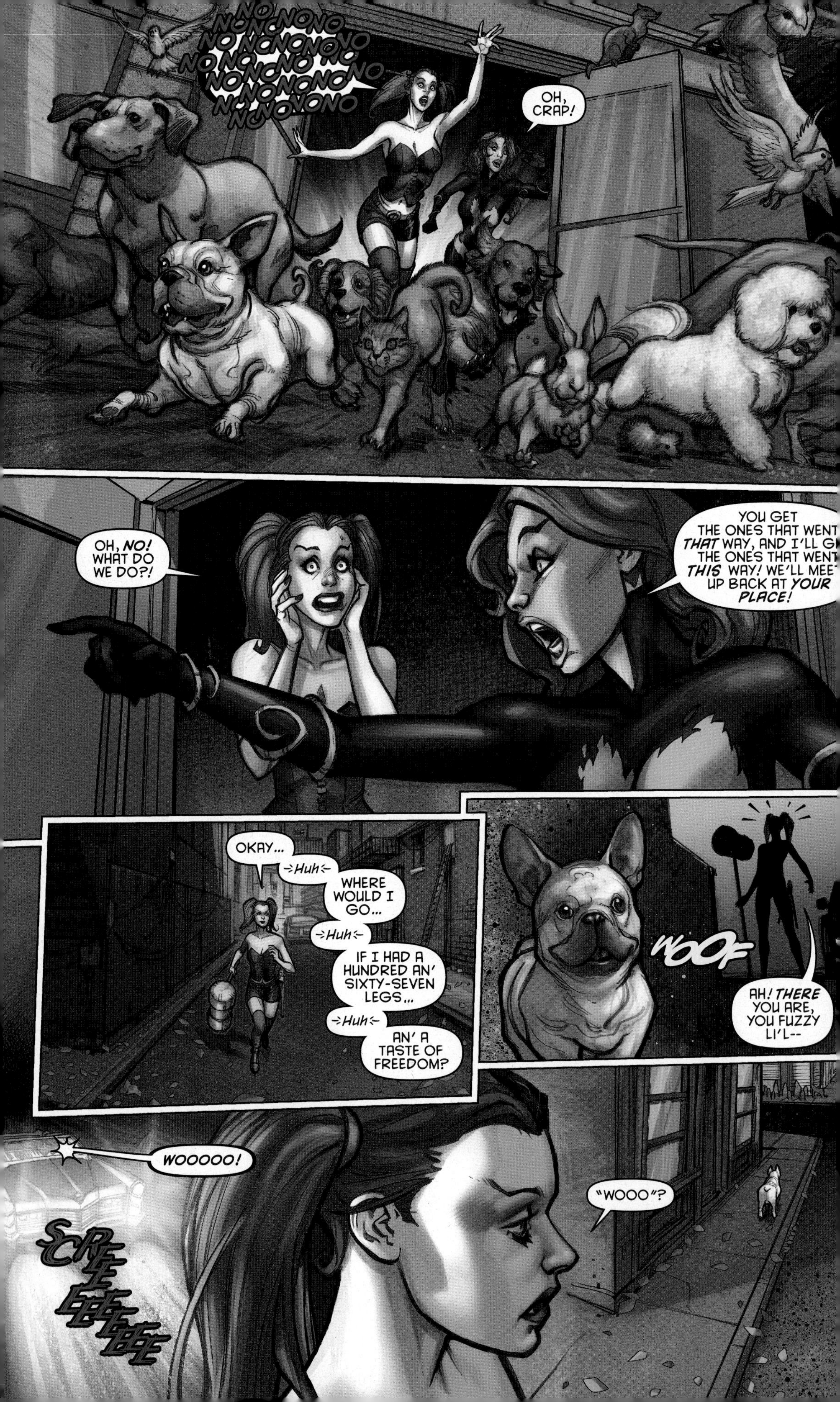
NO NO NO NO NO NO NO NO NO NO NO NO NO NO NO NO NO NO NO NO NO NO NO NO NO
OH, CRAP!
OH, NO! WHAT DO WE DO?!
YOU GET THE ONES THAT WENT THAT WAY, AND I'LL G THE ONES THAT WENT THIS WAY! WE'LL MEET UP BACK AT YOUR PLACE!
OKAY...
Huh
WHERE WOULD I GO...
Huh
IF I HAD A HUNDRED AN' SIXTY-SEVEN LEGS...
Huh
AN' A TASTE OF FREEDOM?
WOOF
AH! THERE YOU ARE, YOU FUZZY LI'L--
WOOOOO!
SCREEEEEEEEE
"WOOO"?

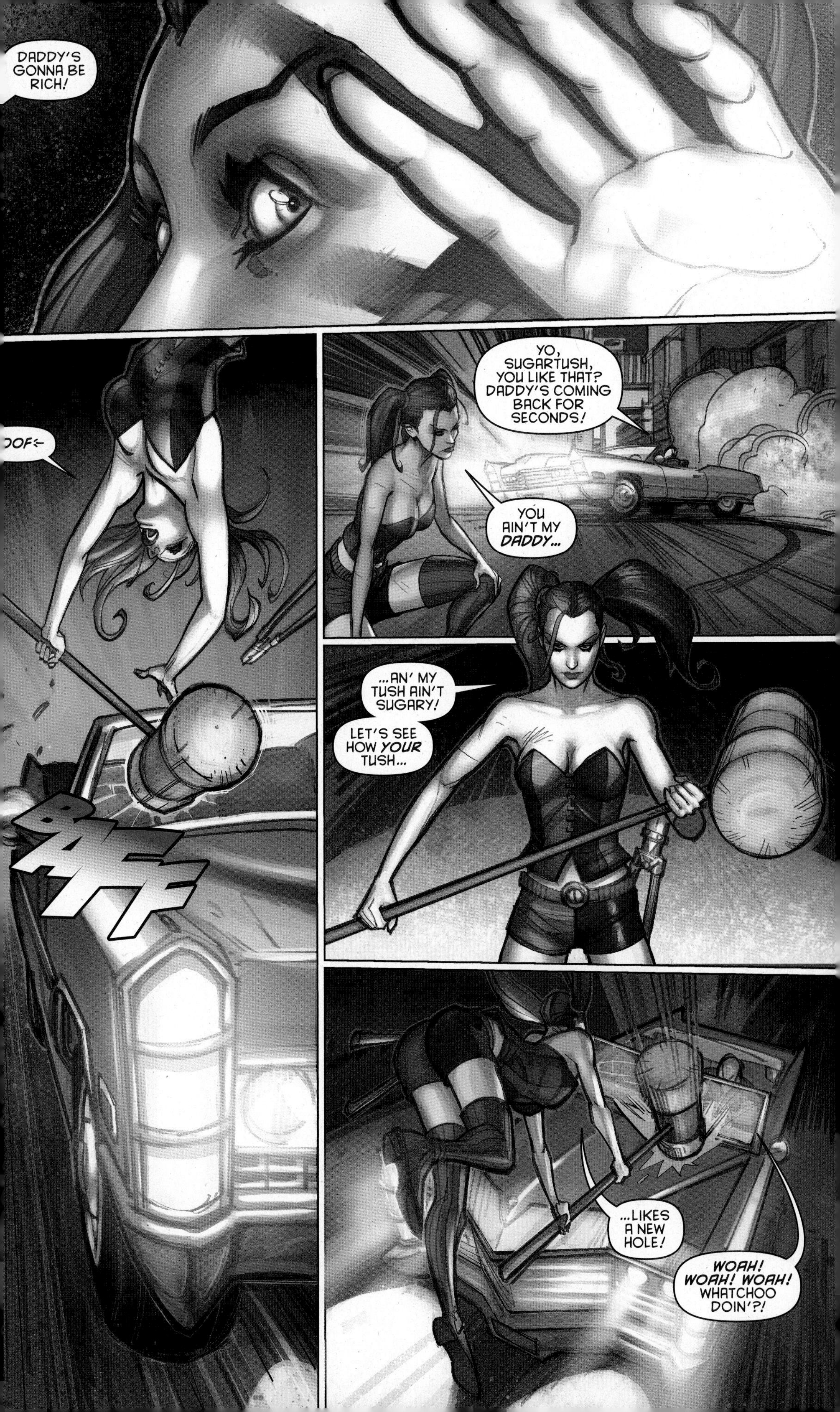
DADDY'S GONNA BE RICH!
OOF
BAFF
YO, SUGARTUSH, YOU LIKE THAT? DADDY'S COMING BACK FOR SECONDS!
YOU AIN'T MY *DADDY*...
...AN' MY TUSH AIN'T SUGARY!
LET'S SEE HOW *YOUR* TUSH...
...LIKES A NEW HOLE!
*WOAH! WOAH! WOAH!* WHATCHOO DOIN'?!

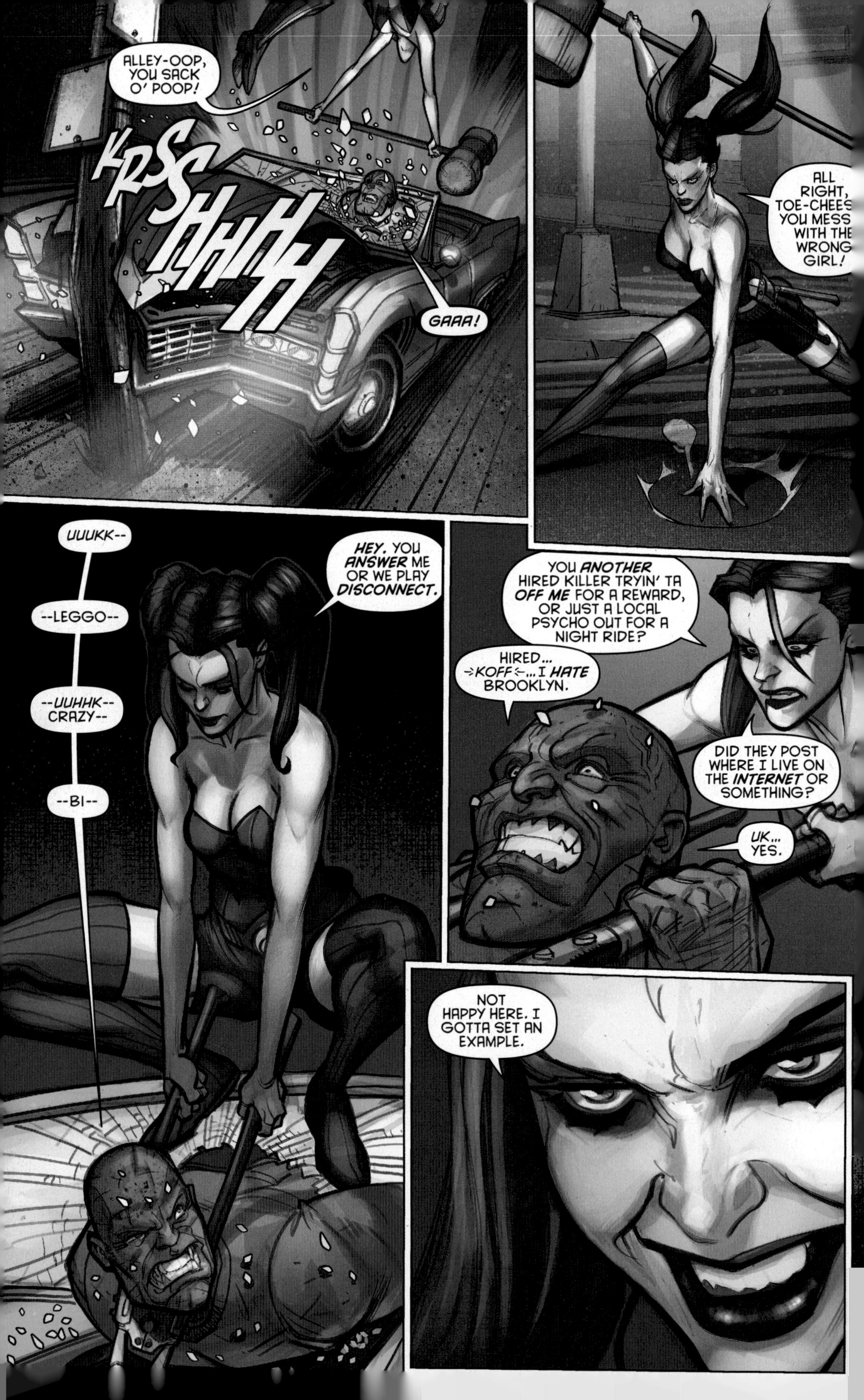
ALLEY-OOP, YOU SACK O' POOP!
KRSSHHHH
GAAA!
ALL RIGHT, TOE-CHEES YOU MESS WITH THE WRONG GIRL!
UUUKK--
--LEGGO--
--UUHHK-- CRAZY--
--BI--
HEY. YOU ANSWER ME OR WE PLAY DISCONNECT.
YOU ANOTHER HIRED KILLER TRYIN' TA OFF ME FOR A REWARD, OR JUST A LOCAL PSYCHO OUT FOR A NIGHT RIDE?
HIRED... KOFF ...I HATE BROOKLYN.
DID THEY POST WHERE I LIVE ON THE INTERNET OR SOMETHING?
UK... YES.
NOT HAPPY HERE. I GOTTA SET AN EXAMPLE.

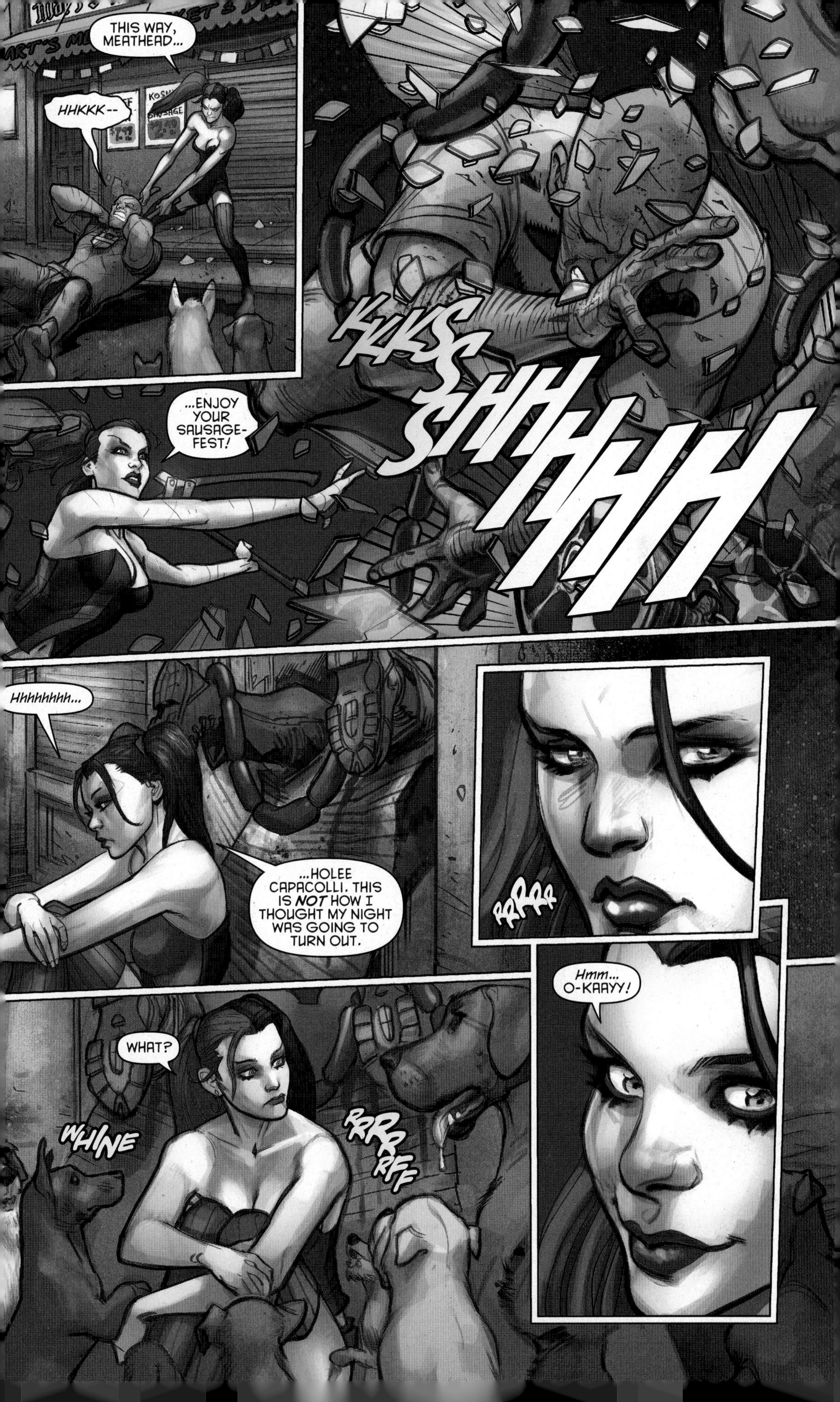
THIS WAY, MEATHEAD...
HHKKK--
KOSHER
SAUSAGE
...ENJOY YOUR SAUSAGE-FEST!
KLKSSHHHHHH
Hhhhhhhh...
...HOLEE CAPACOLLI. THIS IS NOT HOW I THOUGHT MY NIGHT WAS GOING TO TURN OUT.
RRRRR
WHAT?
WHINE
RRRRRFF
Hmm... O-KAAYY!

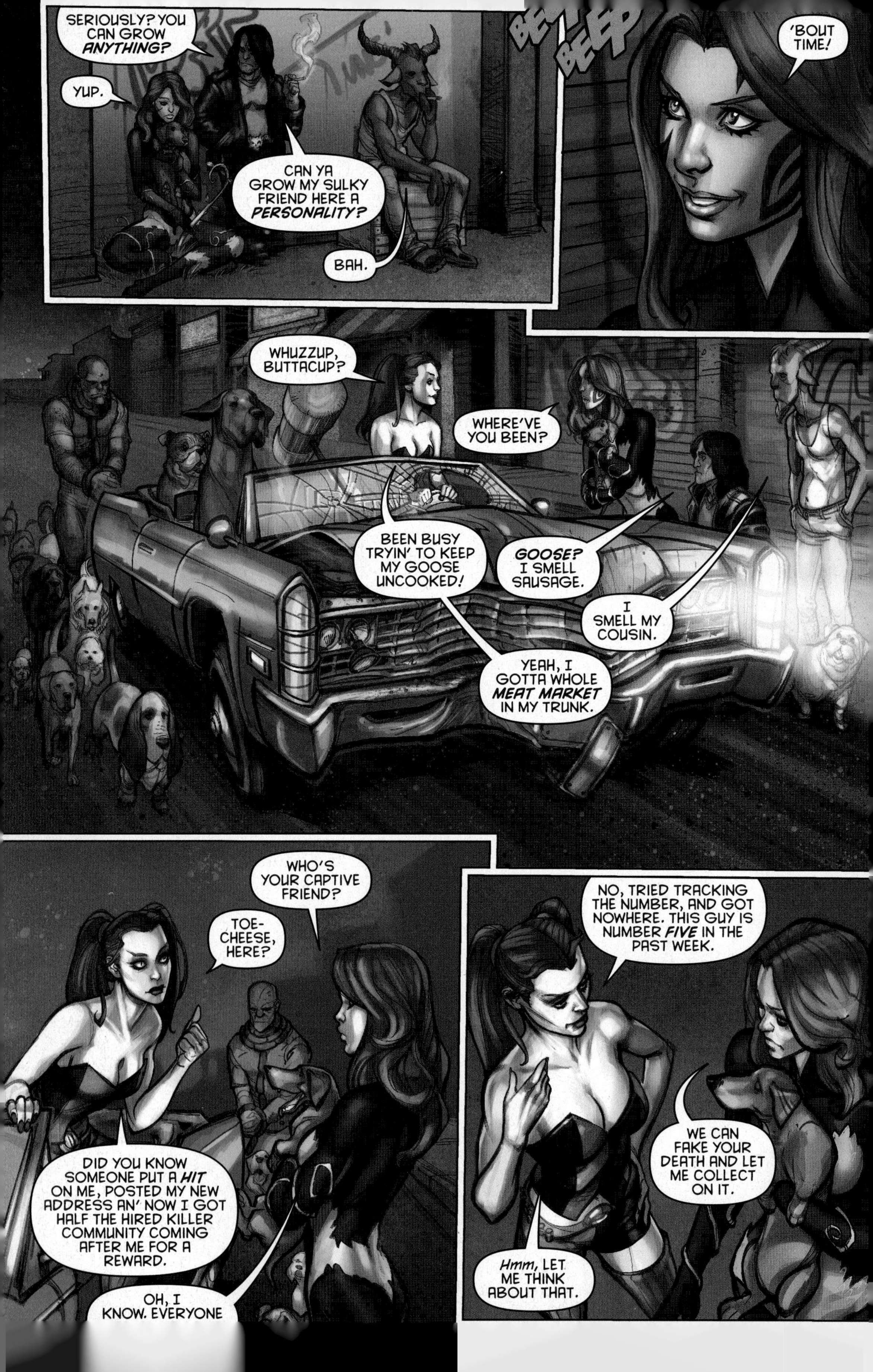
SERIOUSLY? YOU CAN GROW *ANYTHING?*
YUP.
CAN YA GROW MY SULKY FRIEND HERE A *PERSONALITY?*
BAH.
BEEP BEEP
'BOUT TIME!
WHUZZUP, BUTTACUP?
WHERE'VE YOU BEEN?
BEEN BUSY TRYIN' TO KEEP MY GOOSE UNCOOKED!
*GOOSE?* I SMELL SAUSAGE.
I SMELL MY COUSIN.
YEAH, I GOTTA WHOLE *MEAT MARKET* IN MY TRUNK.
WHO'S YOUR CAPTIVE FRIEND?
TOE-CHEESE, HERE?
DID YOU KNOW SOMEONE PUT A *HIT* ON ME, POSTED MY NEW ADDRESS AN' NOW I GOT HALF THE HIRED KILLER COMMUNITY COMING AFTER ME FOR A REWARD.
OH, I KNOW. EVERYONE
NO, TRIED TRACKING THE NUMBER, AND GOT NOWHERE. THIS GUY IS NUMBER *FIVE* IN THE PAST WEEK.
WE CAN FAKE YOUR DEATH AND LET ME COLLECT ON IT.
*Hmm,* LET ME THINK ABOUT THAT.

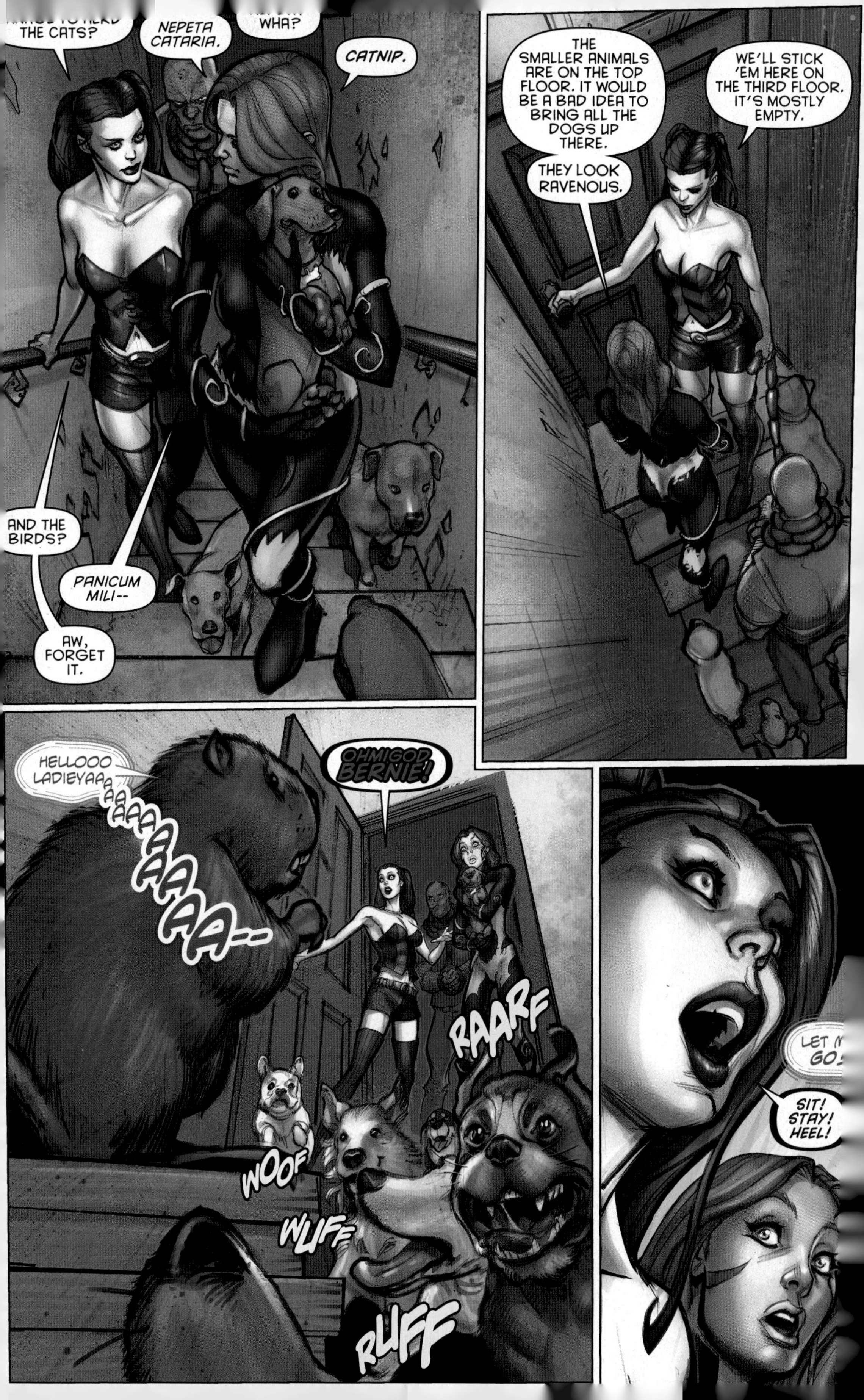

THE CATS?
NEPETA CATARIA.
WHA?
CATNIP.
AND THE BIRDS?
PANICUM MILI--
AW, FORGET IT.
THE SMALLER ANIMALS ARE ON THE TOP FLOOR. IT WOULD BE A BAD IDEA TO BRING ALL THE DOGS UP THERE.
THEY LOOK RAVENOUS.
WE'LL STICK 'EM HERE ON THE THIRD FLOOR. IT'S MOSTLY EMPTY.
HELLOOO LADIEYAAAAAAAAAAAA--
OHMIGOD BERNIE!
RAARF
WOOF
WUFF
RUFF
SIT! STAY! HEEL!

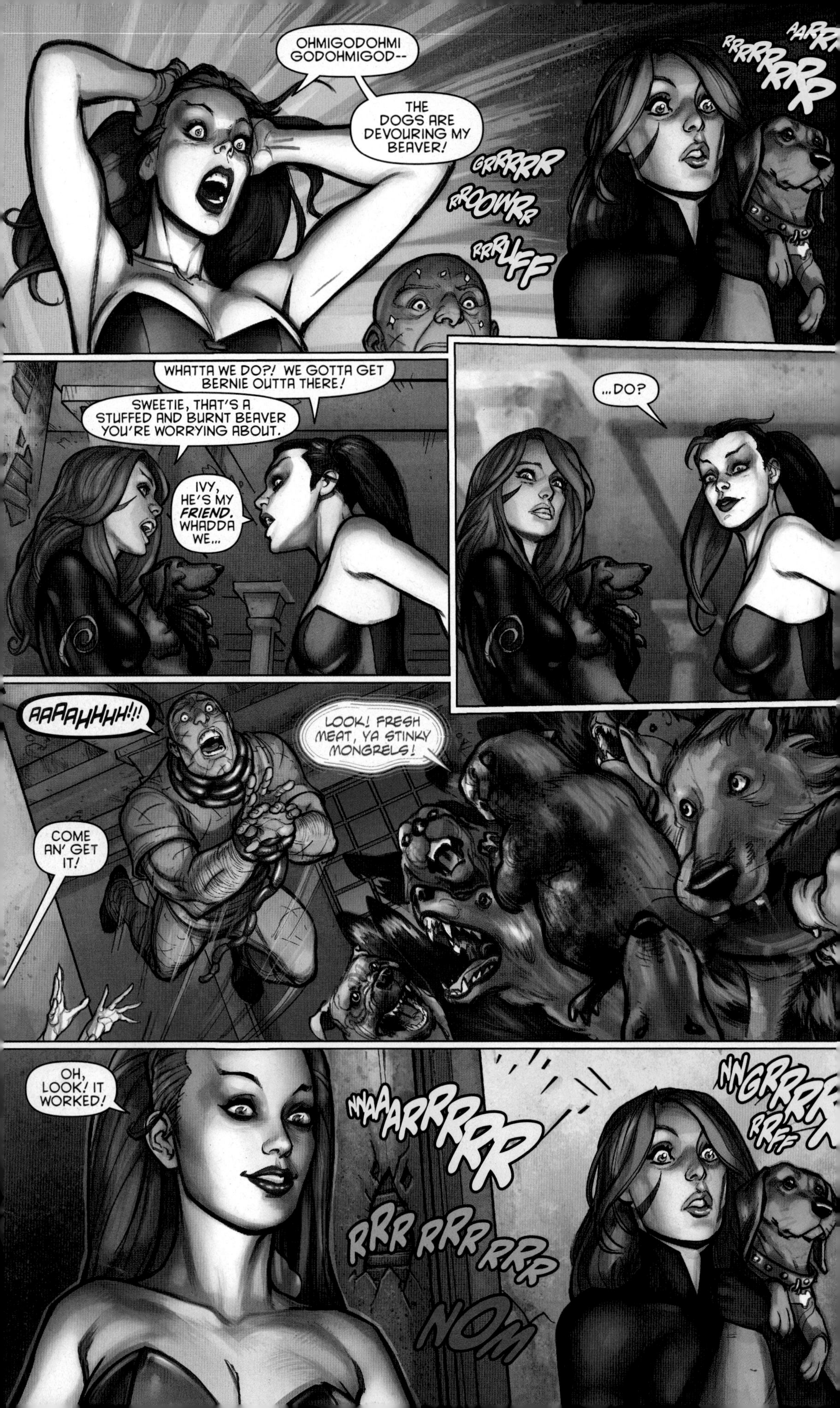
OHMIGODOHMI GODOHMIGOD--
THE DOGS ARE DEVOURING MY BEAVER!
GRRRRRR
RROOWRR
RRRUFF
AARR
RRRRRRRR
WHATTA WE DO?! WE GOTTA GET BERNIE OUTTA THERE!
SWEETIE, THAT'S A STUFFED AND BURNT BEAVER YOU'RE WORRYING ABOUT.
IVY, HE'S MY *FRIEND.* WHADDA WE...
...DO?
AAAAHHHH!!!
LOOK! FRESH MEAT, YA STINKY MONGRELS!
COME AN' GET IT!
OH, LOOK! IT WORKED!
NNAAARRRRRR
NNGRRRRR
RRFF
RRR RRR RRRR
NOM

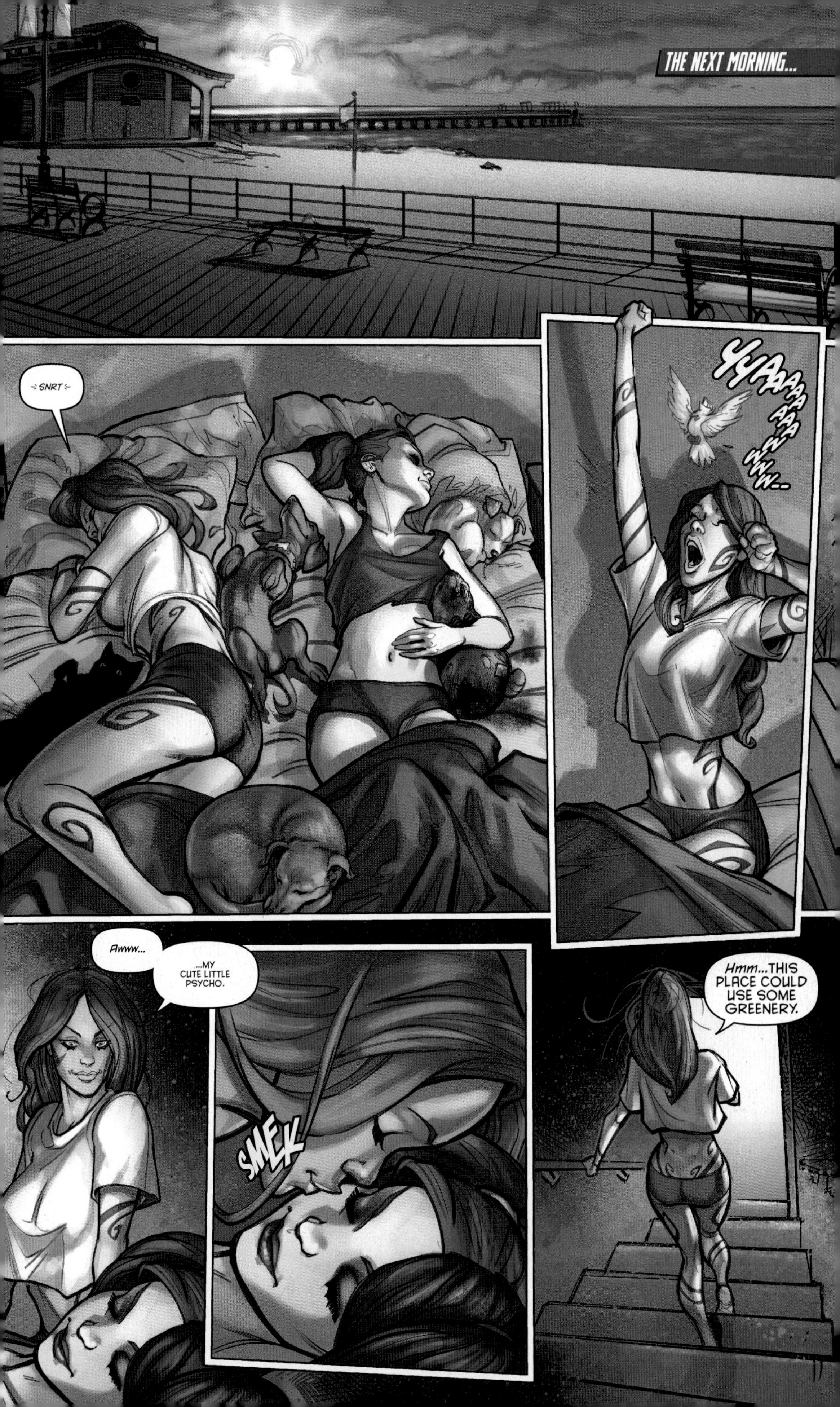
THE NEXT MORNING...
SNRT
YYAAAAAAAAAWWW...
Awww...
...MY CUTE LITTLE PSYCHO.
SMEK
Hmm...THIS PLACE COULD USE SOME GREENERY.

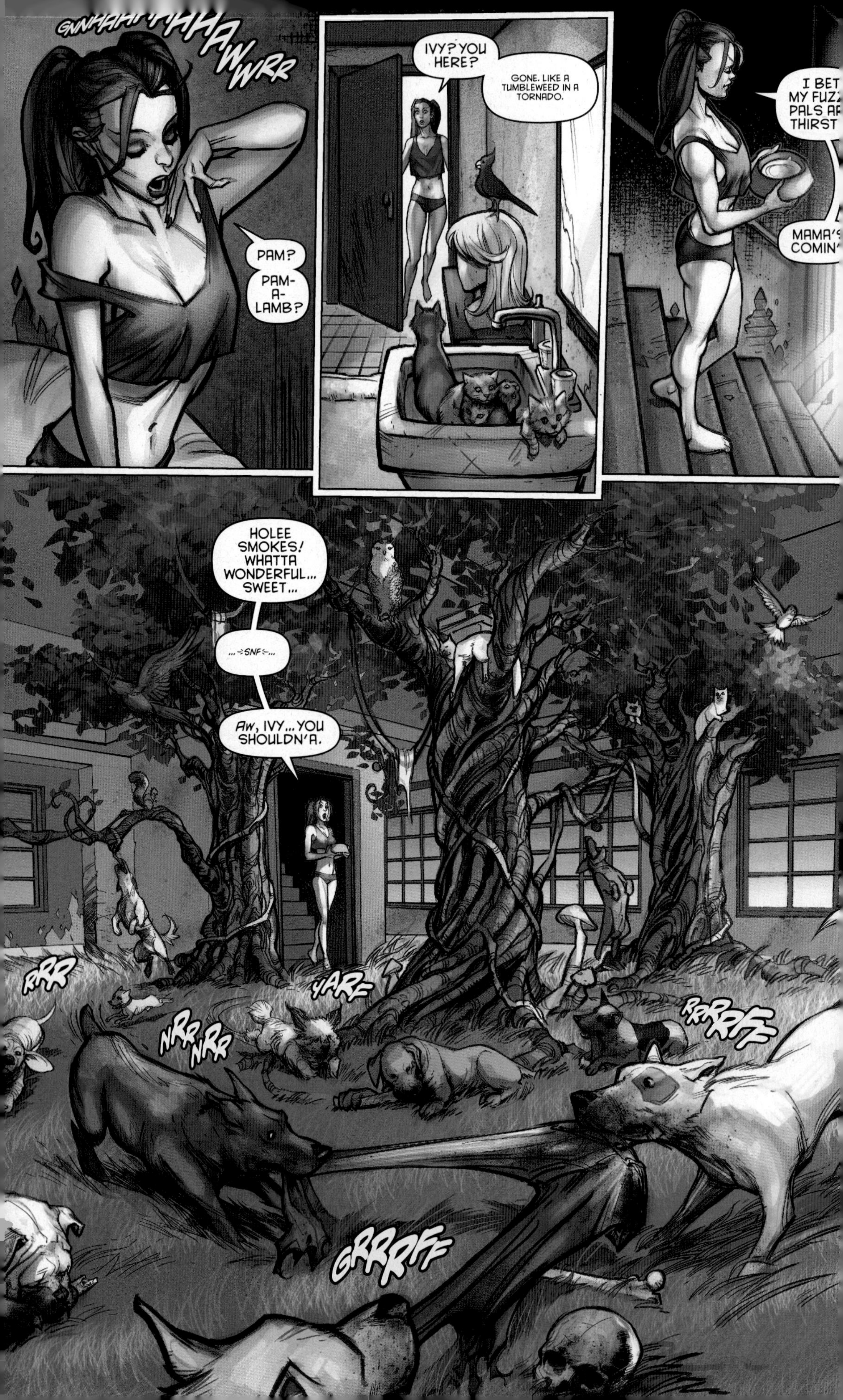
GNHAAAHHHAAWWRR
PAM?
PAM-A-LAMB?
IVY? YOU HERE?
GONE. LIKE A TUMBLEWEED IN A TORNADO.
I BET MY FUZZ PALS AR THIRST
MAMA'S COMIN'
HOLEE SMOKES! WHATTA WONDERFUL... SWEET...
...SNF...
AW, IVY... YOU SHOULDN'A.
RRR
YARF
NRR NRR
RRRRFF
GRRRFF

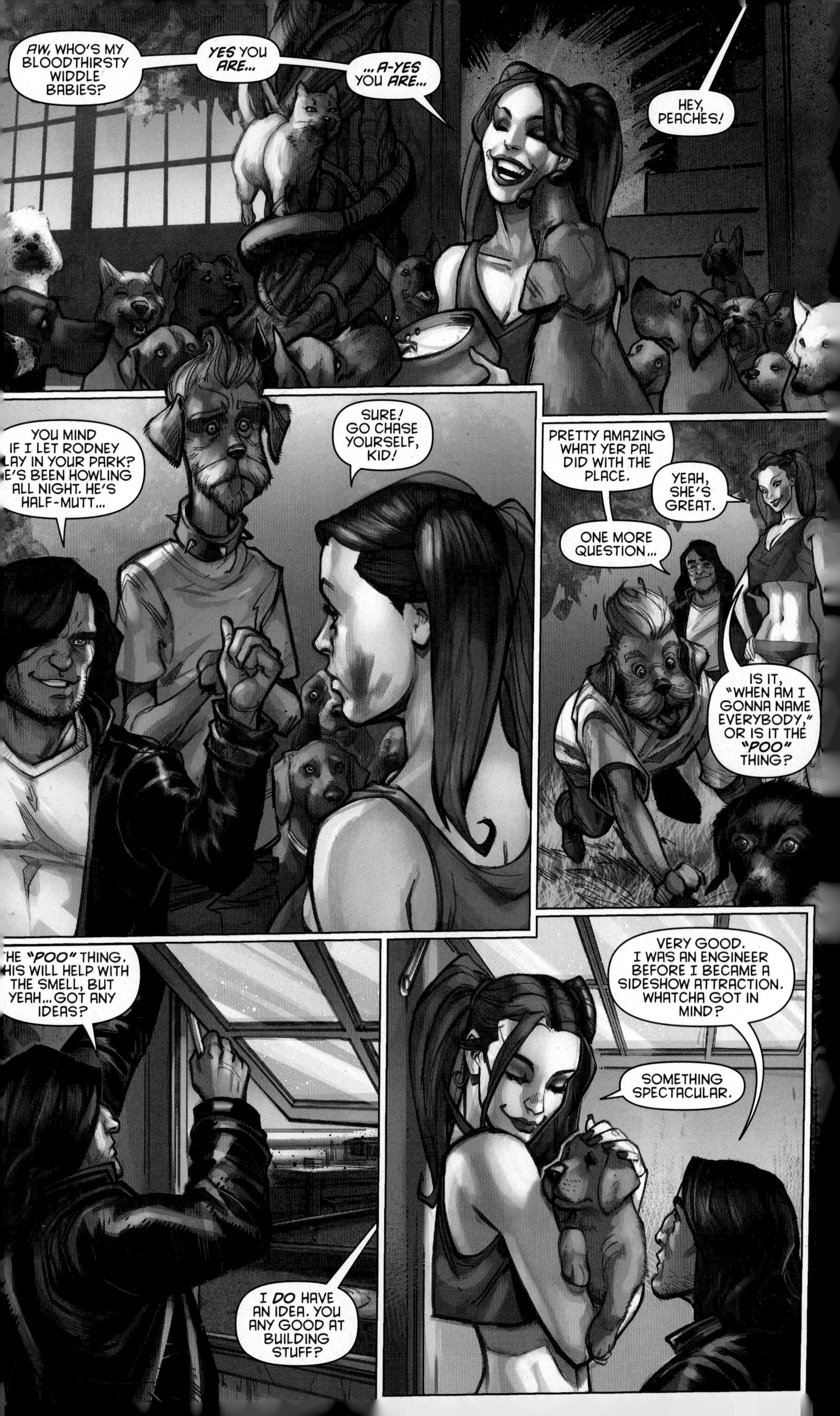
AW, WHO'S MY BLOODTHIRSTY WIDDLE BABIES?
YES YOU ARE...
...A-YES YOU ARE...
HEY, PEACHES!
YOU MIND IF I LET RODNEY PLAY IN YOUR PARK? HE'S BEEN HOWLING ALL NIGHT. HE'S HALF-MUTT...
SURE! GO CHASE YOURSELF, KID!
PRETTY AMAZING WHAT YER PAL DID WITH THE PLACE.
YEAH, SHE'S GREAT.
ONE MORE QUESTION...
IS IT, "WHEN AM I GONNA NAME EVERYBODY," OR IS IT THE "POO" THING?
THE "POO" THING. THIS WILL HELP WITH THE SMELL, BUT YEAH... GOT ANY IDEAS?
I DO HAVE AN IDEA. YOU ANY GOOD AT BUILDING STUFF?
VERY GOOD. I WAS AN ENGINEER BEFORE I BECAME A SIDESHOW ATTRACTION. WHATCHA GOT IN MIND?
SOMETHING SPECTACULAR.

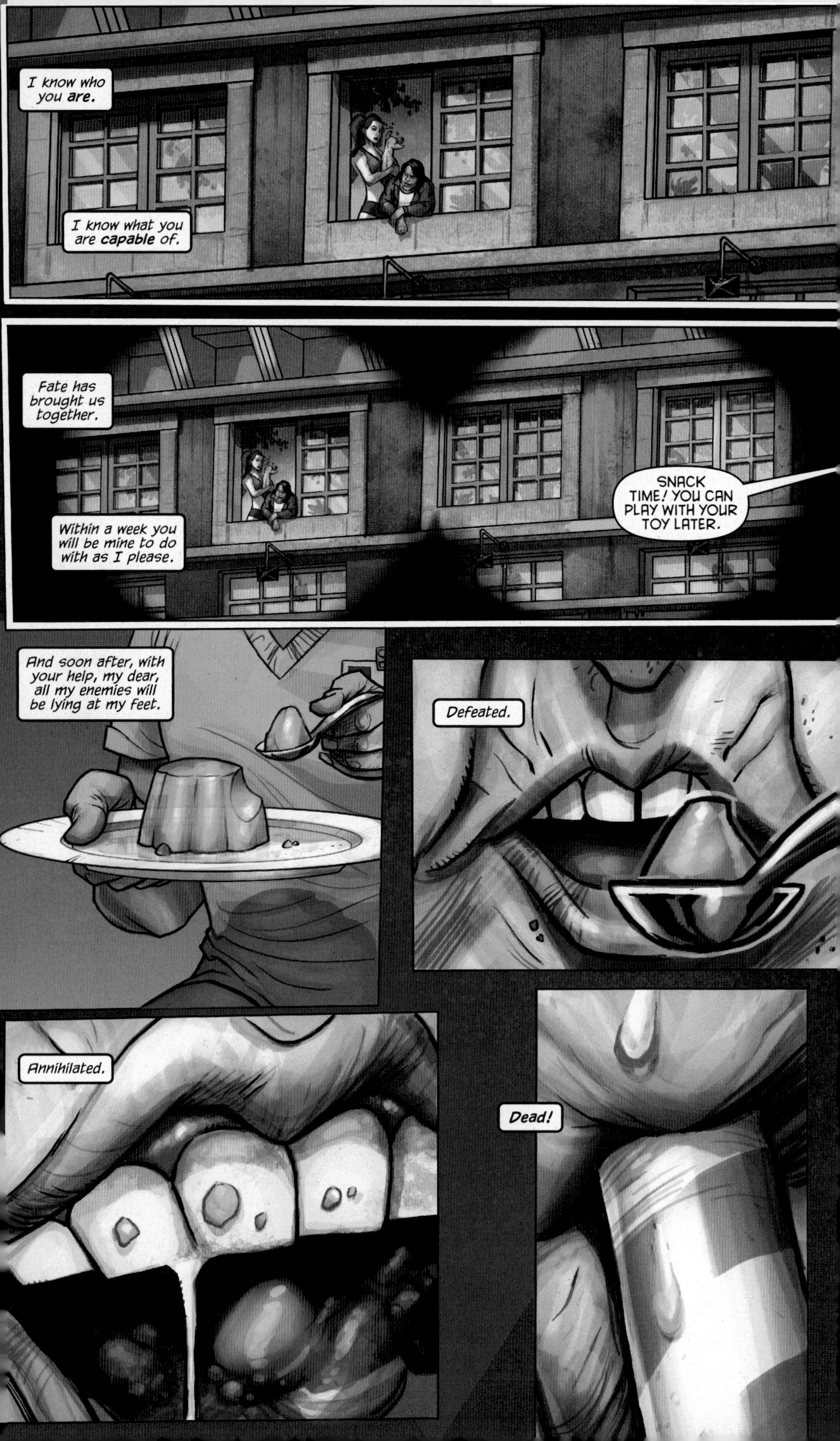
I know who you are.
I know what you are capable of.
Fate has brought us together.
Within a week you will be mine to do with as I please.
SNACK TIME! YOU CAN PLAY WITH YOUR TOY LATER.
And soon after, with your help, my dear, all my enemies will be lying at my feet.
Defeated.
Annihilated.
Dead!

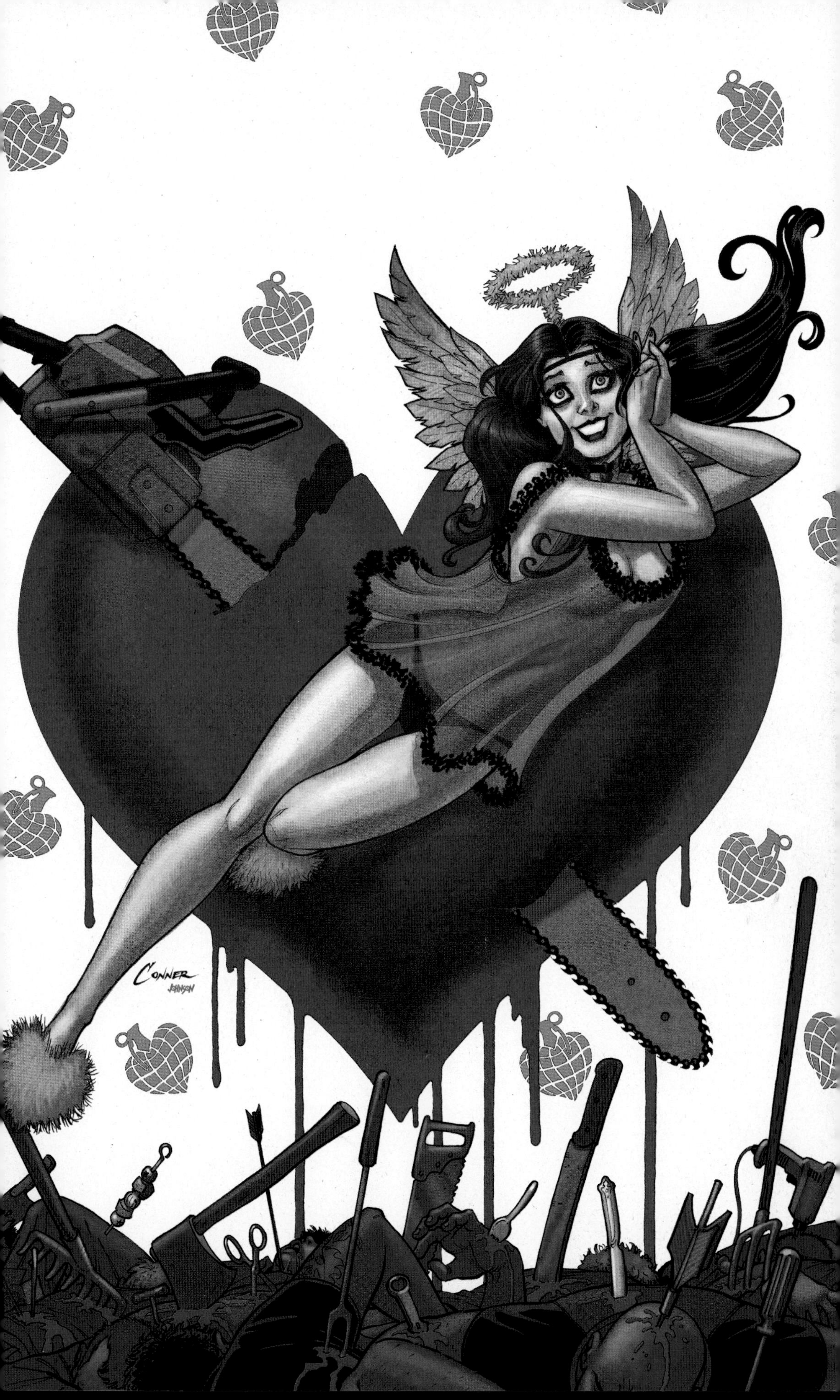
CONNER
JOHNSON

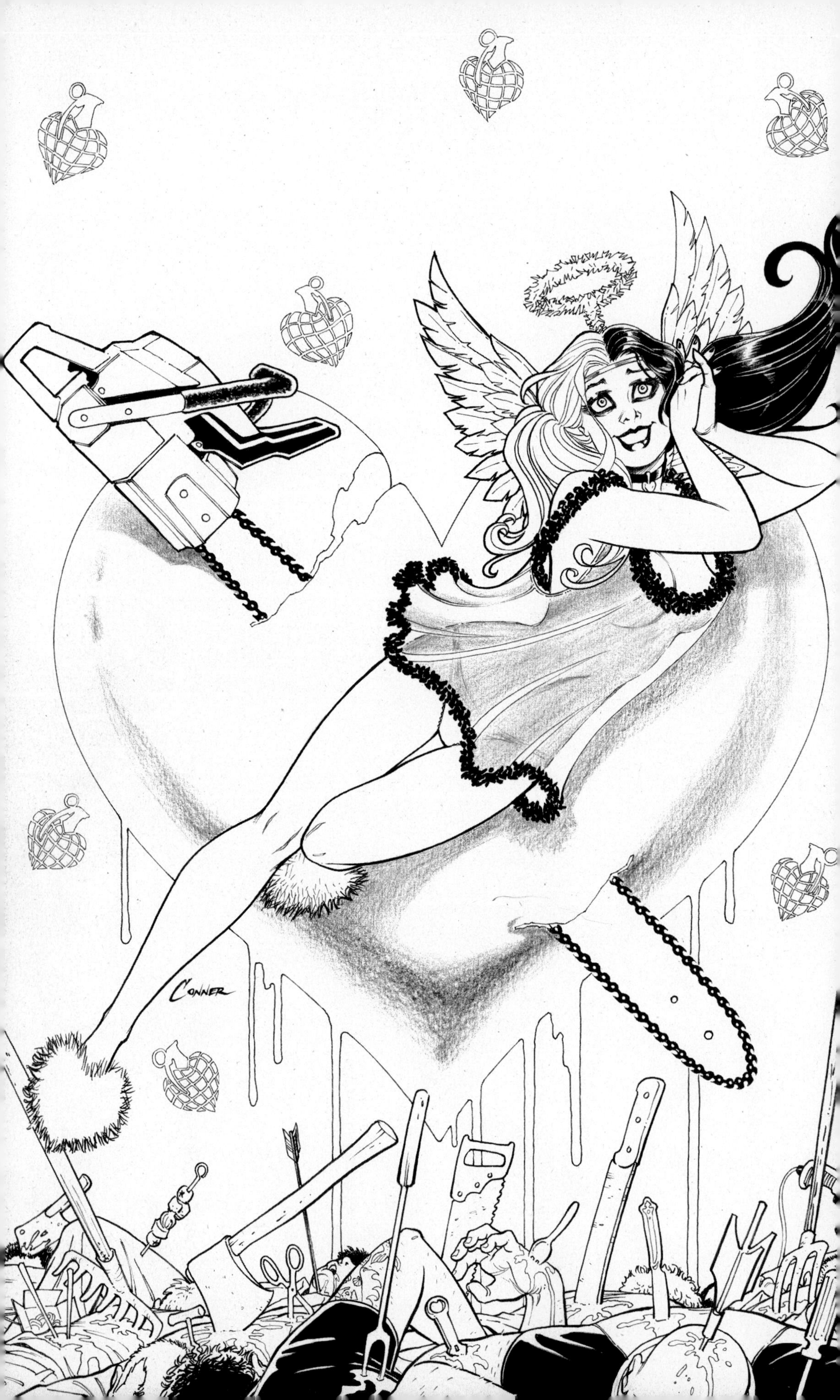
CONNER

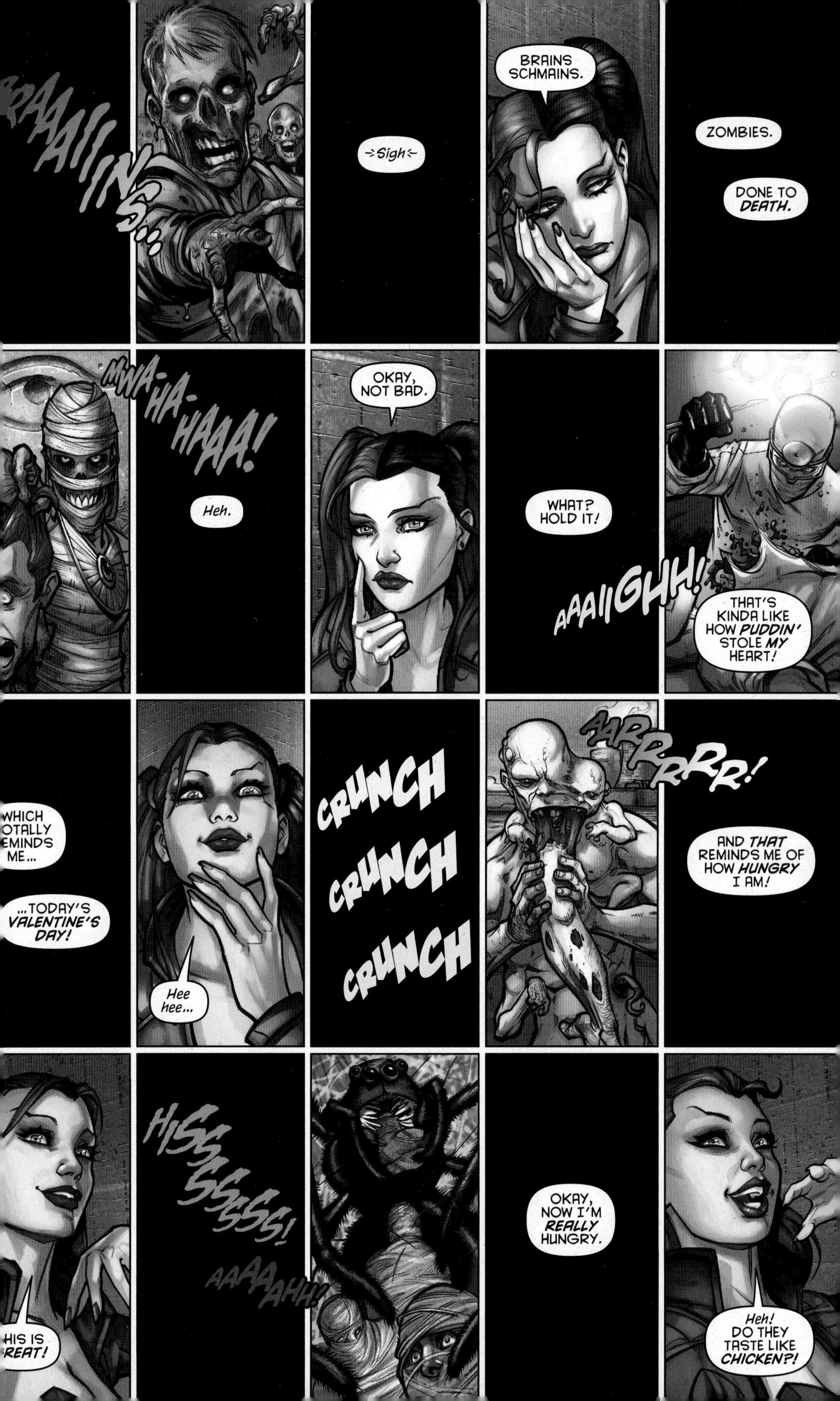

BRAAAAIIIINS...
-Sigh-
BRAINS SCHMAINS.
ZOMBIES.
DONE TO DEATH.
MWA-HA-HAAAA!
Heh.
OKAY, NOT BAD.
WHAT? HOLD IT!
AAAIIGHH!
THAT'S KINDA LIKE HOW PUDDIN' STOLE MY HEART!
WHICH OTALLY EMINDS ME...
...TODAY'S VALENTINE'S DAY!
Hee hee...
CRUNCH
CRUNCH
CRUNCH
AARRRRRR!
AND THAT REMINDS ME OF HOW HUNGRY I AM!
HIS IS REAT!
HISSSSSSS!
AAAAAHH!
OKAY, NOW I'M REALLY HUNGRY.
Heh! DO THEY TASTE LIKE CHICKEN?!

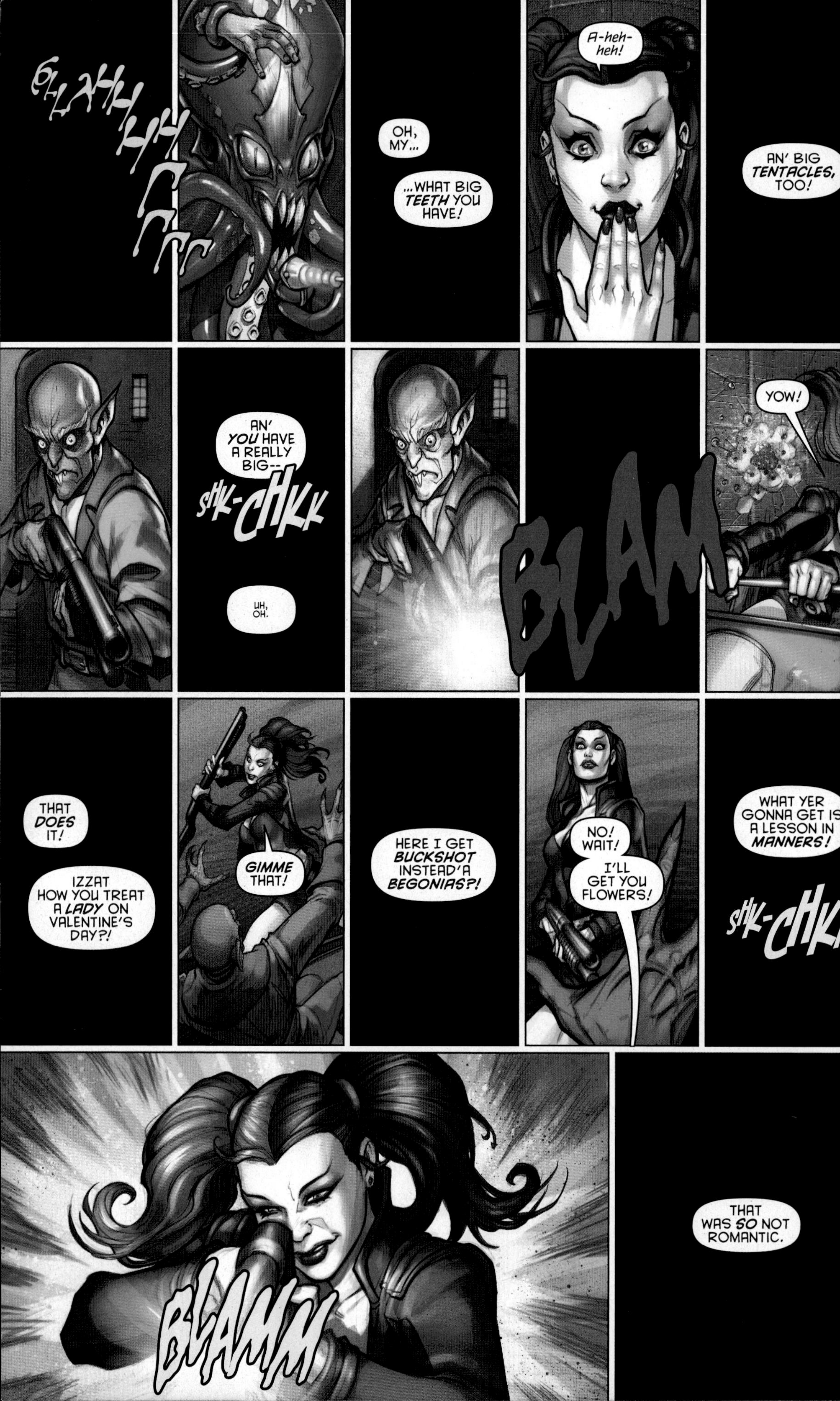

OH, MY...
...WHAT BIG TEETH YOU HAVE!
A-heh-heh!
AN' BIG TENTACLES, TOO!
AN' YOU HAVE A REALLY BIG--
SHK-CHKK
UH, OH.
BLAM
YOW!
THAT DOES IT!
IZZAT HOW YOU TREAT A LADY ON VALENTINE'S DAY?!
GIMME THAT!
HERE I GET BUCKSHOT INSTEAD'A BEGONIAS?!
NO! WAIT!
I'LL GET YOU FLOWERS!
WHAT YER GONNA GET IS A LESSON IN MANNERS!
BLAMM
THAT WAS SO NOT ROMANTIC.

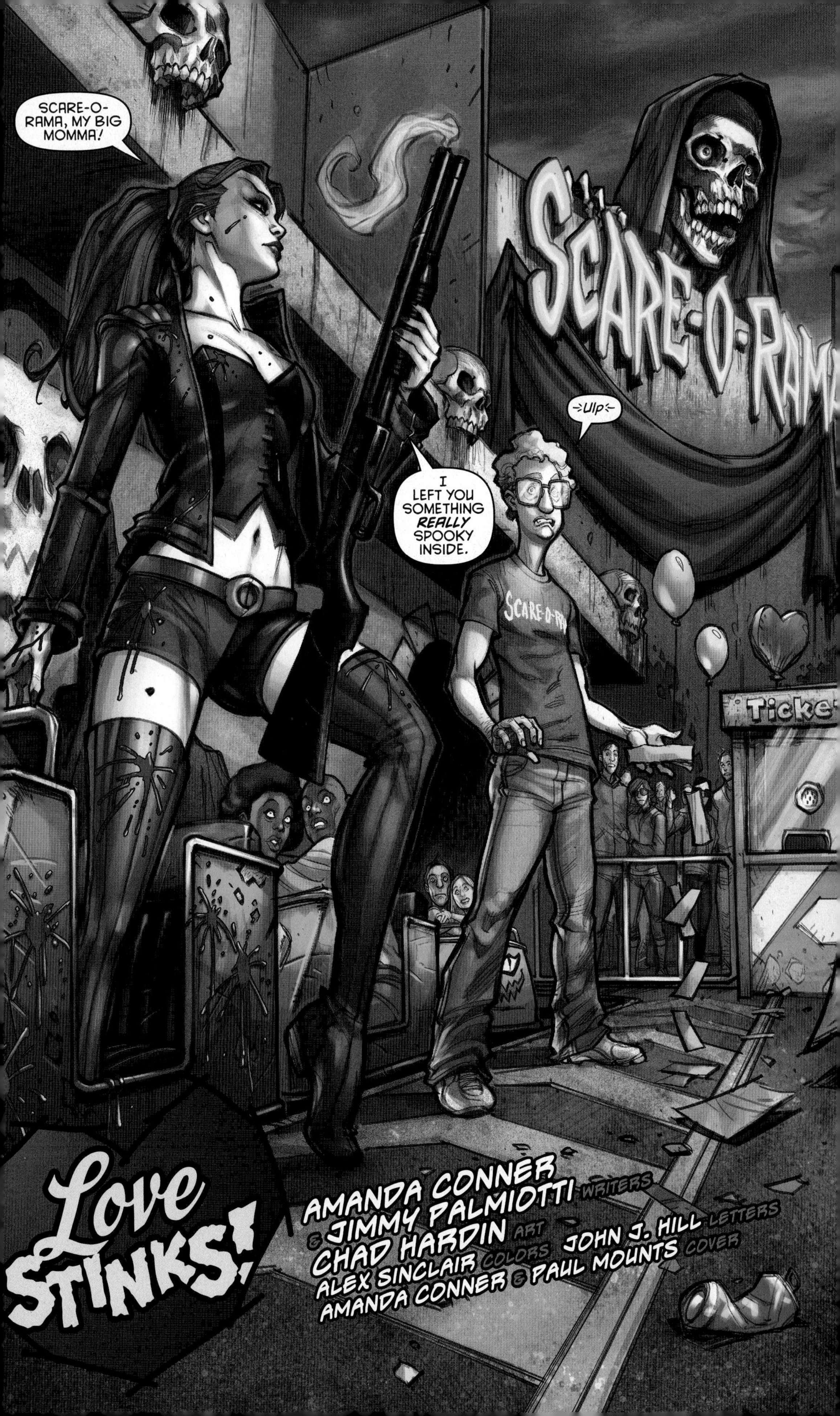
SCARE-O-RAMA, MY BIG MOMMA!
I LEFT YOU SOMETHING REALLY SPOOKY INSIDE.
~Ulp~
SCARE-O-RAMA
SCARE-O-RAMA
Ticke
Love STINKS!
AMANDA CONNER & JIMMY PALMIOTTI WRITERS
CHAD HARDIN ART
ALEX SINCLAIR COLORS JOHN J. HILL LETTERS
AMANDA CONNER & PAUL MOUNTS COVER

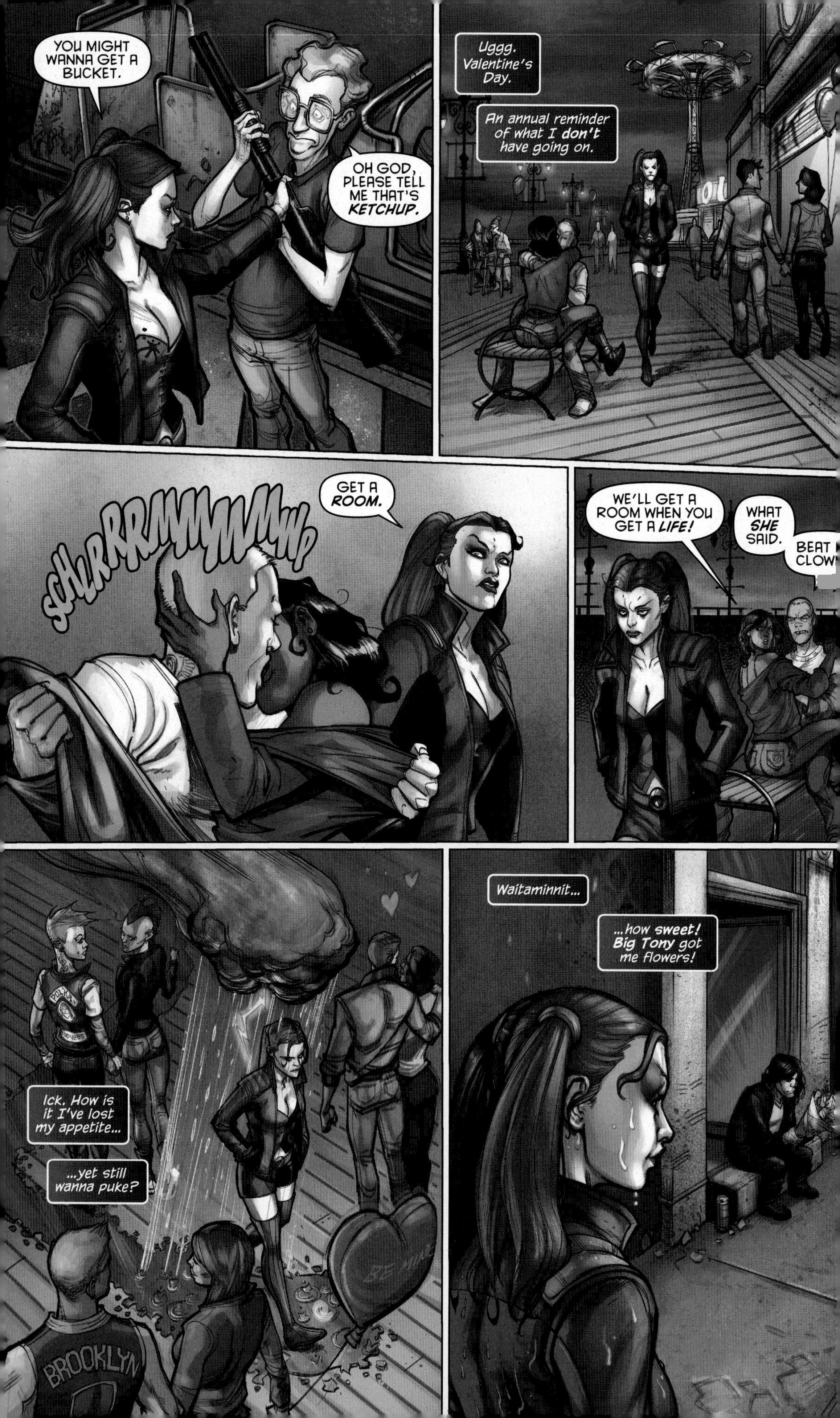
YOU MIGHT WANNA GET A BUCKET.
OH GOD, PLEASE TELL ME THAT'S KETCHUP.
Uggg. Valentine's Day.
An annual reminder of what I don't have going on.
GET A ROOM.
SCHLRRRMMMMMWP
WE'LL GET A ROOM WHEN YOU GET A LIFE!
WHAT SHE SAID.
BEAT CLOW
Ick. How is it I've lost my appetite...
...yet still wanna puke?
BROOKLYN
Waitaminnit...
...how sweet! Big Tony got me flowers!

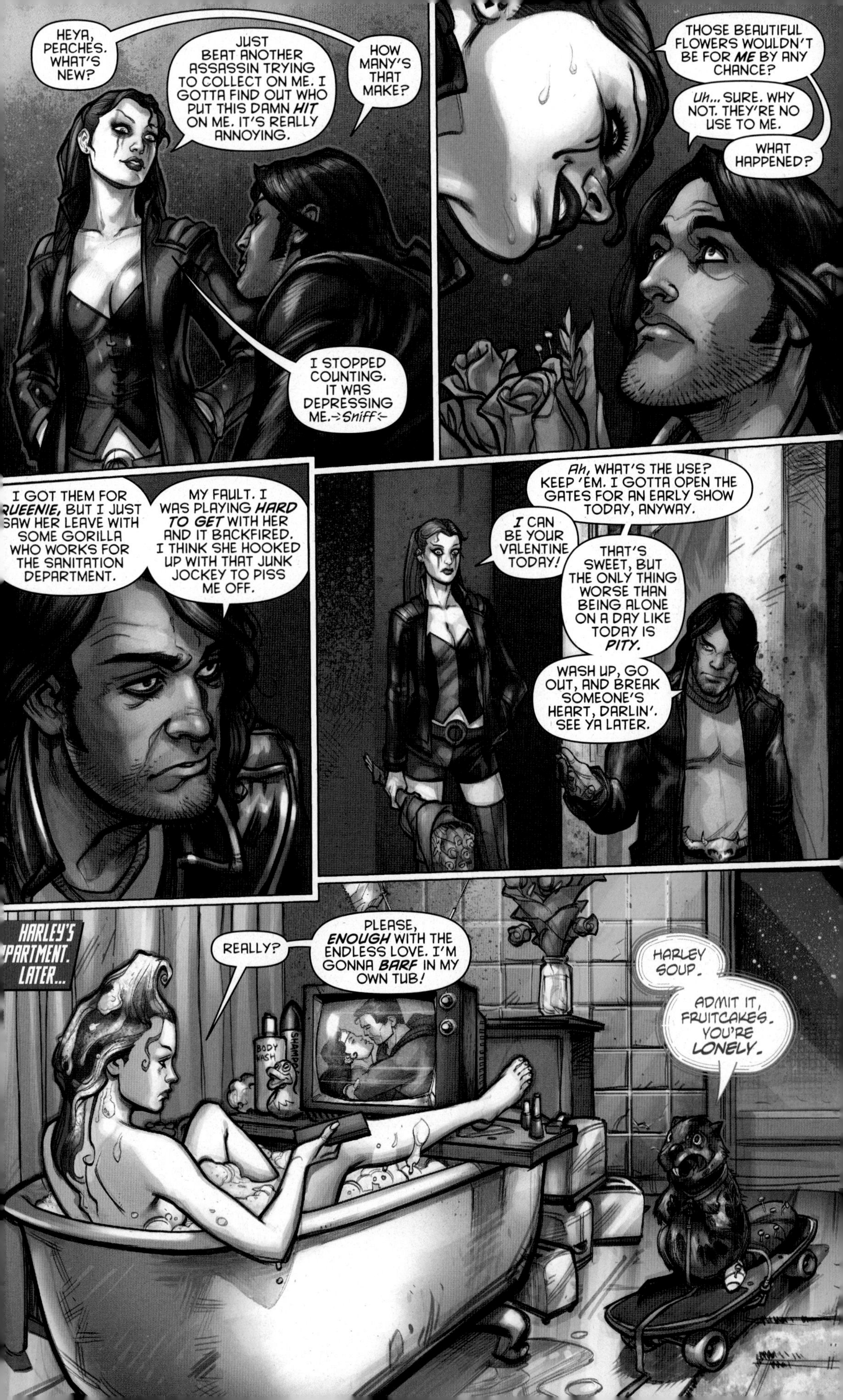
HEYA, PEACHES. WHAT'S NEW?
JUST BEAT ANOTHER ASSASSIN TRYING TO COLLECT ON ME. I GOTTA FIND OUT WHO PUT THIS DAMN HIT ON ME. IT'S REALLY ANNOYING.
HOW MANY'S THAT MAKE?
I STOPPED COUNTING. IT WAS DEPRESSING ME. >SNIFF<
THOSE BEAUTIFUL FLOWERS WOULDN'T BE FOR ME BY ANY CHANCE?
UH... SURE. WHY NOT. THEY'RE NO USE TO ME.
WHAT HAPPENED?
I GOT THEM FOR QUEENIE, BUT I JUST SAW HER LEAVE WITH SOME GORILLA WHO WORKS FOR THE SANITATION DEPARTMENT.
MY FAULT. I WAS PLAYING HARD TO GET WITH HER AND IT BACKFIRED. I THINK SHE HOOKED UP WITH THAT JUNK JOCKEY TO PISS ME OFF.
AH, WHAT'S THE USE? KEEP 'EM. I GOTTA OPEN THE GATES FOR AN EARLY SHOW TODAY, ANYWAY.
I CAN BE YOUR VALENTINE TODAY!
THAT'S SWEET, BUT THE ONLY THING WORSE THAN BEING ALONE ON A DAY LIKE TODAY IS PITY.
WASH UP, GO OUT, AND BREAK SOMEONE'S HEART, DARLIN'. SEE YA LATER.
HARLEY'S APARTMENT. LATER...
REALLY?
PLEASE, ENOUGH WITH THE ENDLESS LOVE. I'M GONNA BARF IN MY OWN TUB!
HARLEY SOUP.
ADMIT IT, FRUITCAKES. YOU'RE LONELY.
BODY WASH
SHAMPOO

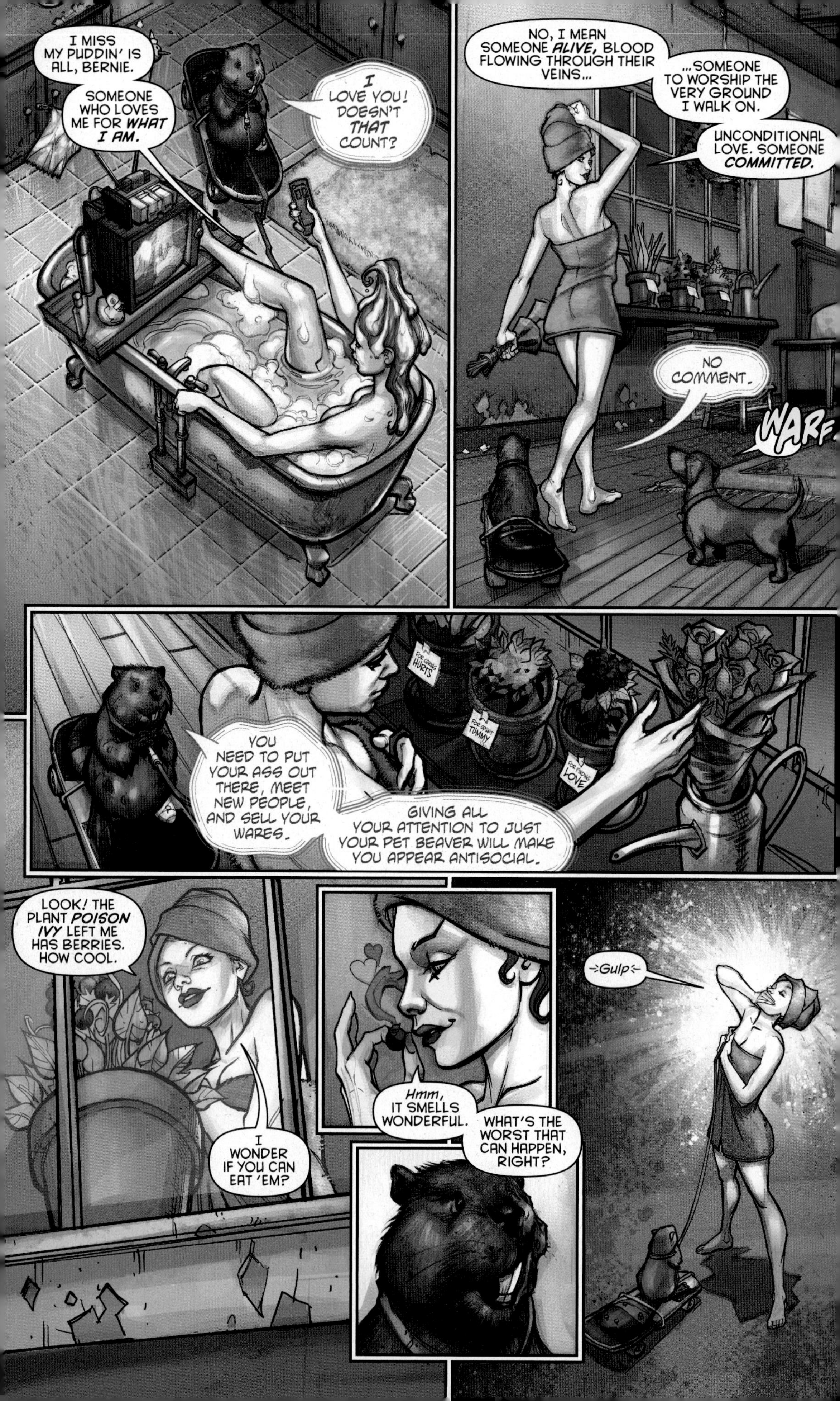
I MISS MY PUDDIN' IS ALL, BERNIE.
SOMEONE WHO LOVES ME FOR *WHAT I AM.*
I LOVE YOU! DOESN'T *THAT* COUNT?
NO, I MEAN SOMEONE *ALIVE,* BLOOD FLOWING THROUGH THEIR VEINS...
...SOMEONE TO WORSHIP THE VERY GROUND I WALK ON.
UNCONDITIONAL LOVE. SOMEONE *COMMITTED.*
NO COMMENT.
WARF.
FOR ACHING HURTS
FOR UPSET TUMMY
FOR FINDING LOVE
YOU NEED TO PUT YOUR ASS OUT THERE, MEET NEW PEOPLE, AND SELL YOUR WARES.
GIVING ALL YOUR ATTENTION TO JUST YOUR PET BEAVER WILL MAKE YOU APPEAR ANTISOCIAL.
LOOK! THE PLANT *POISON IVY* LEFT ME HAS BERRIES. HOW COOL.
I WONDER IF YOU CAN EAT 'EM?
*Hmm,* IT SMELLS WONDERFUL.
WHAT'S THE WORST THAT CAN HAPPEN, RIGHT?
*Gulp*

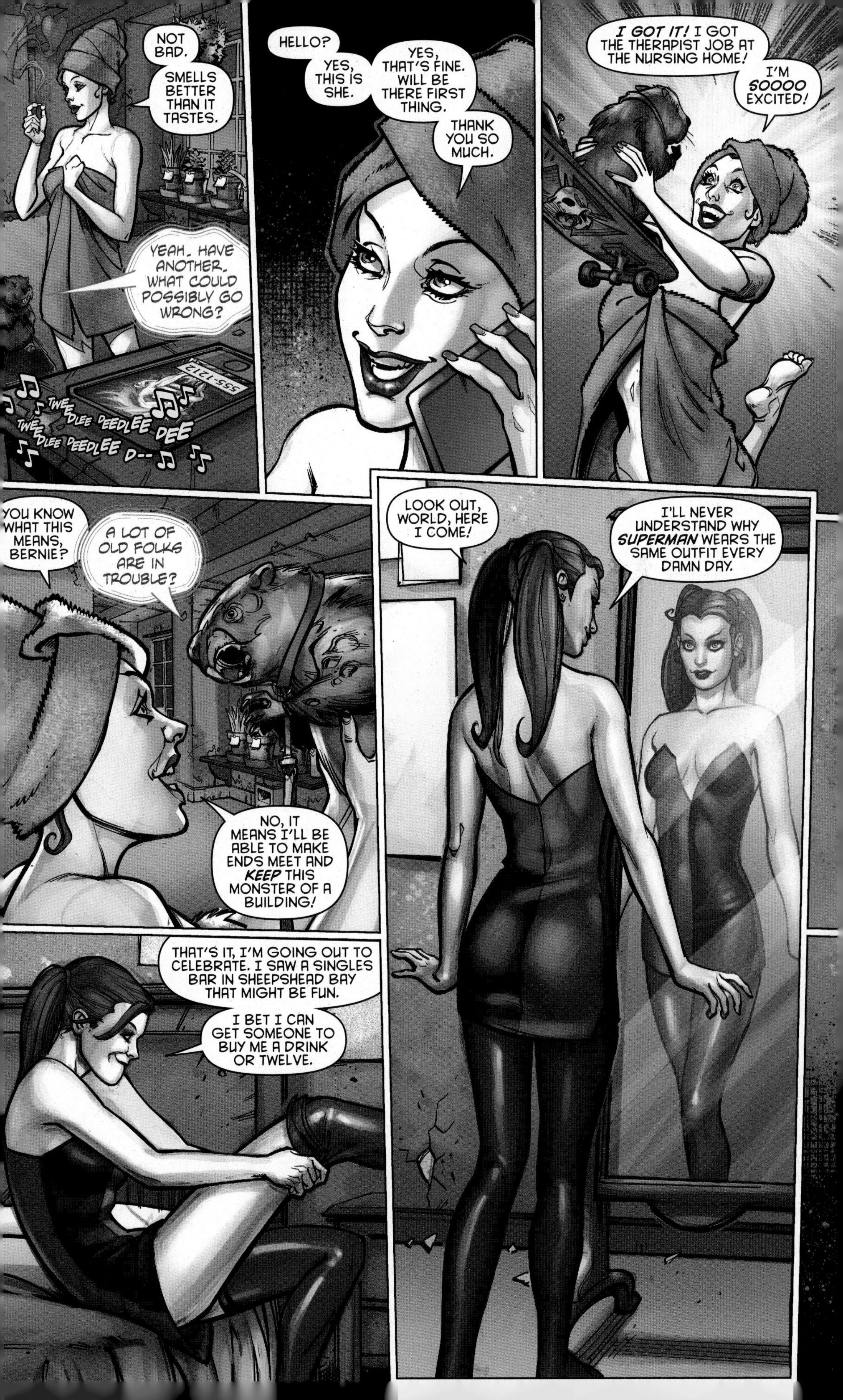

NOT BAD.
SMELLS BETTER THAN IT TASTES.
YEAH. HAVE ANOTHER. WHAT COULD POSSIBLY GO WRONG?
555-1212
TWEEDLEE DEEDLEE DEE
TWEEDLEE DEEDLEE D--
HELLO?
YES, THIS IS SHE.
YES, THAT'S FINE. WILL BE THERE FIRST THING.
THANK YOU SO MUCH.
I GOT IT! I GOT THE THERAPIST JOB AT THE NURSING HOME!
I'M SOOOO EXCITED!
YOU KNOW WHAT THIS MEANS, BERNIE?
A LOT OF OLD FOLKS ARE IN TROUBLE?
NO, IT MEANS I'LL BE ABLE TO MAKE ENDS MEET AND KEEP THIS MONSTER OF A BUILDING!
THAT'S IT, I'M GOING OUT TO CELEBRATE. I SAW A SINGLES BAR IN SHEEPSHEAD BAY THAT MIGHT BE FUN.
I BET I CAN GET SOMEONE TO BUY ME A DRINK OR TWELVE.
LOOK OUT, WORLD, HERE I COME!
I'LL NEVER UNDERSTAND WHY SUPERMAN WEARS THE SAME OUTFIT EVERY DAMN DAY.

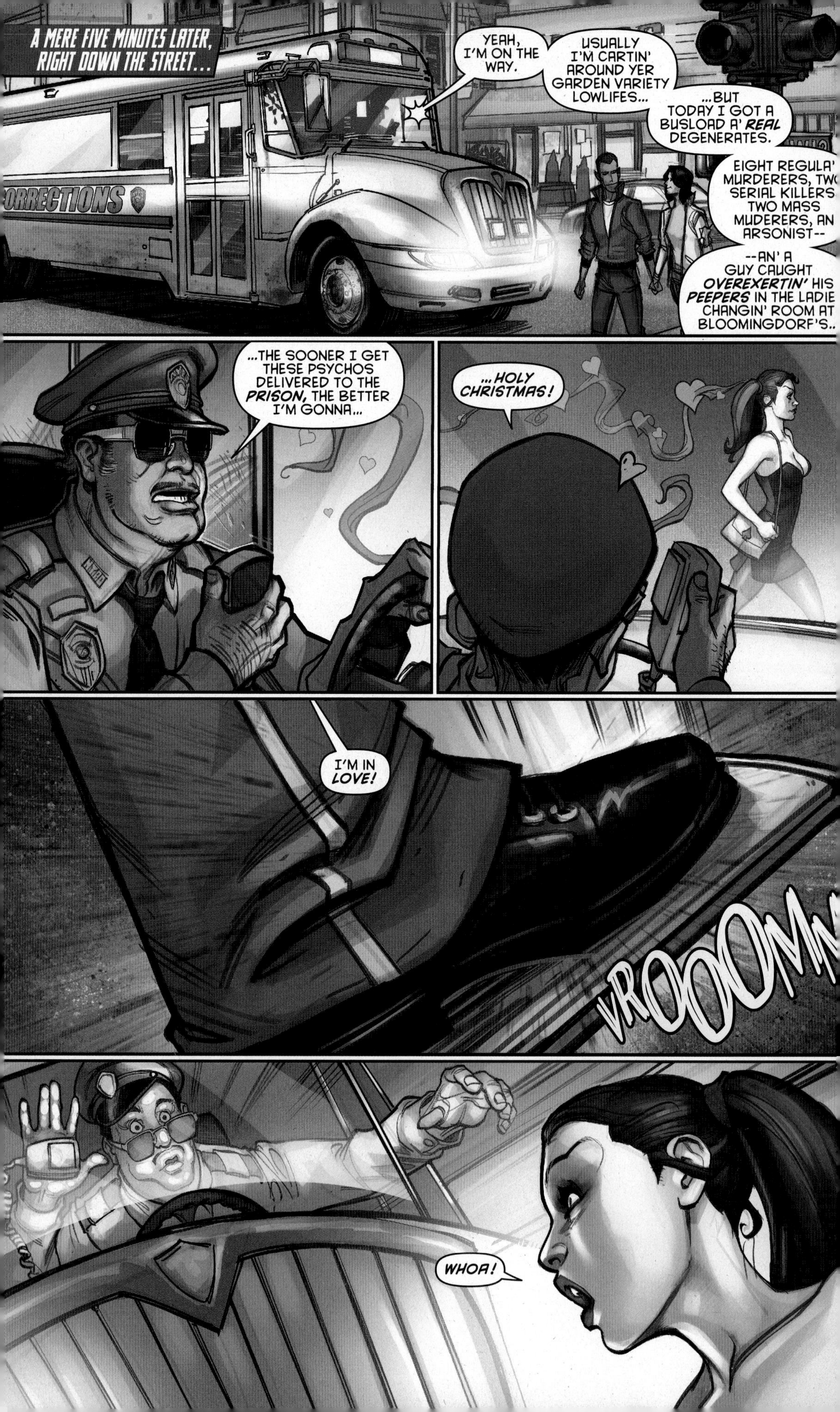
A MERE FIVE MINUTES LATER, RIGHT DOWN THE STREET...
YEAH, I'M ON THE WAY.
USUALLY I'M CARTIN' AROUND YER GARDEN VARIETY LOWLIFES...
...BUT TODAY I GOT A BUSLOAD A' REAL DEGENERATES.
EIGHT REGULA' MURDERERS, TWO SERIAL KILLERS, TWO MASS MUDERERS, AN ARSONIST--
--AN' A GUY CAUGHT OVEREXERTIN' HIS PEEPERS IN THE LADIE CHANGIN' ROOM AT BLOOMINGDORF'S..
CORRECTIONS
...THE SOONER I GET THESE PSYCHOS DELIVERED TO THE PRISON, THE BETTER I'M GONNA...
...HOLY CHRISTMAS!
I'M IN LOVE!
VROOOMM
WHOA!

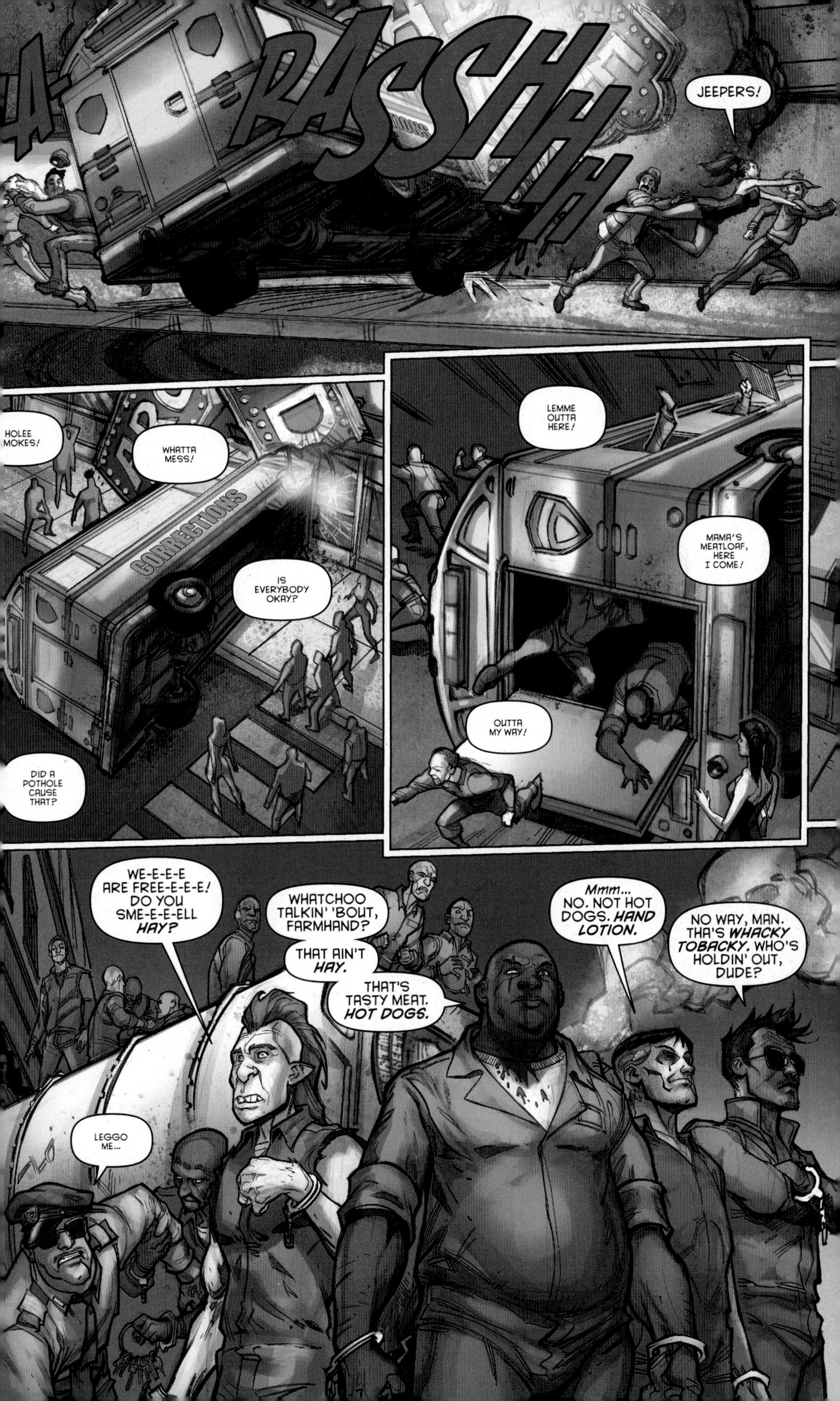
A-RASSHHH
JEEPERS!
HOLEE SMOKES!
WHATTA MESS!
IS EVERYBODY OKAY?
DID A POTHOLE CAUSE THAT?
CORRECTIONS
LEMME OUTTA HERE!
MAMA'S MEATLOAF, HERE I COME!
OUTTA MY WAY!
WE-E-E-E ARE FREE-E-E-E! DO YOU SME-E-E-ELL HAY?
WHATCHOO TALKIN' 'BOUT, FARMHAND?
THAT AIN'T HAY.
THAT'S TASTY MEAT. HOT DOGS.
Mmm... NO. NOT HOT DOGS. HAND LOTION.
NO WAY, MAN. THA'S WHACKY TOBACKY. WHO'S HOLDIN' OUT, DUDE?
LEGGO ME...

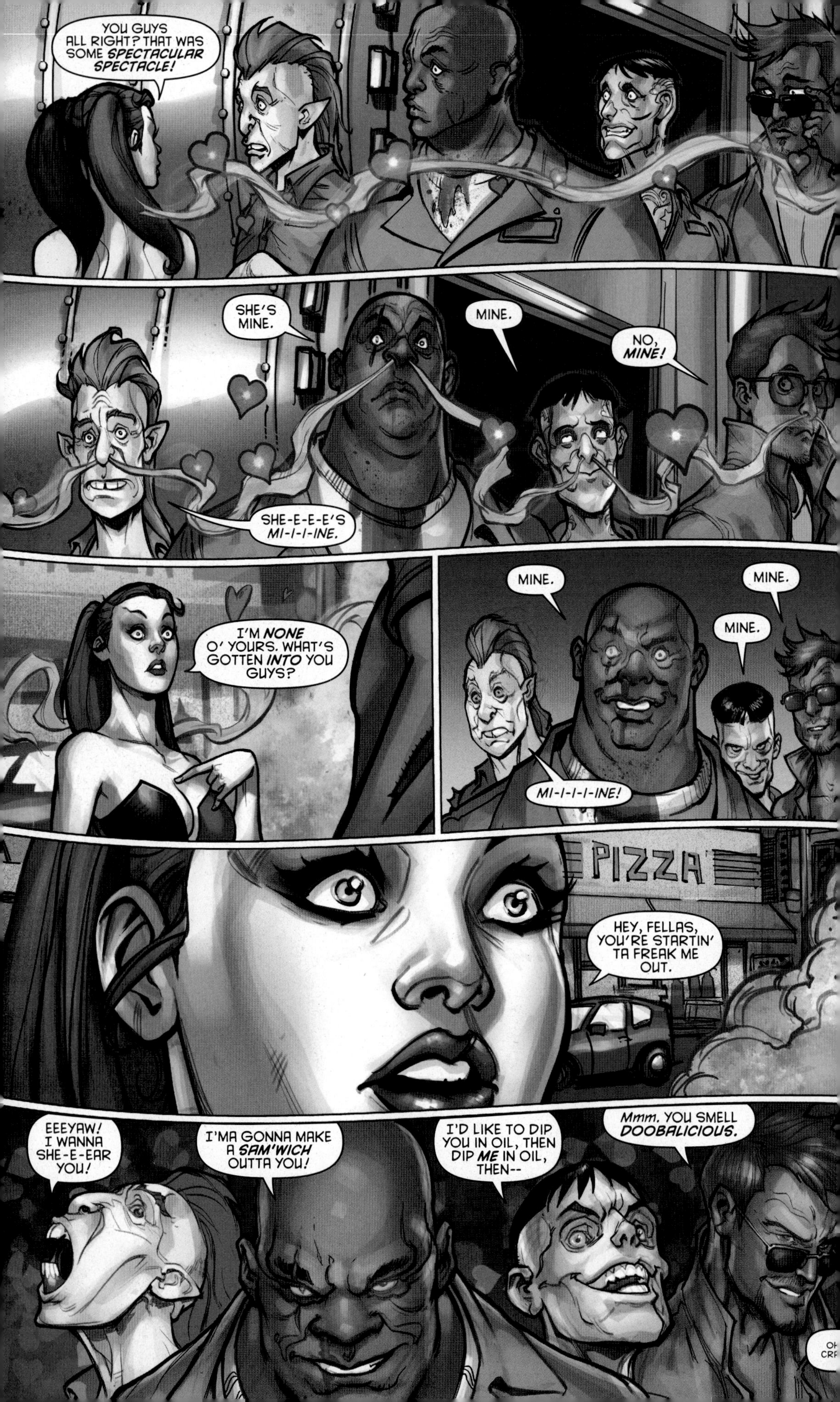
YOU GUYS ALL RIGHT? THAT WAS SOME SPECTACULAR SPECTACLE!
SHE'S MINE.
MINE.
NO, MINE!
SHE-E-E-E'S MI-I-I-INE.
I'M NONE O' YOURS. WHAT'S GOTTEN INTO YOU GUYS?
MINE.
MINE.
MINE.
MI-I-I-I-INE!
PIZZA
HEY, FELLAS, YOU'RE STARTIN' TA FREAK ME OUT.
EEEYAW! I WANNA SHE-E-EAR YOU!
I'MA GONNA MAKE A SAM'WICH OUTTA YOU!
I'D LIKE TO DIP YOU IN OIL, THEN DIP ME IN OIL, THEN--
Mmm. YOU SMELL DOOBALICIOUS.

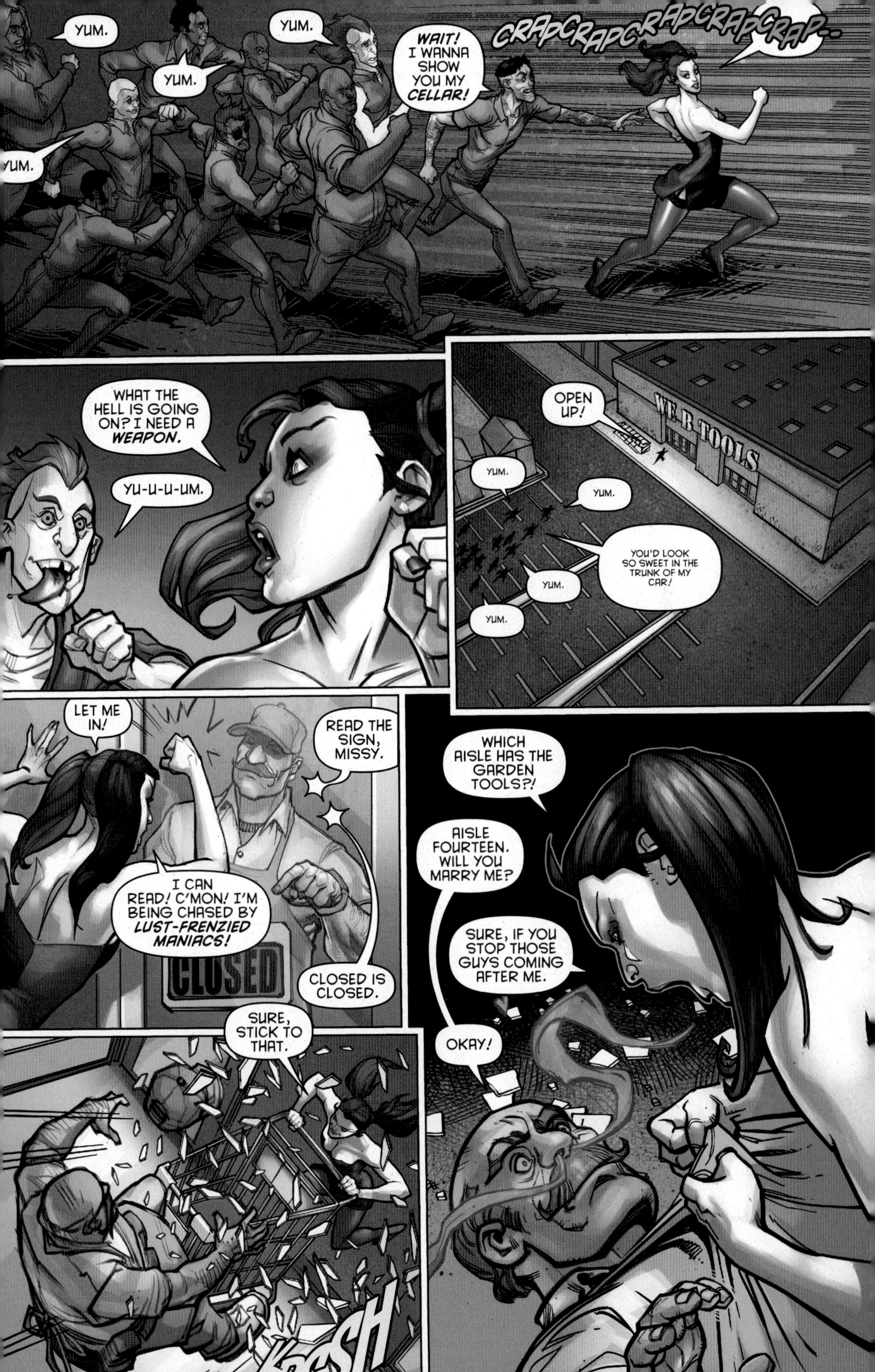
YUM.
YUM.
YUM.
YUM.
WAIT! I WANNA SHOW YOU MY CELLAR!
CRAPCRAPCRAPCRAPCRAP..
WHAT THE HELL IS GOING ON? I NEED A WEAPON.
YU-U-U-UM.
OPEN UP!
YUM.
YUM.
YOU'D LOOK SO SWEET IN THE TRUNK OF MY CAR!
YUM.
YUM.
W.E.B TOOLS
LET ME IN!
READ THE SIGN, MISSY.
I CAN READ! C'MON! I'M BEING CHASED BY LUST-FRENZIED MANIACS!
CLOSED
CLOSED IS CLOSED.
SURE, STICK TO THAT.
KRSSH
WHICH AISLE HAS THE GARDEN TOOLS?!
AISLE FOURTEEN. WILL YOU MARRY ME?
SURE, IF YOU STOP THOSE GUYS COMING AFTER ME.
OKAY!

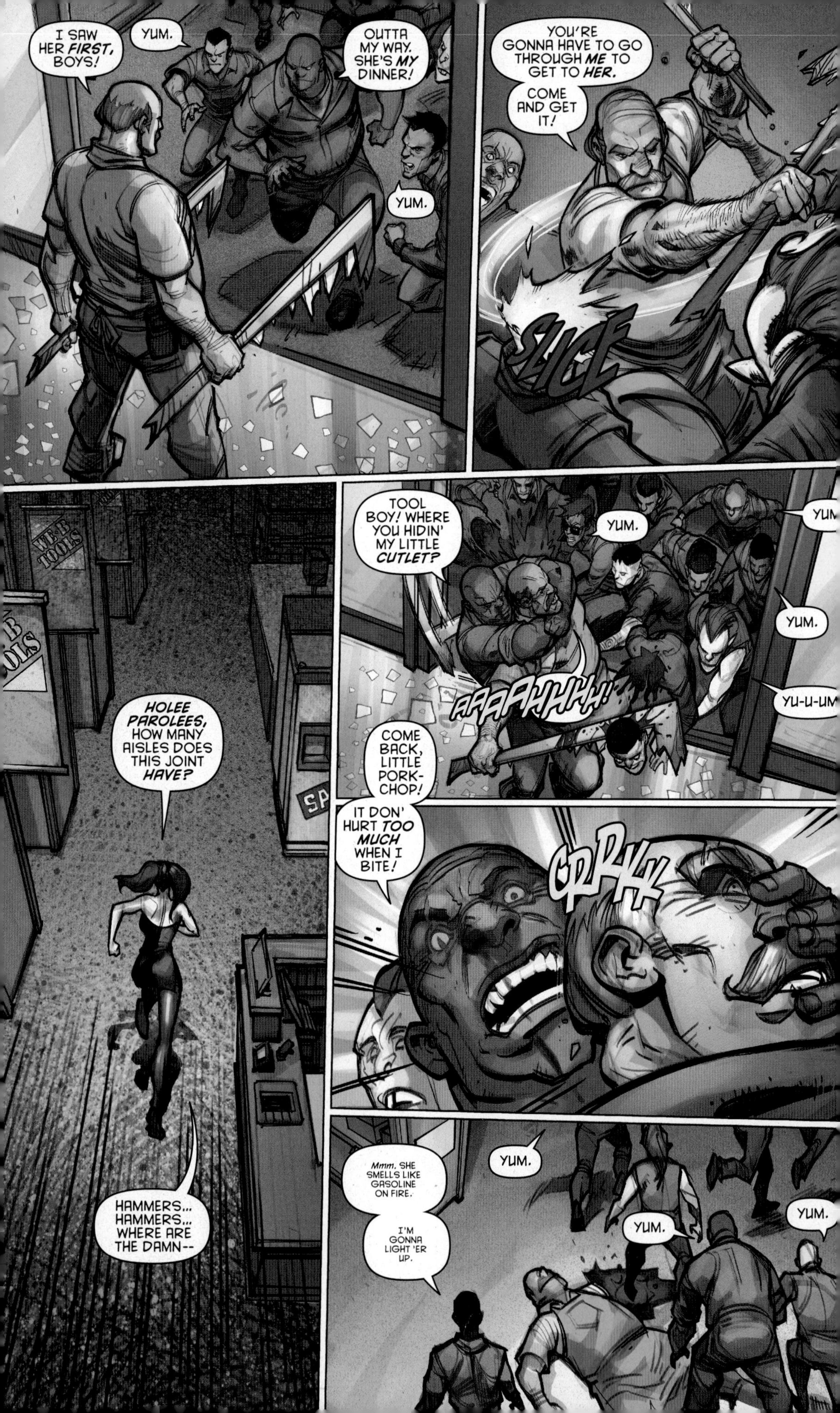
I SAW HER *FIRST*, BOYS!
YUM.
OUTTA MY WAY. SHE'S *MY* DINNER!
YUM.
YOU'RE GONNA HAVE TO GO THROUGH *ME* TO GET TO *HER*.
COME AND GET IT!
SLICE
WE B TOOLS
*HOLEE PAROLEES*, HOW MANY AISLES DOES THIS JOINT *HAVE?*
HAMMERS... HAMMERS... WHERE ARE THE DAMN--
TOOL BOY! WHERE YOU HIDIN' MY LITTLE *CUTLET?*
YUM.
YUM.
AAAAHHHH!
YU-U-UM
COME BACK, LITTLE PORK-CHOP!
IT DON' HURT *TOO MUCH* WHEN I BITE!
CRRKK
*Mmm.* SHE SMELLS LIKE GASOLINE ON FIRE.
I'M GONNA LIGHT 'ER UP.
YUM.
YUM.
YUM.

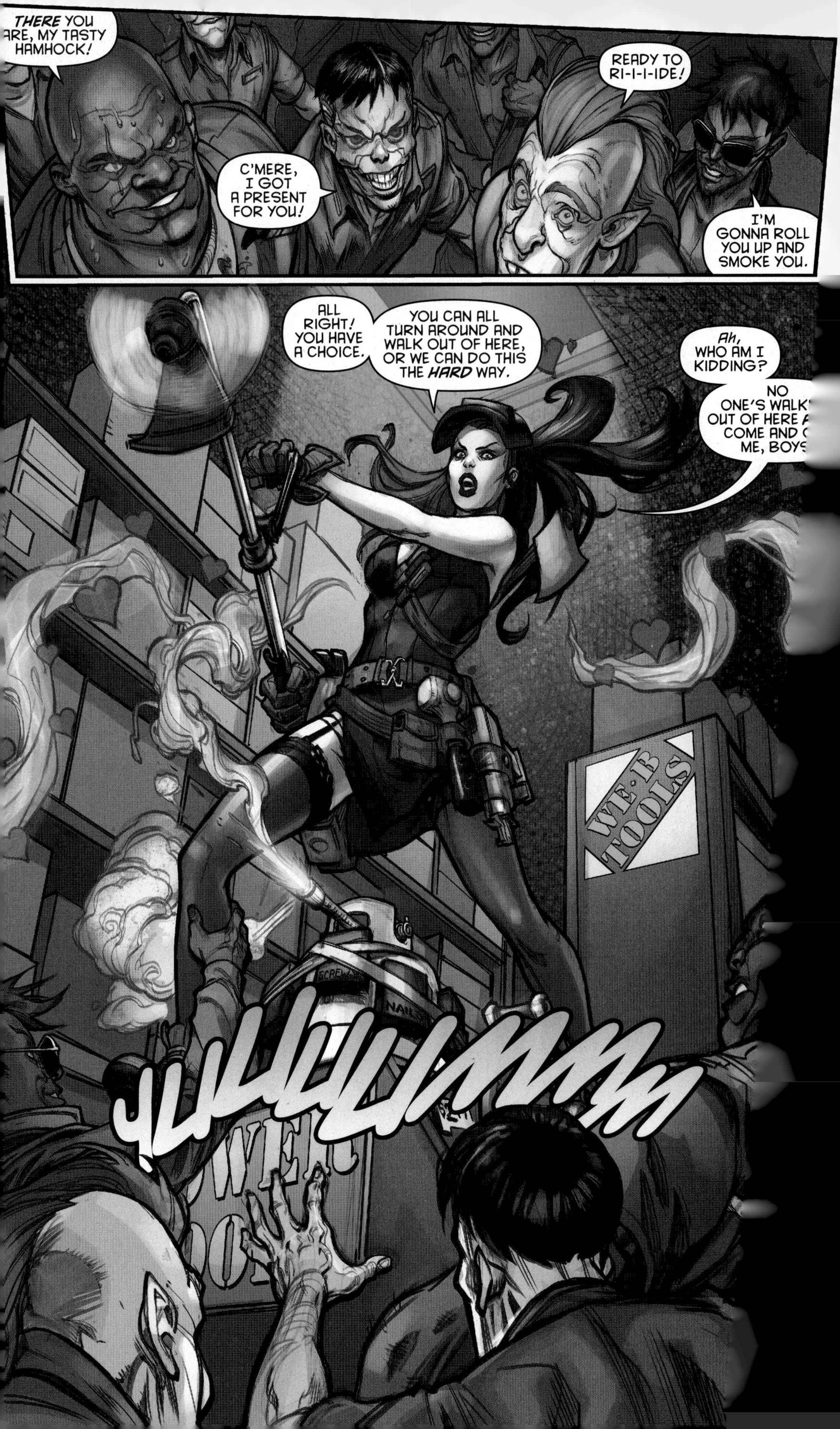
THERE YOU ARE, MY TASTY HAMHOCK!
C'MERE, I GOT A PRESENT FOR YOU!
READY TO RI-I-I-IDE!
I'M GONNA ROLL YOU UP AND SMOKE YOU.
ALL RIGHT! YOU HAVE A CHOICE.
YOU CAN ALL TURN AROUND AND WALK OUT OF HERE, OR WE CAN DO THIS THE HARD WAY.
AH, WHO AM I KIDDING?
NO ONE'S OUT OF HERE COME AND ME,
WE-B TOOLS

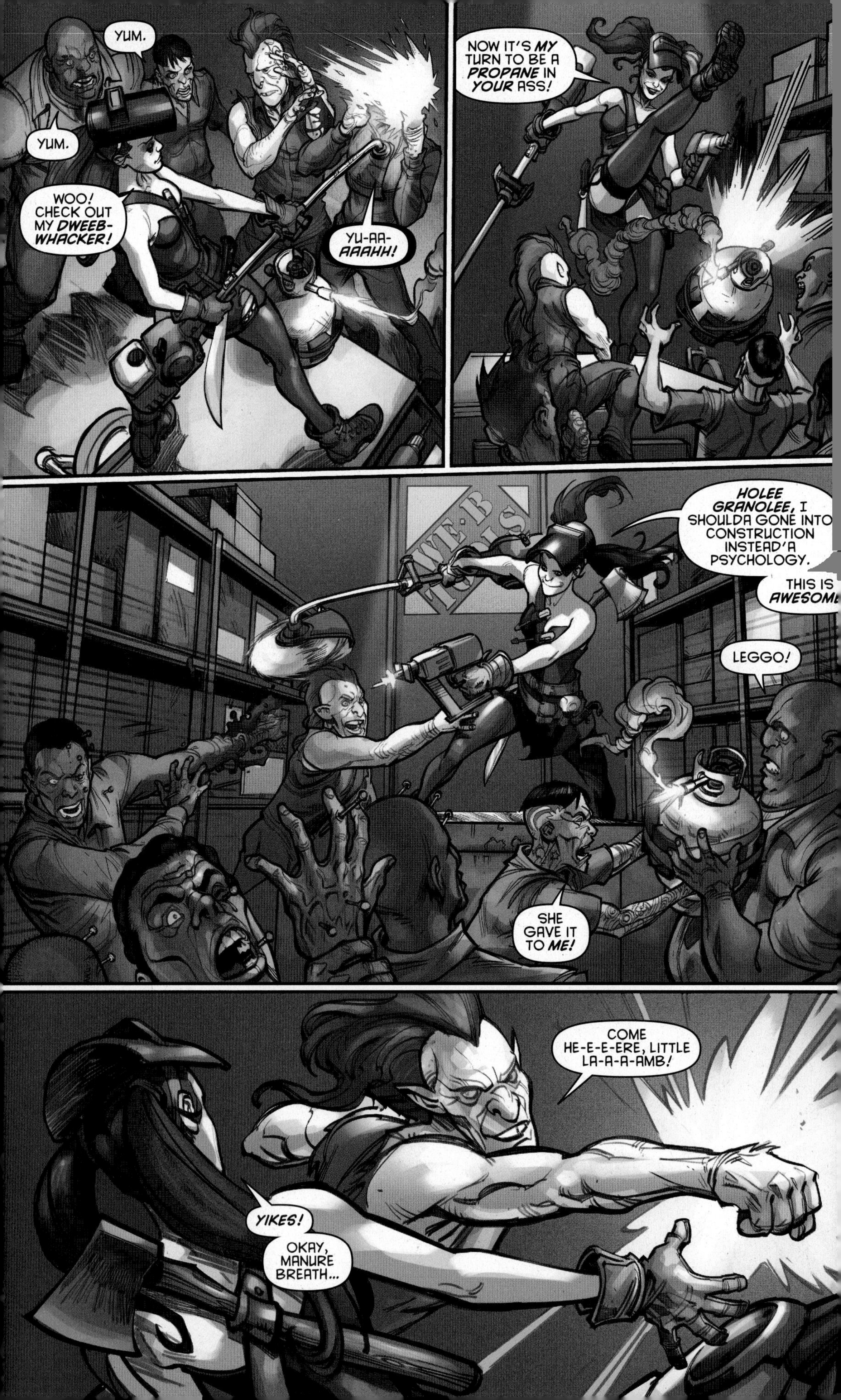
YUM.
YUM.
WOO! CHECK OUT MY *DWEEB-WHACKER!*
YU-AA-*AAAHH!*
NOW IT'S *MY* TURN TO BE A *PROPANE* IN *YOUR* ASS!
*HOLEE GRANOLEE*, I SHOULDA GONE INTO CONSTRUCTION INSTEAD'A PSYCHOLOGY.
THIS IS *AWESOME*
LEGGO!
SHE GAVE IT TO *ME!*
COME HE-E-E-ERE, LITTLE LA-A-A-AMB!
*YIKES!*
OKAY, MANURE BREATH...

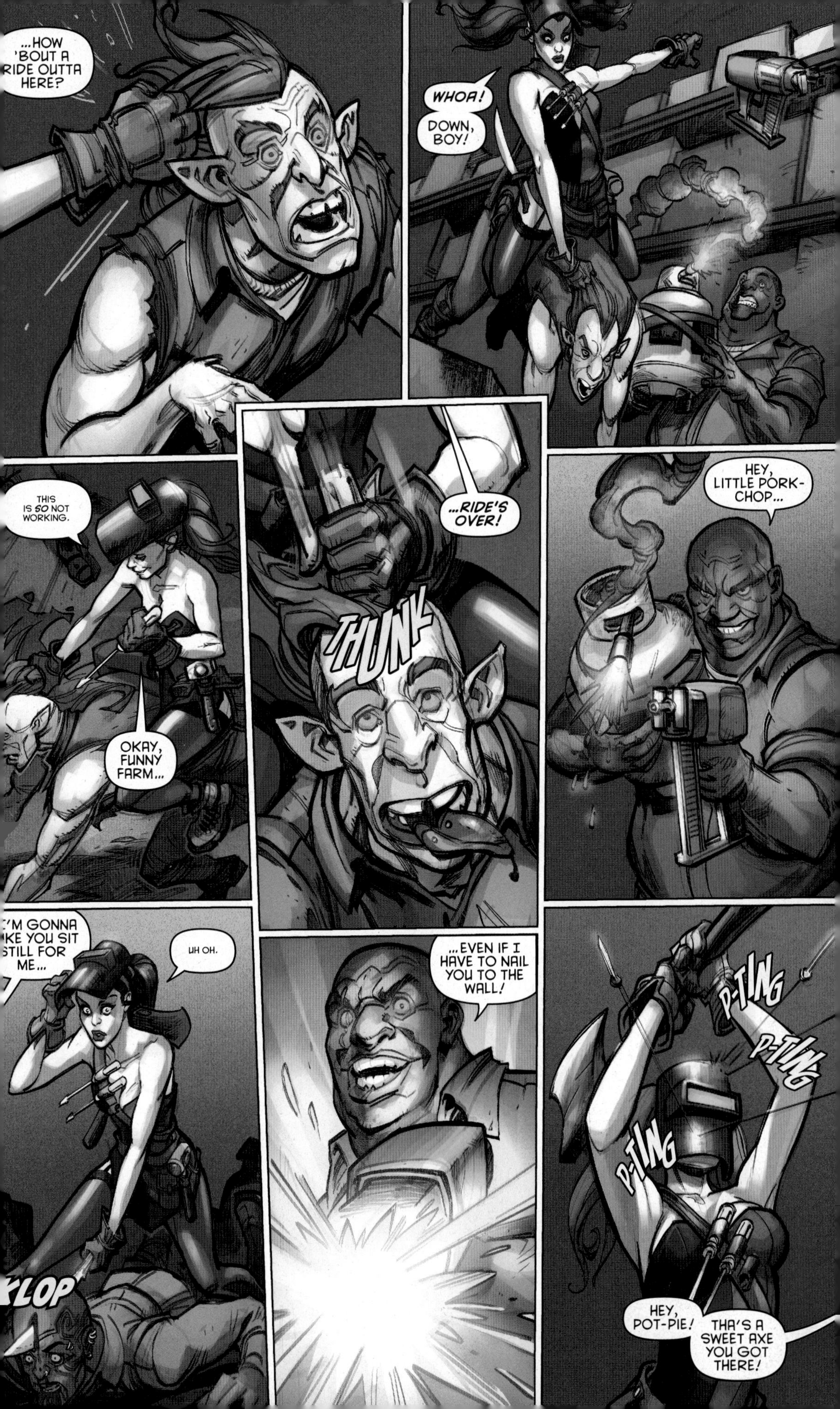
...HOW 'BOUT A RIDE OUTTA HERE?
WHOA!
DOWN, BOY!
THIS IS SO NOT WORKING.
OKAY, FUNNY FARM...
...RIDE'S OVER!
THUNK
HEY, LITTLE PORK-CHOP...
I'M GONNA MAKE YOU SIT STILL FOR ME...
UH OH.
KLOP
...EVEN IF I HAVE TO NAIL YOU TO THE WALL!
P-TING
P-TING
P-TING
HEY, POT-PIE!
THA'S A SWEET AXE YOU GOT THERE!

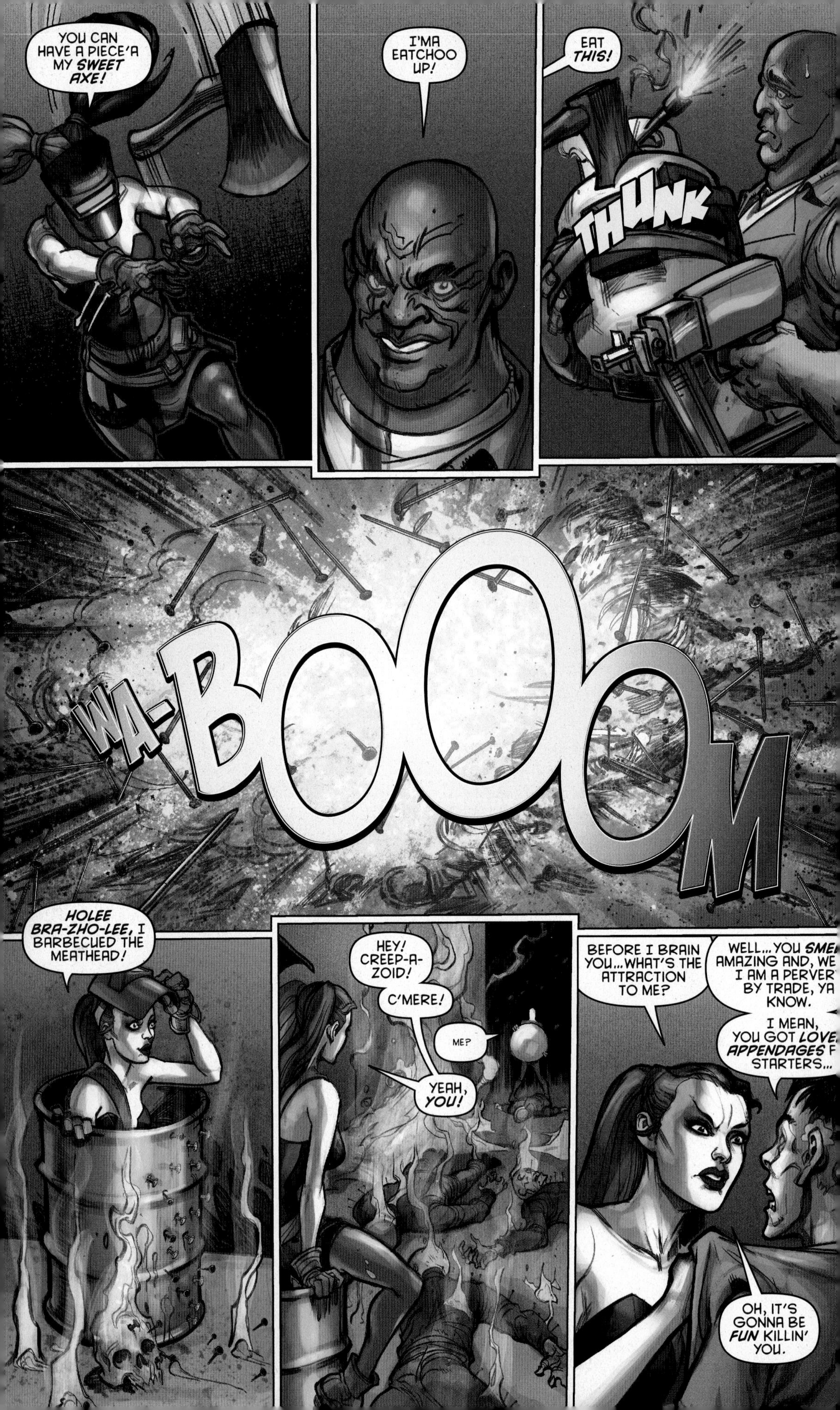

YOU CAN HAVE A PIECE'A MY *SWEET AXE!*
I'MA EATCHOO UP!
EAT *THIS!*
THUNK
WA-BOOOM
*HOLEE BRA-ZHO-LEE,* I BARBECUED THE MEATHEAD!
HEY! CREEP-A-ZOID!
C'MERE!
ME?
YEAH, *YOU!*
BEFORE I BRAIN YOU...WHAT'S THE ATTRACTION TO ME?
WELL...YOU *SME* AMAZING AND, WE I AM A PERVER BY TRADE, YA KNOW.
I MEAN, YOU GOT *LOVE APPENDAGES* F STARTERS...
OH, IT'S GONNA BE *FUN* KILLIN' YOU.

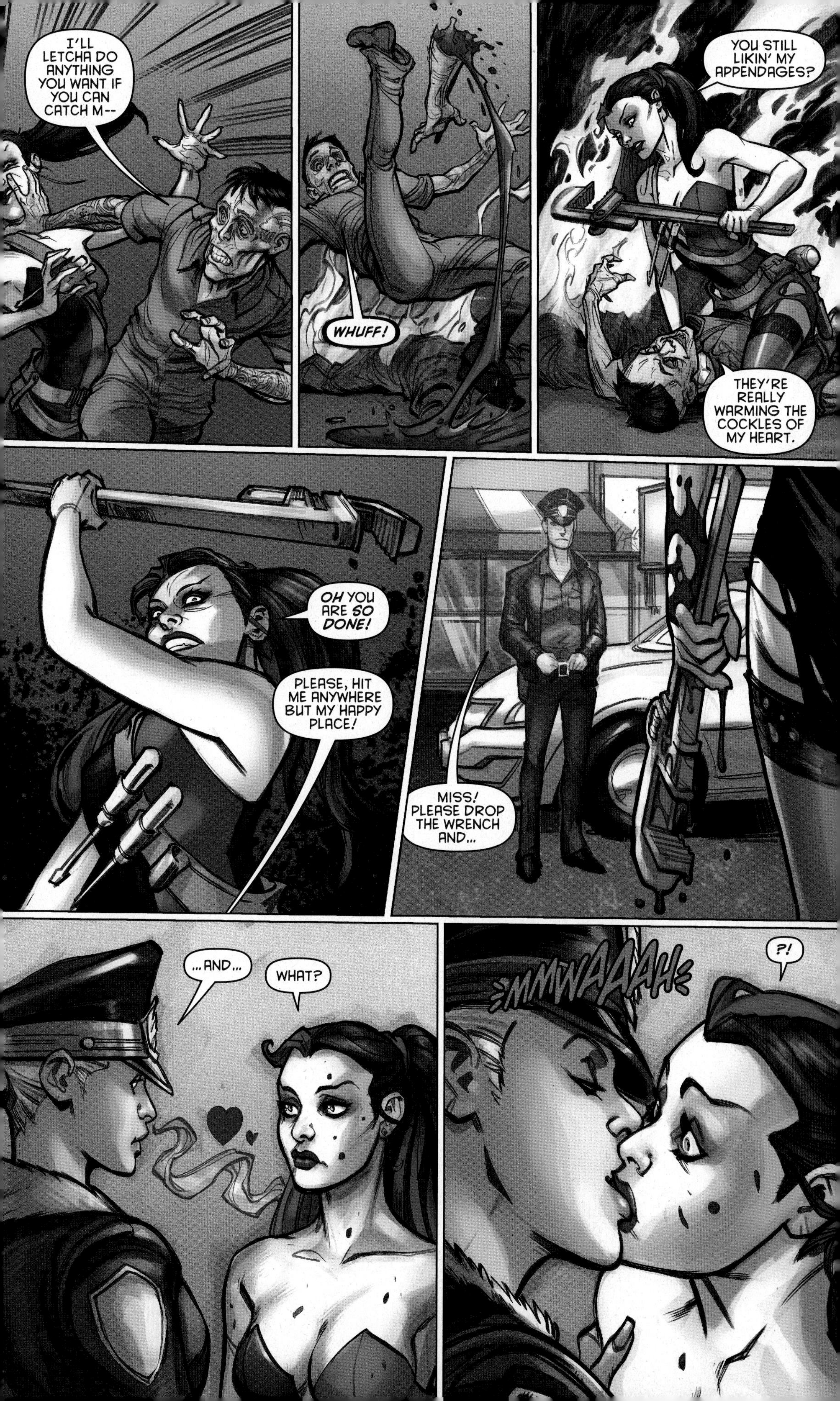
I'LL LETCHA DO ANYTHING YOU WANT IF YOU CAN CATCH M--
WHUFF!
YOU STILL LIKIN' MY APPENDAGES?
THEY'RE REALLY WARMING THE COCKLES OF MY HEART.
OH YOU ARE SO DONE!
PLEASE, HIT ME ANYWHERE BUT MY HAPPY PLACE!
MISS! PLEASE DROP THE WRENCH AND...
...AND...
WHAT?
MMWAAAAH
?!

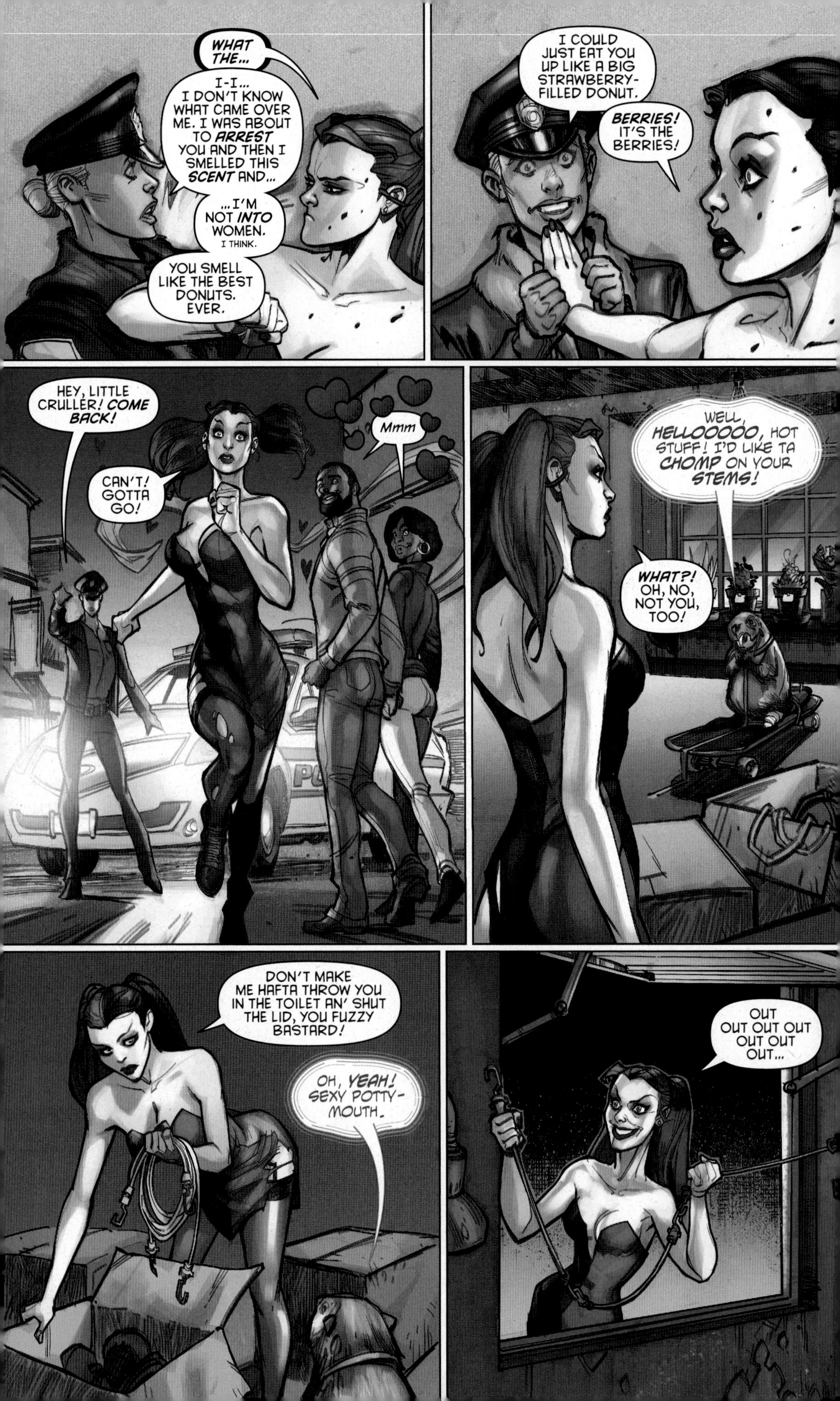
WHAT THE...
I-I... I DON'T KNOW WHAT CAME OVER ME. I WAS ABOUT TO ARREST YOU AND THEN I SMELLED THIS SCENT AND...
...I'M NOT INTO WOMEN. I THINK.
YOU SMELL LIKE THE BEST DONUTS. EVER.
I COULD JUST EAT YOU UP LIKE A BIG STRAWBERRY-FILLED DONUT.
BERRIES! IT'S THE BERRIES!
HEY, LITTLE CRULLER! COME BACK!
CAN'T! GOTTA GO!
Mmm
WELL, HELLOOOOO, HOT STUFF! I'D LIKE TA CHOMP ON YOUR STEMS!
WHAT?! OH, NO, NOT YOU, TOO!
DON'T MAKE ME HAFTA THROW YOU IN THE TOILET AN' SHUT THE LID, YOU FUZZY BASTARD!
OH, YEAH! SEXY POTTY-MOUTH.
OUT OUT OUT OUT OUT OUT OUT...

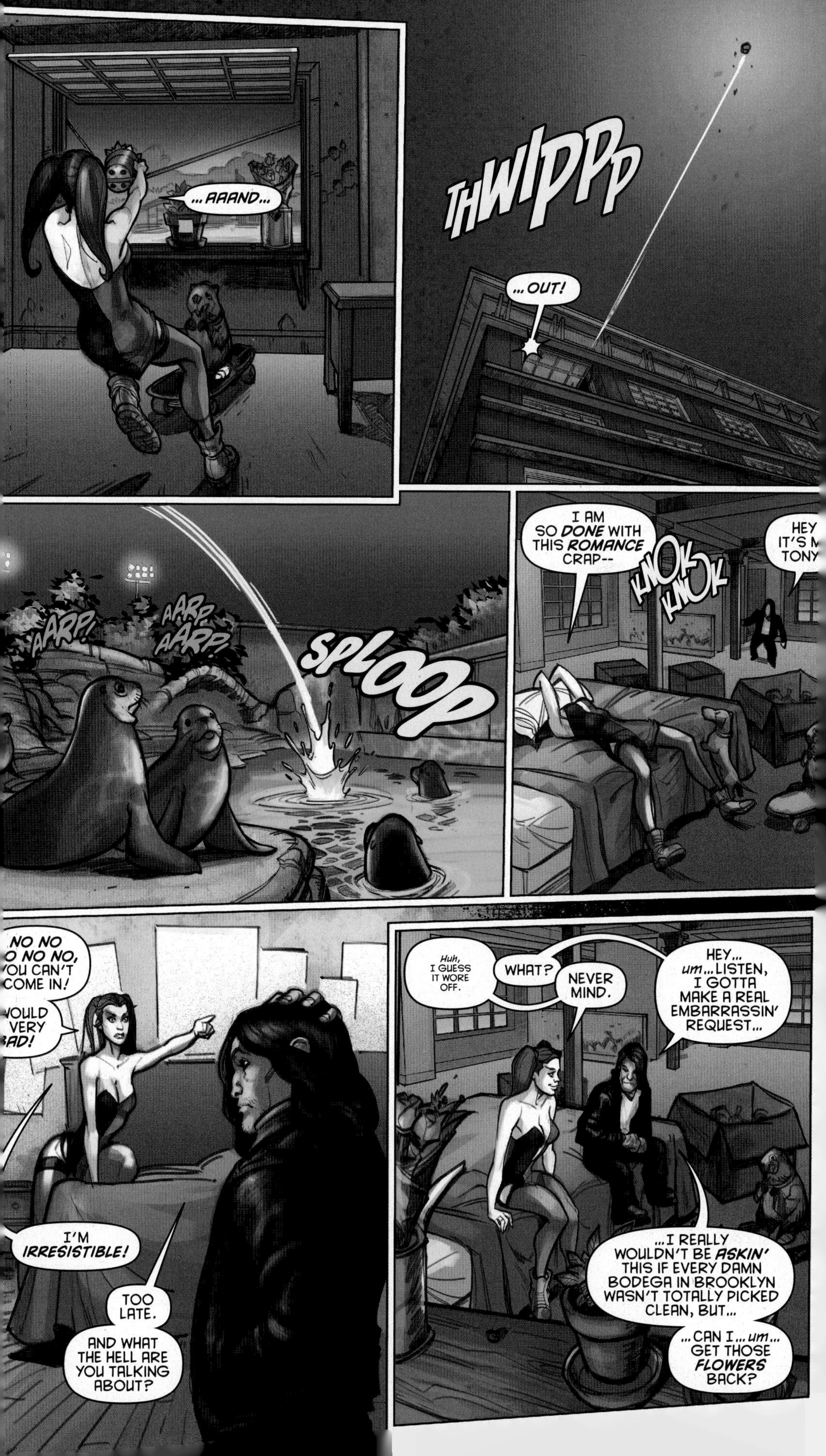
...AAAND...
THWIPPP
...OUT!
AARP!
AARP, AARP!
SPLOOP
I AM SO DONE WITH THIS ROMANCE CRAP--
KNOK KNOK
HEY IT'S M TONY
NO NO NO NO NO, YOU CAN'T COME IN!
WOULD VERY BAD!
I'M IRRESISTIBLE!
TOO LATE.
AND WHAT THE HELL ARE YOU TALKING ABOUT?
Huh, I GUESS IT WORE OFF.
WHAT?
NEVER MIND.
HEY... um...LISTEN, I GOTTA MAKE A REAL EMBARRASSIN' REQUEST...
...I REALLY WOULDN'T BE ASKIN' THIS IF EVERY DAMN BODEGA IN BROOKLYN WASN'T TOTALLY PICKED CLEAN, BUT...
...CAN I...um... GET THOSE FLOWERS BACK?

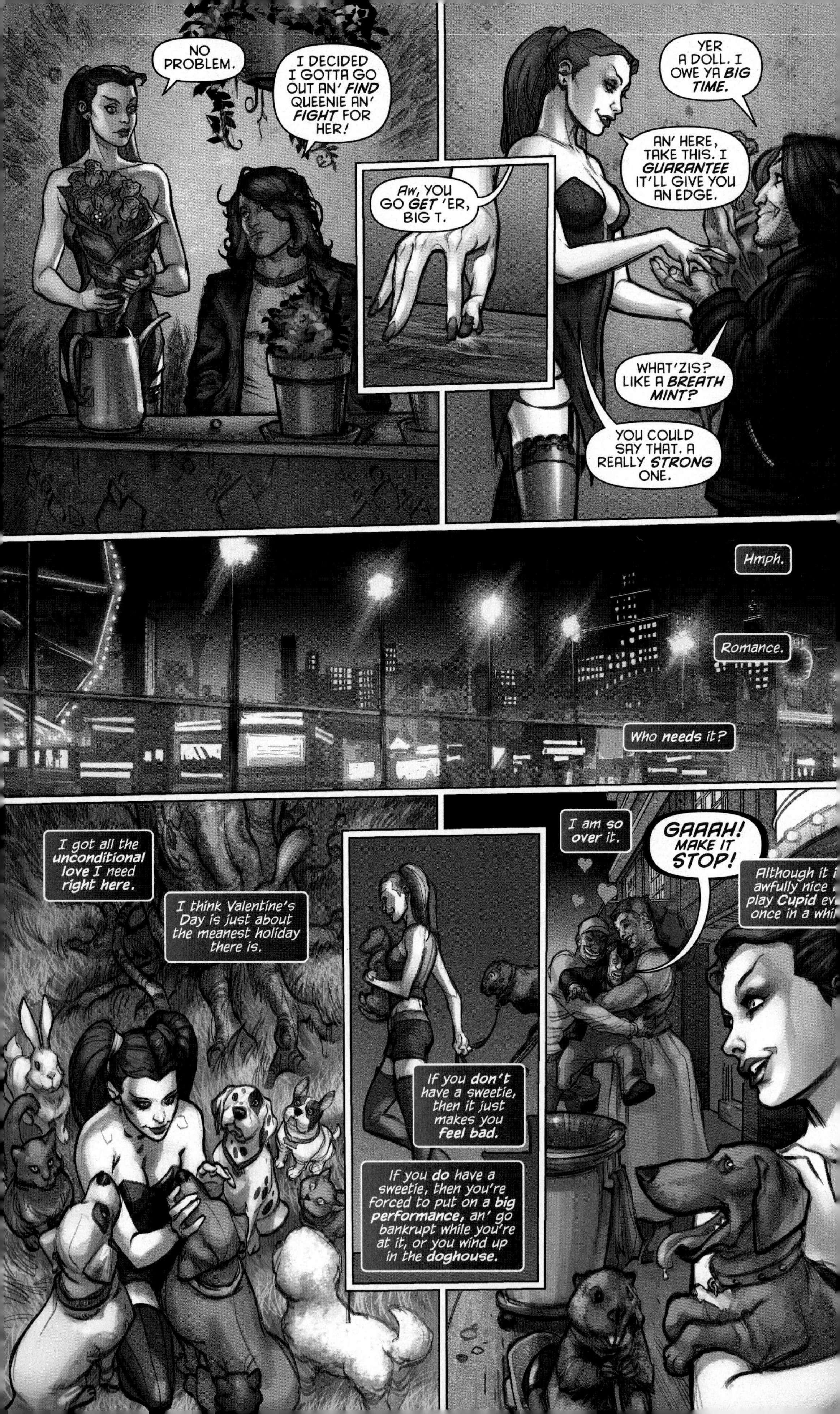
NO PROBLEM.
I DECIDED I GOTTA GO OUT AN' FIND QUEENIE AN' FIGHT FOR HER!
Aw, YOU GO GET 'ER, BIG T.
YER A DOLL. I OWE YA BIG TIME.
AN' HERE, TAKE THIS. I GUARANTEE IT'LL GIVE YOU AN EDGE.
WHAT'ZIS? LIKE A BREATH MINT?
YOU COULD SAY THAT. A REALLY STRONG ONE.
Hmph.
Romance.
Who needs it?
I got all the unconditional love I need right here.
I think Valentine's Day is just about the meanest holiday there is.
If you don't have a sweetie, then it just makes you feel bad.
If you do have a sweetie, then you're forced to put on a big performance, an' go bankrupt while you're at it, or you wind up in the doghouse.
I am so over it.
GAAAH! MAKE IT STOP!

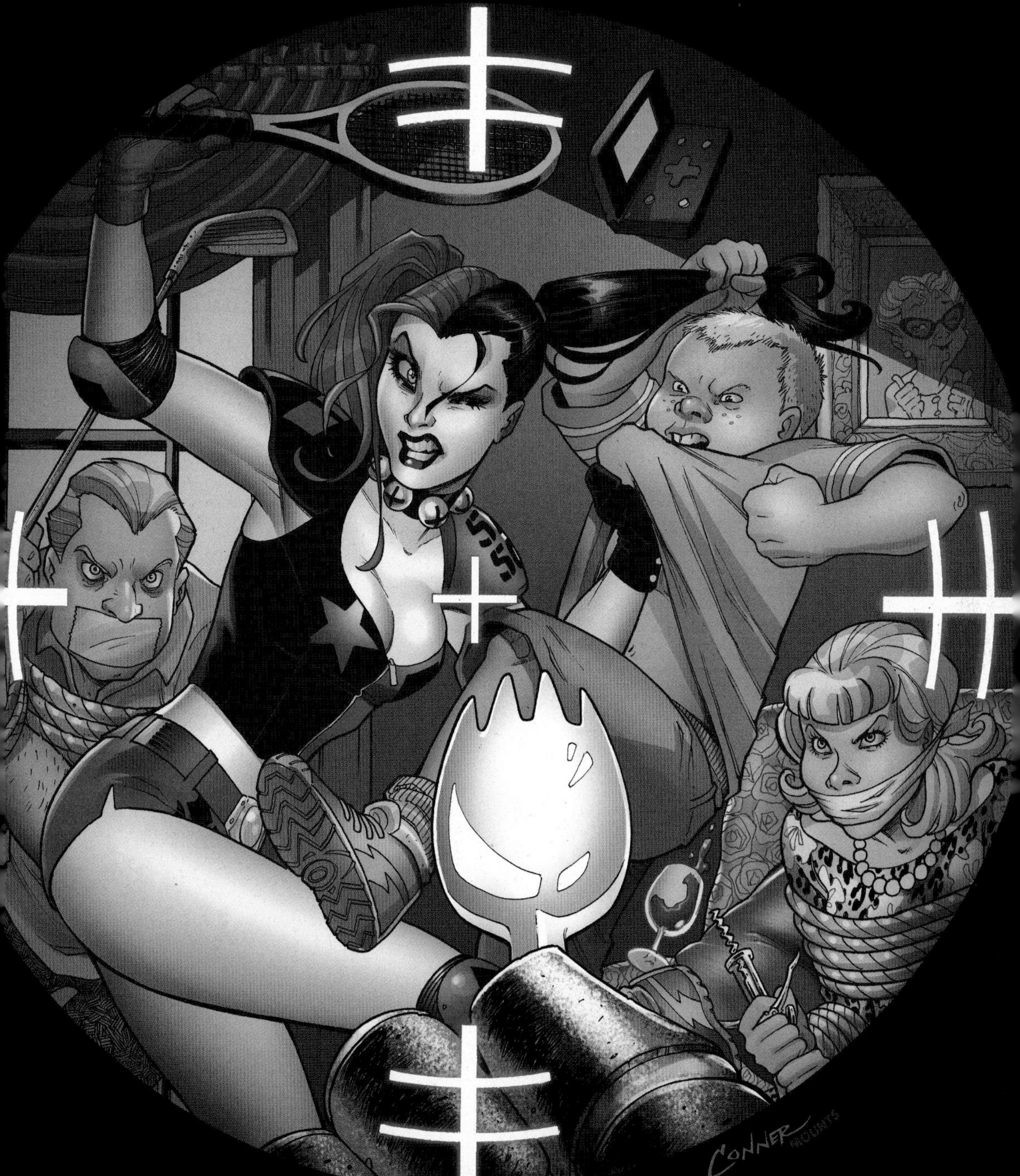
CONNER

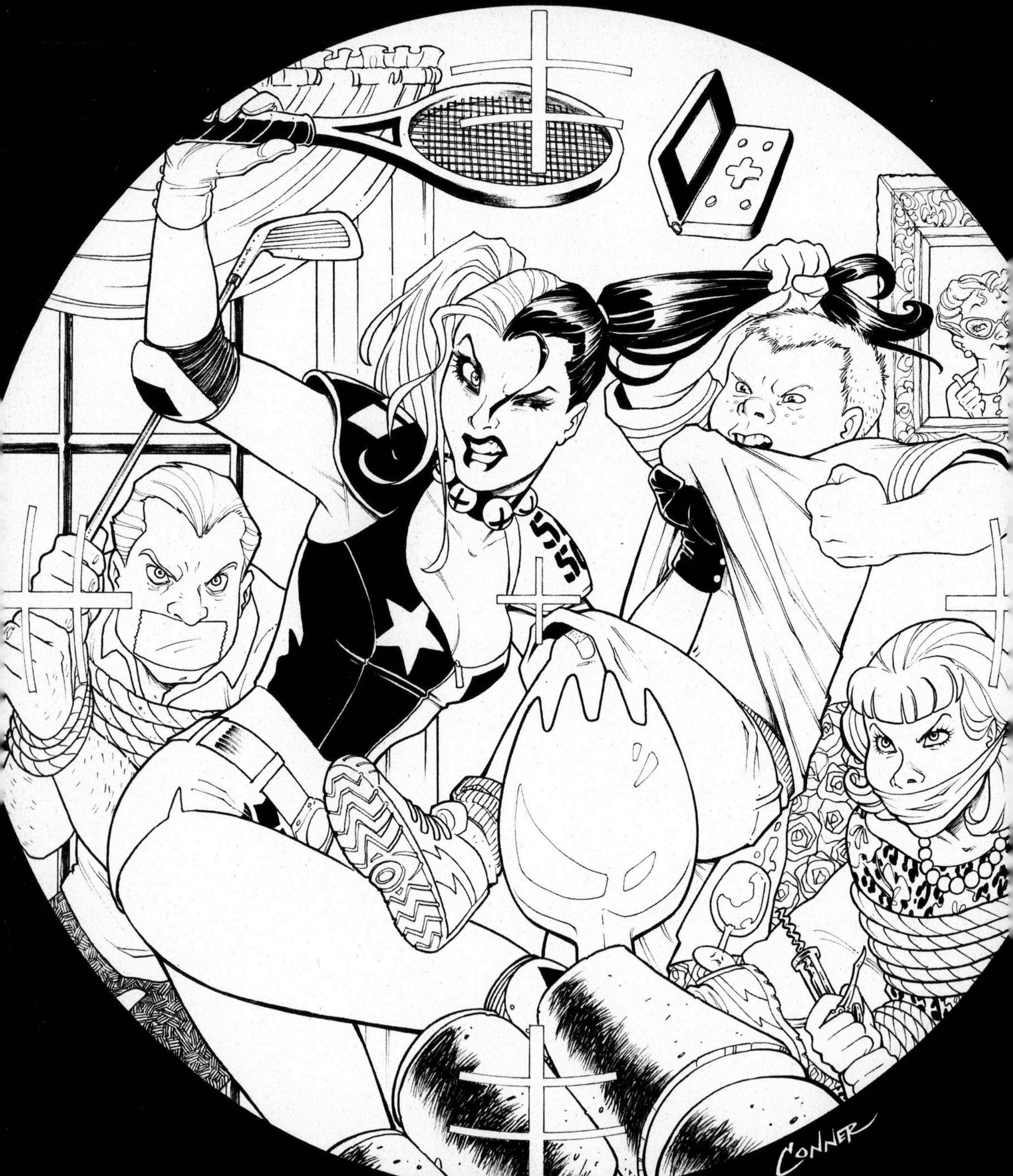
CONNER

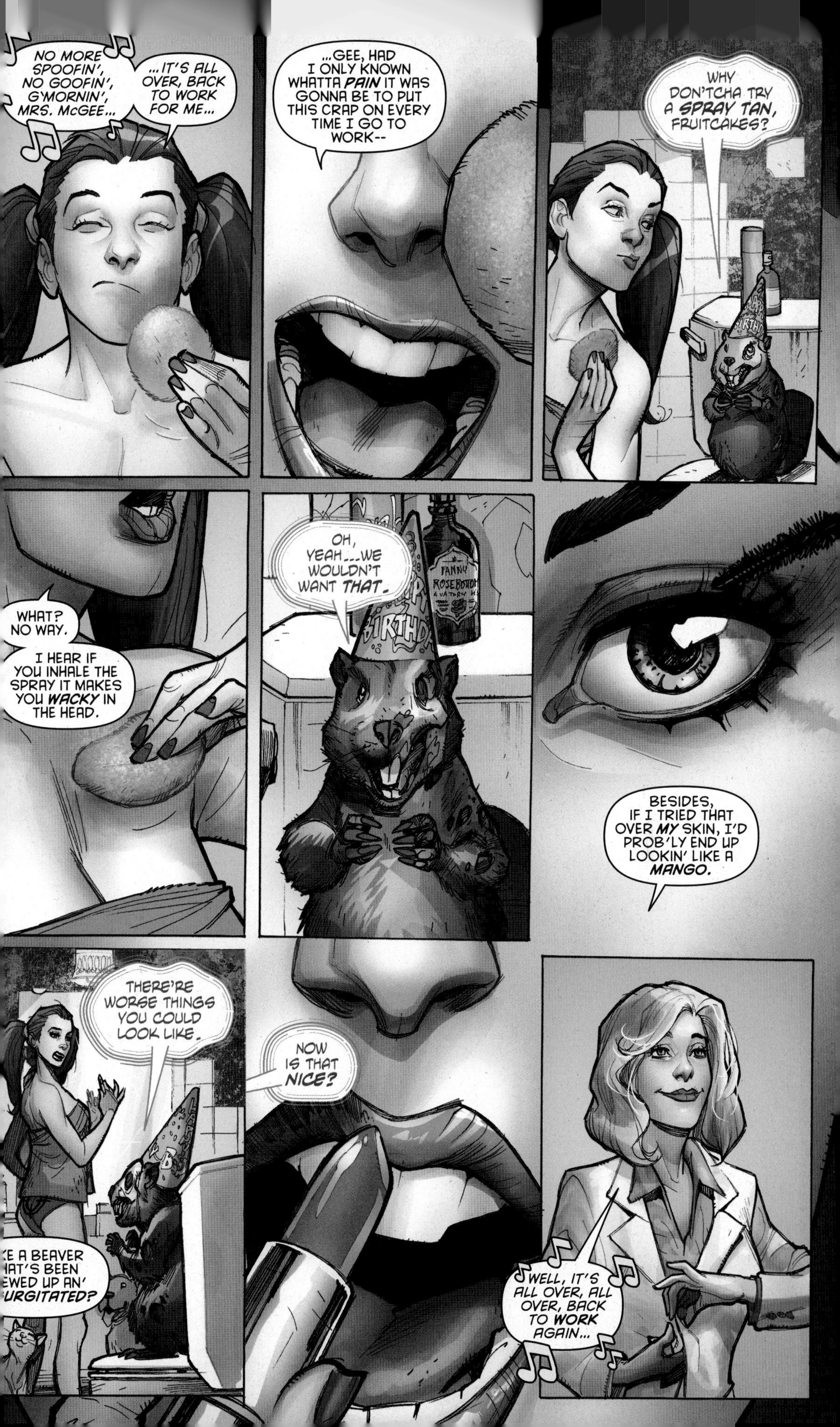
NO MORE SPOOFIN', NO GOOFIN', G'MORNIN', MRS. McGEE...
...IT'S ALL OVER, BACK TO WORK FOR ME...
...GEE, HAD I ONLY KNOWN WHATTA PAIN IT WAS GONNA BE TO PUT THIS CRAP ON EVERY TIME I GO TO WORK--
WHY DON'TCHA TRY A SPRAY TAN, FRUITCAKES?
WHAT? NO WAY.
I HEAR IF YOU INHALE THE SPRAY IT MAKES YOU WACKY IN THE HEAD.
OH, YEAH...WE WOULDN'T WANT THAT.
BESIDES, IF I TRIED THAT OVER MY SKIN, I'D PROB'LY END UP LOOKIN' LIKE A MANGO.
THERE'RE WORSE THINGS YOU COULD LOOK LIKE.
NOW IS THAT NICE?
WELL, IT'S ALL OVER, ALL OVER, BACK TO WORK AGAIN...

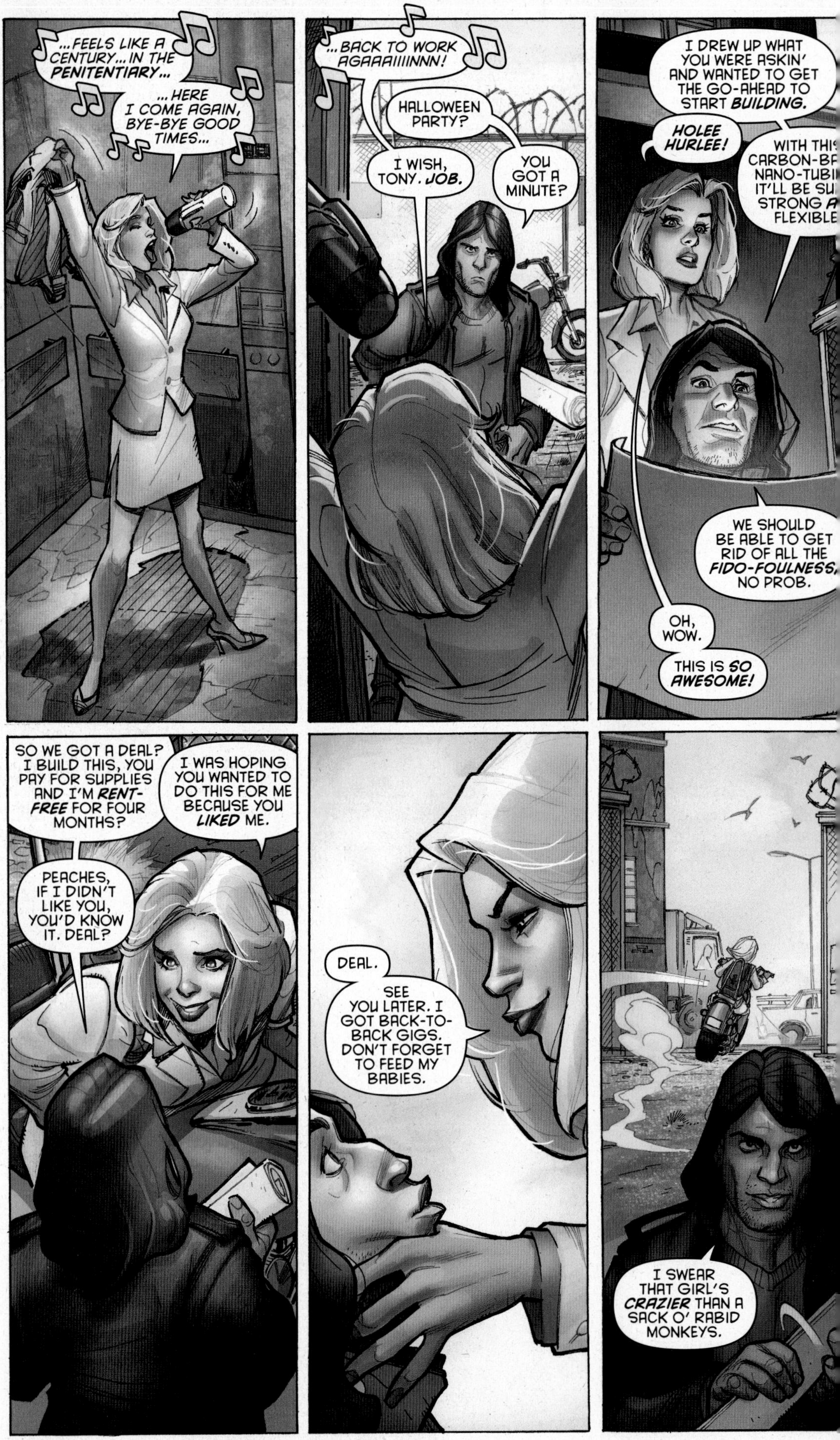
...FEELS LIKE A CENTURY... IN THE PENITENTIARY...
... HERE I COME AGAIN, BYE-BYE GOOD TIMES...
...BACK TO WORK AGAAAAIIIINNN!
HALLOWEEN PARTY?
I WISH, TONY. JOB.
YOU GOT A MINUTE?
I DREW UP WHAT YOU WERE ASKIN' AND WANTED TO GET THE GO-AHEAD TO START BUILDING.
HOLEE HURLEE!
WITH THIS CARBON-BA NANO-TUBI IT'LL BE SU STRONG A FLEXIBLE
WE SHOULD BE ABLE TO GET RID OF ALL THE FIDO-FOULNESS, NO PROB.
OH, WOW.
THIS IS SO AWESOME!
SO WE GOT A DEAL? I BUILD THIS, YOU PAY FOR SUPPLIES AND I'M RENT-FREE FOR FOUR MONTHS?
I WAS HOPING YOU WANTED TO DO THIS FOR ME BECAUSE YOU LIKED ME.
PEACHES, IF I DIDN'T LIKE YOU, YOU'D KNOW IT. DEAL?
DEAL.
SEE YOU LATER. I GOT BACK-TO-BACK GIGS. DON'T FORGET TO FEED MY BABIES.
I SWEAR THAT GIRL'S CRAZIER THAN A SACK O' RABID MONKEYS.

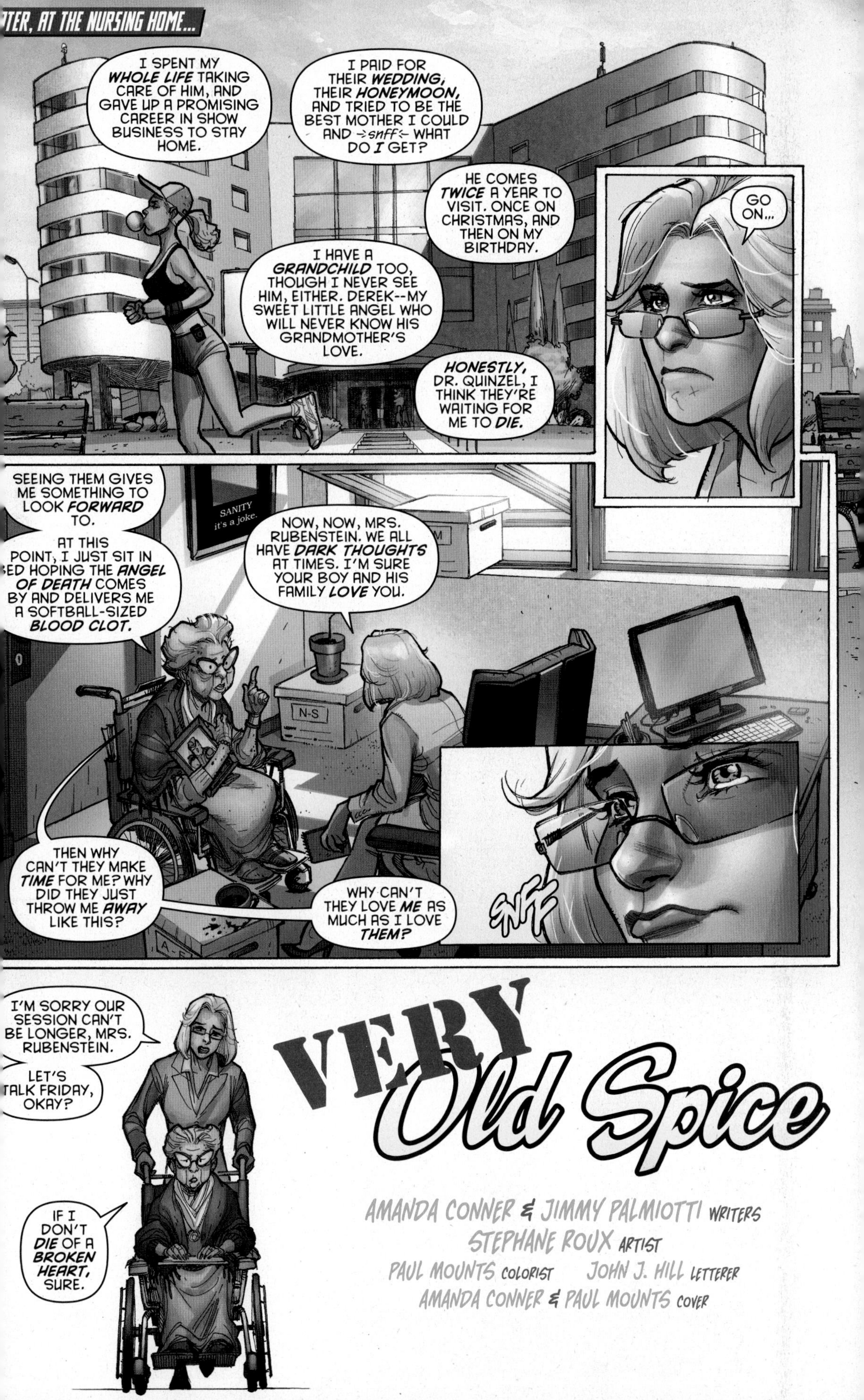

TER, AT THE NURSING HOME...
I SPENT MY WHOLE LIFE TAKING CARE OF HIM, AND GAVE UP A PROMISING CAREER IN SHOW BUSINESS TO STAY HOME.
I PAID FOR THEIR WEDDING, THEIR HONEYMOON, AND TRIED TO BE THE BEST MOTHER I COULD AND ->snff<- WHAT DO I GET?
HE COMES TWICE A YEAR TO VISIT. ONCE ON CHRISTMAS, AND THEN ON MY BIRTHDAY.
I HAVE A GRANDCHILD TOO, THOUGH I NEVER SEE HIM, EITHER. DEREK--MY SWEET LITTLE ANGEL WHO WILL NEVER KNOW HIS GRANDMOTHER'S LOVE.
HONESTLY, DR. QUINZEL, I THINK THEY'RE WAITING FOR ME TO DIE.
GO ON...
SEEING THEM GIVES ME SOMETHING TO LOOK FORWARD TO.
AT THIS POINT, I JUST SIT IN ED HOPING THE ANGEL OF DEATH COMES BY AND DELIVERS ME A SOFTBALL-SIZED BLOOD CLOT.
SANITY it's a joke.
NOW, NOW, MRS. RUBENSTEIN. WE ALL HAVE DARK THOUGHTS AT TIMES. I'M SURE YOUR BOY AND HIS FAMILY LOVE YOU.
N-S
THEN WHY CAN'T THEY MAKE TIME FOR ME? WHY DID THEY JUST THROW ME AWAY LIKE THIS?
WHY CAN'T THEY LOVE ME AS MUCH AS I LOVE THEM?
SNFF
I'M SORRY OUR SESSION CAN'T BE LONGER, MRS. RUBENSTEIN.
LET'S TALK FRIDAY, OKAY?
IF I DON'T DIE OF A BROKEN HEART, SURE.
VERY Old Spice
AMANDA CONNER & JIMMY PALMIOTTI WRITERS
STEPHANE ROUX ARTIST
PAUL MOUNTS COLORIST
JOHN J. HILL LETTERER
AMANDA CONNER & PAUL MOUNTS COVER

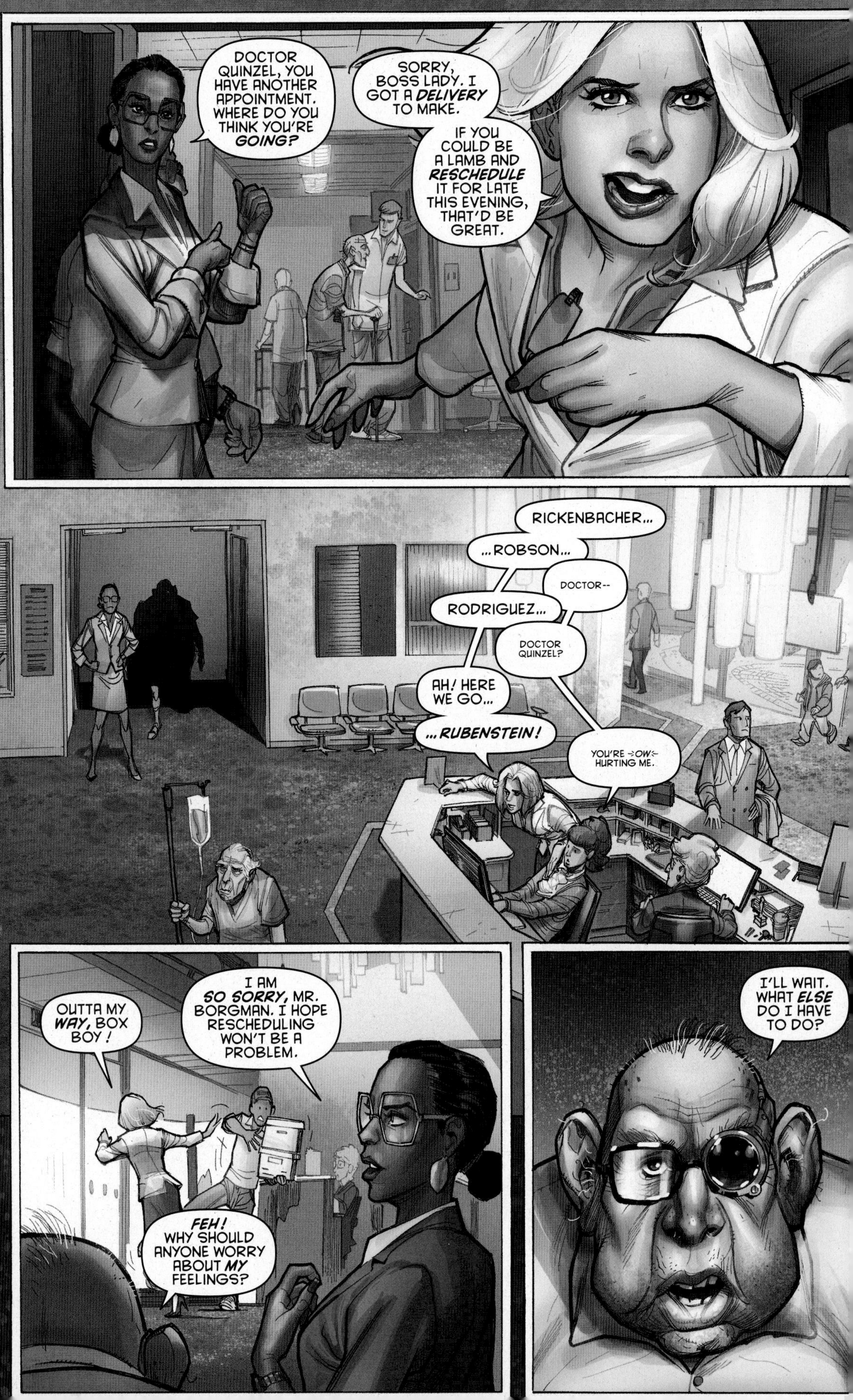
DOCTOR QUINZEL, YOU HAVE ANOTHER APPOINTMENT. WHERE DO YOU THINK YOU'RE *GOING?*
SORRY, BOSS LADY. I GOT A *DELIVERY* TO MAKE.
IF YOU COULD BE A LAMB AND *RESCHEDULE* IT FOR LATE THIS EVENING, THAT'D BE GREAT.
RICKENBACHER...
...ROBSON...
DOCTOR--
RODRIGUEZ...
DOCTOR QUINZEL?
AH! HERE WE GO...
*...RUBENSTEIN!*
YOU'RE *OW* HURTING ME.
OUTTA MY *WAY*, BOX BOY!
I AM *SO SORRY*, MR. BORGMAN. I HOPE RESCHEDULING WON'T BE A PROBLEM.
*FEH!* WHY SHOULD ANYONE WORRY ABOUT *MY* FEELINGS?
I'LL WAIT. WHAT *ELSE* DO I HAVE TO DO?

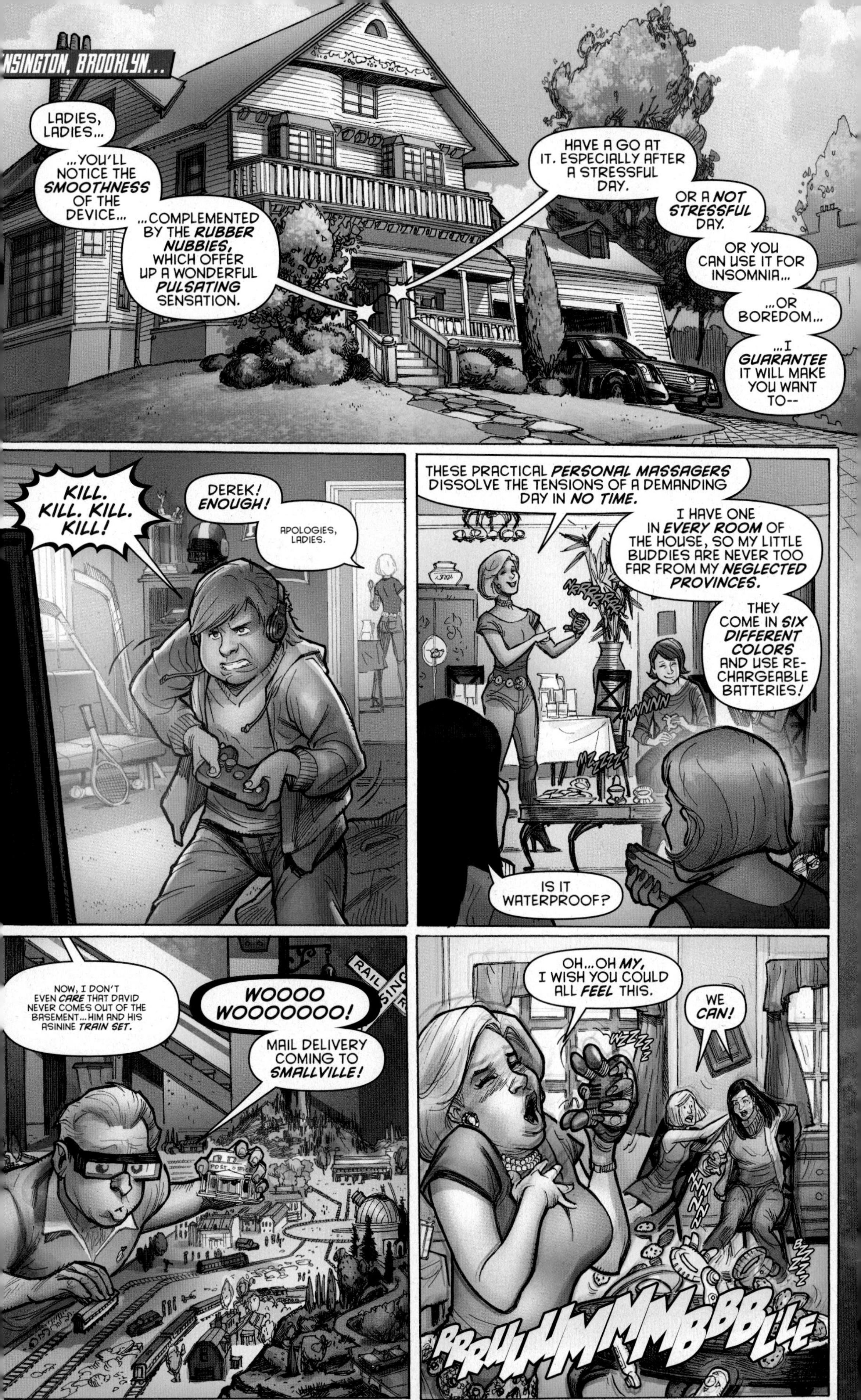
NSINGTON, BROOKLYN...
LADIES, LADIES...
...YOU'LL NOTICE THE SMOOTHNESS OF THE DEVICE...
...COMPLEMENTED BY THE RUBBER NUBBIES, WHICH OFFER UP A WONDERFUL PULSATING SENSATION.
HAVE A GO AT IT. ESPECIALLY AFTER A STRESSFUL DAY.
OR A NOT STRESSFUL DAY.
OR YOU CAN USE IT FOR INSOMNIA...
...OR BOREDOM...
...I GUARANTEE IT WILL MAKE YOU WANT TO--
KILL. KILL. KILL. KILL!
DEREK! ENOUGH!
APOLOGIES, LADIES.
THESE PRACTICAL PERSONAL MASSAGERS DISSOLVE THE TENSIONS OF A DEMANDING DAY IN NO TIME.
I HAVE ONE IN EVERY ROOM OF THE HOUSE, SO MY LITTLE BUDDIES ARE NEVER TOO FAR FROM MY NEGLECTED PROVINCES.
THEY COME IN SIX DIFFERENT COLORS AND USE RE-CHARGEABLE BATTERIES!
IS IT WATERPROOF?
NOW, I DON'T EVEN CARE THAT DAVID NEVER COMES OUT OF THE BASEMENT...HIM AND HIS ASININE TRAIN SET.
WOOOO WOOOOOOO!
MAIL DELIVERY COMING TO SMALLVILLE!
OH...OH MY, I WISH YOU COULD ALL FEEL THIS.
WE CAN!
RRRUUMMMMBBBLLE

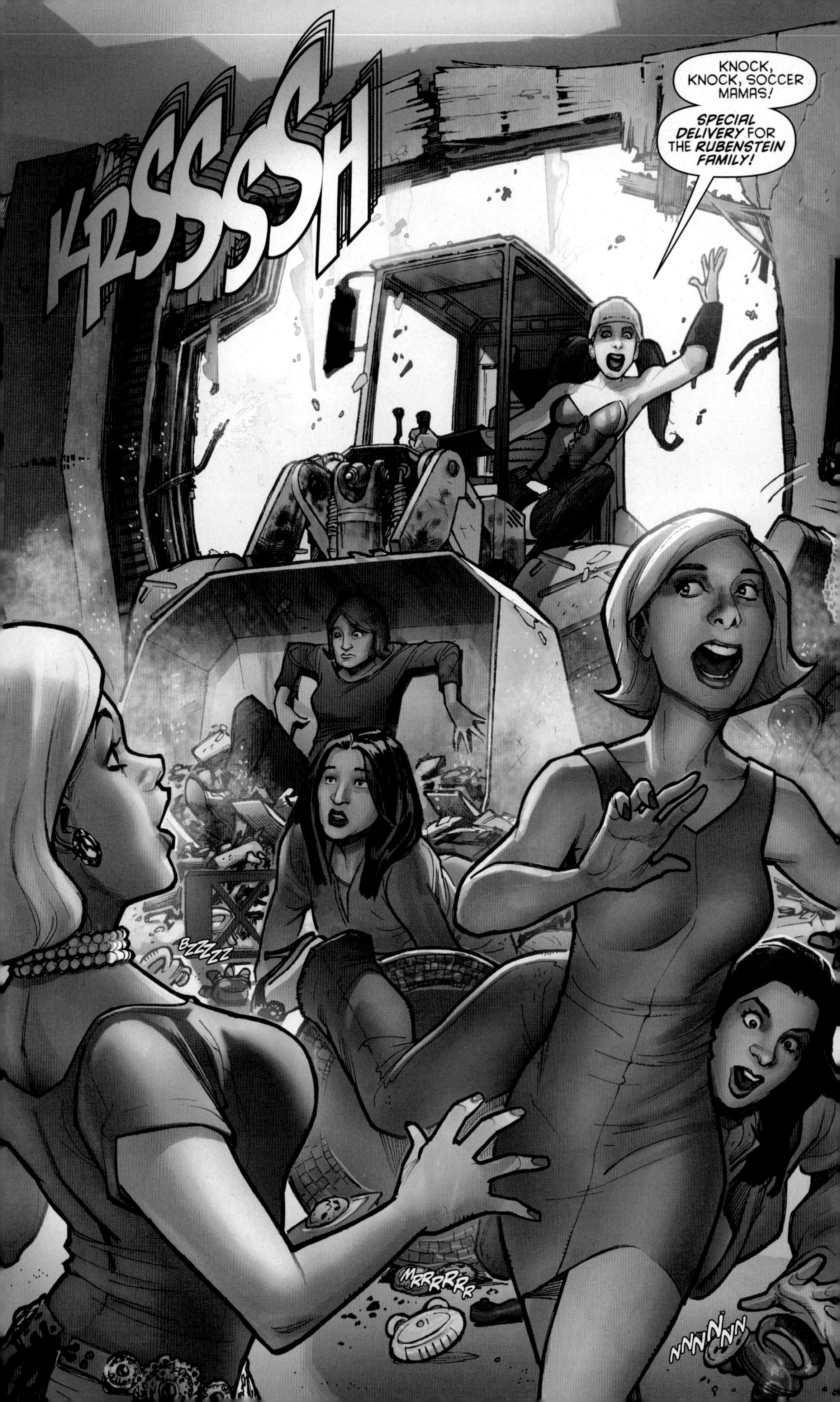
KRSSSSH
KNOCK, KNOCK, SOCCER MAMAS!
SPECIAL DELIVERY FOR THE RUBENSTEIN FAMILY!
BZZZZZ
MRRRRRR
NNNNNN

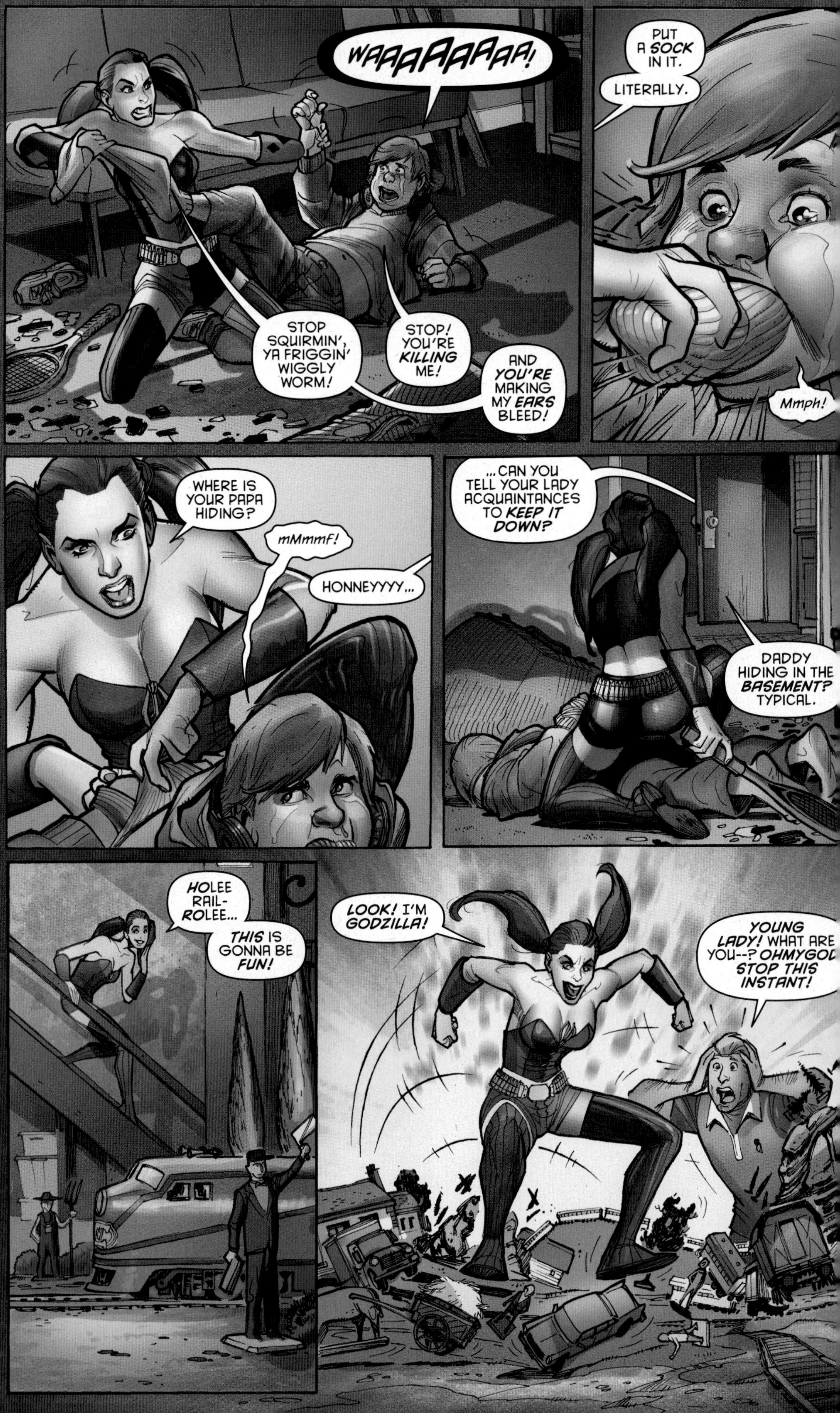
WAAAAAAAA!
STOP SQUIRMIN', YA FRIGGIN' WIGGLY WORM!
STOP! YOU'RE KILLING ME!
AND YOU'RE MAKING MY EARS BLEED!
PUT A SOCK IN IT.
LITERALLY.
Mmph!
WHERE IS YOUR PAPA HIDING?
mMmmf!
HONNEYYYY...
...CAN YOU TELL YOUR LADY ACQUAINTANCES TO KEEP IT DOWN?
DADDY HIDING IN THE BASEMENT? TYPICAL.
HOLEE RAIL-ROLEE...
THIS IS GONNA BE FUN!
LOOK! I'M GODZILLA!
YOUNG LADY! WHAT ARE YOU--? OHMYGOD STOP THIS INSTANT!

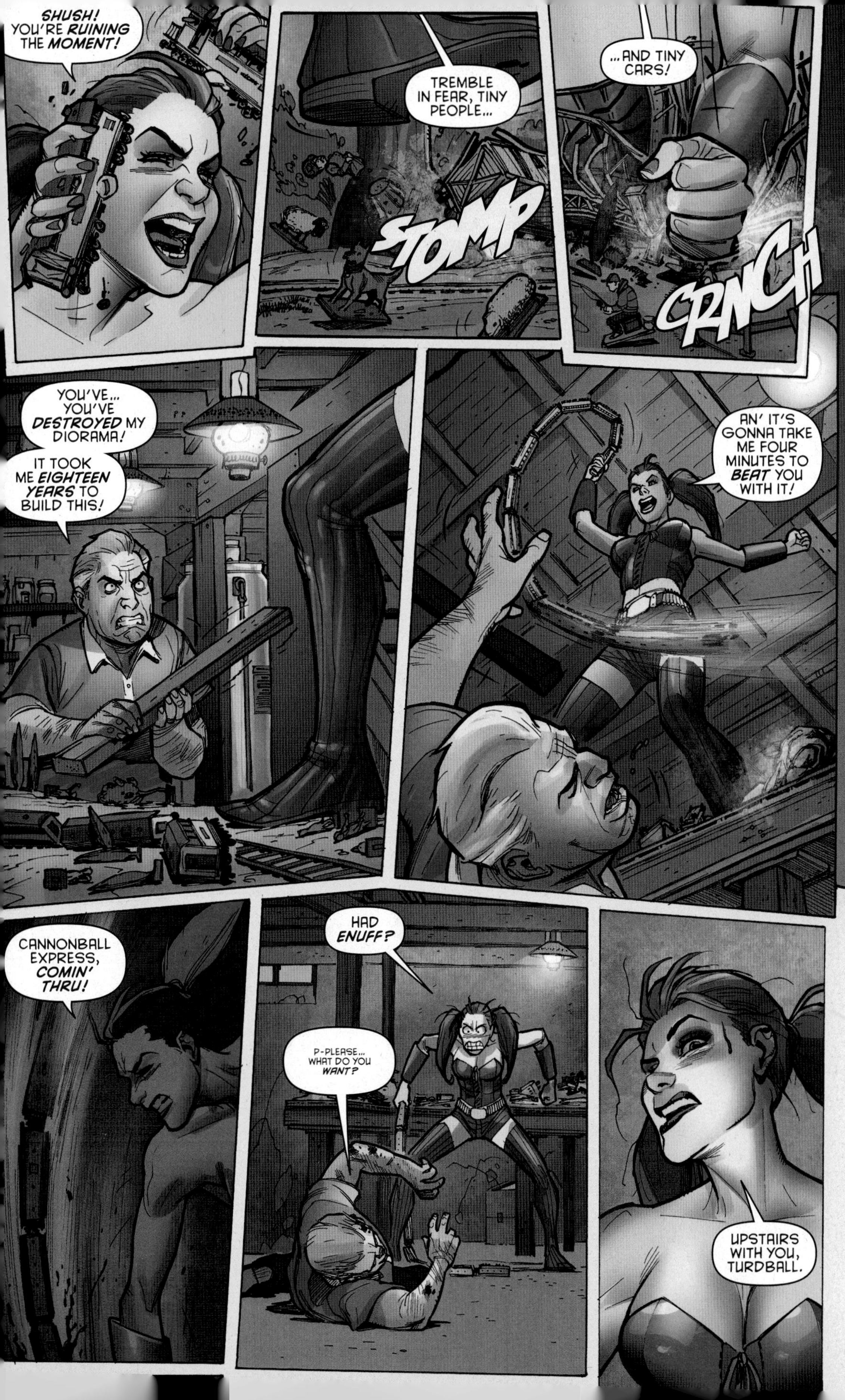

SHUSH! YOU'RE RUINING THE MOMENT!
TREMBLE IN FEAR, TINY PEOPLE...
STOMP
...AND TINY CARS!
CRNCH
YOU'VE... YOU'VE DESTROYED MY DIORAMA!
IT TOOK ME EIGHTEEN YEARS TO BUILD THIS!
AN' IT'S GONNA TAKE ME FOUR MINUTES TO BEAT YOU WITH IT!
CANNONBALL EXPRESS, COMIN' THRU!
HAD ENUFF?
P-PLEASE... WHAT DO YOU WANT?
UPSTAIRS WITH YOU, TURDBALL.

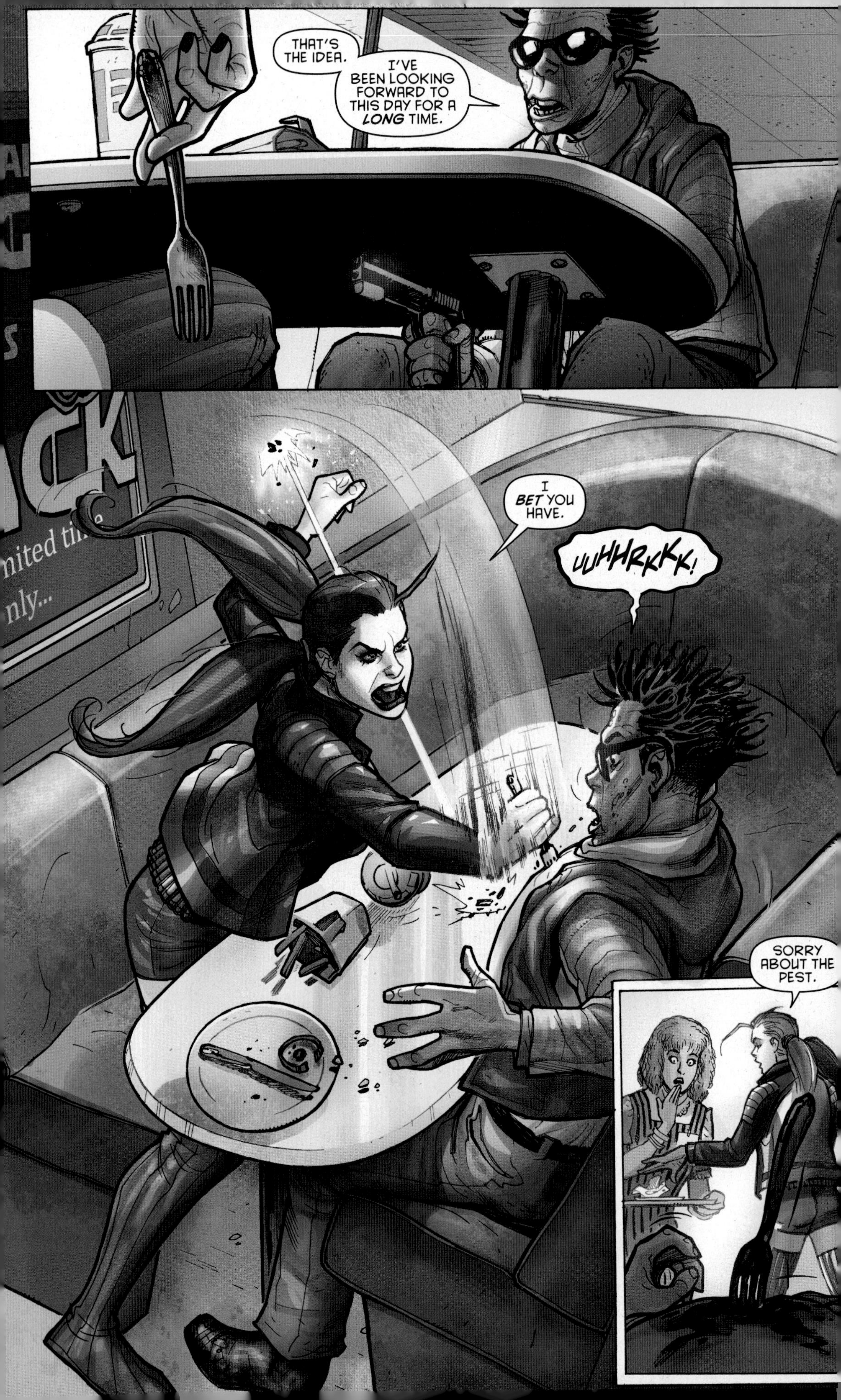

THAT'S THE IDEA.
I'VE BEEN LOOKING FORWARD TO THIS DAY FOR A *LONG* TIME.
I *BET* YOU HAVE.
UUHHRKKK!
SORRY ABOUT THE PEST.

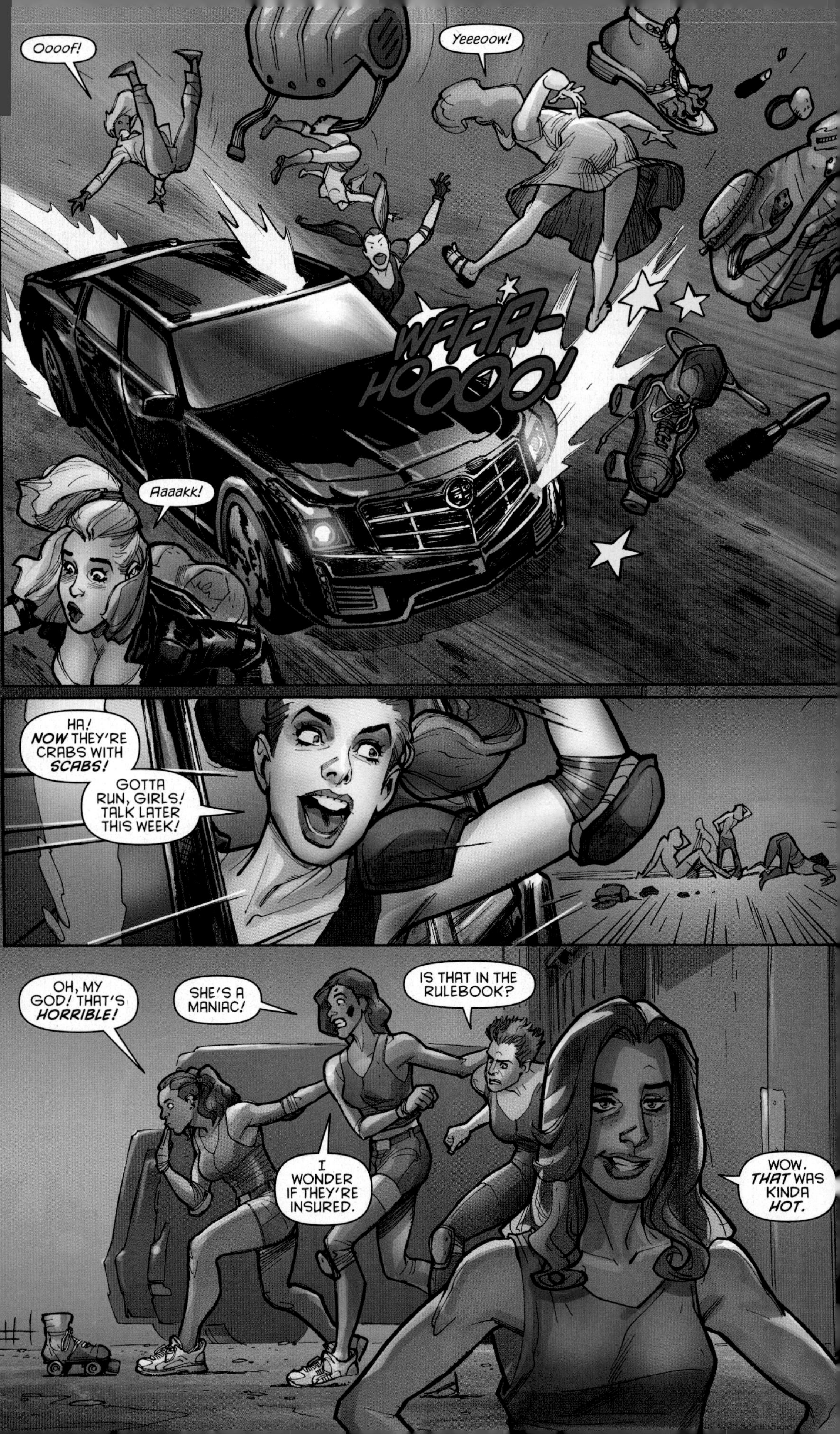
Oooof!
Yeeeoow!
WAAA-HOOOO!
Aaaakk!
HA! NOW THEY'RE CRABS WITH SCABS!
GOTTA RUN, GIRLS! TALK LATER THIS WEEK!
OH, MY GOD! THAT'S HORRIBLE!
SHE'S A MANIAC!
IS THAT IN THE RULEBOOK?
I WONDER IF THEY'RE INSURED.
WOW. THAT WAS KINDA HOT.

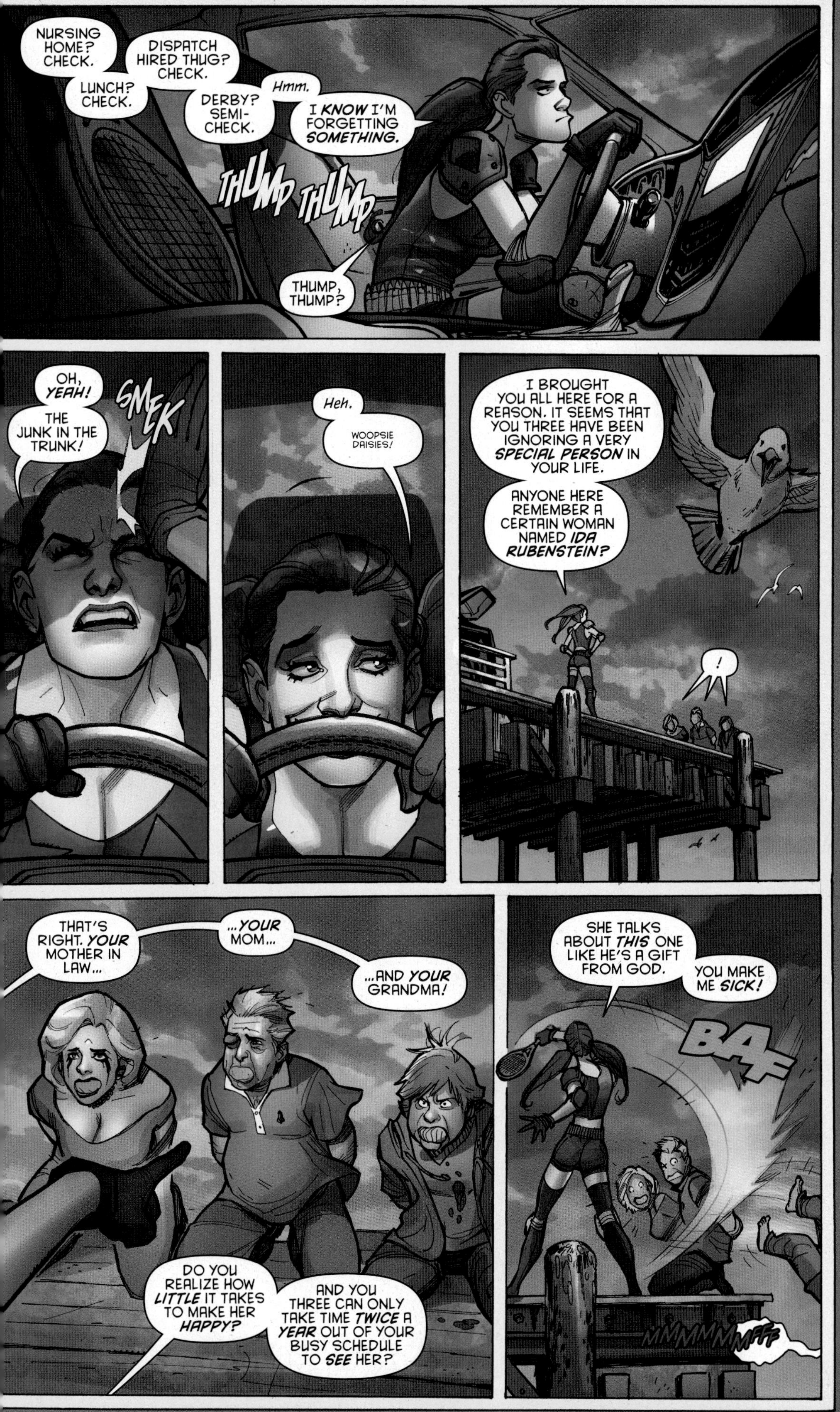
NURSING HOME? CHECK.
LUNCH? CHECK.
DISPATCH HIRED THUG? CHECK.
DERBY? SEMI-CHECK.
Hmm.
I KNOW I'M FORGETTING SOMETHING.
THUMP THUMP
THUMP, THUMP?
OH, YEAH!
THE JUNK IN THE TRUNK!
SMEK
Heh.
WOOPSIE DAISIES!
I BROUGHT YOU ALL HERE FOR A REASON. IT SEEMS THAT YOU THREE HAVE BEEN IGNORING A VERY SPECIAL PERSON IN YOUR LIFE.
ANYONE HERE REMEMBER A CERTAIN WOMAN NAMED IDA RUBENSTEIN?
!
THAT'S RIGHT. YOUR MOTHER IN LAW...
...YOUR MOM...
...AND YOUR GRANDMA!
DO YOU REALIZE HOW LITTLE IT TAKES TO MAKE HER HAPPY?
AND YOU THREE CAN ONLY TAKE TIME TWICE A YEAR OUT OF YOUR BUSY SCHEDULE TO SEE HER?
SHE TALKS ABOUT THIS ONE LIKE HE'S A GIFT FROM GOD.
YOU MAKE ME SICK!
BAF
MMMMMMFFF

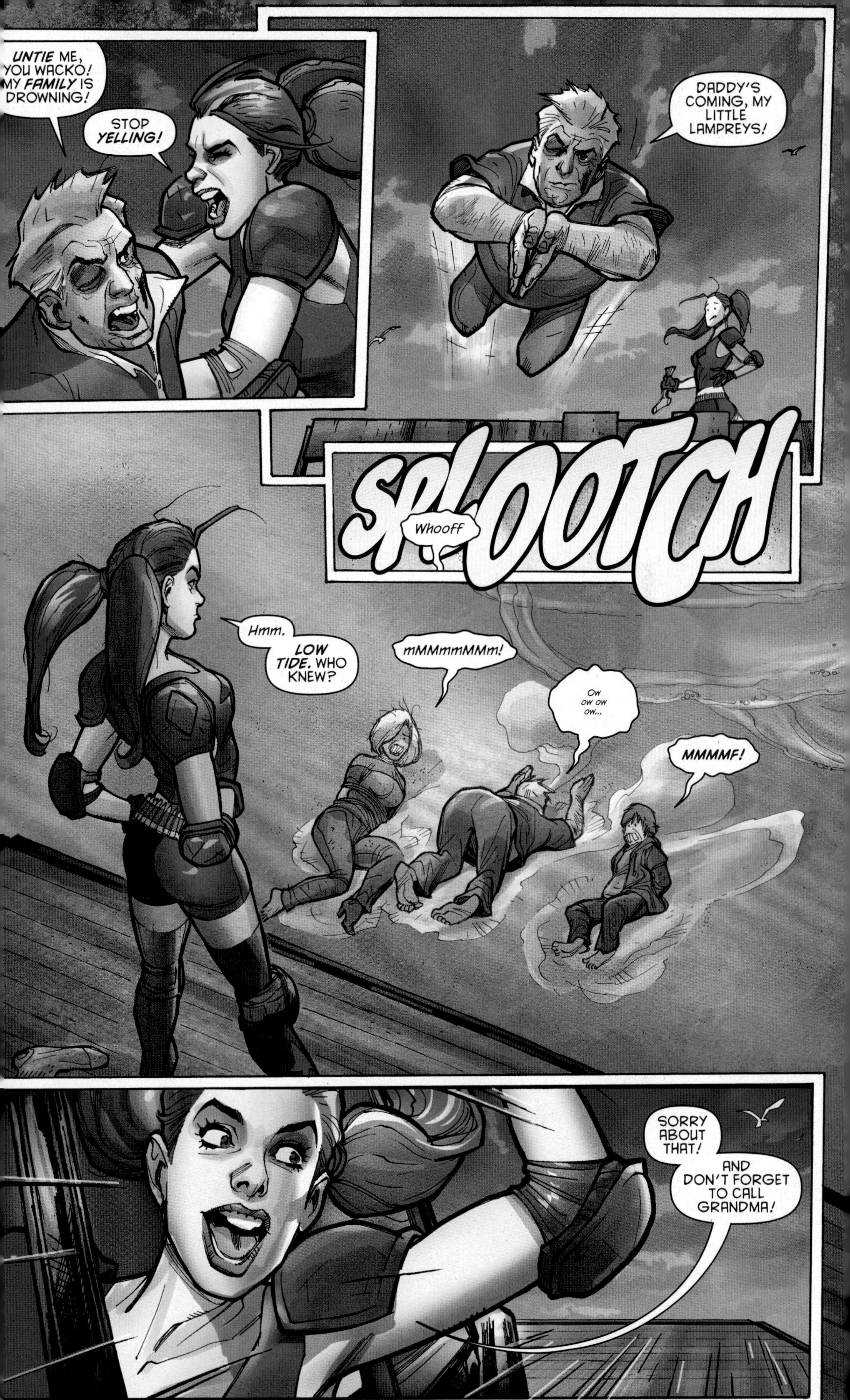
UNTIE ME, YOU WACKO! MY FAMILY IS DROWNING!
STOP YELLING!
DADDY'S COMING, MY LITTLE LAMPREYS!
SPLOOTCH
Whooff
Hmm.
LOW TIDE. WHO KNEW?
mMMmmMMm!
OW OW OW OW...
MMMMF!
SORRY ABOUT THAT!
AND DON'T FORGET TO CALL GRANDMA!

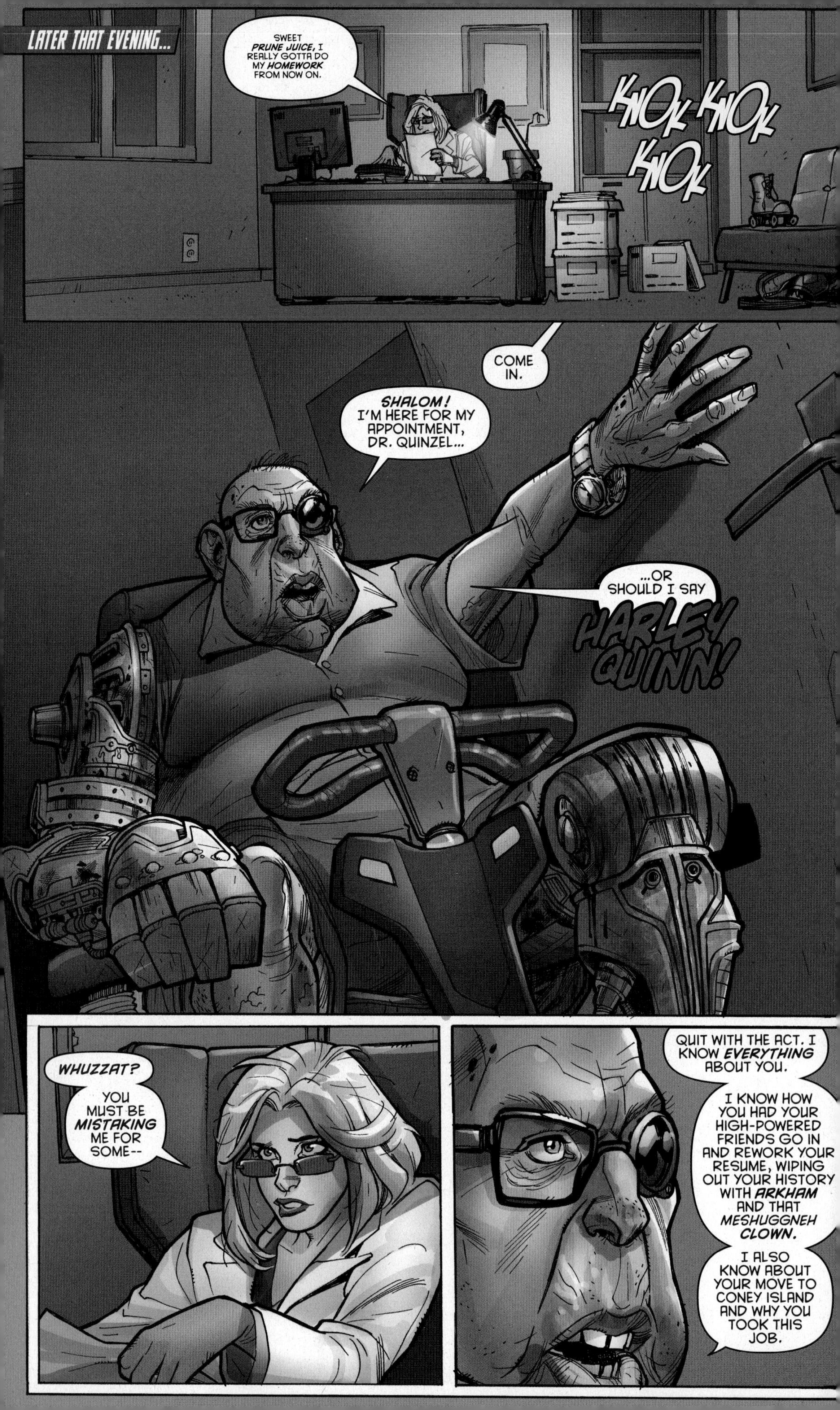

LATER THAT EVENING...
SWEET PRUNE JUICE, I REALLY GOTTA DO MY HOMEWORK FROM NOW ON.
KNOK KNOK KNOK
COME IN.
SHALOM! I'M HERE FOR MY APPOINTMENT, DR. QUINZEL...
...OR SHOULD I SAY HARLEY QUINN!
WHUZZAT?
YOU MUST BE MISTAKING ME FOR SOME--
QUIT WITH THE ACT. I KNOW EVERYTHING ABOUT YOU.
I KNOW HOW YOU HAD YOUR HIGH-POWERED FRIENDS GO IN AND REWORK YOUR RESUME, WIPING OUT YOUR HISTORY WITH ARKHAM AND THAT MESHUGGNEH CLOWN.
I ALSO KNOW ABOUT YOUR MOVE TO CONEY ISLAND AND WHY YOU TOOK THIS JOB.

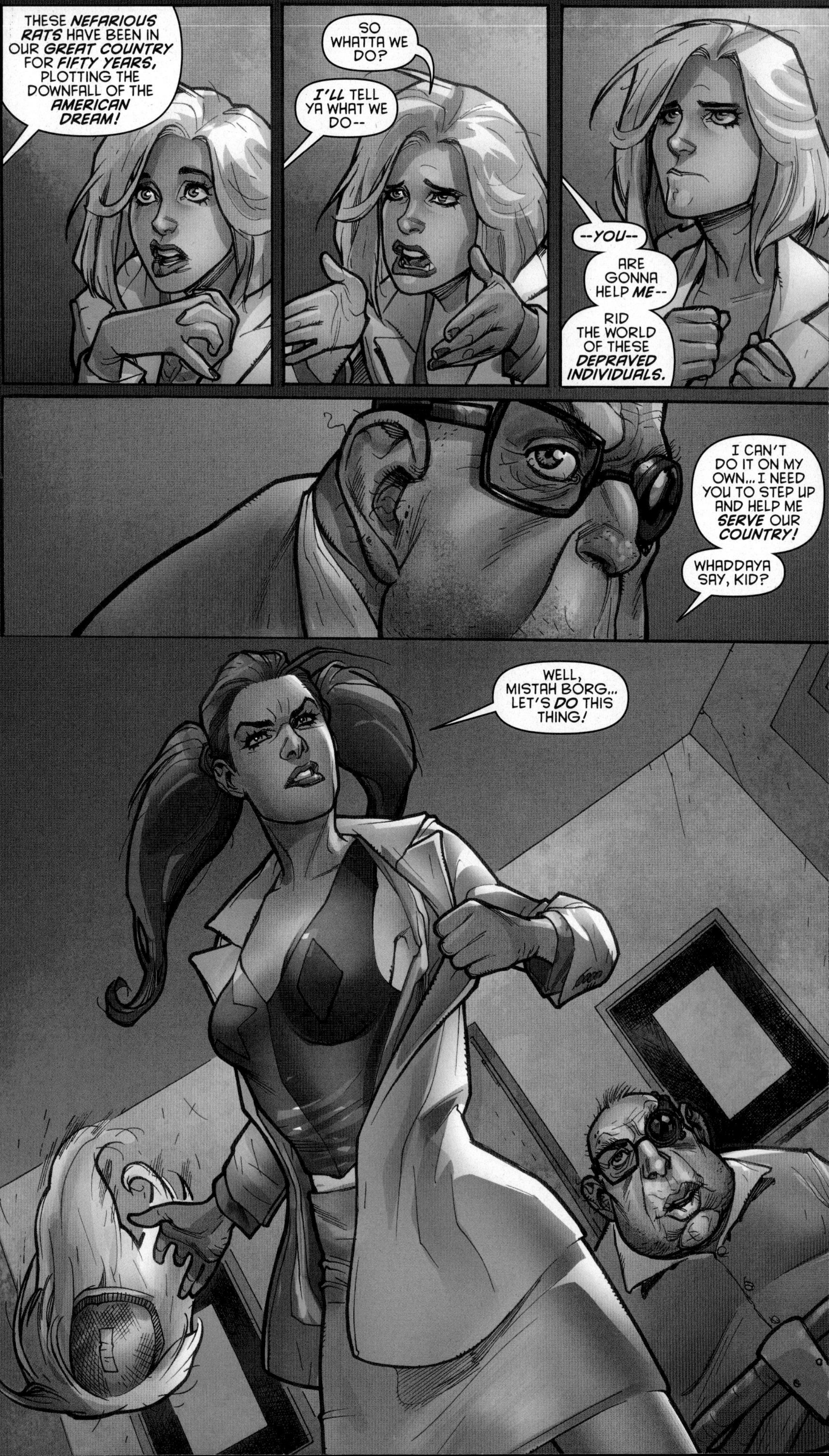

THESE *NEFARIOUS RATS* HAVE BEEN IN OUR *GREAT COUNTRY* FOR *FIFTY YEARS,* PLOTTING THE DOWNFALL OF THE *AMERICAN DREAM!*
SO WHATTA WE DO?
*I'LL* TELL YA WHAT WE DO--
--*YOU*--
ARE GONNA HELP *ME*--
RID THE WORLD OF THESE *DEPRAVED INDIVIDUALS.*
I CAN'T DO IT ON MY OWN... I NEED YOU TO STEP UP AND HELP ME *SERVE* OUR *COUNTRY!*
WHADDAYA SAY, KID?
WELL, MISTAH BORG... LET'S *DO* THIS THING!

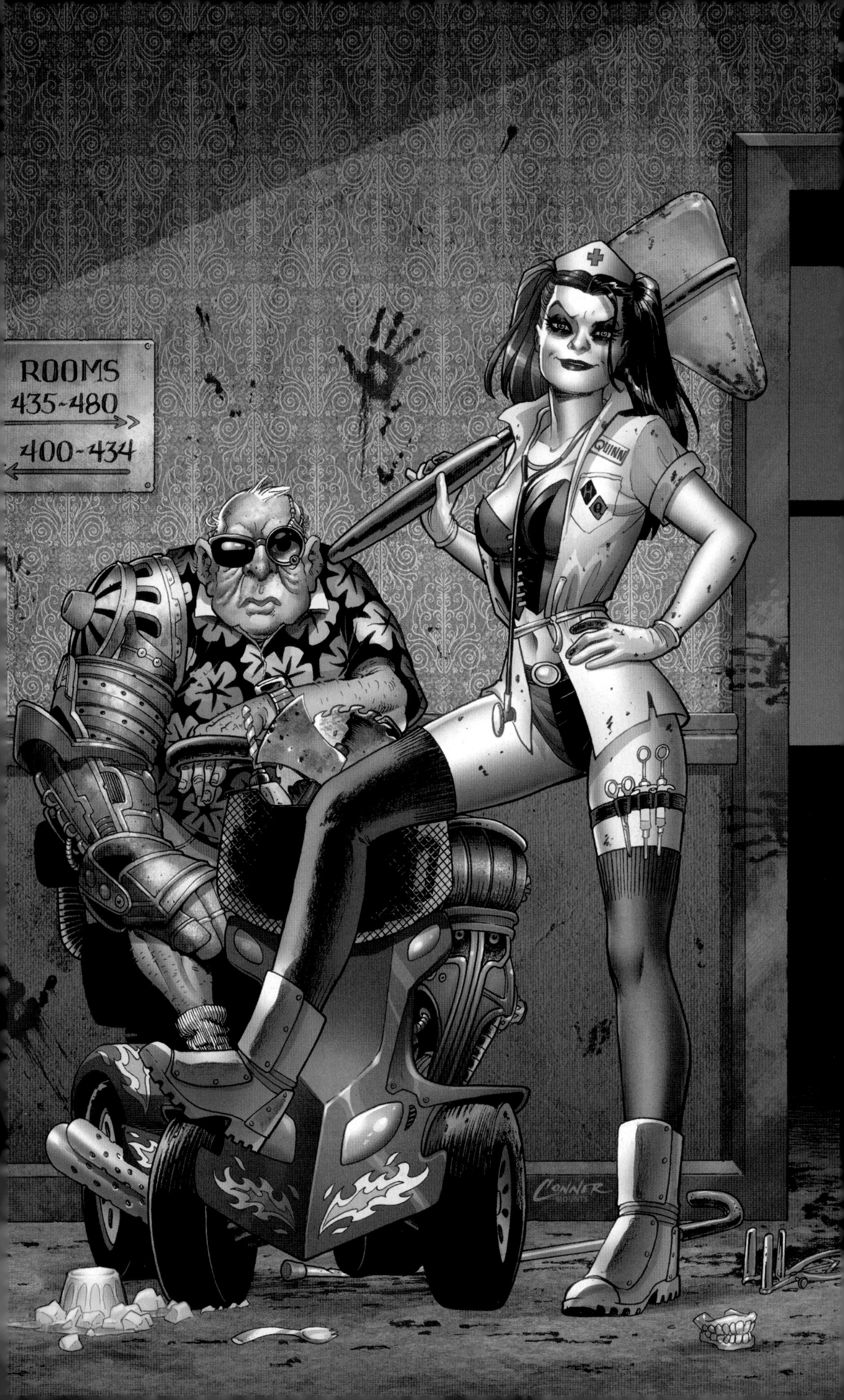

ROOMS
435-480
400-434
QUINN
CONNER

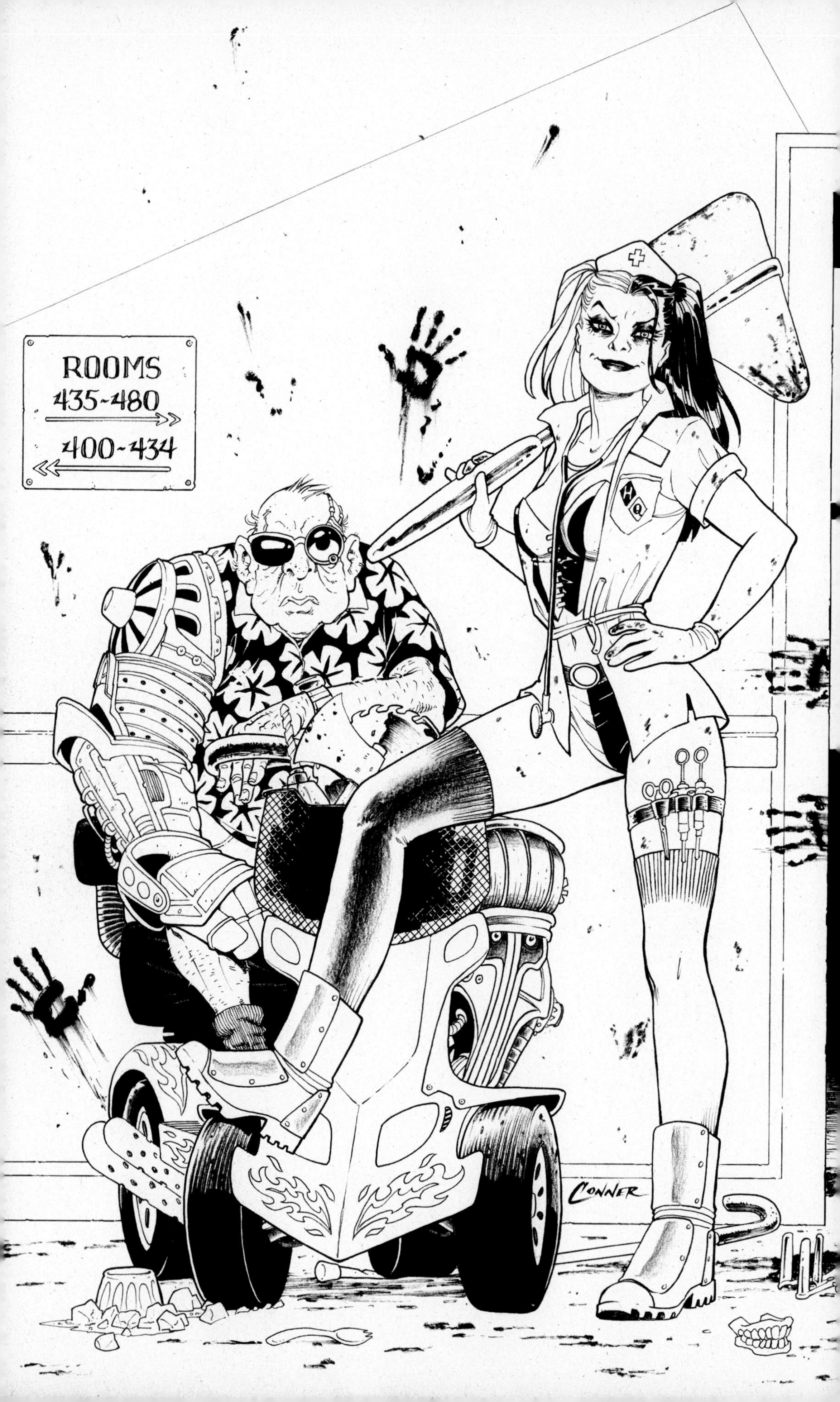
ROOMS
435-480
400-434
HQ
CONNER

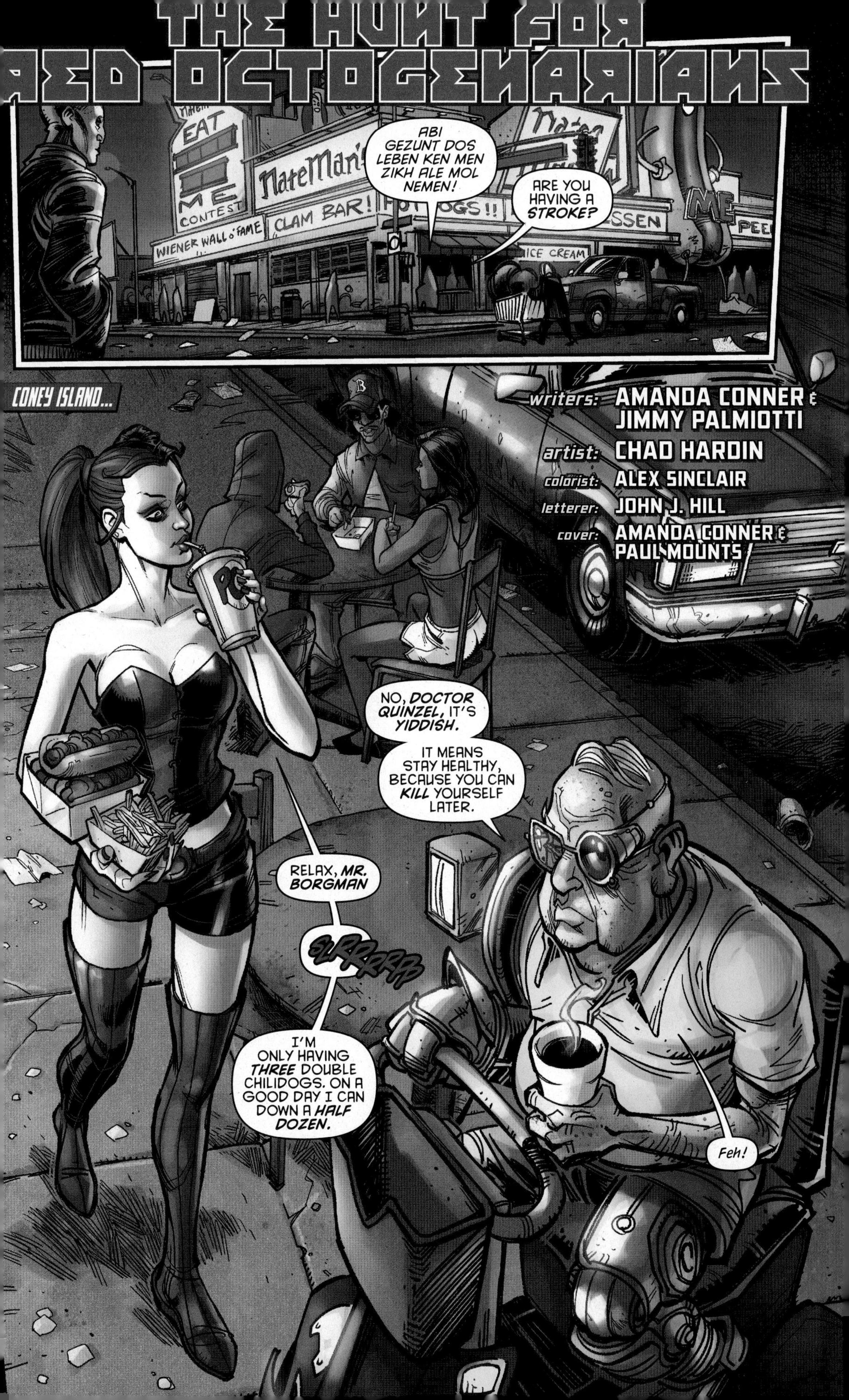
THE HUNT FOR
RED OCTOGENARIANS
NateMan's
CLAM BAR!
WIENER WALL o' FAME
ICE CREAM
ABI GEZUNT DOS LEBEN KEN MEN ZIKH ALE MOL NEMEN!
ARE YOU HAVING A STROKE?
CONEY ISLAND...
writers: AMANDA CONNER & JIMMY PALMIOTTI
artist: CHAD HARDIN
colorist: ALEX SINCLAIR
letterer: JOHN J. HILL
cover: AMANDA CONNER & PAUL MOUNTS
NO, DOCTOR QUINZEL, IT'S YIDDISH.
IT MEANS STAY HEALTHY, BECAUSE YOU CAN KILL YOURSELF LATER.
RELAX, MR. BORGMAN
SLRRRRP
I'M ONLY HAVING THREE DOUBLE CHILIDOGS. ON A GOOD DAY I CAN DOWN A HALF DOZEN.
Feh!

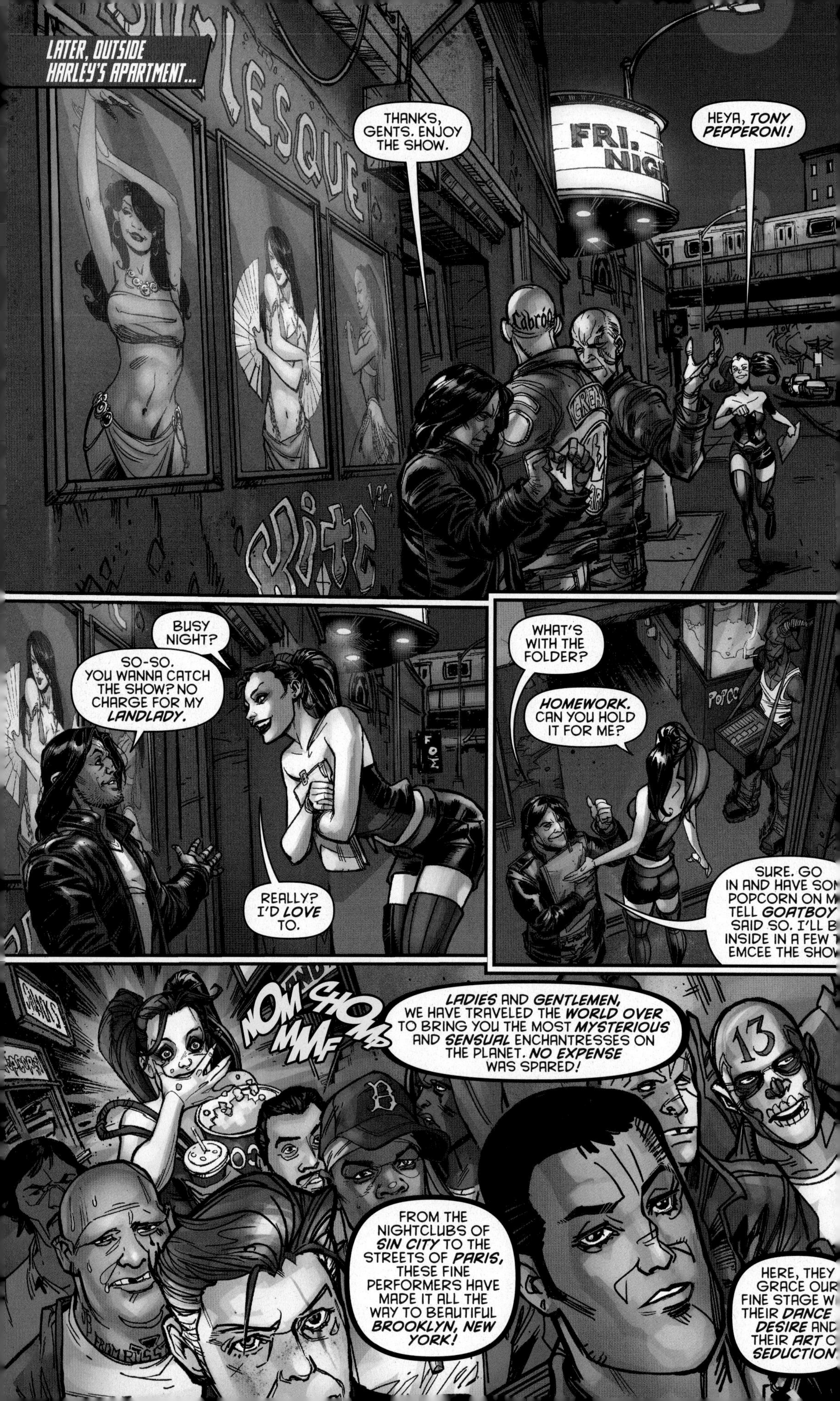
LATER, OUTSIDE HARLEY'S APARTMENT...
THANKS, GENTS. ENJOY THE SHOW.
FRI. NIGH
HEYA, *TONY PEPPERONI!*
BUSY NIGHT?
SO-SO. YOU WANNA CATCH THE SHOW? NO CHARGE FOR MY *LANDLADY*.
REALLY? I'D *LOVE* TO.
WHAT'S WITH THE FOLDER?
*HOMEWORK.* CAN YOU HOLD IT FOR ME?
SURE. GO IN AND HAVE SON POPCORN ON M TELL *GOATBOY* SAID SO. I'LL B INSIDE IN A FEW T EMCEE THE SHOW
NOM CHOMP MMF
*LADIES* AND *GENTLEMEN,* WE HAVE TRAVELED THE *WORLD OVER* TO BRING YOU THE MOST *MYSTERIOUS* AND *SENSUAL* ENCHANTRESSES ON THE PLANET. *NO EXPENSE* WAS SPARED!
FROM THE NIGHTCLUBS OF *SIN CITY* TO THE STREETS OF *PARIS,* THESE FINE PERFORMERS HAVE MADE IT ALL THE WAY TO BEAUTIFUL *BROOKLYN, NEW YORK!*
HERE, THEY GRACE OUR FINE STAGE W THEIR *DANCE DESIRE* AND THEIR *ART* O *SEDUCTION*
13

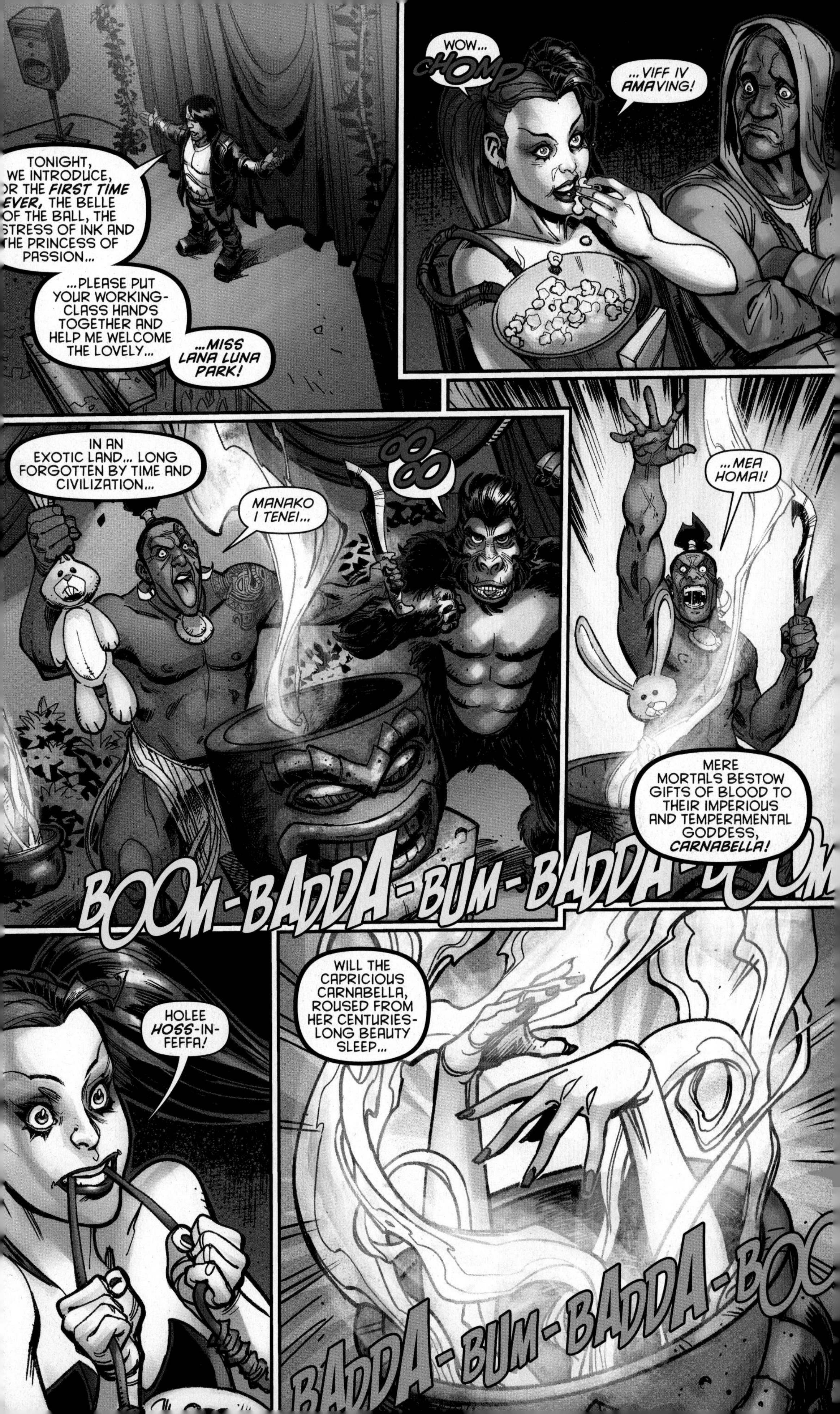
TONIGHT, WE INTRODUCE, FOR THE FIRST TIME EVER, THE BELLE OF THE BALL, THE MISTRESS OF INK AND THE PRINCESS OF PASSION...
...PLEASE PUT YOUR WORKING-CLASS HANDS TOGETHER AND HELP ME WELCOME THE LOVELY...
...MISS LANA LUNA PARK!
WOW...
CHOMP
...VIFF IV AMAVING!
IN AN EXOTIC LAND... LONG FORGOTTEN BY TIME AND CIVILIZATION...
MANAKO I TENEI...
...MEA HOMAI!
MERE MORTALS BESTOW GIFTS OF BLOOD TO THEIR IMPERIOUS AND TEMPERAMENTAL GODDESS, CARNABELLA!
BOOM-BADDA-BUM-BADDA-
HOLEE HOSS-IN-FEFFA!
WILL THE CAPRICIOUS CARNABELLA, ROUSED FROM HER CENTURIES-LONG BEAUTY SLEEP...
BADDA-BUM-BADDA-BO

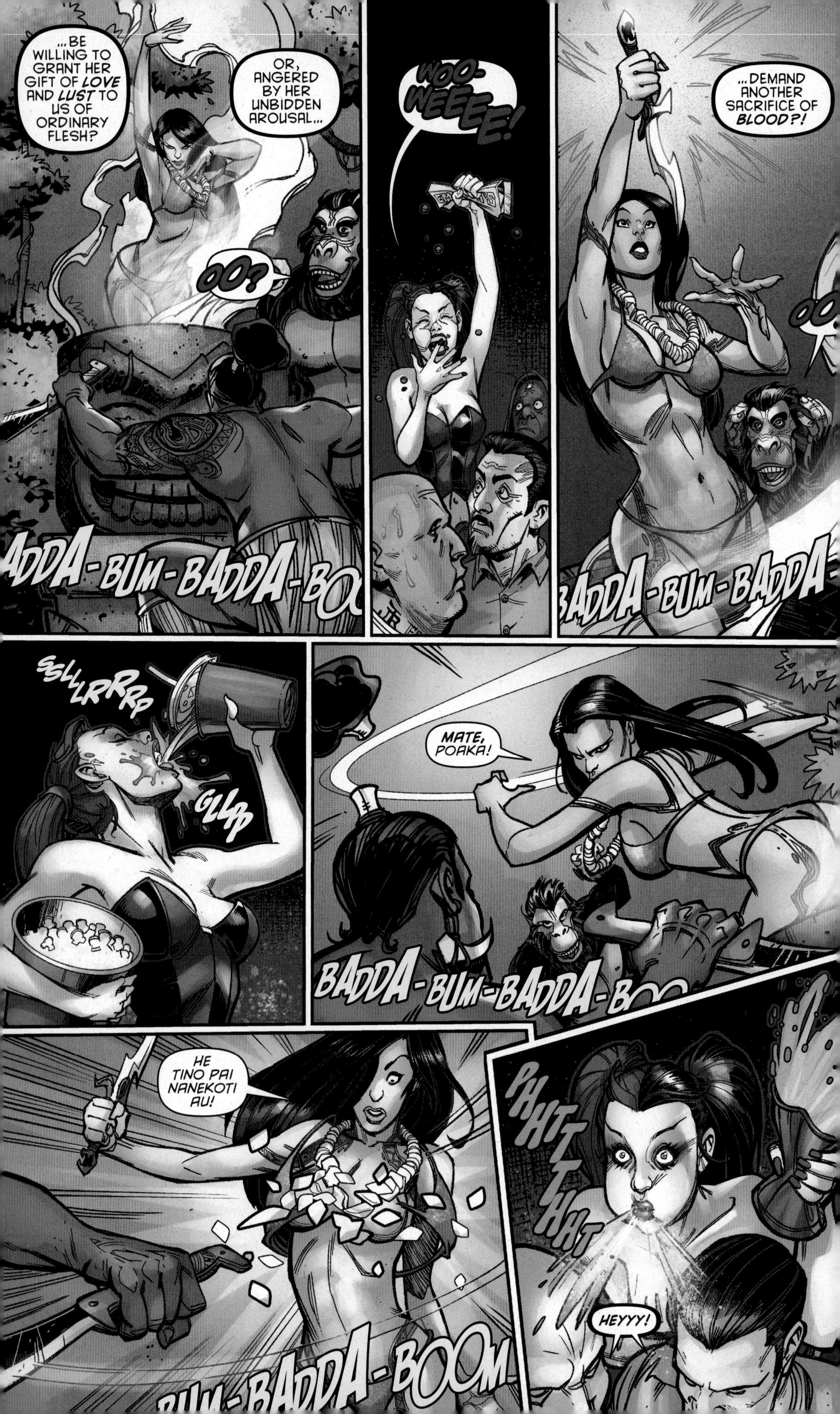

...BE WILLING TO GRANT HER GIFT OF *LOVE* AND *LUST* TO US OF ORDINARY FLESH?
OR, ANGERED BY HER UNBIDDEN AROUSAL...
OO?
ADDA-BUM-BADDA-BO
WOO-WEEEEE!
...DEMAND ANOTHER SACRIFICE OF *BLOOD?!*
BADDA-BUM-BADDA-
SSLLLRRRP
GLLRP
MATE, POAKA!
BADDA-BUM-BADDA-BO
HE TINO PAI NANEKOTI AU!
BUM-BADDA-BOOM
PHHTTTHHT
HEYYY!

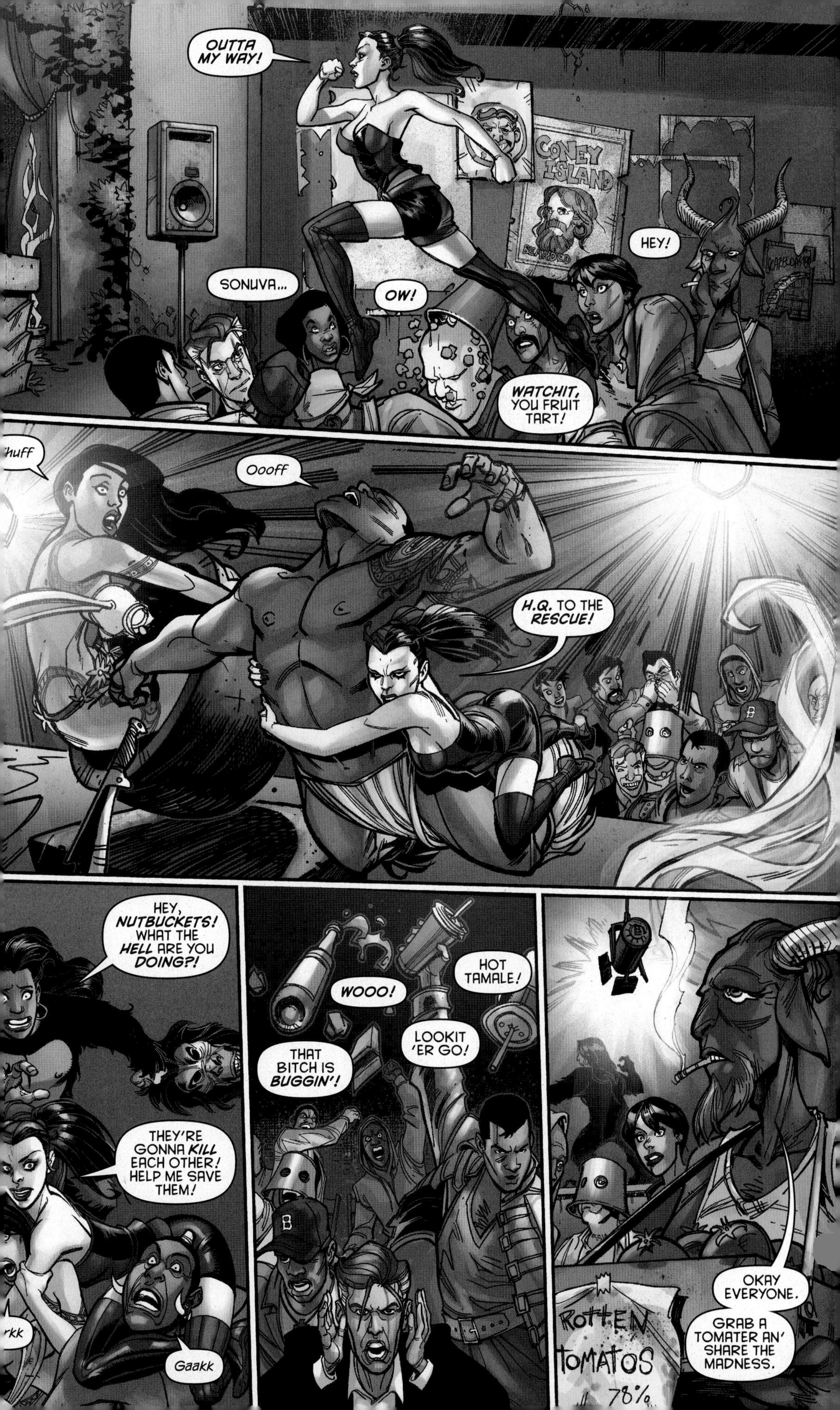
OUTTA MY WAY!
CONEY ISLAND
BEARDED
SONUVA...
OW!
HEY!
WATCHIT, YOU FRUIT TART!
huff
Oooff
H.Q. TO THE RESCUE!
HEY, NUTBUCKETS! WHAT THE HELL ARE YOU DOING?!
THEY'RE GONNA KILL EACH OTHER! HELP ME SAVE THEM!
rkk
Gaakk
WOOO!
HOT TAMALE!
LOOKIT 'ER GO!
THAT BITCH IS BUGGIN'!
ROTTEN TOMATOS 78%
OKAY EVERYONE.
GRAB A TOMATER AN' SHARE THE MADNESS.

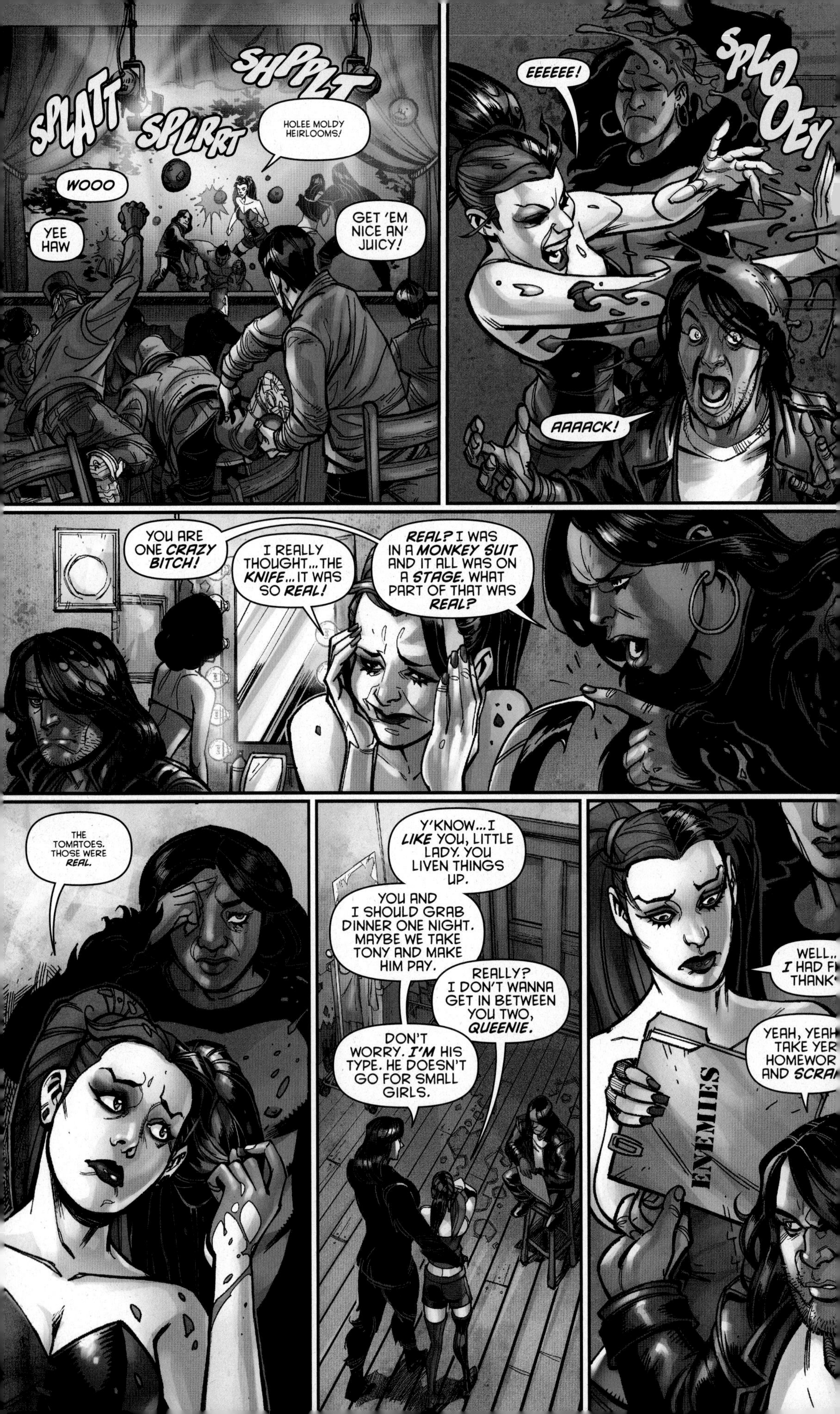
SPLATT
SPLRRT
SHPPLT
HOLEE MOLDY HEIRLOOMS!
WOOO
YEE HAW
GET 'EM NICE AN' JUICY!
EEEEEE!
SPLOOEY
AAAACK!
YOU ARE ONE CRAZY BITCH!
I REALLY THOUGHT... THE KNIFE... IT WAS SO REAL!
REAL? I WAS IN A MONKEY SUIT AND IT ALL WAS ON A STAGE. WHAT PART OF THAT WAS REAL?
THE TOMATOES. THOSE WERE REAL.
Y'KNOW... I LIKE YOU, LITTLE LADY. YOU LIVEN THINGS UP.
YOU AND I SHOULD GRAB DINNER ONE NIGHT. MAYBE WE TAKE TONY AND MAKE HIM PAY.
REALLY? I DON'T WANNA GET IN BETWEEN YOU TWO, QUEENIE.
DON'T WORRY. I'M HIS TYPE. HE DOESN'T GO FOR SMALL GIRLS.
ENEMIES

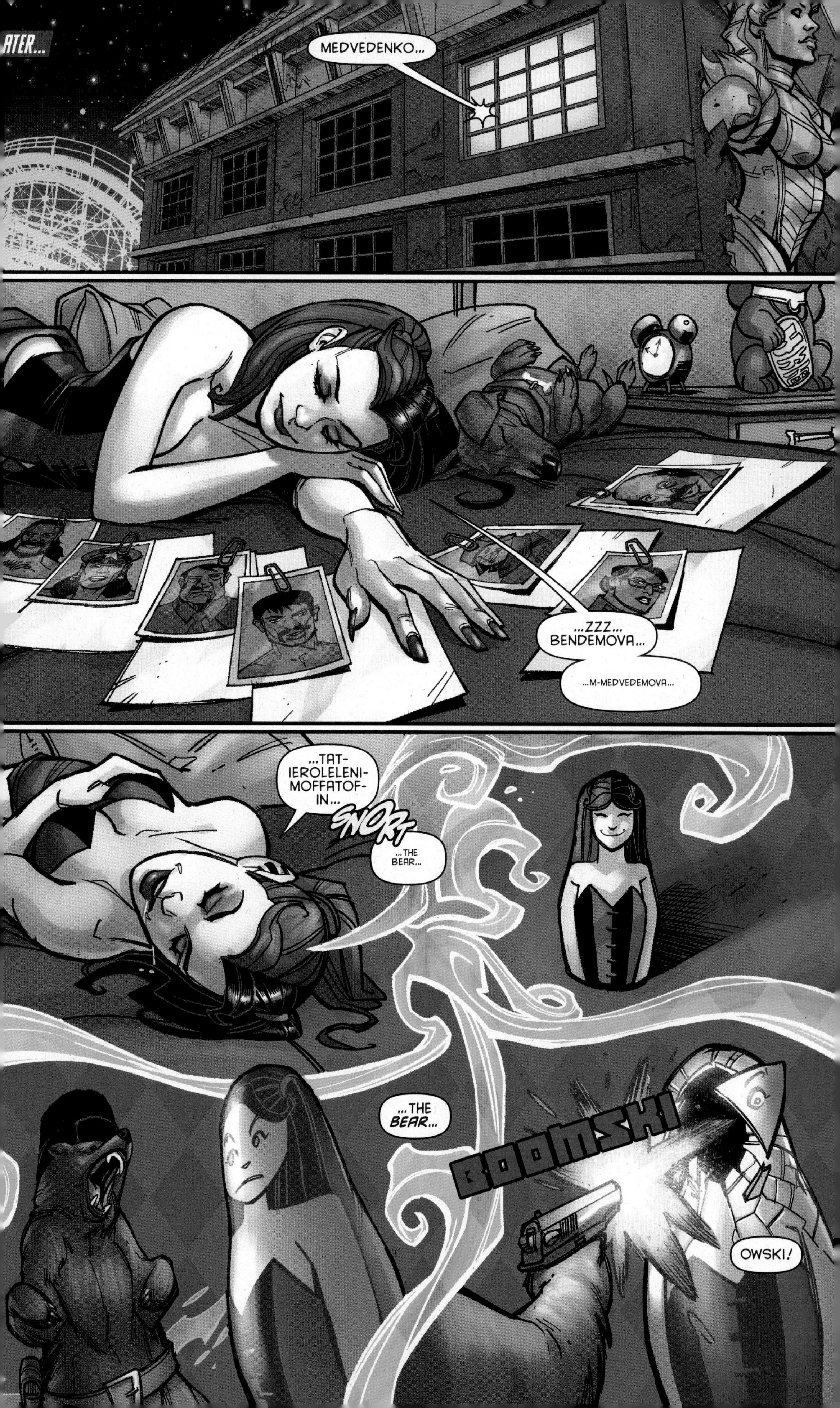

ATER...
MEDVEDENKO...
...ZZZ... BENDEMOVA...
...M-MEDVEDEMOVA...
...TAT-IEROLELENI-MOFFATOF-IN...
SNORT
...THE BEAR...
...THE BEAR...
BOOMSKI
OWSKI!

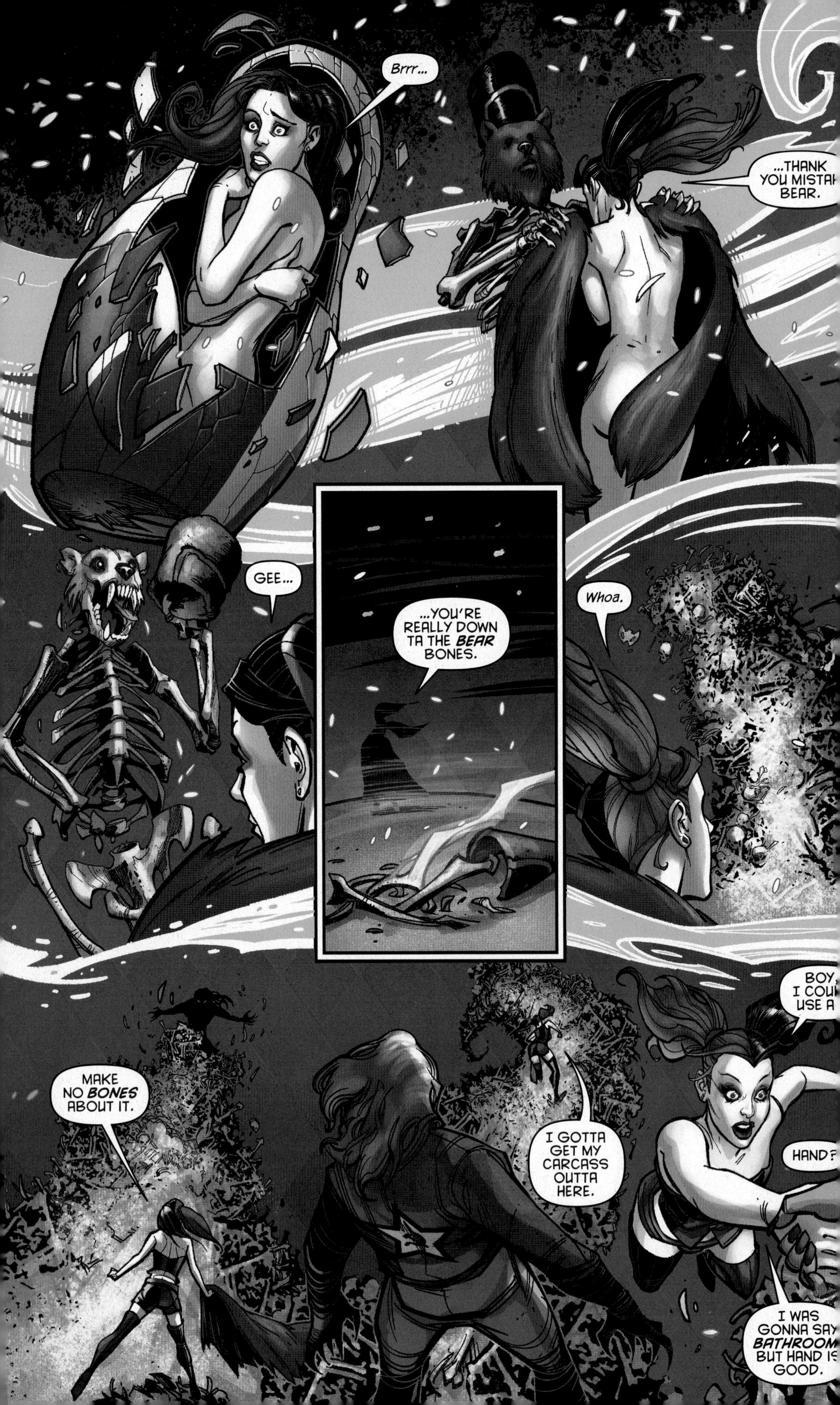

Brrr...
...THANK YOU MISTA
BEAR.
GEE...
...YOU'RE REALLY DOWN TA THE *BEAR* BONES.
Whoa.
MAKE NO *BONES* ABOUT IT.
I GOTTA GET MY CARCASS OUTTA HERE.
BOY, I COU USE A
HAND?
I WAS GONNA SAY *BATHROOM* BUT HAND IS GOOD.

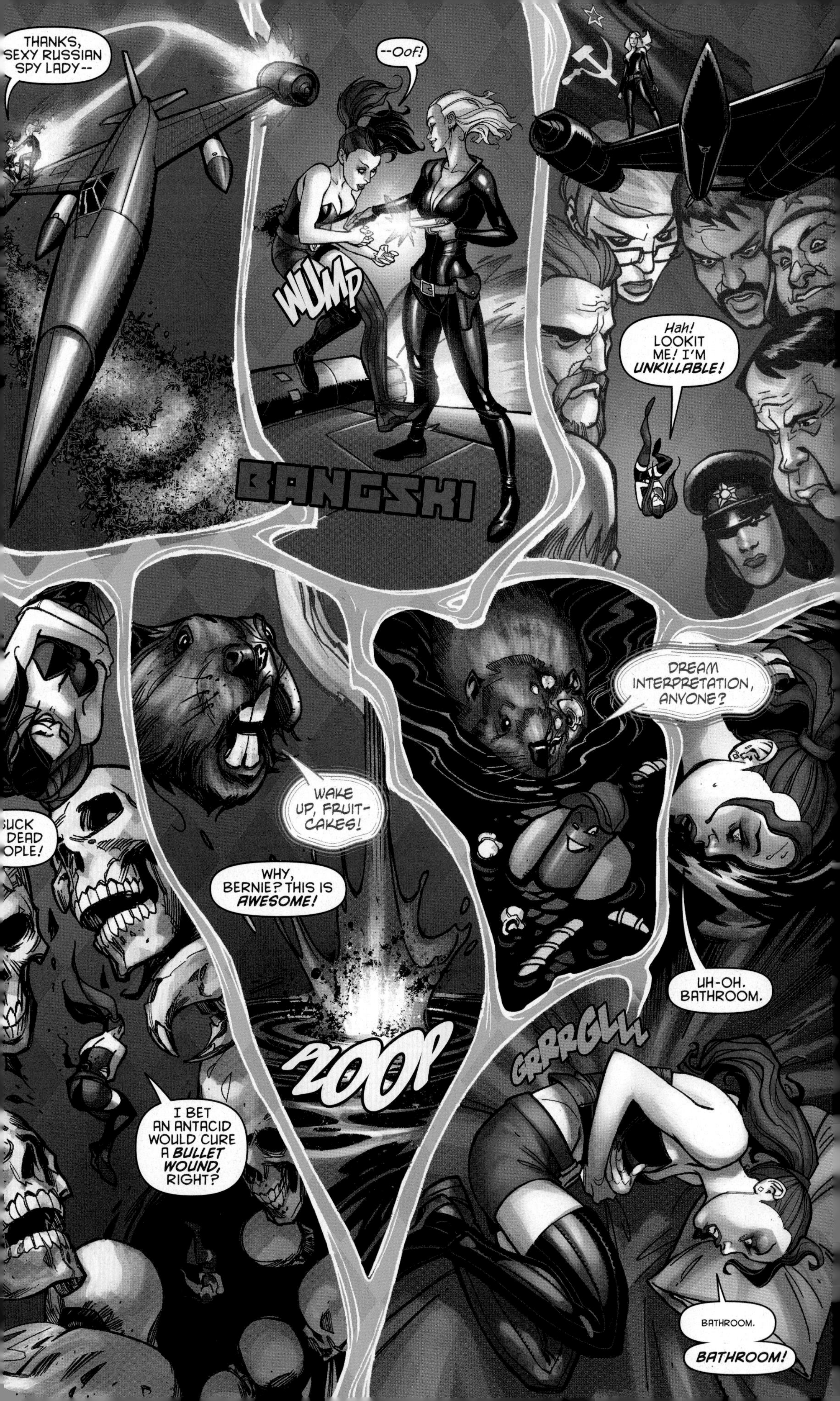

THANKS, SEXY RUSSIAN SPY LADY--
--Oof!
WUMP
BANGSKI
Hah! LOOKIT ME! I'M UNKILLABLE!
SUCK DEAD OPLE!
WAKE UP, FRUIT-CAKES!
WHY, BERNIE? THIS IS AWESOME!
ZOOP
DREAM INTERPRETATION, ANYONE?
UH-OH. BATHROOM.
GRRRGLLL
I BET AN ANTACID WOULD CURE A BULLET WOUND, RIGHT?
BATHROOM.
BATHROOM!

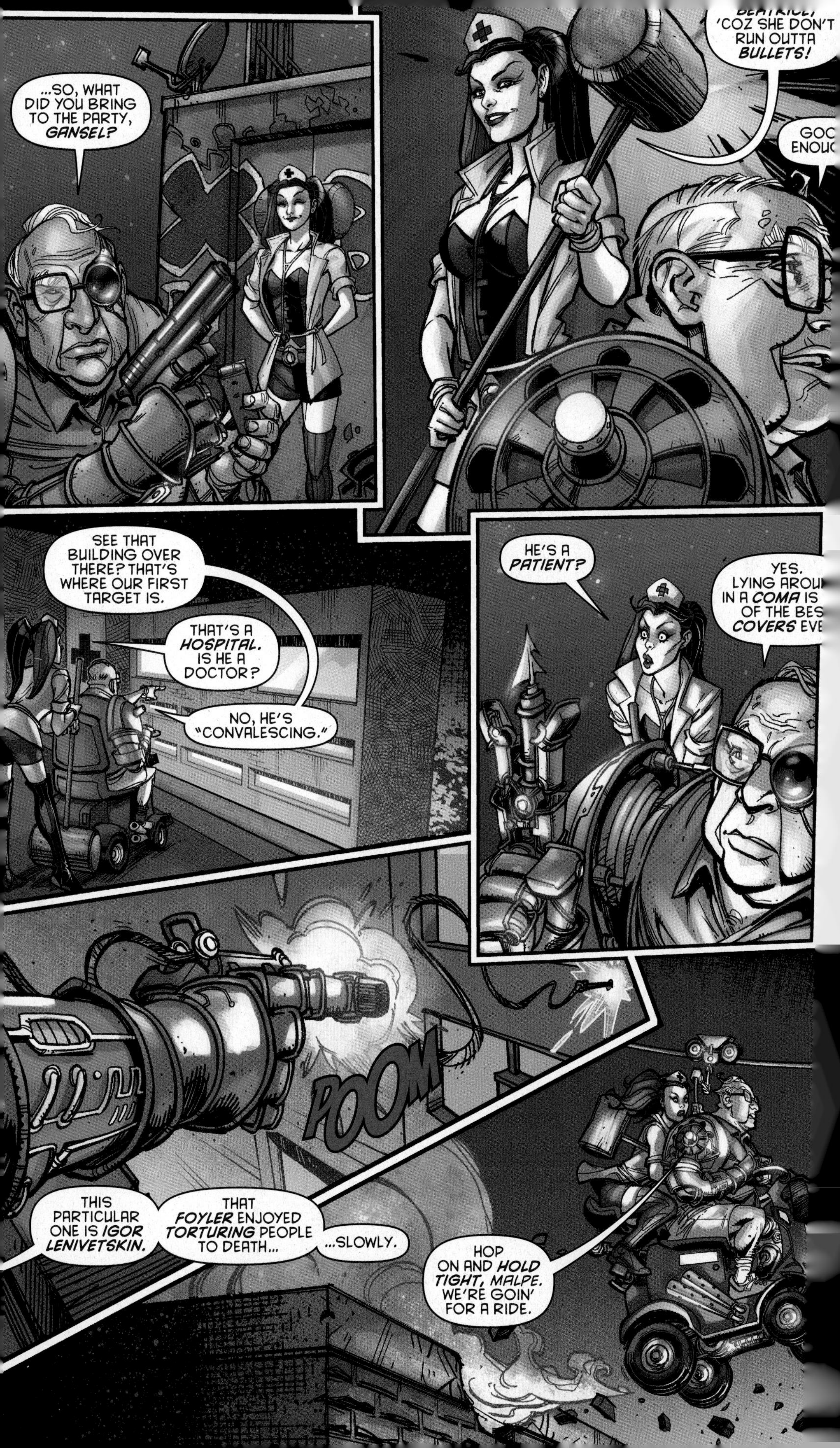

...SO, WHAT DID YOU BRING TO THE PARTY, GANSEL?
'COZ SHE DON'T RUN OUTTA BULLETS!
SEE THAT BUILDING OVER THERE? THAT'S WHERE OUR FIRST TARGET IS.
THAT'S A HOSPITAL. IS HE A DOCTOR?
NO, HE'S "CONVALESCING."
HE'S A PATIENT?
YES.
IN A COMA IS
POOM
THIS PARTICULAR ONE IS IGOR LENIVETSKIN.
THAT FOYLER ENJOYED TORTURING PEOPLE TO DEATH...
...SLOWLY.
HOP ON AND HOLD TIGHT, MALPE. WE'RE GOIN' FOR A RIDE.

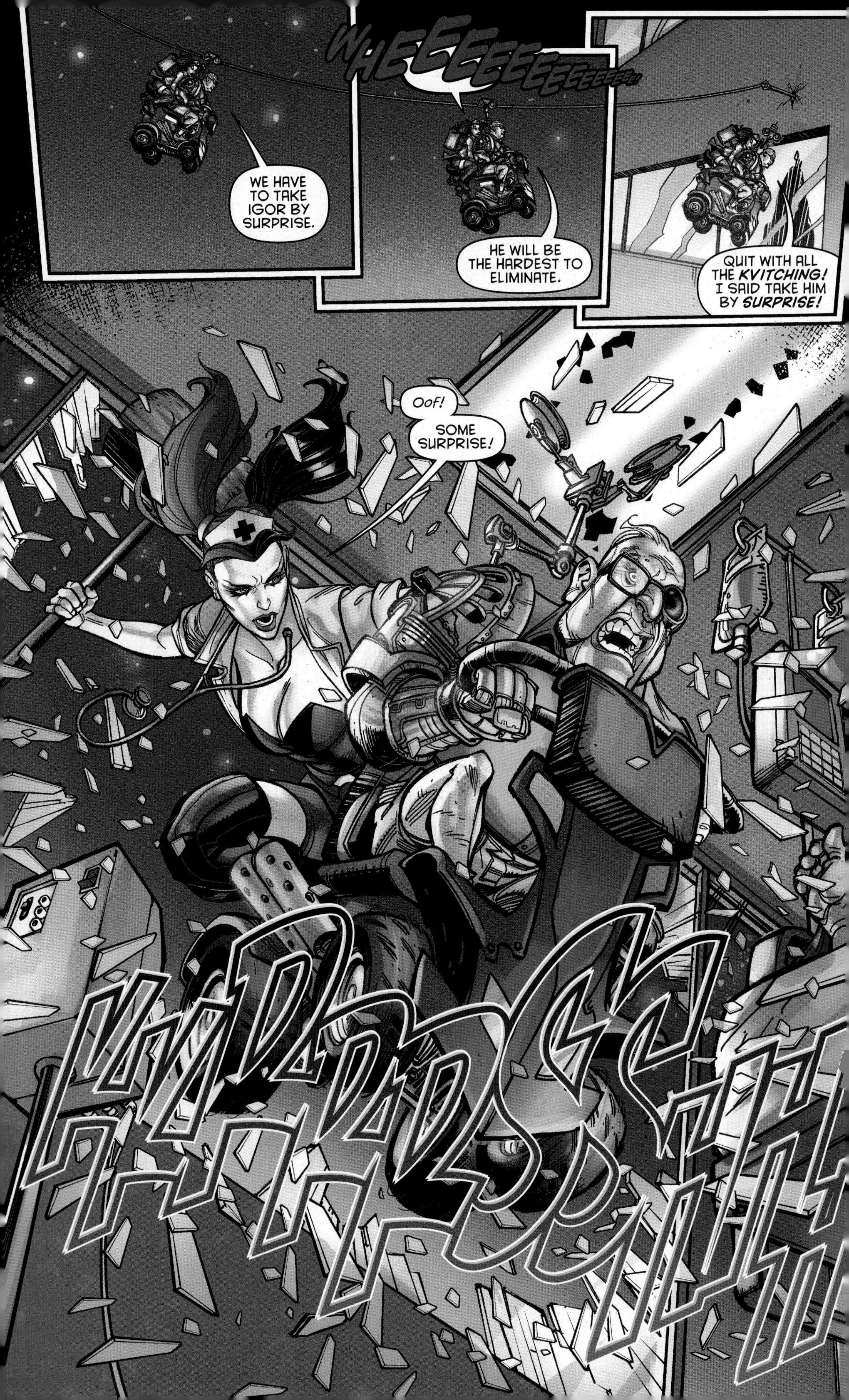
WHEEEEEEEEEeeeeee...
WE HAVE TO TAKE IGOR BY SURPRISE.
HE WILL BE THE HARDEST TO ELIMINATE.
QUIT WITH ALL THE *KVITCHING!* I SAID TAKE HIM BY *SURPRISE!*
*Oof!*
SOME SURPRISE!

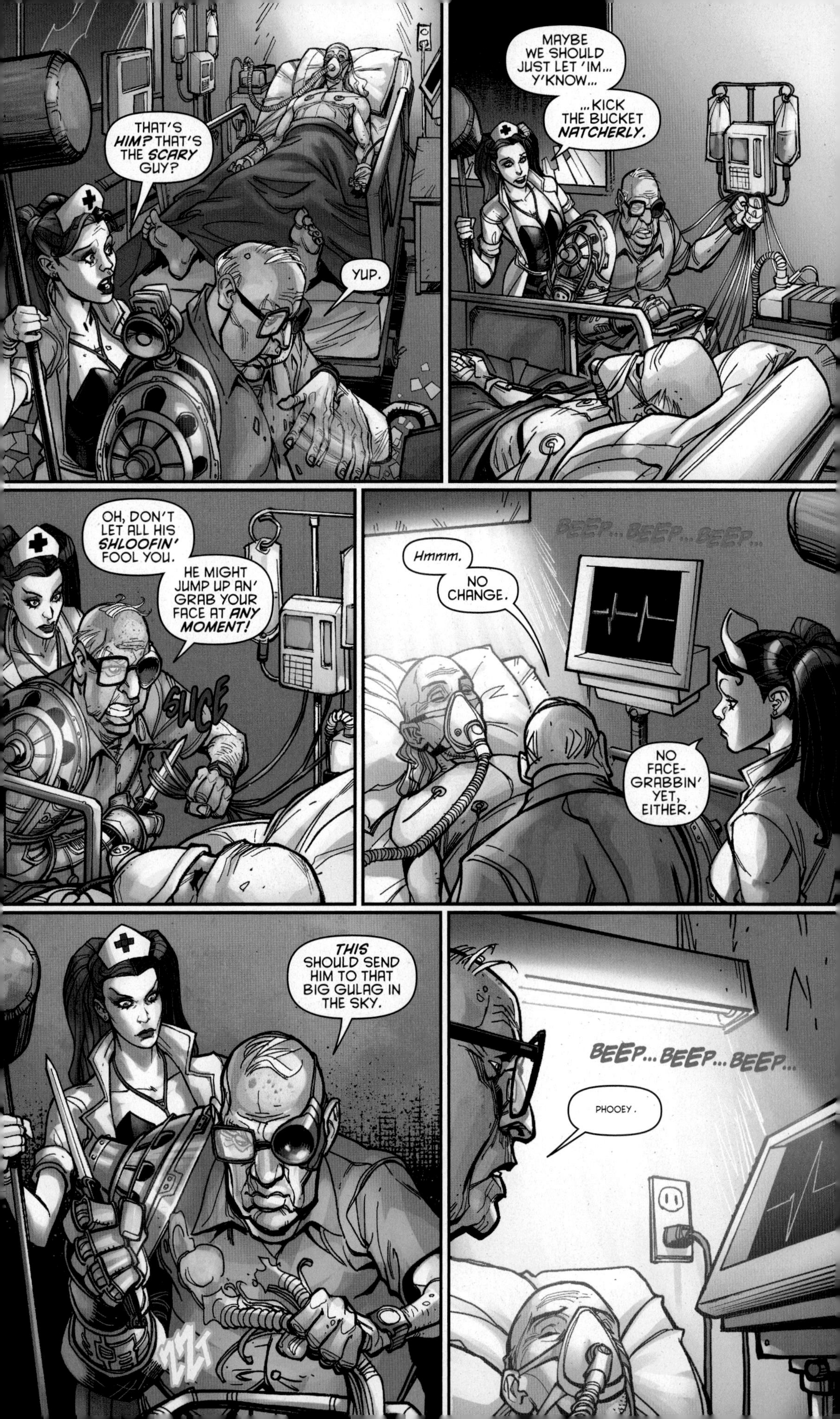
THAT'S HIM? THAT'S THE SCARY GUY?
YUP.
MAYBE WE SHOULD JUST LET 'IM... Y'KNOW...
...KICK THE BUCKET NATCHERLY.
OH, DON'T LET ALL HIS SHLOOFIN' FOOL YOU.
HE MIGHT JUMP UP AN' GRAB YOUR FACE AT ANY MOMENT!
SLICE
BEEP...BEEP...BEEP...
Hmmm.
NO CHANGE.
NO FACE-GRABBIN' YET, EITHER.
THIS SHOULD SEND HIM TO THAT BIG GULAG IN THE SKY.
ZZZT
BEEP...BEEP...BEEP...
PHOOEY.

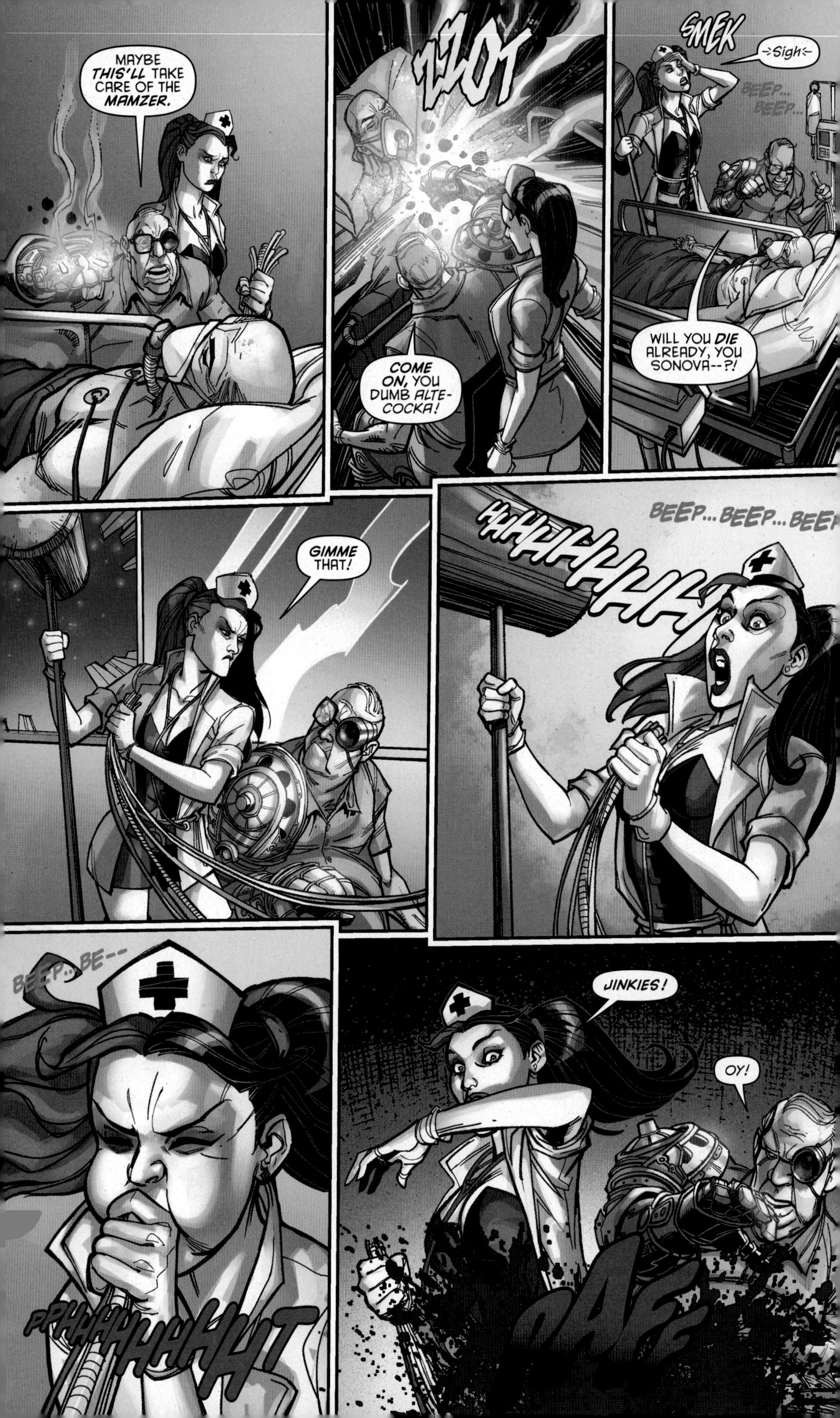
MAYBE THIS'LL TAKE CARE OF THE MAMZER.
ZZLOT
COME ON, YOU DUMB ALTE-COCKA!
SMEK
Sigh
BEEP... BEEP...
WILL YOU DIE ALREADY, YOU SONOVA--?!
GIMME THAT!
HHHHHHHHHK
BEEP...BEEP...BEEP
BEEP...BE--
PPHHHHHHHHT
JINKIES!
OY!

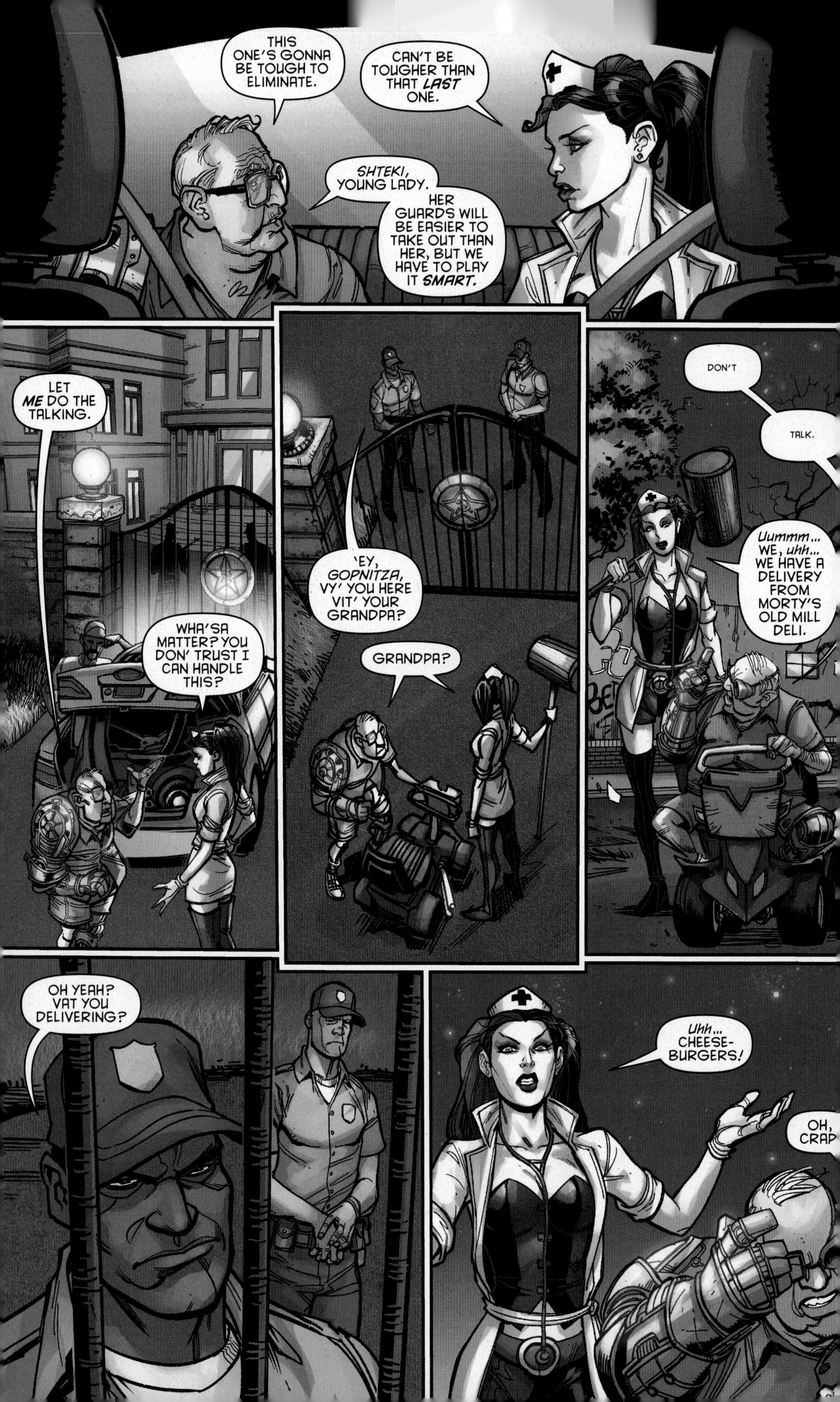

THIS ONE'S GONNA BE TOUGH TO ELIMINATE.
CAN'T BE TOUGHER THAN THAT *LAST* ONE.
*SHTEKI*, YOUNG LADY.
HER GUARDS WILL BE EASIER TO TAKE OUT THAN HER, BUT WE HAVE TO PLAY IT ***SMART.***
LET ***ME*** DO THE TALKING.
WHA'SA MATTER? YOU DON' TRUST I CAN HANDLE THIS?
'EY, *GOPNITZA*, VY' YOU HERE VIT' YOUR GRANDPA?
GRANDPA?
DON'T
TALK.
*Uummm...* WE, *uhh...* WE HAVE A DELIVERY FROM MORTY'S OLD MILL DELI.
OH YEAH? VAT YOU DELIVERING?
*Uhh...* CHEESE-BURGERS!
OH, CRAP

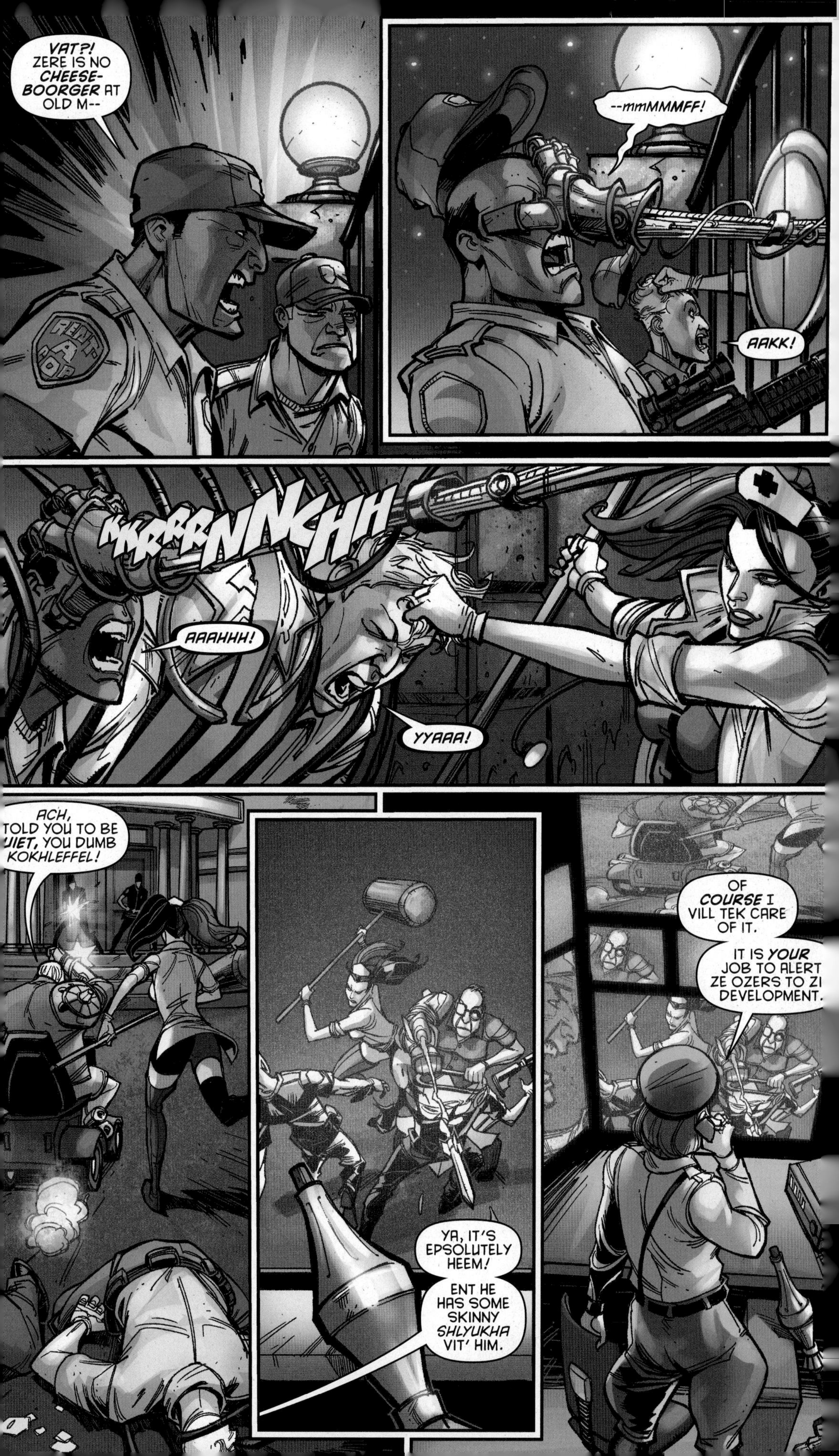
VAT?! ZERE IS NO CHEESE-BOORGER AT OLD M--
--mmMMMFF!
AAKK!
KKRRRNNCHH
AAAHHH!
YYAAA!
ACH, TOLD YOU TO BE UIET, YOU DUMB KOKHLEFFEL!
YA, IT'S EPSOLUTELY HEEM!
ENT HE HAS SOME SKINNY SHLYUKHA VIT' HIM.
OF COURSE I VILL TEK CARE OF IT.
IT IS YOUR JOB TO ALERT ZE OZERS TO ZI DEVELOPMENT.

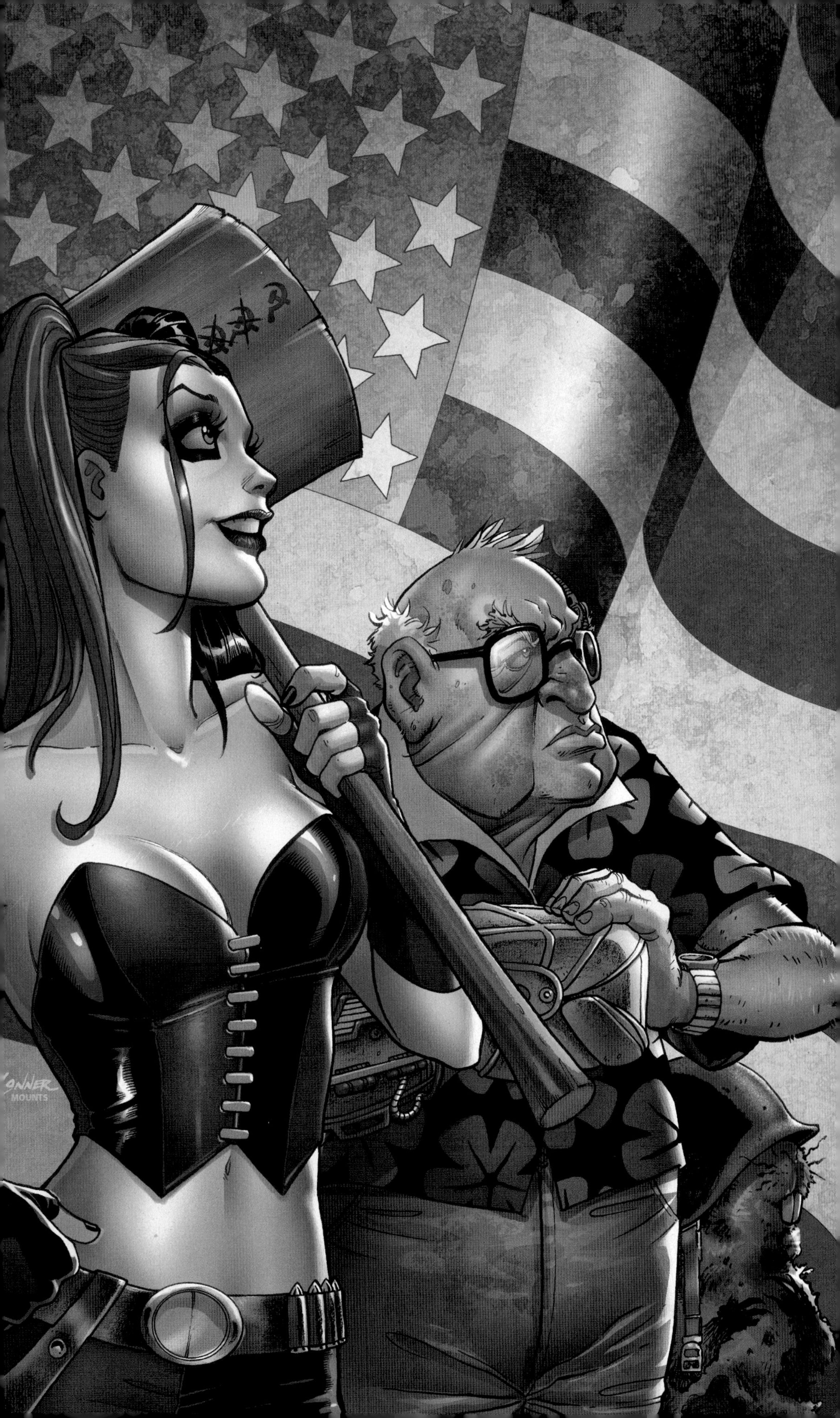
MOUNTS

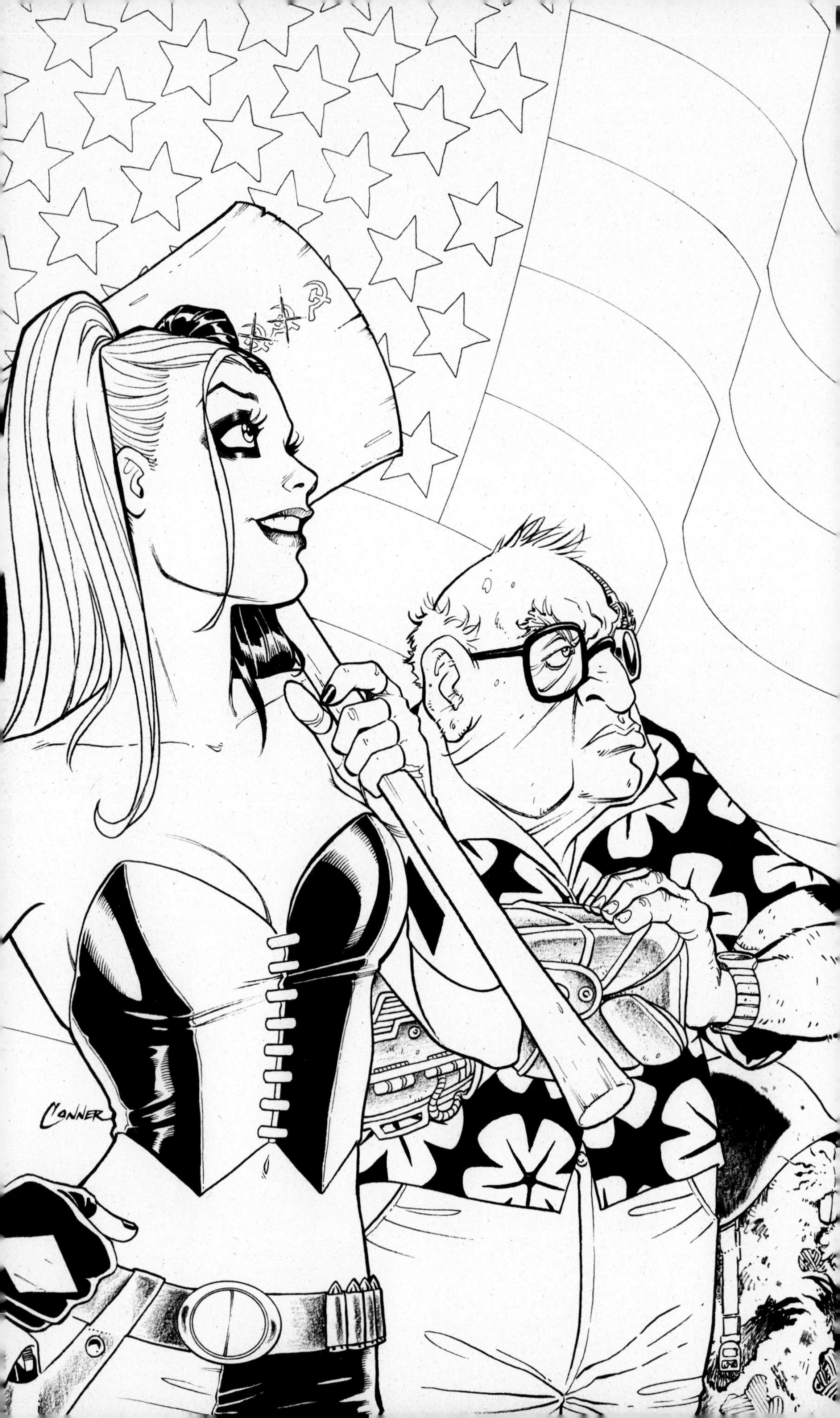
CONNER

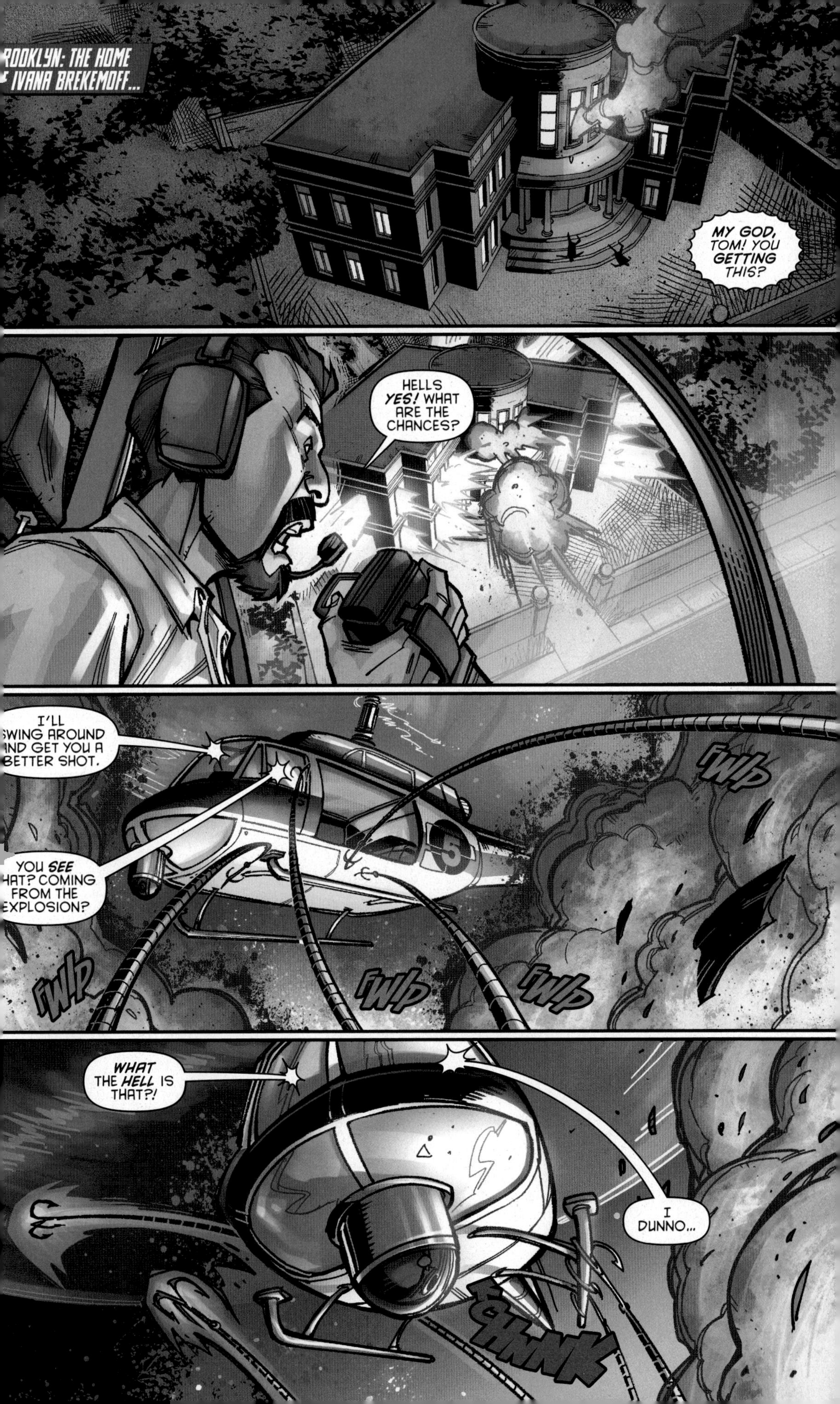

ROOKLYN: THE HOME
F IVANA BREKEMOFF...
MY GOD, TOM! YOU GETTING THIS?
HELLS YES! WHAT ARE THE CHANCES?
I'LL SWING AROUND AND GET YOU A BETTER SHOT.
YOU SEE THAT? COMING FROM THE EXPLOSION?
FWIP
FWIP
FWIP
FWIP
WHAT THE HELL IS THAT?!
I DUNNO...
CHUNK

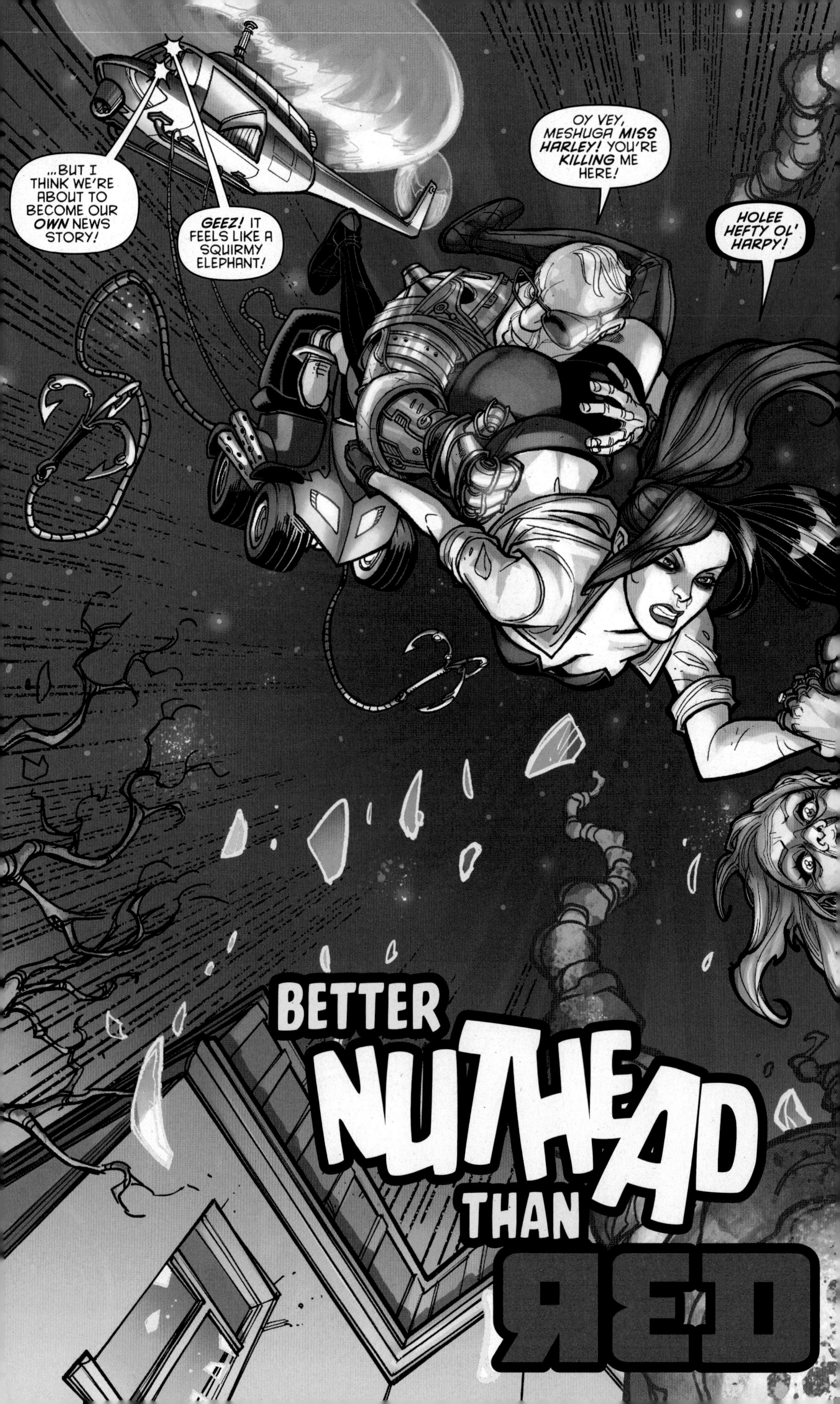
...BUT I THINK WE'RE ABOUT TO BECOME OUR OWN NEWS STORY!
GEEZ! IT FEELS LIKE A SQUIRMY ELEPHANT!
OY VEY, MESHUGA MISS HARLEY! YOU'RE KILLING ME HERE!
HOLEE HEFTY OL' HARPY!
BETTER NUTHEAD THAN RED

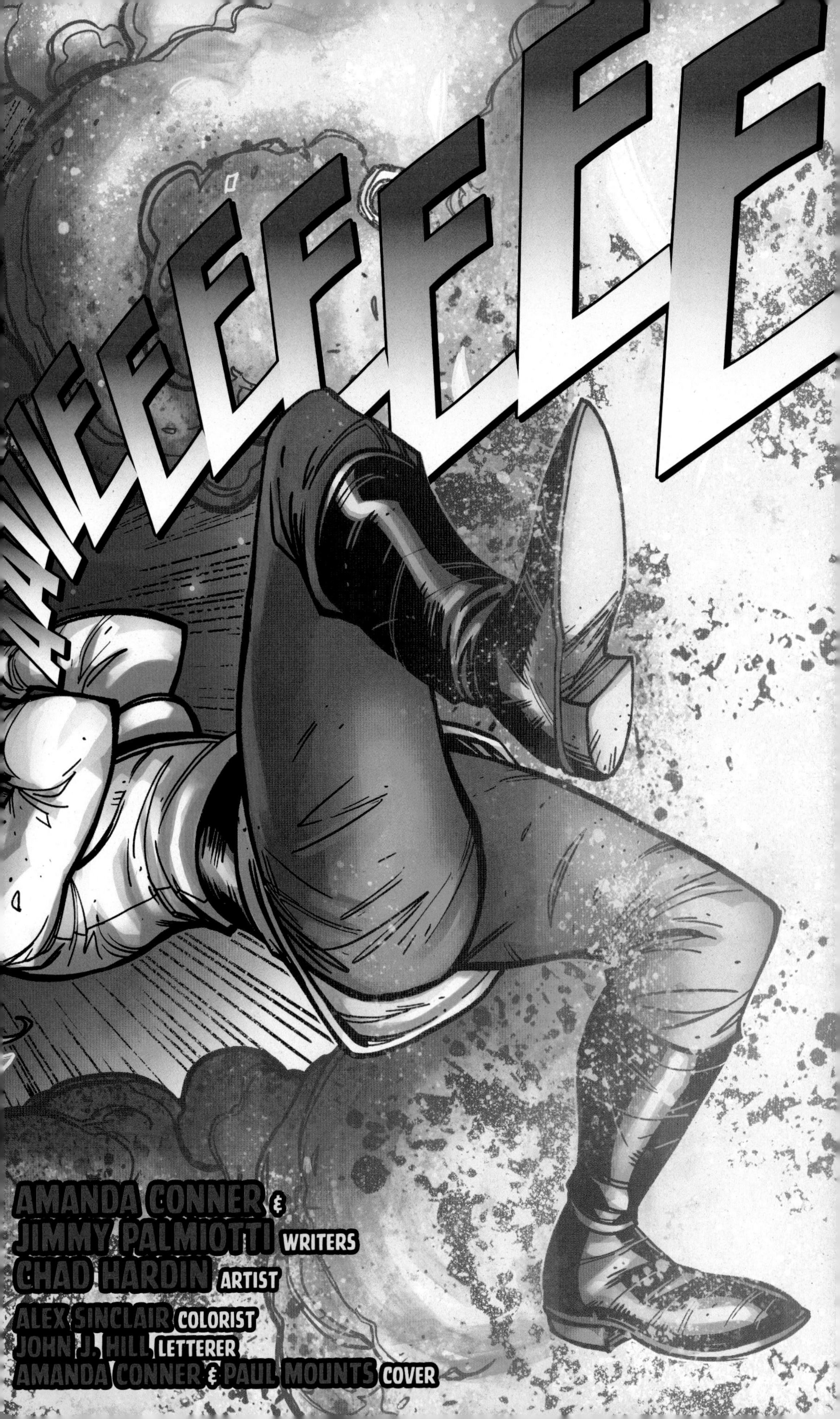

WHEEEEEEEE
AMANDA CONNER & JIMMY PALMIOTTI WRITERS
CHAD HARDIN ARTIST
ALEX SINCLAIR COLORIST
JOHN J. HILL LETTERER
AMANDA CONNER & PAUL MOUNTS COVER

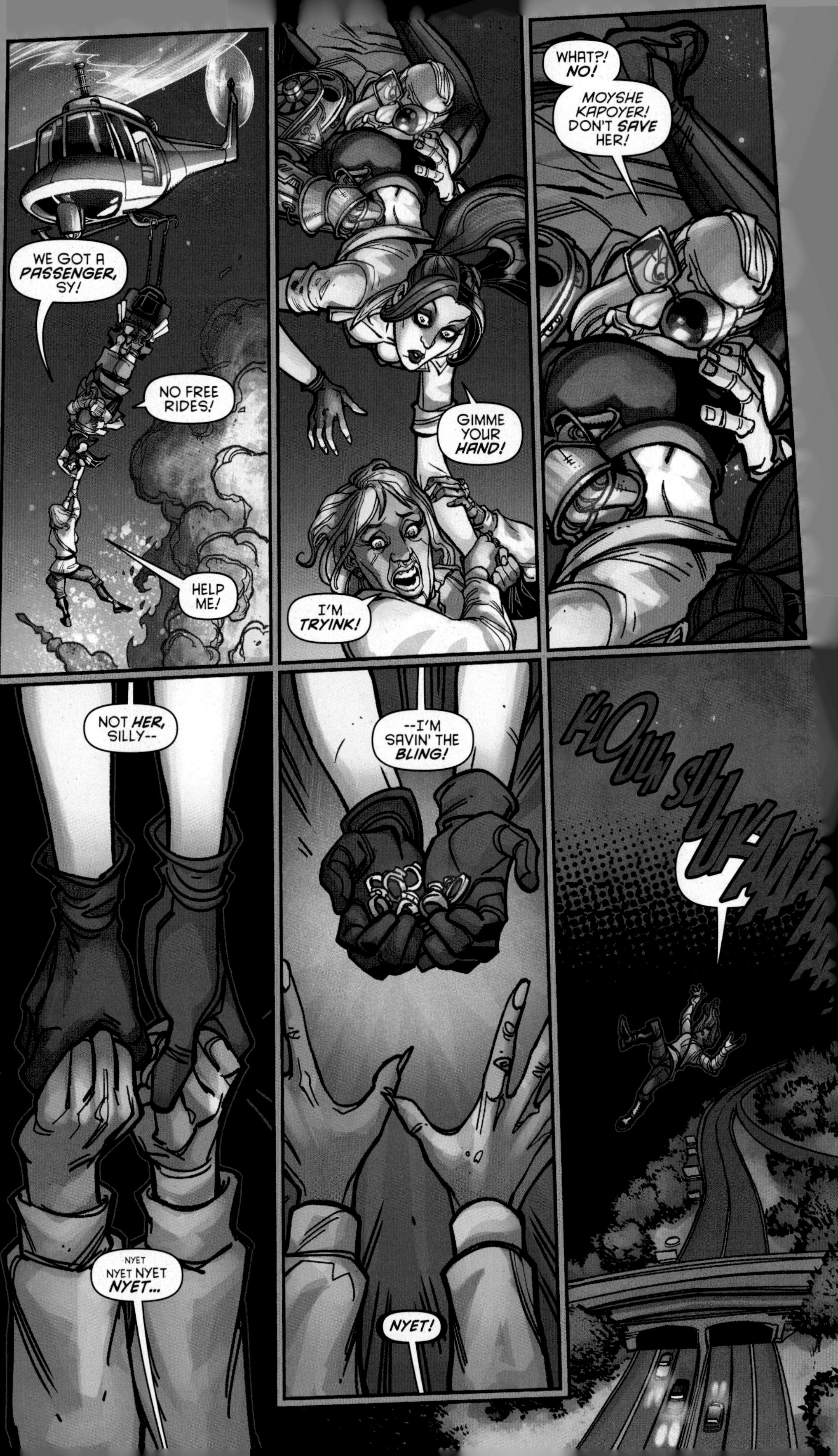
WE GOT A PASSENGER, SY!
NO FREE RIDES!
HELP ME!
GIMME YOUR HAND!
I'M TRYINK!
WHAT?! NO!
MOYSHE KAPOYER! DON'T SAVE HER!
NOT HER, SILLY--
--I'M SAVIN' THE BLING!
NYET NYET NYET NYET...
NYET!

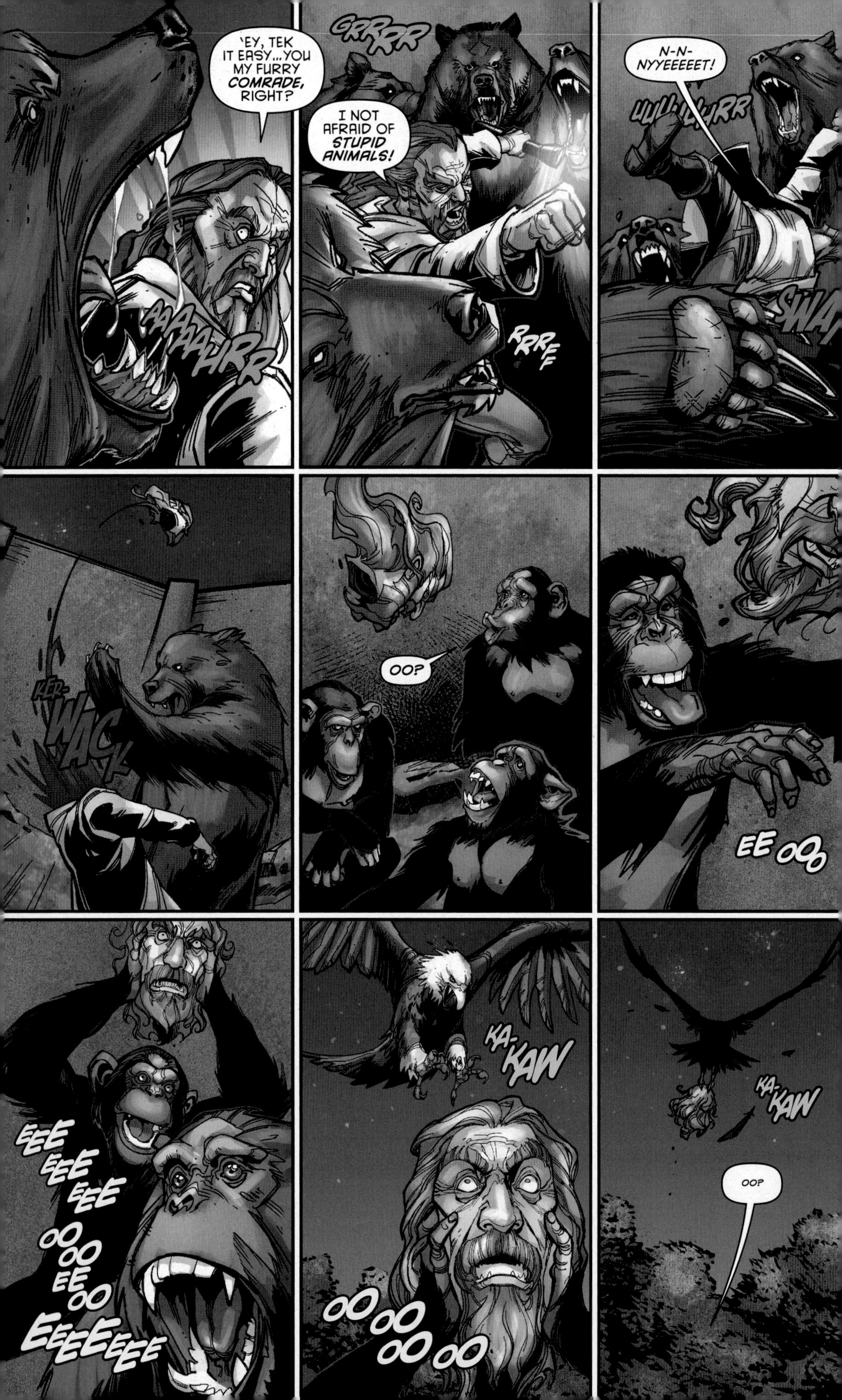
'EY, TEK IT EASY...YOU MY FURRY COMRADE, RIGHT?
AAAAAUHRR
GRRRRR
I NOT AFRAID OF STUPID ANIMALS!
RRRFF
N-N-NYYEEEEET!
UUUUUHRR
SWAP
HER-WACK
OO?
EE OOO
EEEEEEEEE OOOOEEOO EEEEEEEE
KA-KAW
OOOOO OOOOO
KA-KAW
OO?

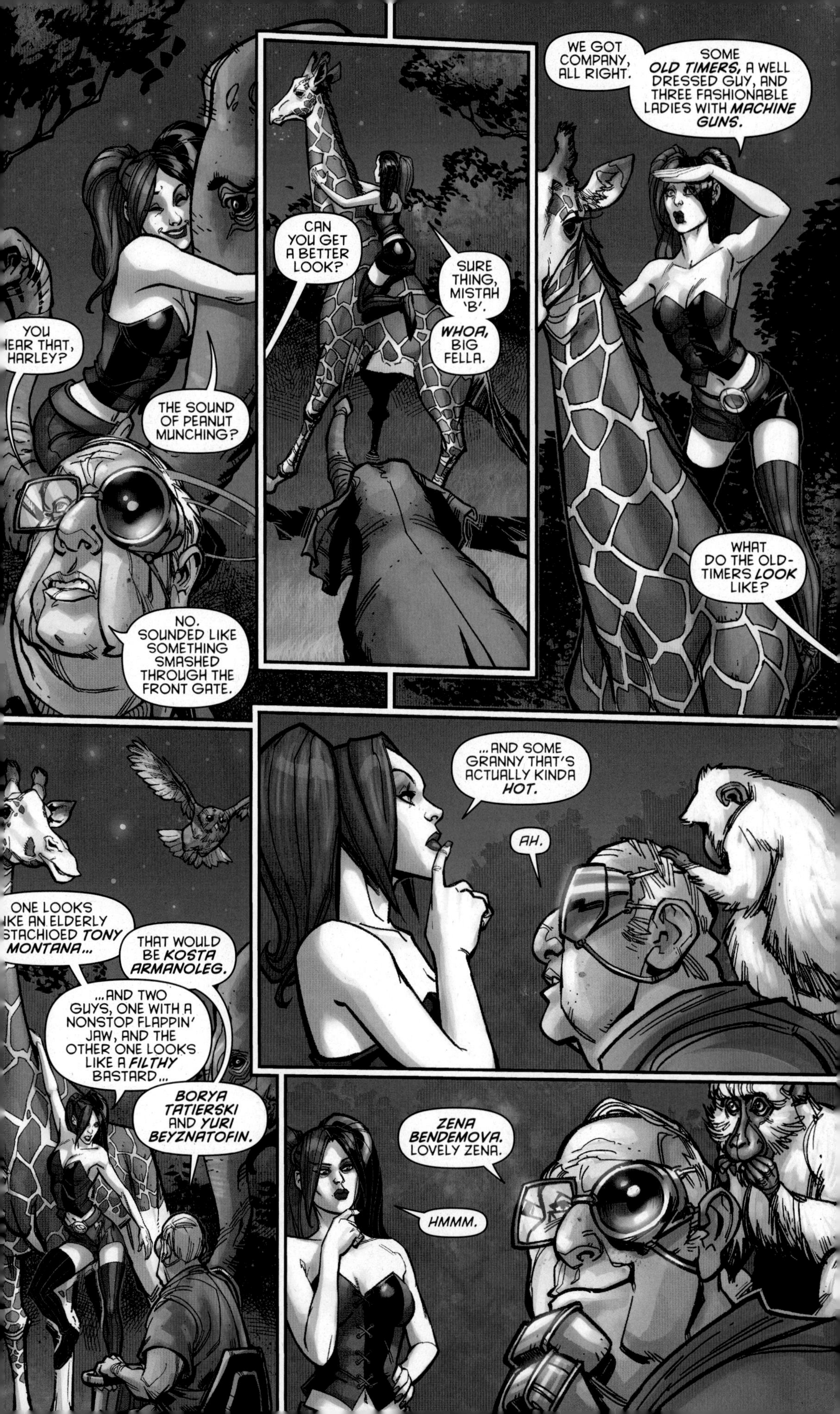
YOU HEAR THAT, HARLEY?
THE SOUND OF PEANUT MUNCHING?
NO. SOUNDED LIKE SOMETHING SMASHED THROUGH THE FRONT GATE.
CAN YOU GET A BETTER LOOK?
SURE THING, MISTAH 'B'.
WHOA, BIG FELLA.
WE GOT COMPANY, ALL RIGHT.
SOME OLD TIMERS, A WELL DRESSED GUY, AND THREE FASHIONABLE LADIES WITH MACHINE GUNS.
WHAT DO THE OLD-TIMERS LOOK LIKE?
ONE LOOKS LIKE AN ELDERLY STACHIOED TONY MONTANA...
THAT WOULD BE KOSTA ARMANOLEG.
...AND TWO GUYS, ONE WITH A NONSTOP FLAPPIN' JAW, AND THE OTHER ONE LOOKS LIKE A FILTHY BASTARD...
BORYA TATIERSKI AND YURI BEYZNATOFIN.
...AND SOME GRANNY THAT'S ACTUALLY KINDA HOT.
AH.
ZENA BENDEMOVA. LOVELY ZENA.
HMMM.

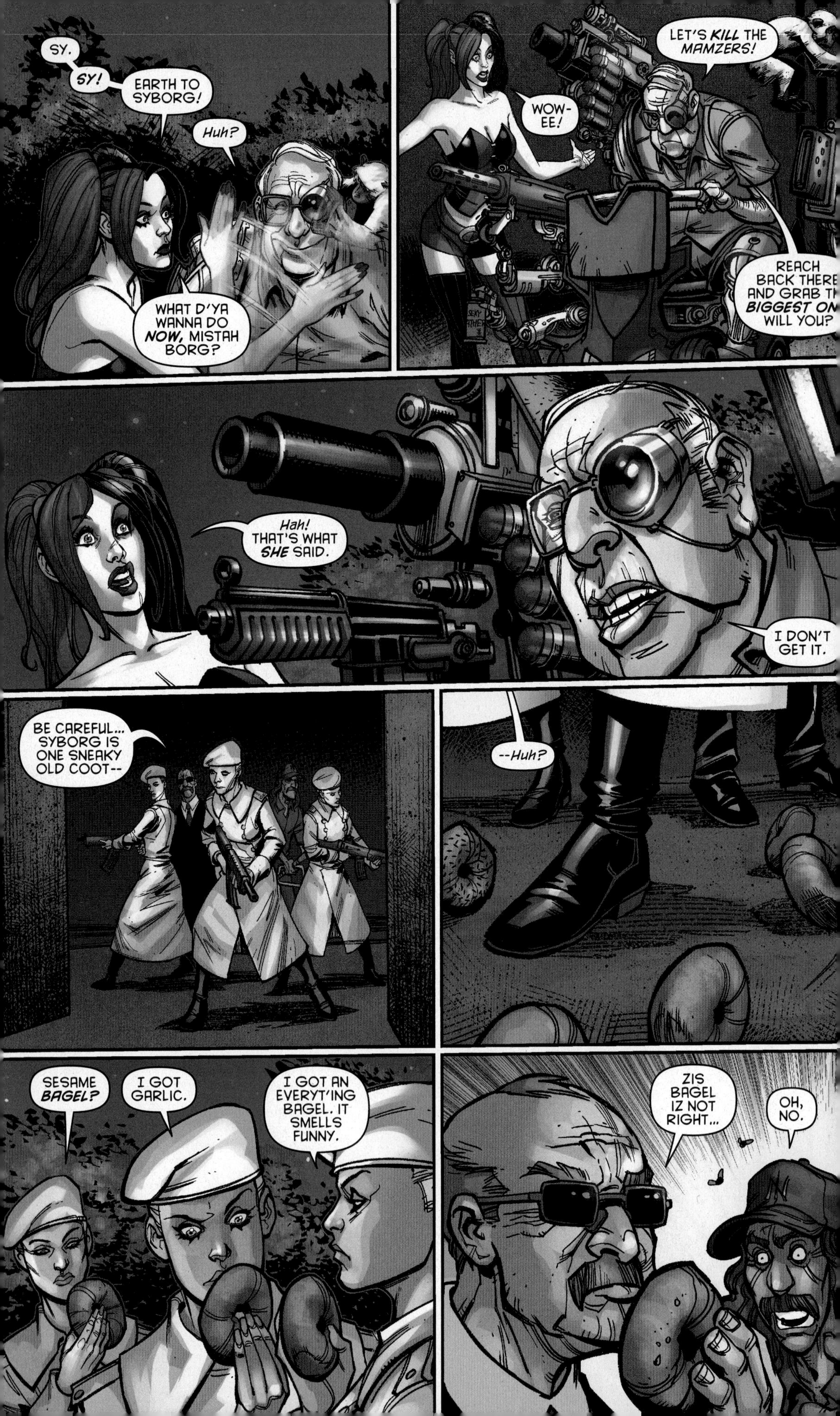
SY.
SY!
EARTH TO SYBORG!
Huh?
WHAT D'YA WANNA DO NOW, MISTAH BORG?
LET'S KILL THE MAMZERS!
WOW-EE!
REACH BACK THERE AND GRAB TH BIGGEST ON WILL YOU?
Hah! THAT'S WHAT SHE SAID.
I DON'T GET IT.
BE CAREFUL... SYBORG IS ONE SNEAKY OLD COOT--
--Huh?
SESAME BAGEL?
I GOT GARLIC.
I GOT AN EVERYT'ING BAGEL. IT SMELLS FUNNY.
ZIS BAGEL IZ NOT RIGHT...
OH, NO.

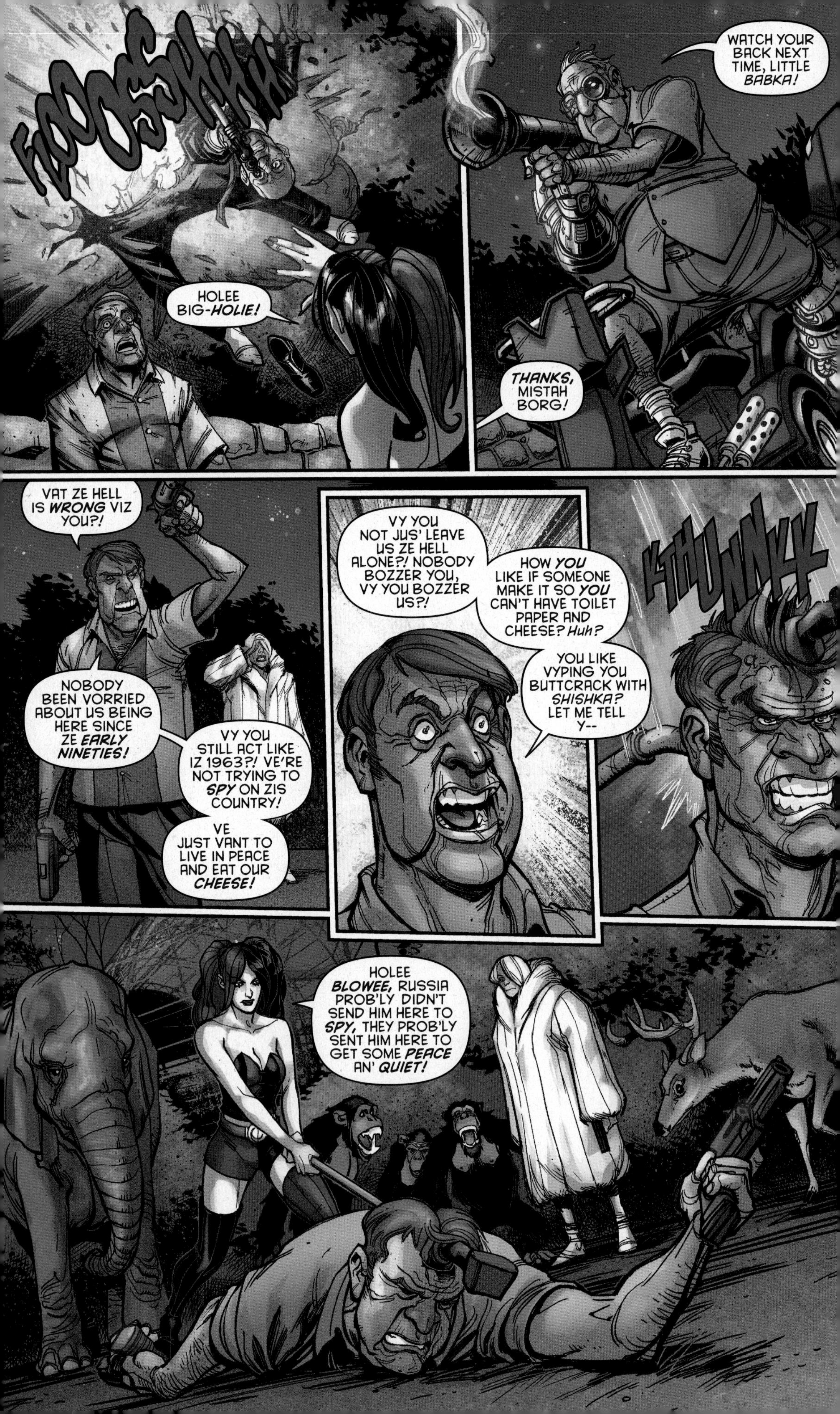
FOOOSSHHH
HOLEE BIG-*HOLIE!*
WATCH YOUR BACK NEXT TIME, LITTLE *BABKA!*
*THANKS,* MISTAH BORG!
VAT ZE HELL IS *WRONG* VIZ YOU?!
NOBODY BEEN VORRIED ABOUT US BEING HERE SINCE ZE *EARLY NINETIES!*
VY YOU STILL ACT LIKE IZ 1963?! VE'RE NOT TRYING TO *SPY* ON ZIS COUNTRY!
VE JUST VANT TO LIVE IN PEACE AND EAT OUR *CHEESE!*
VY YOU NOT JUS' LEAVE US ZE HELL ALONE?! NOBODY BOZZER YOU, VY YOU BOZZER US?!
HOW *YOU* LIKE IF SOMEONE MAKE IT SO *YOU* CAN'T HAVE TOILET PAPER AND CHEESE? *Huh?*
YOU LIKE VYPING YOU BUTTCRACK WITH *SHISHKA?* LET ME TELL Y--
KTHUNNKK
HOLEE *BLOWEE,* RUSSIA PROB'LY DIDN'T SEND HIM HERE TO *SPY,* THEY PROB'LY SENT HIM HERE TO GET SOME *PEACE* AN' *QUIET!*

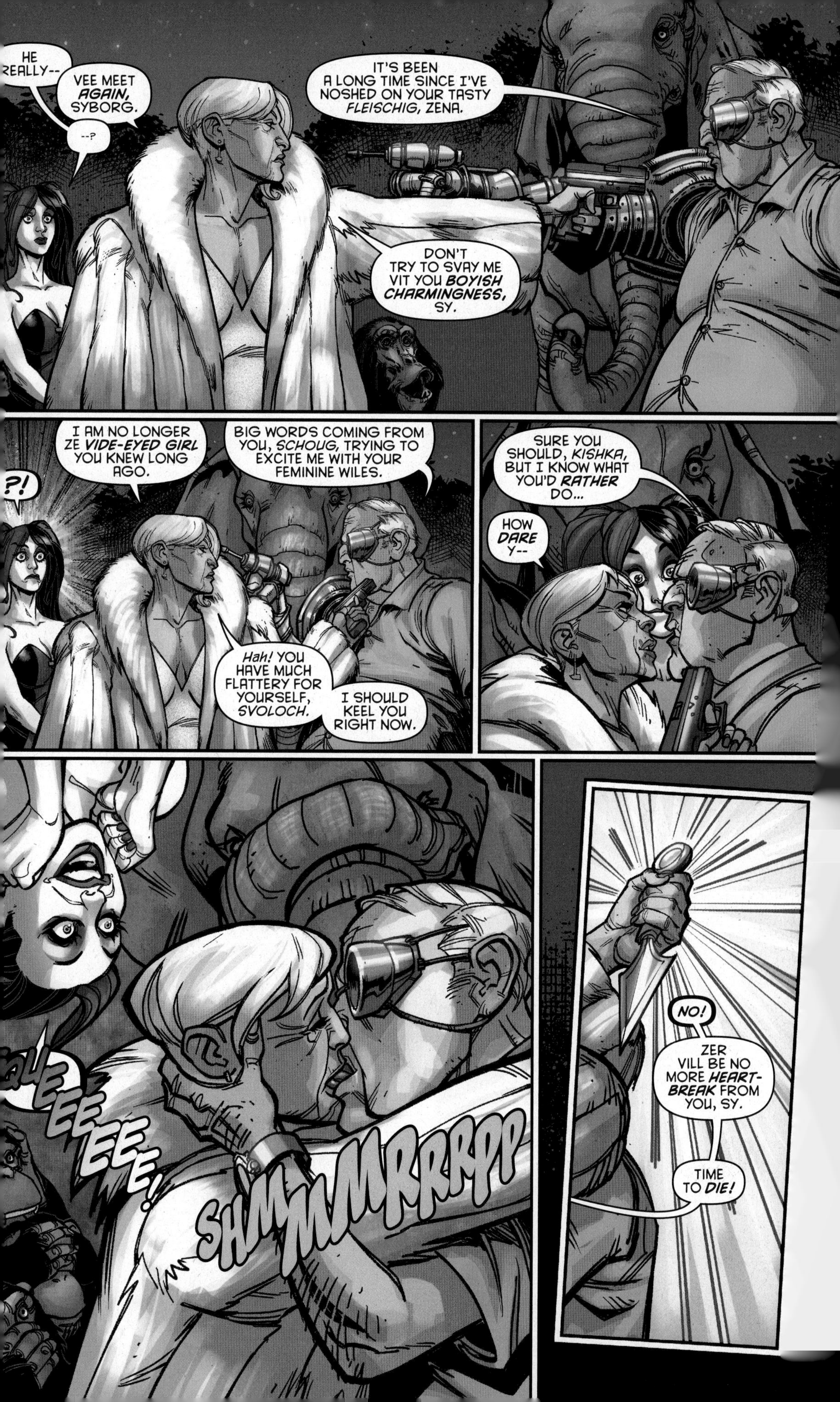

HE REALLY--
VEE MEET AGAIN, SYBORG.
--?
IT'S BEEN A LONG TIME SINCE I'VE NOSHED ON YOUR TASTY FLEISCHIG, ZENA.
DON'T TRY TO SVAY ME VIT YOU BOYISH CHARMINGNESS, SY.
I AM NO LONGER ZE VIDE-EYED GIRL YOU KNEW LONG AGO.
BIG WORDS COMING FROM YOU, SCHOUG, TRYING TO EXCITE ME WITH YOUR FEMININE WILES.
?!
Hah! YOU HAVE MUCH FLATTERY FOR YOURSELF, SVOLOCH.
I SHOULD KEEL YOU RIGHT NOW.
SURE YOU SHOULD, KISHKA, BUT I KNOW WHAT YOU'D RATHER DO...
HOW DARE Y--
SQUEEEEEEEE!
SHMMMMRRRPP
NO!
ZER VILL BE NO MORE HEART-BREAK FROM YOU, SY.
TIME TO DIE!

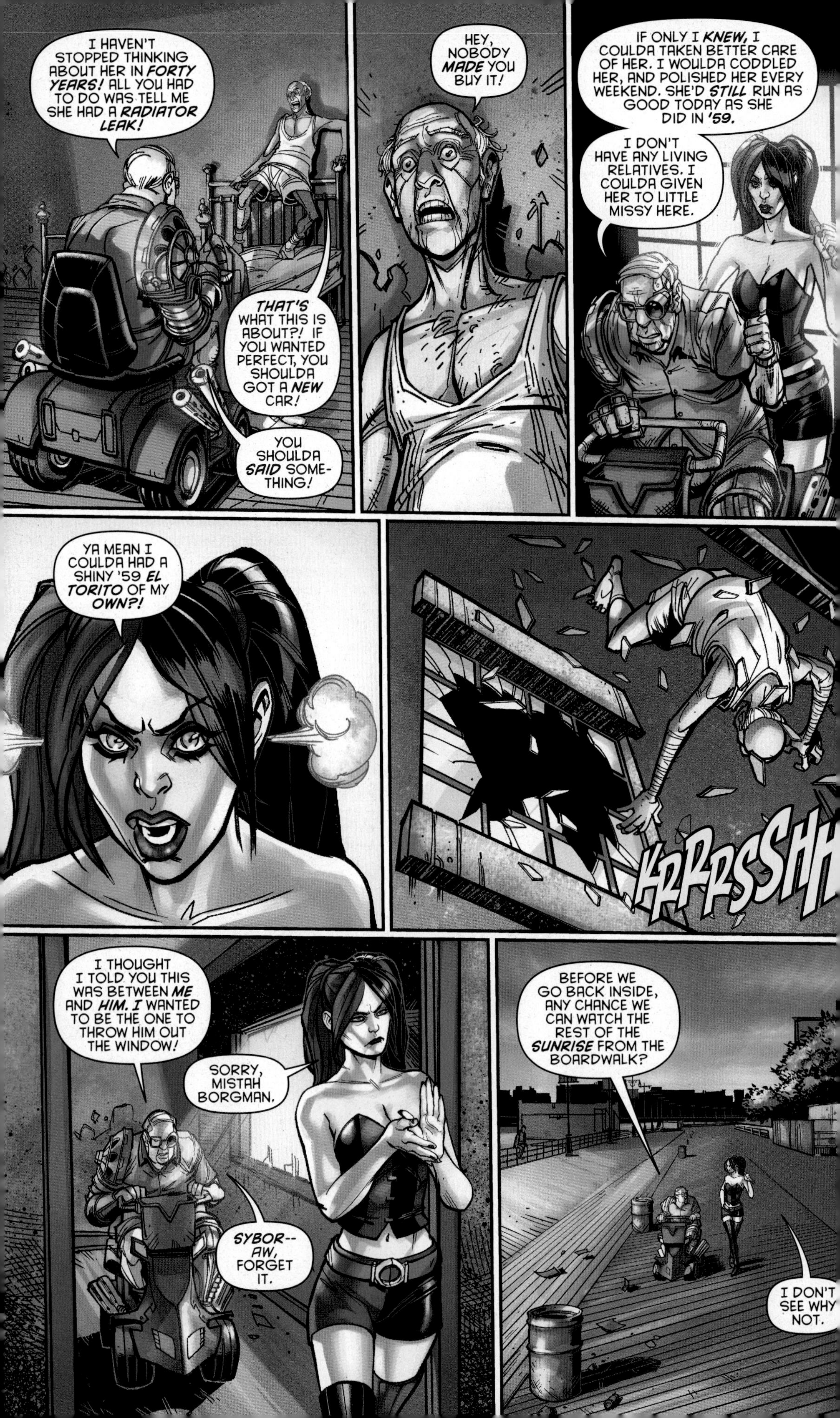
I HAVEN'T STOPPED THINKING ABOUT HER IN *FORTY YEARS!* ALL YOU HAD TO DO WAS TELL ME SHE HAD A *RADIATOR LEAK!*
*THAT'S* WHAT THIS IS ABOUT?! IF YOU WANTED PERFECT, YOU SHOULDA GOT A *NEW* CAR!
YOU SHOULDA *SAID* SOME-THING!
HEY, NOBODY *MADE* YOU BUY IT!
IF ONLY I *KNEW,* I COULDA TAKEN BETTER CARE OF HER. I WOULDA CODDLED HER, AND POLISHED HER EVERY WEEKEND. SHE'D *STILL* RUN AS GOOD TODAY AS SHE DID IN *'59.*
I DON'T HAVE ANY LIVING RELATIVES. I COULDA GIVEN HER TO LITTLE MISSY HERE.
YA MEAN I COULDA HAD A SHINY '59 *EL TORITO* OF MY *OWN?!*
KRRRSSHH
I THOUGHT I TOLD YOU THIS WAS BETWEEN *ME* AND *HIM. I* WANTED TO BE THE ONE TO THROW HIM OUT THE WINDOW!
SORRY, MISTAH BORGMAN.
*SYBOR*-- AW, FORGET IT.
BEFORE WE GO BACK INSIDE, ANY CHANCE WE CAN WATCH THE REST OF THE *SUNRISE* FROM THE BOARDWALK?
I DON'T SEE WHY NOT.

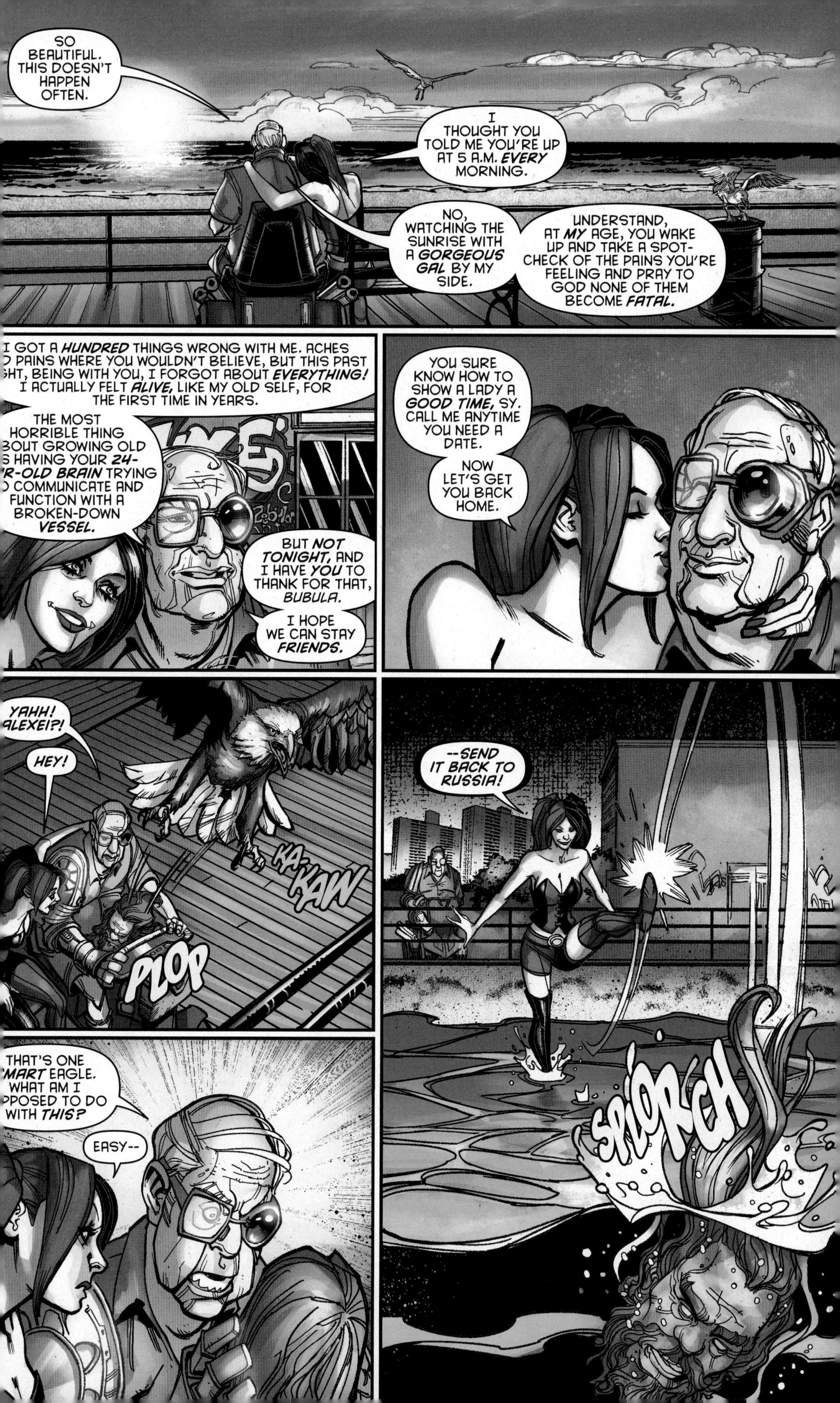

SO BEAUTIFUL. THIS DOESN'T HAPPEN OFTEN.
I THOUGHT YOU TOLD ME YOU'RE UP AT 5 A.M. EVERY MORNING.
NO, WATCHING THE SUNRISE WITH A GORGEOUS GAL BY MY SIDE.
UNDERSTAND, AT MY AGE, YOU WAKE UP AND TAKE A SPOT-CHECK OF THE PAINS YOU'RE FEELING AND PRAY TO GOD NONE OF THEM BECOME FATAL.
I GOT A HUNDRED THINGS WRONG WITH ME. ACHES D PAINS WHERE YOU WOULDN'T BELIEVE, BUT THIS PAST GHT, BEING WITH YOU, I FORGOT ABOUT EVERYTHING! I ACTUALLY FELT ALIVE, LIKE MY OLD SELF, FOR THE FIRST TIME IN YEARS.
THE MOST HORRIBLE THING BOUT GROWING OLD S HAVING YOUR 24-R-OLD BRAIN TRYING O COMMUNICATE AND FUNCTION WITH A BROKEN-DOWN VESSEL.
BUT NOT TONIGHT, AND I HAVE YOU TO THANK FOR THAT, BUBULA.
I HOPE WE CAN STAY FRIENDS.
YOU SURE KNOW HOW TO SHOW A LADY A GOOD TIME, SY. CALL ME ANYTIME YOU NEED A DATE.
NOW LET'S GET YOU BACK HOME.
YAHH! ALEXEI?!
HEY!
KA-KAW
PLOP
THAT'S ONE MART EAGLE. WHAT AM I PPOSED TO DO WITH THIS?
EASY--
--SEND IT BACK TO RUSSIA!
SPLORCH

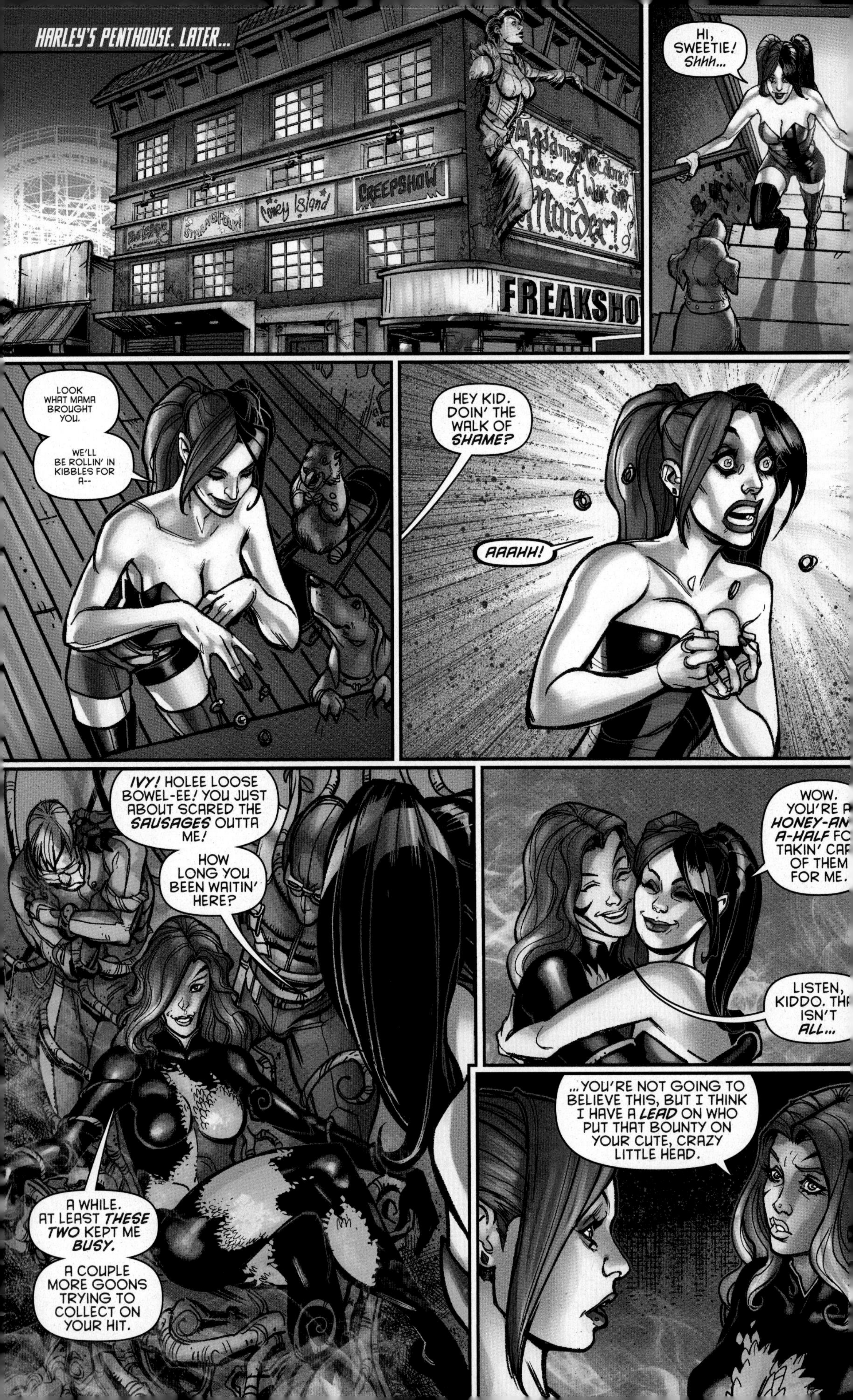
HARLEY'S PENTHOUSE. LATER...
Madame Macabre's House of Wax and Murder!
CREEPSHOW
Coney Island
FREAKSHOW
HI, SWEETIE! Shhh...
LOOK WHAT MAMA BROUGHT YOU.
WE'LL BE ROLLIN' IN KIBBLES FOR A--
HEY KID. DOIN' THE WALK OF SHAME?
AAAHH!
IVY! HOLEE LOOSE BOWEL-EE! YOU JUST ABOUT SCARED THE SAUSAGES OUTTA ME!
HOW LONG YOU BEEN WAITIN' HERE?
A WHILE. AT LEAST THESE TWO KEPT ME BUSY.
A COUPLE MORE GOONS TRYING TO COLLECT ON YOUR HIT.
WOW. YOU'RE A HONEY-AN A-HALF FO TAKIN' CAR OF THEM FOR ME.
LISTEN, KIDDO. TH ISN'T ALL...
...YOU'RE NOT GOING TO BELIEVE THIS, BUT I THINK I HAVE A LEAD ON WHO PUT THAT BOUNTY ON YOUR CUTE, CRAZY LITTLE HEAD.

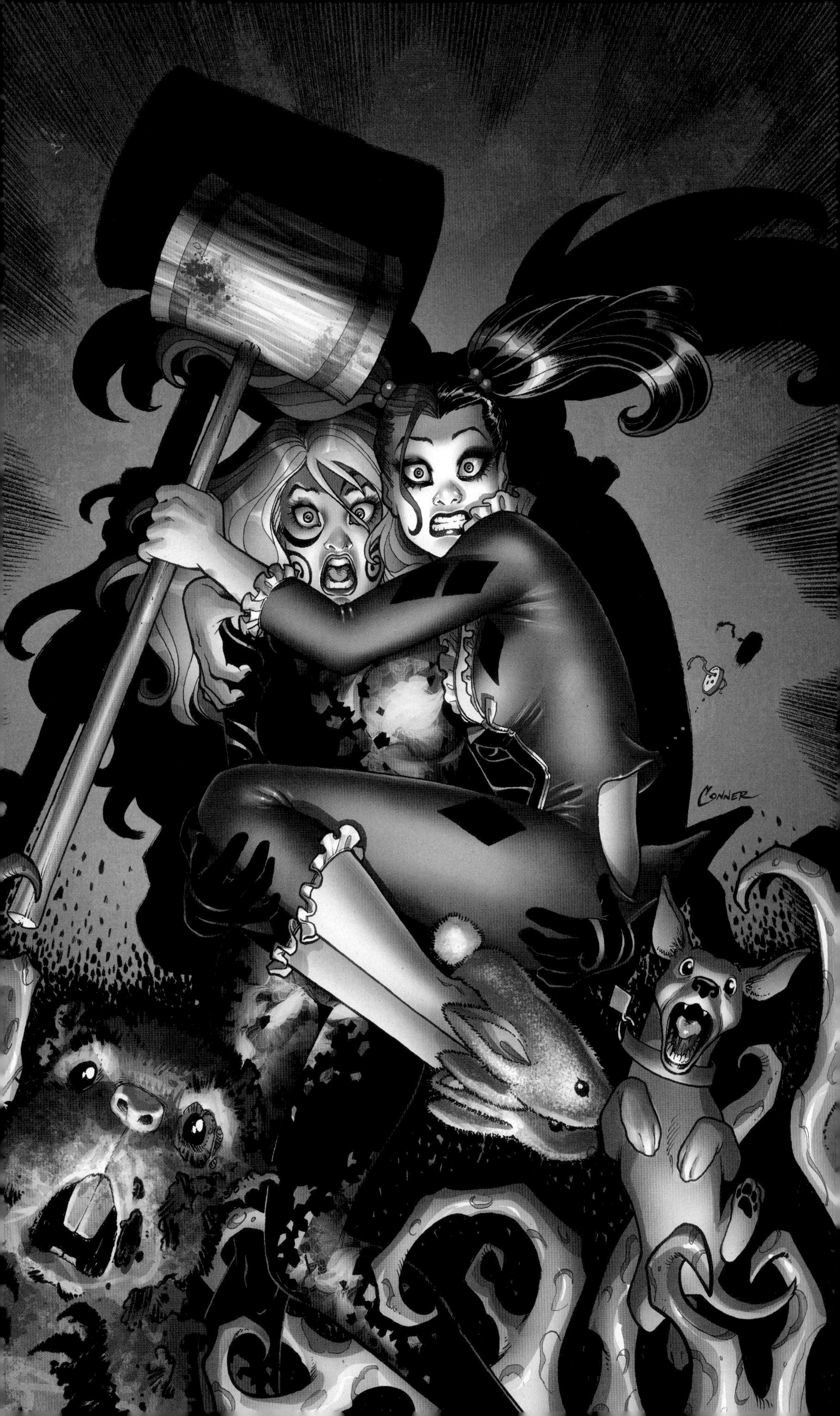
CONNER

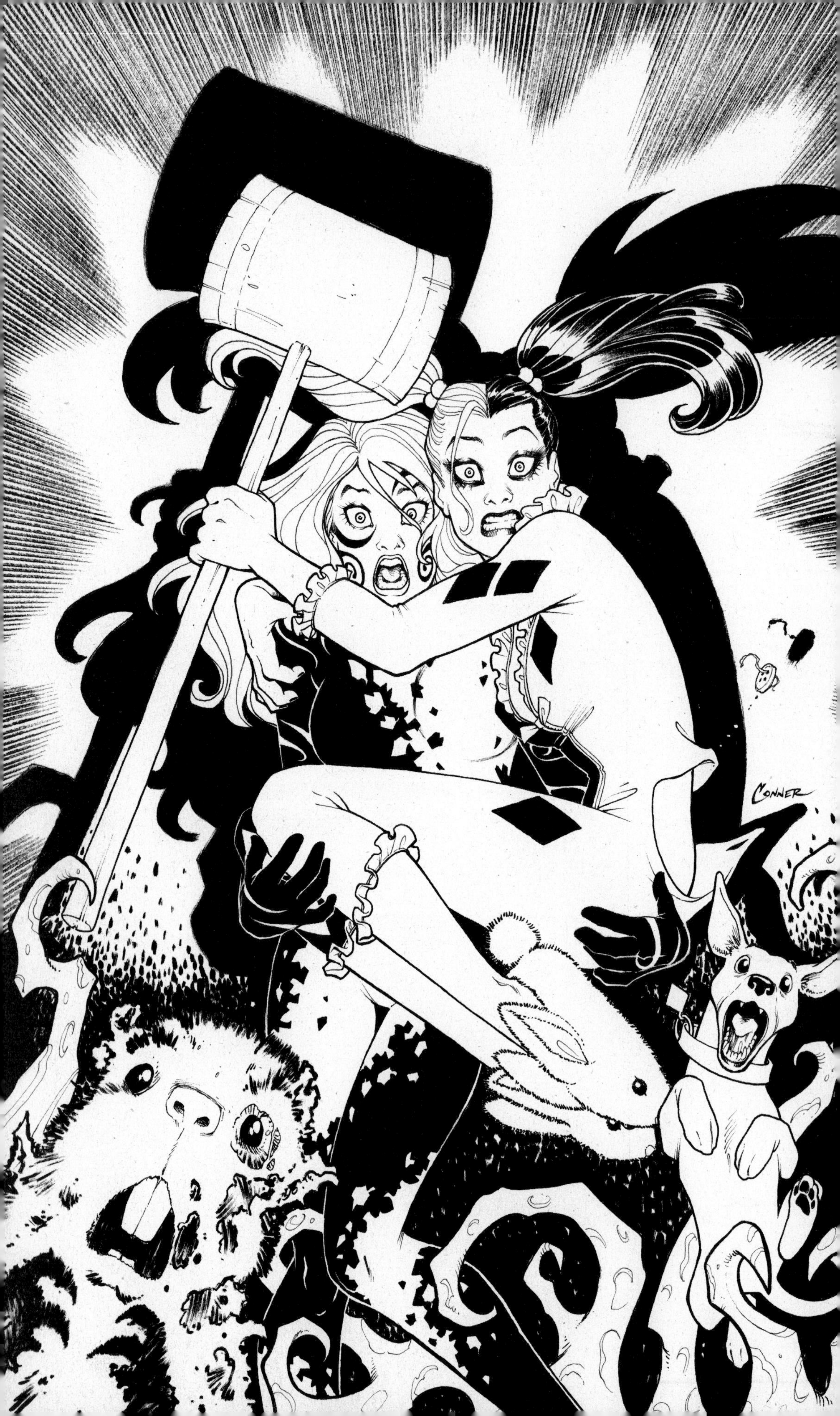
CONNER

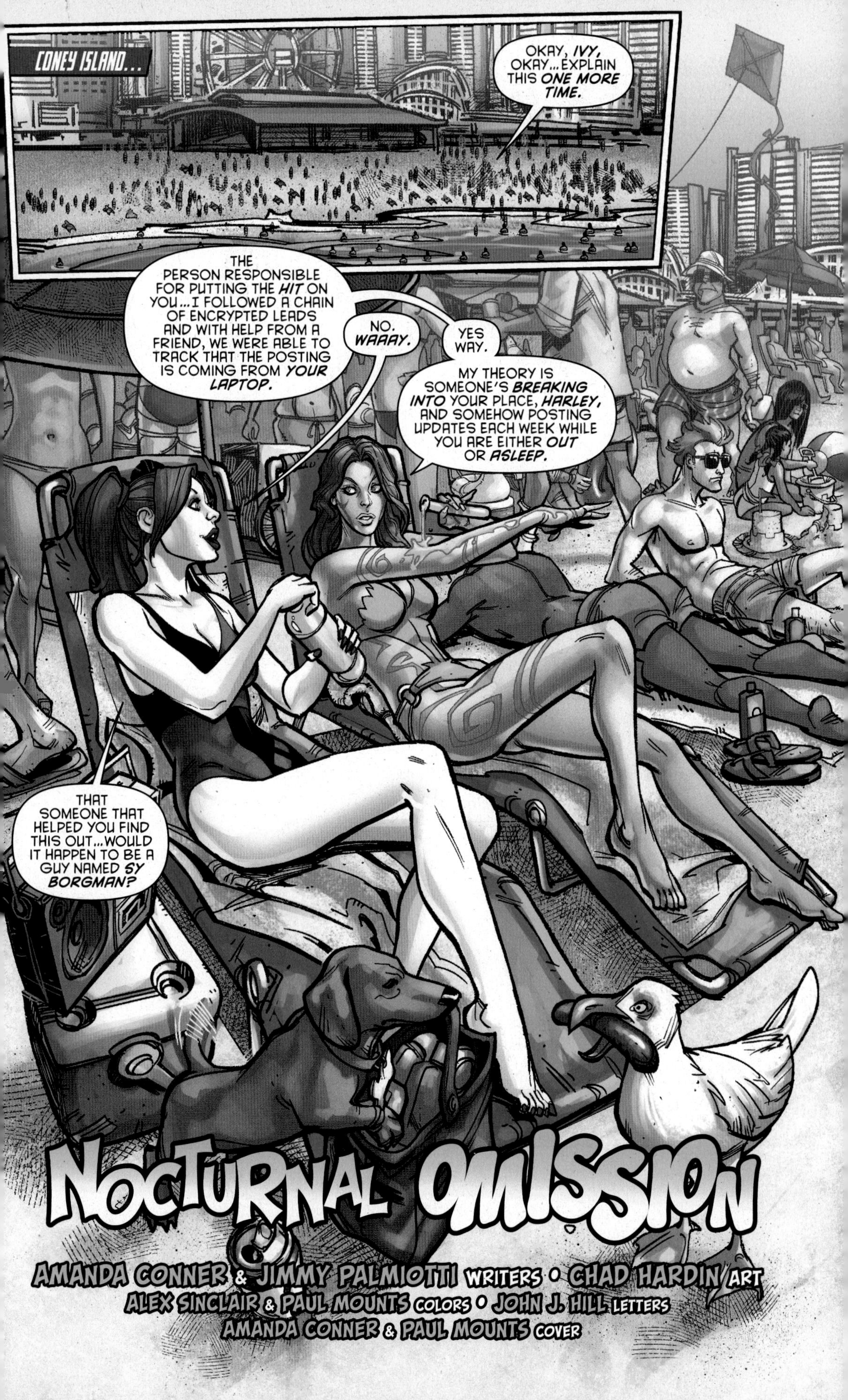
CONEY ISLAND...
OKAY, IVY, OKAY...EXPLAIN THIS ONE MORE TIME.
THE PERSON RESPONSIBLE FOR PUTTING THE HIT ON YOU...I FOLLOWED A CHAIN OF ENCRYPTED LEADS AND WITH HELP FROM A FRIEND, WE WERE ABLE TO TRACK THAT THE POSTING IS COMING FROM YOUR LAPTOP.
NO. WAAAY.
YES WAY.
MY THEORY IS SOMEONE'S BREAKING INTO YOUR PLACE, HARLEY, AND SOMEHOW POSTING UPDATES EACH WEEK WHILE YOU ARE EITHER OUT OR ASLEEP.
THAT SOMEONE THAT HELPED YOU FIND THIS OUT...WOULD IT HAPPEN TO BE A GUY NAMED SY BORGMAN?
NOCTURNAL OMISSION
AMANDA CONNER & JIMMY PALMIOTTI WRITERS • CHAD HARDIN ART
ALEX SINCLAIR & PAUL MOUNTS COLORS • JOHN J. HILL LETTERS
AMANDA CONNER & PAUL MOUNTS COVER

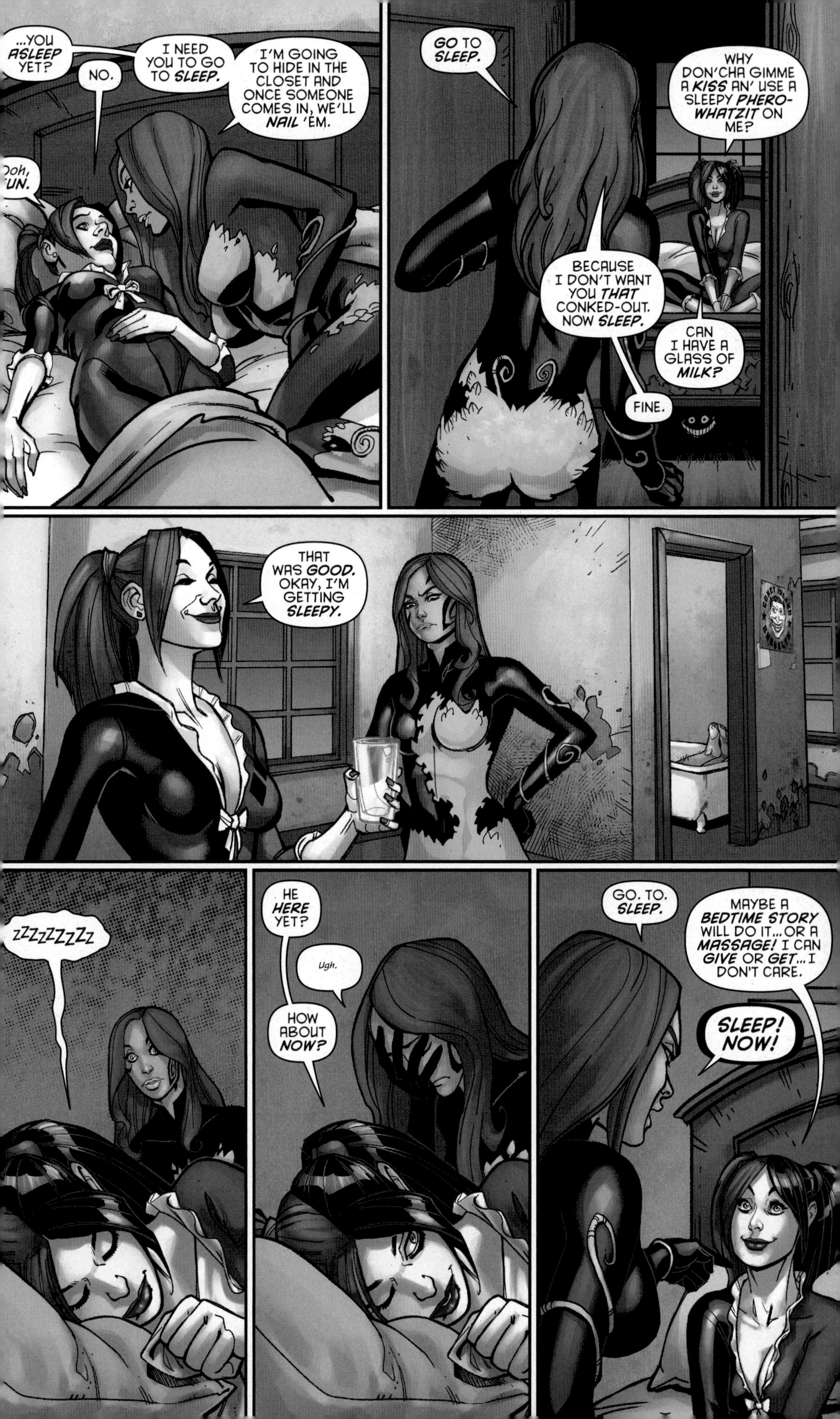
...YOU ASLEEP YET?
NO.
I NEED YOU TO GO TO SLEEP.
I'M GOING TO HIDE IN THE CLOSET AND ONCE SOMEONE COMES IN, WE'LL NAIL 'EM.
Ooh, FUN.
GO TO SLEEP.
WHY DON'CHA GIMME A KISS AN' USE A SLEEPY PHERO-WHATZIT ON ME?
BECAUSE I DON'T WANT YOU THAT CONKED-OUT. NOW SLEEP.
CAN I HAVE A GLASS OF MILK?
FINE.
THAT WAS GOOD. OKAY, I'M GETTING SLEEPY.
ZZZZZZZZZ
HE HERE YET?
Ugh.
HOW ABOUT NOW?
GO. TO. SLEEP.
MAYBE A BEDTIME STORY WILL DO IT...OR A MASSAGE! I CAN GIVE OR GET...I DON'T CARE.
SLEEP! NOW!

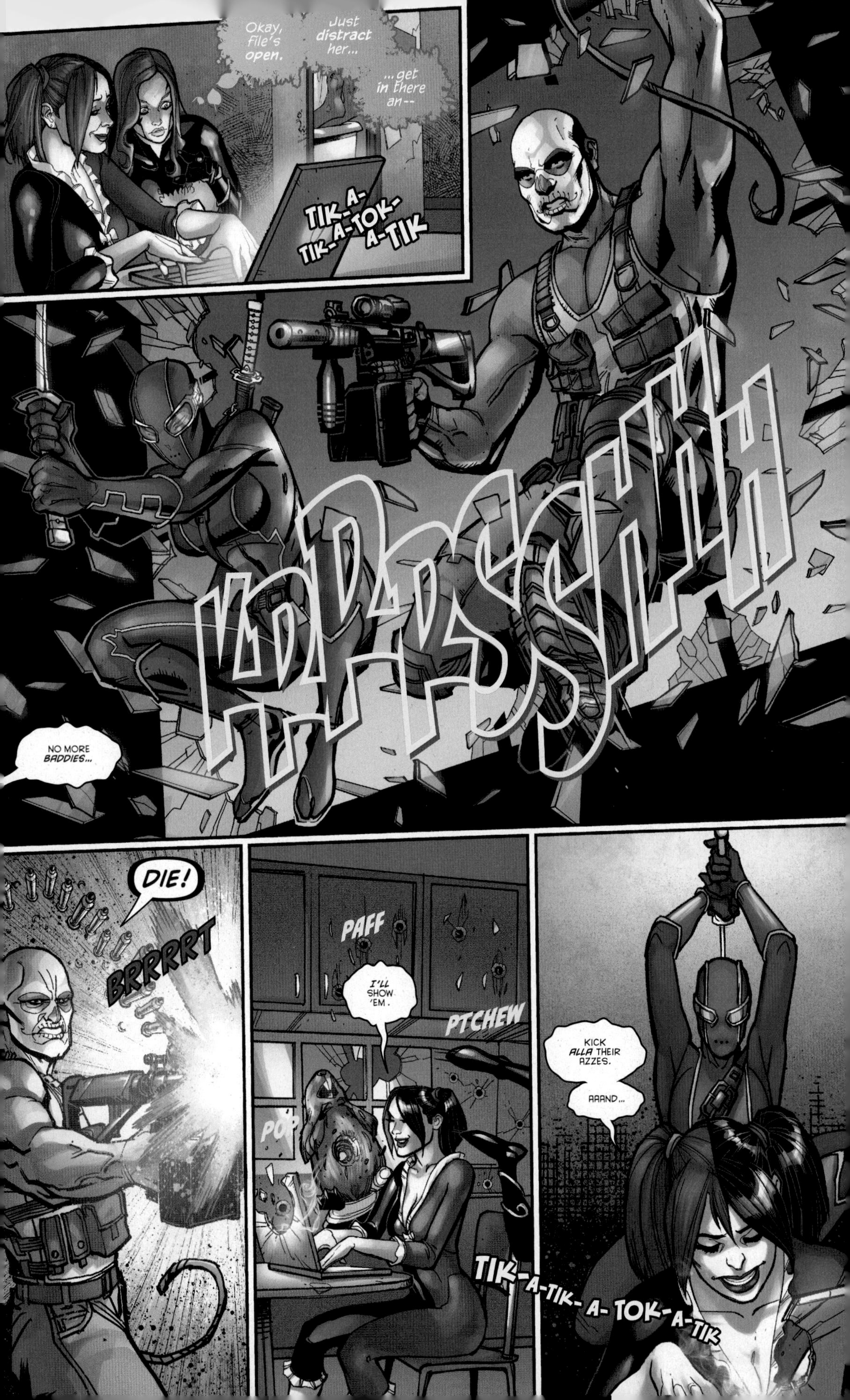

Okay, file's open.
Just distract her...
...get in there an--
TIK-A-TIK-A-TOK-A-TIK
NO MORE BADDIES...
KRRASSHHH
DIE!
BRRRRT
PAFF
I'LL SHOW 'EM.
PTCHEW
POP
KICK ALLA THEIR AZZES.
AAAND...
TIK-A-TIK-A-TOK-A-TIK

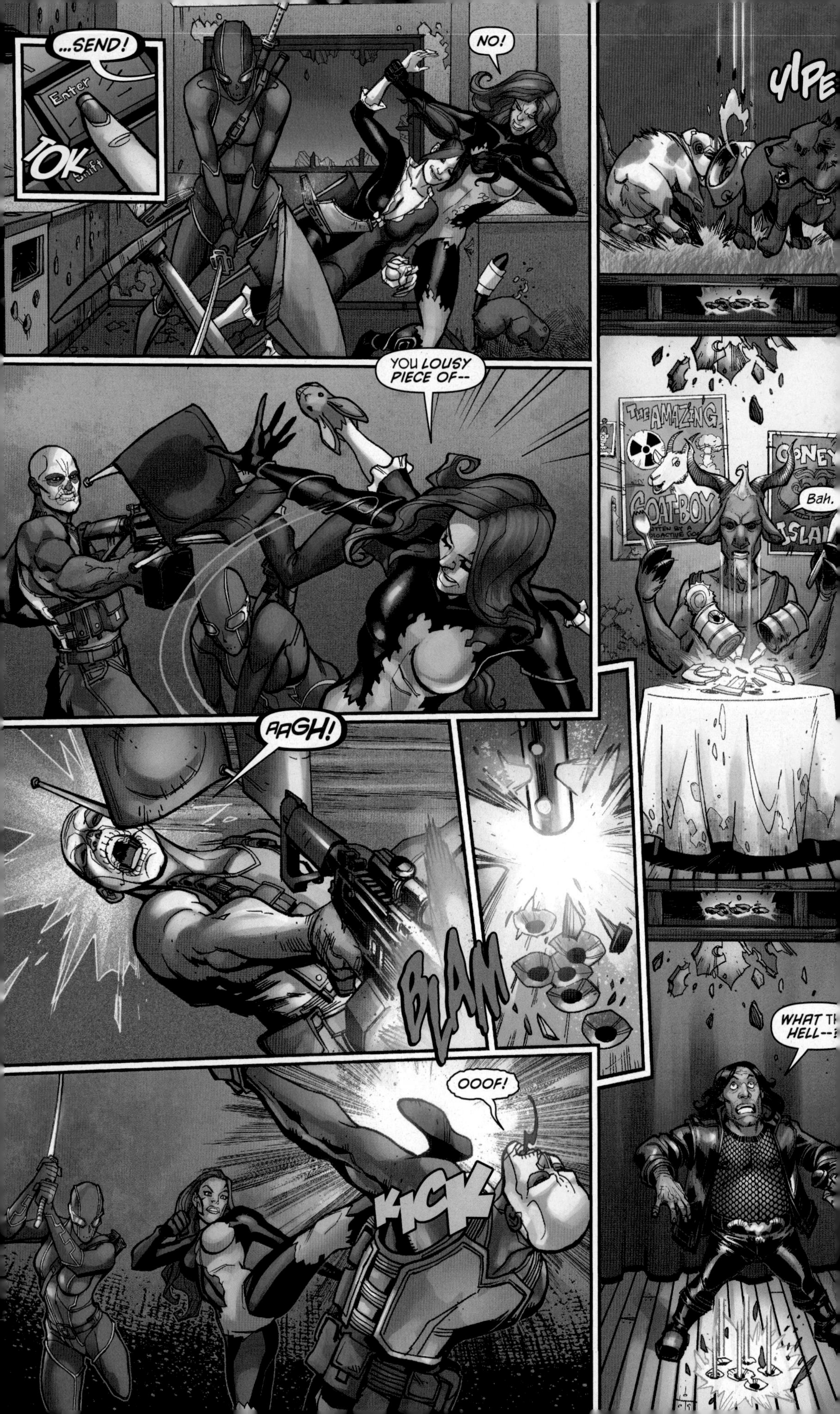
...SEND!
TOK
NO!
YIPE
YOU LOUSY PIECE OF--
THE AMAZING
GOAT-BOY
Bah.
AAGH!
BLAM
OOOF!
KICK
WHAT TH
HELL--

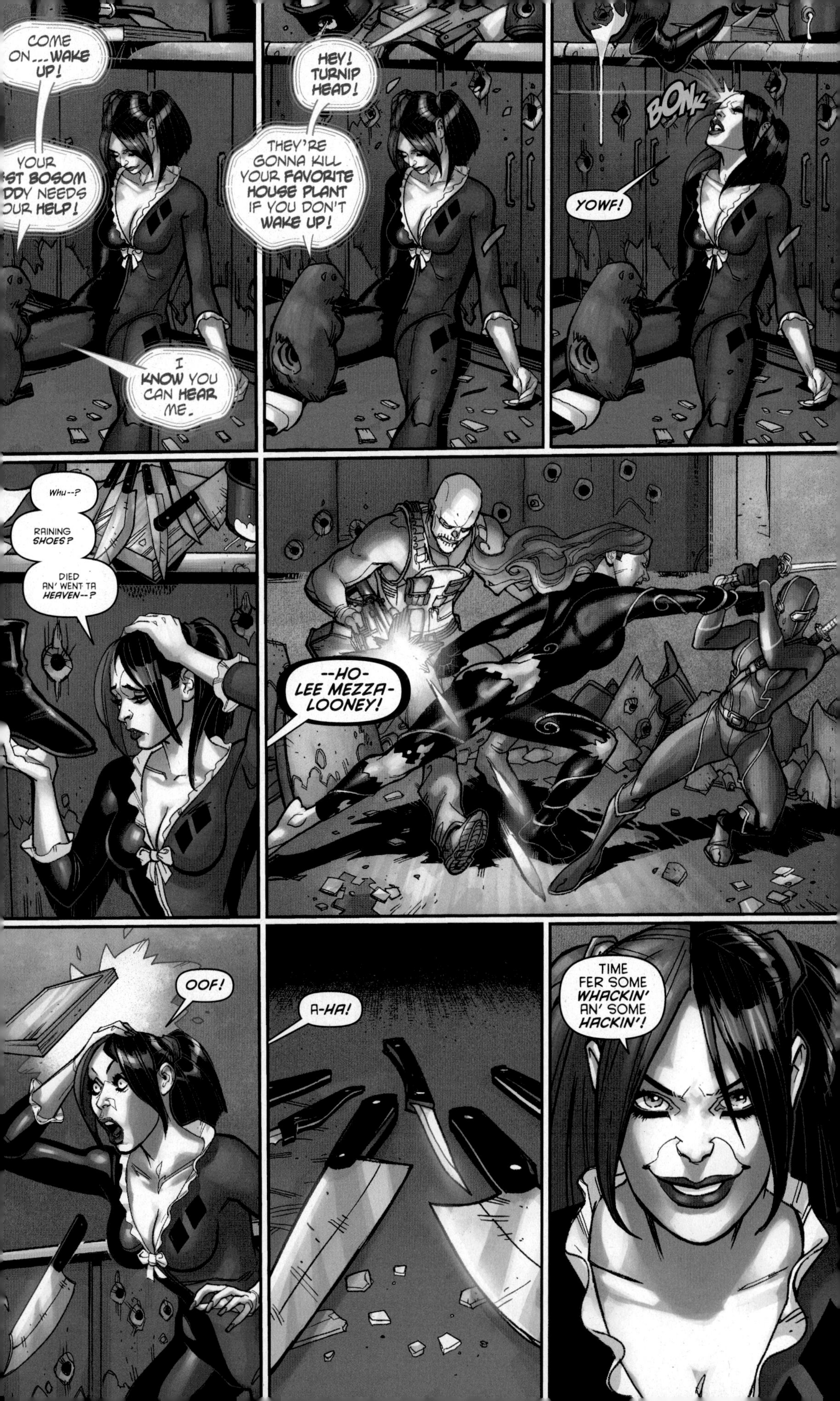

COME ON...WAKE UP!
YOUR ...ST BOSOM ...DDY NEEDS ...OUR HELP!
I KNOW YOU CAN HEAR ME.
HEY! TURNIP HEAD!
THEY'RE GONNA KILL YOUR FAVORITE HOUSE PLANT IF YOU DON'T WAKE UP!
BONK
YOWF!
Whu--?
RAINING SHOES?
DIED AN' WENT TA HEAVEN--?
--HO-LEE MEZZA-LOONEY!
OOF!
A-HA!
TIME FER SOME WHACKIN' AN' SOME HACKIN'!

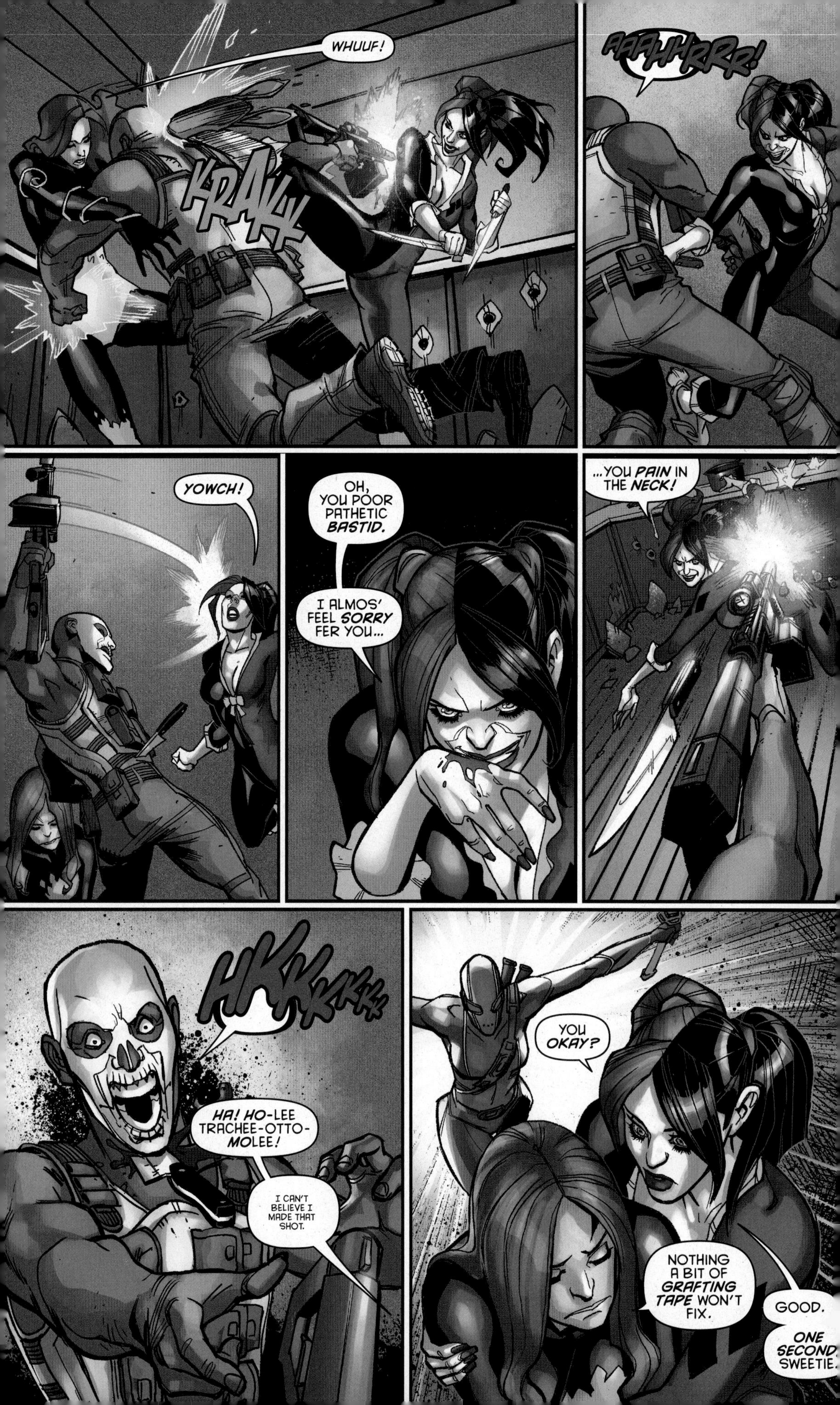
WHUUF!
KRAKK
AAAHHRRR!
YOWCH!
OH, YOU POOR PATHETIC BASTID.
I ALMOS' FEEL SORRY FER YOU...
...YOU PAIN IN THE NECK!
HKKKKKK
HA! HO-LEE TRACHEE-OTTO-MOLEE!
I CAN'T BELIEVE I MADE THAT SHOT.
YOU OKAY?
NOTHING A BIT OF GRAFTING TAPE WON'T FIX.
GOOD.
ONE SECOND SWEETIE.

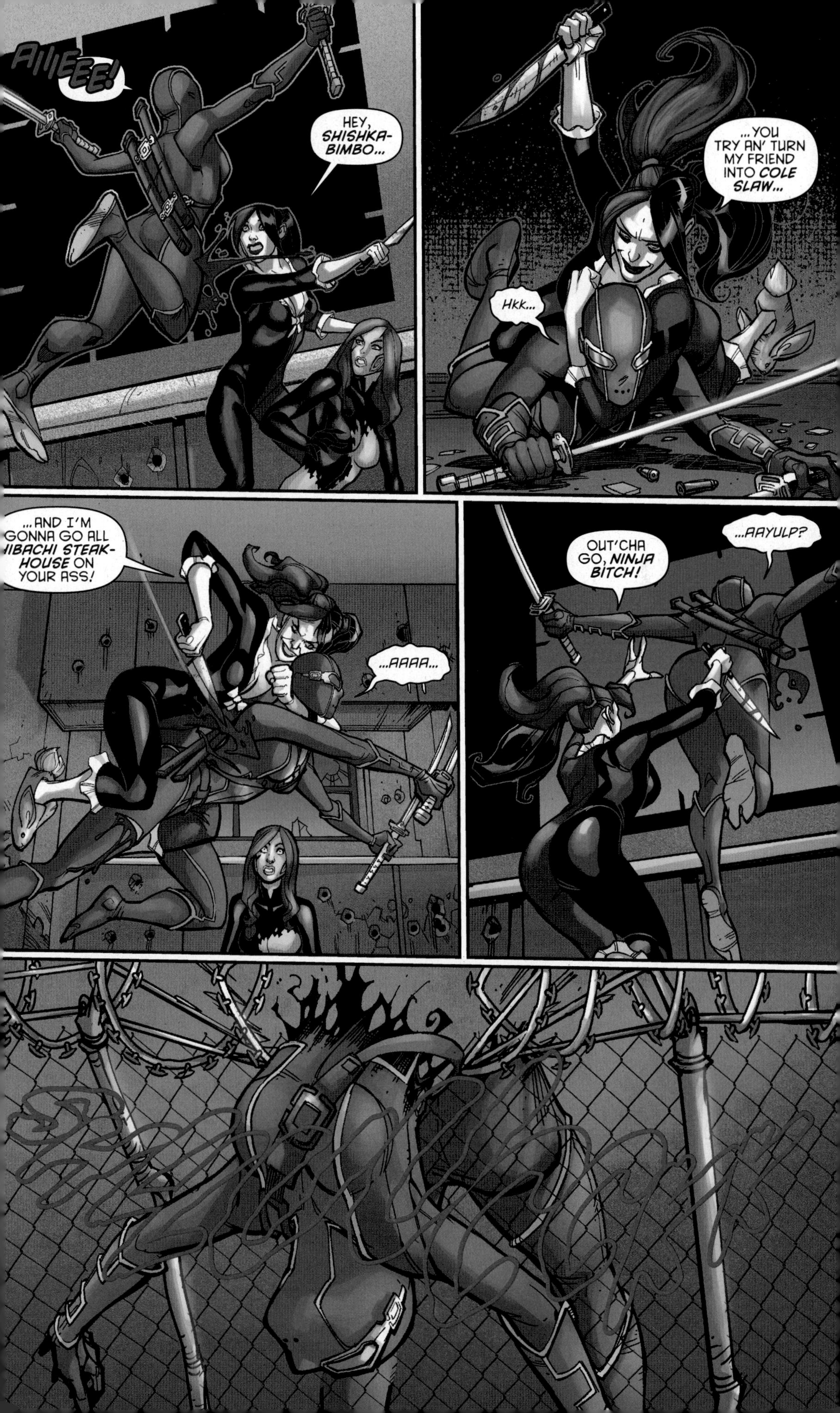
AIIIEEE!
HEY, SHISHKA-BIMBO...
...YOU TRY AN' TURN MY FRIEND INTO COLE SLAW...
HKK...
...AND I'M GONNA GO ALL HIBACHI STEAK-HOUSE ON YOUR ASS!
...AAAA...
OUT'CHA GO, NINJA BITCH!
...AAYULP?

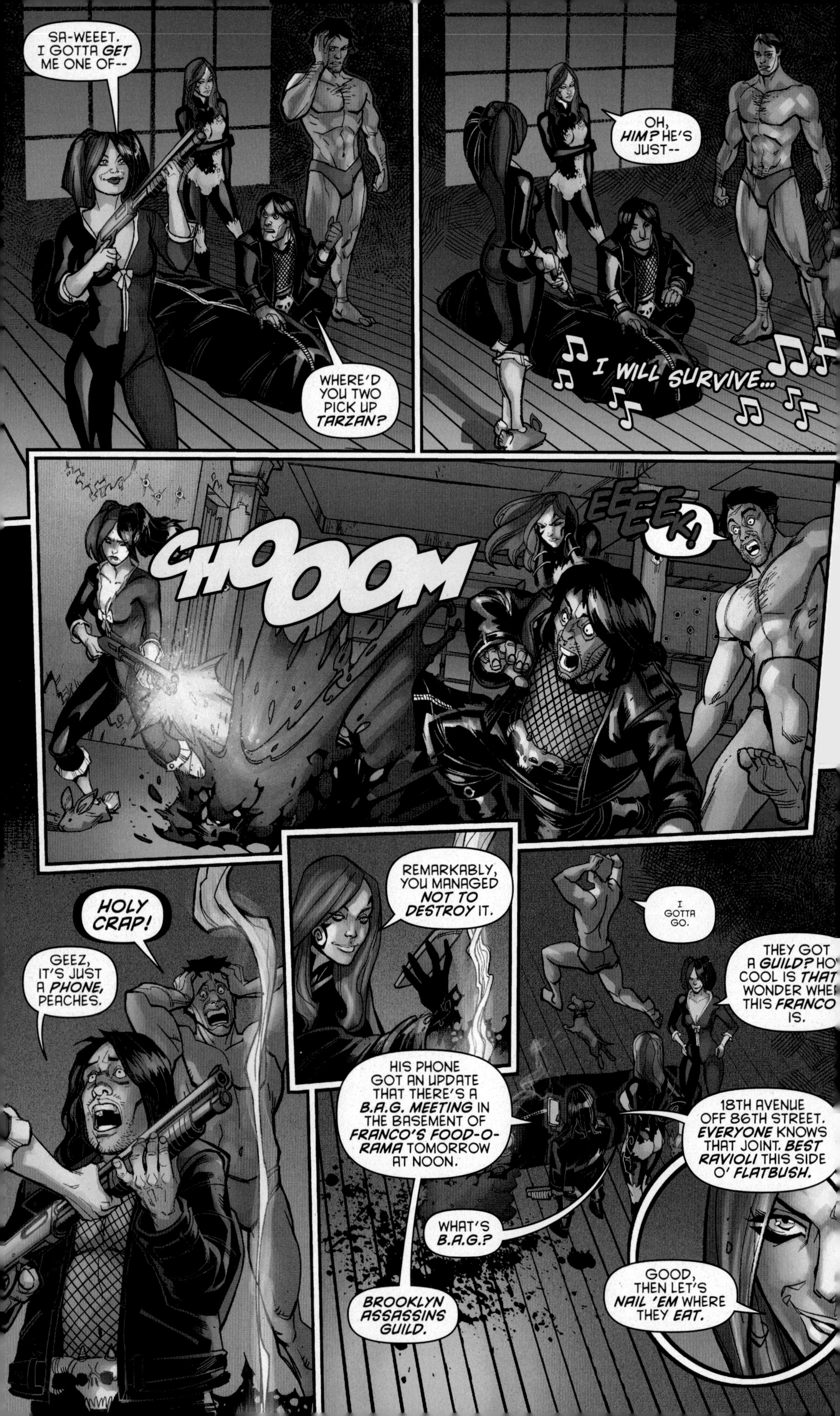

SA-WEEET. I GOTTA GET ME ONE OF--
WHERE'D YOU TWO PICK UP TARZAN?
OH, HIM? HE'S JUST--
I WILL SURVIVE...
CHOOOOM
EEEEEK!
HOLY CRAP!
GEEZ, IT'S JUST A PHONE, PEACHES.
REMARKABLY, YOU MANAGED NOT TO DESTROY IT.
I GOTTA GO.
HIS PHONE GOT AN UPDATE THAT THERE'S A B.A.G. MEETING IN THE BASEMENT OF FRANCO'S FOOD-O-RAMA TOMORROW AT NOON.
WHAT'S B.A.G.?
BROOKLYN ASSASSINS GUILD.
18TH AVENUE OFF 86TH STREET. EVERYONE KNOWS THAT JOINT. BEST RAVIOLI THIS SIDE O' FLATBUSH.
GOOD, THEN LET'S NAIL 'EM WHERE THEY EAT.

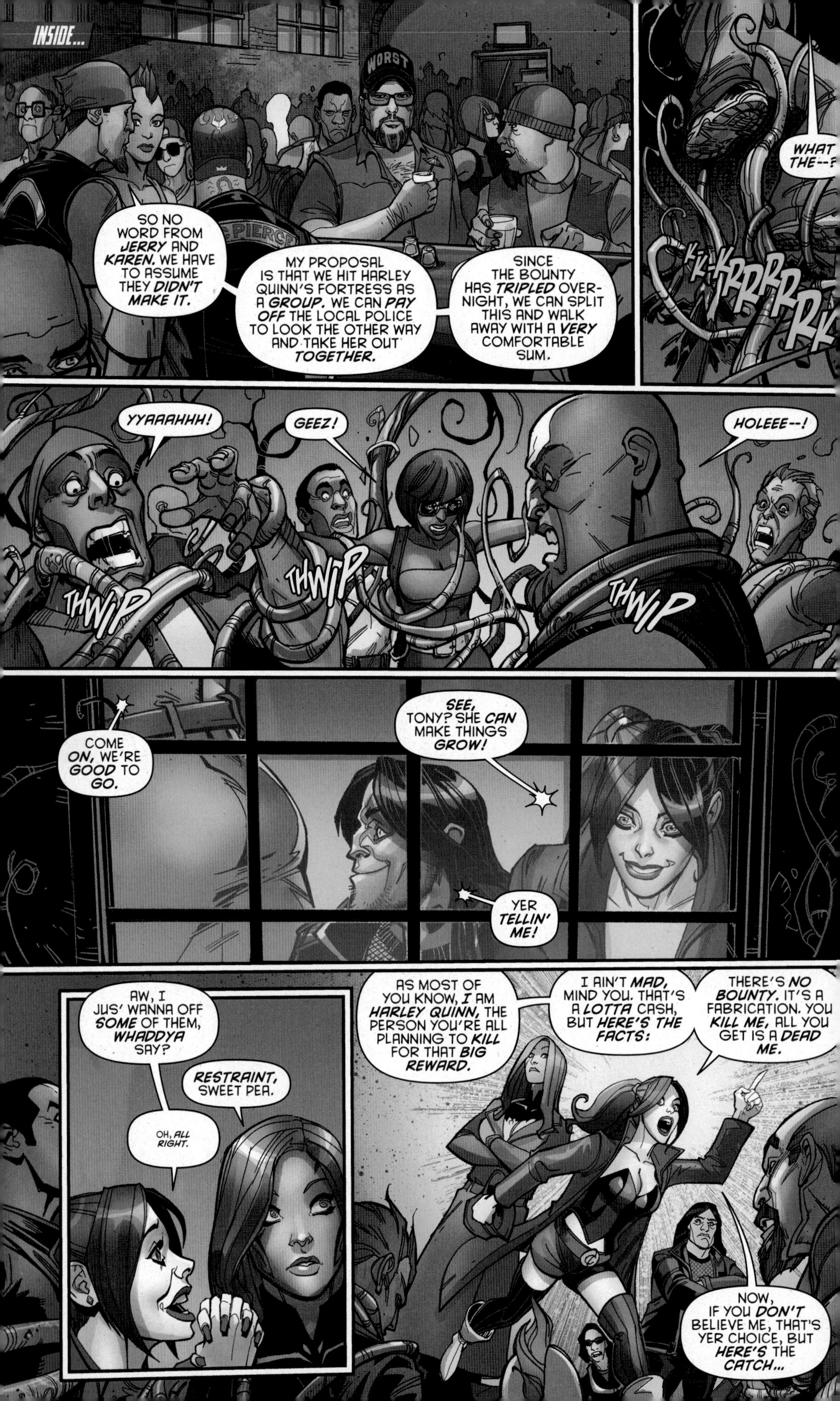
INSIDE...
SO NO WORD FROM JERRY AND KAREN. WE HAVE TO ASSUME THEY DIDN'T MAKE IT.
MY PROPOSAL IS THAT WE HIT HARLEY QUINN'S FORTRESS AS A GROUP. WE CAN PAY OFF THE LOCAL POLICE TO LOOK THE OTHER WAY AND TAKE HER OUT TOGETHER.
SINCE THE BOUNTY HAS TRIPLED OVER-NIGHT, WE CAN SPLIT THIS AND WALK AWAY WITH A VERY COMFORTABLE SUM.
WORST
WHAT THE--?
KK-KRRRRRKK
YYAAAHHH!
GEEZ!
HOLEEE--!
THWIP
THWIP
THWIP
COME ON, WE'RE GOOD TO GO.
SEE, TONY? SHE CAN MAKE THINGS GROW!
YER TELLIN' ME!
AW, I JUS' WANNA OFF SOME OF THEM, WHADDYA SAY?
RESTRAINT, SWEET PEA.
OH, ALL RIGHT.
AS MOST OF YOU KNOW, I AM HARLEY QUINN, THE PERSON YOU'RE ALL PLANNING TO KILL FOR THAT BIG REWARD.
I AIN'T MAD, MIND YOU. THAT'S A LOTTA CASH, BUT HERE'S THE FACTS:
THERE'S NO BOUNTY. IT'S A FABRICATION. YOU KILL ME, ALL YOU GET IS A DEAD ME.
NOW, IF YOU DON'T BELIEVE ME, THAT'S YER CHOICE, BUT HERE'S THE CATCH...

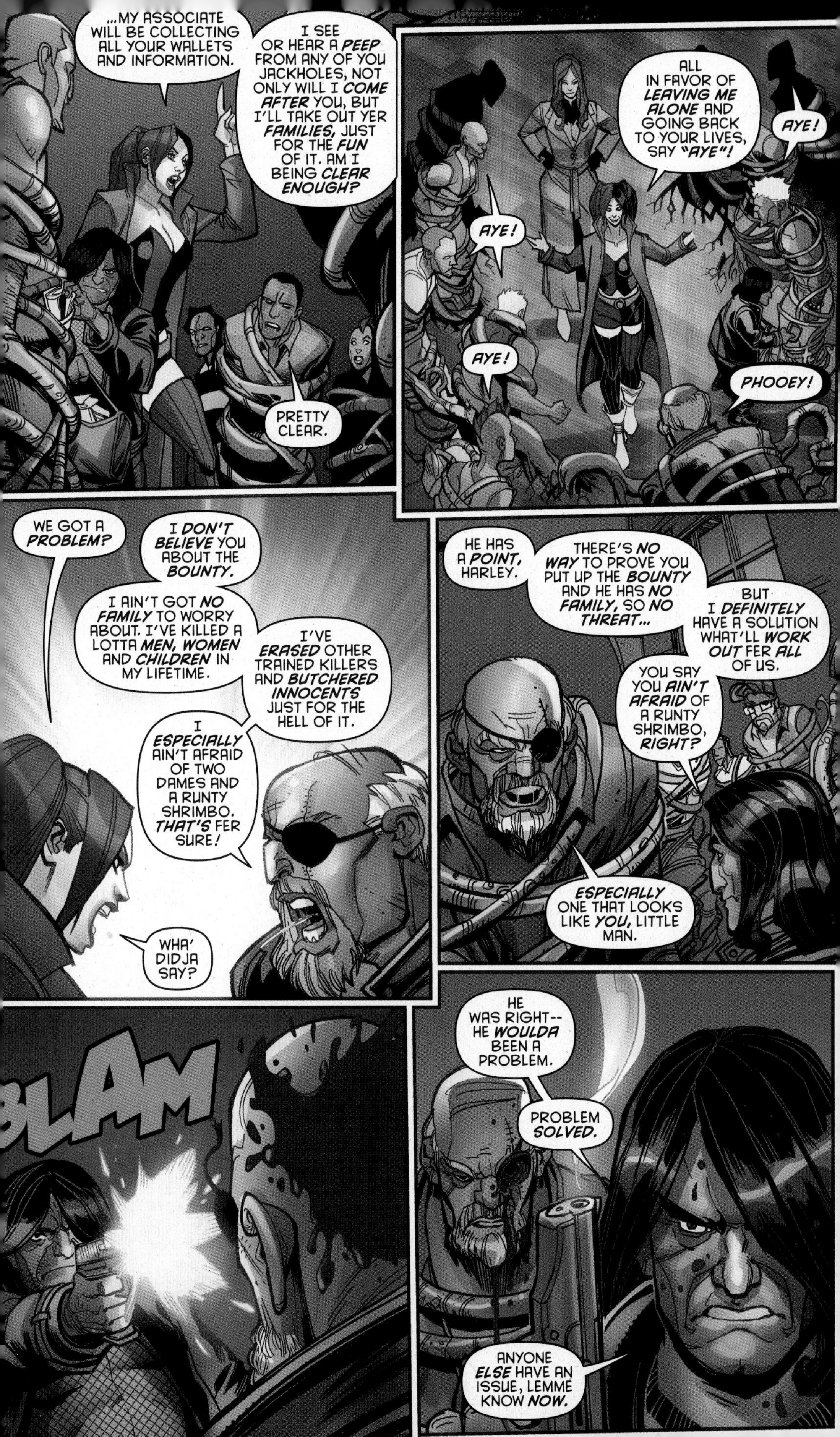
...MY ASSOCIATE WILL BE COLLECTING ALL YOUR WALLETS AND INFORMATION.
I SEE OR HEAR A PEEP FROM ANY OF YOU JACKHOLES, NOT ONLY WILL I COME AFTER YOU, BUT I'LL TAKE OUT YER FAMILIES, JUST FOR THE FUN OF IT. AM I BEING CLEAR ENOUGH?
PRETTY CLEAR.
ALL IN FAVOR OF LEAVING ME ALONE AND GOING BACK TO YOUR LIVES, SAY "AYE"!
AYE!
AYE!
AYE!
PHOOEY!
WE GOT A PROBLEM?
I DON'T BELIEVE YOU ABOUT THE BOUNTY.
I AIN'T GOT NO FAMILY TO WORRY ABOUT. I'VE KILLED A LOTTA MEN, WOMEN AND CHILDREN IN MY LIFETIME.
I'VE ERASED OTHER TRAINED KILLERS AND BUTCHERED INNOCENTS JUST FOR THE HELL OF IT.
I ESPECIALLY AIN'T AFRAID OF TWO DAMES AND A RUNTY SHRIMBO. THAT'S FER SURE!
WHA' DIDJA SAY?
HE HAS A POINT, HARLEY.
THERE'S NO WAY TO PROVE YOU PUT UP THE BOUNTY AND HE HAS NO FAMILY, SO NO THREAT...
BUT I DEFINITELY HAVE A SOLUTION WHAT'LL WORK OUT FER ALL OF US.
YOU SAY YOU AIN'T AFRAID OF A RUNTY SHRIMBO, RIGHT?
ESPECIALLY ONE THAT LOOKS LIKE YOU, LITTLE MAN.
BLAM
HE WAS RIGHT-- HE WOULDA BEEN A PROBLEM.
PROBLEM SOLVED.
ANYONE ELSE HAVE AN ISSUE, LEMME KNOW NOW.

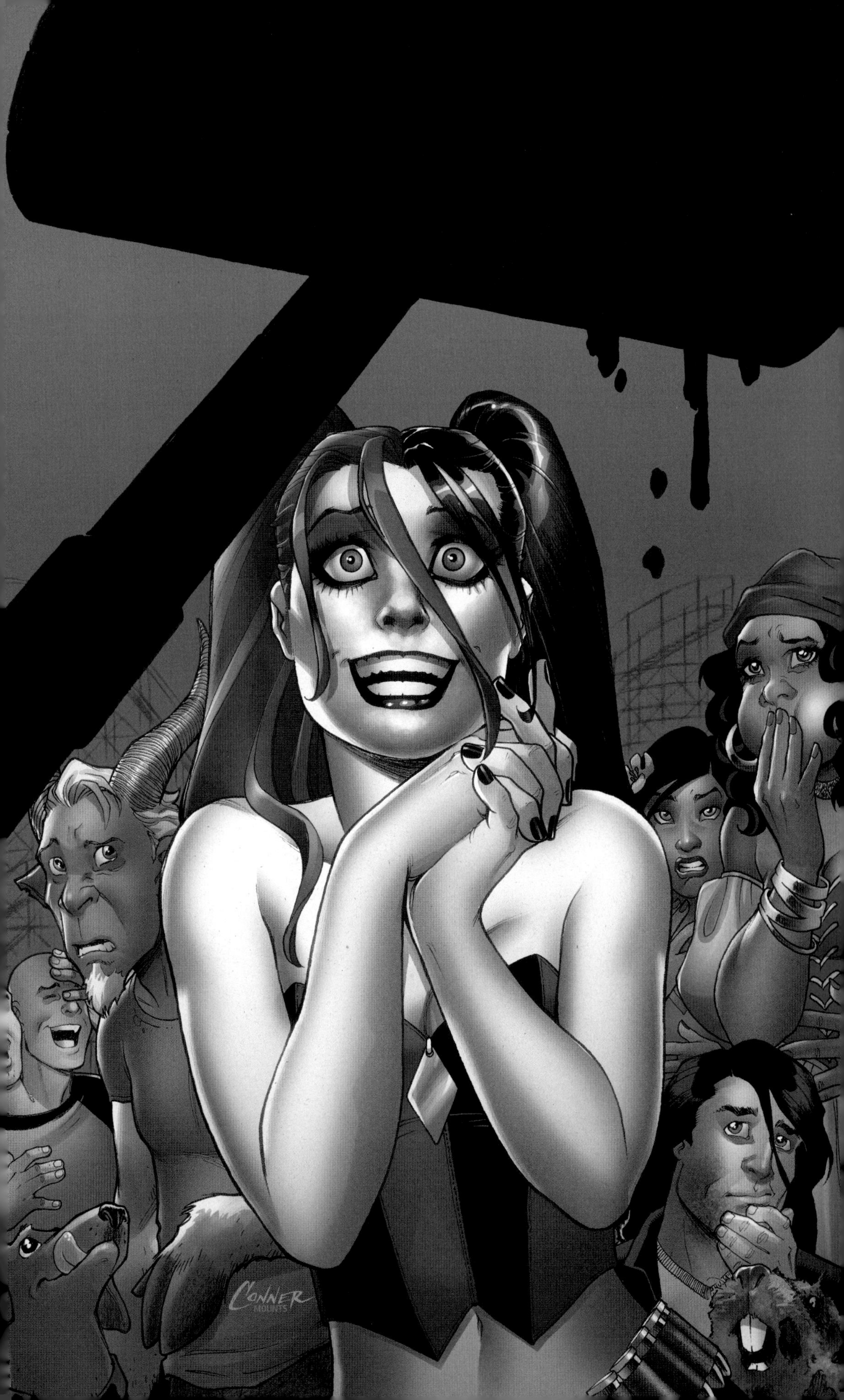
CONNER

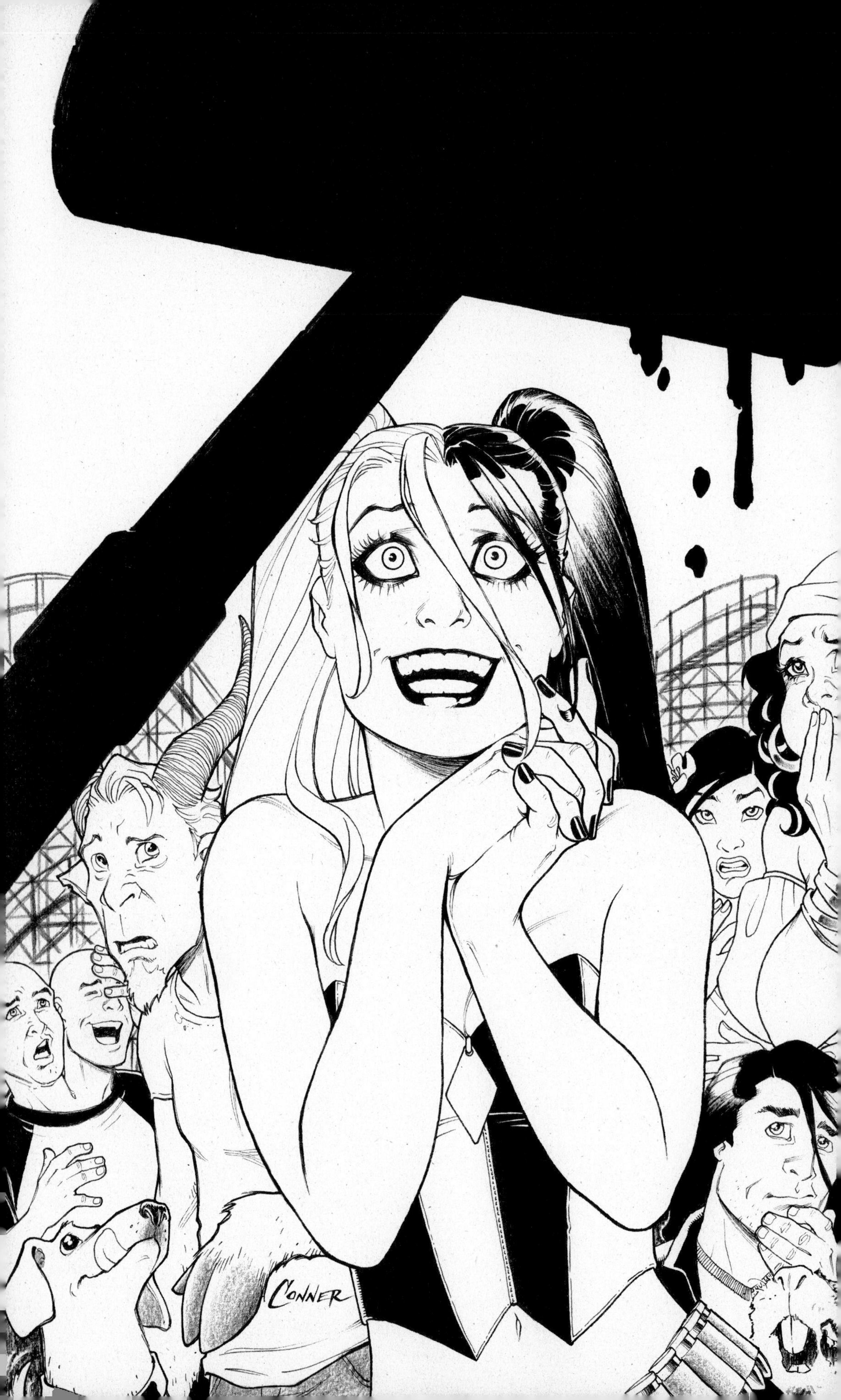
CONNER

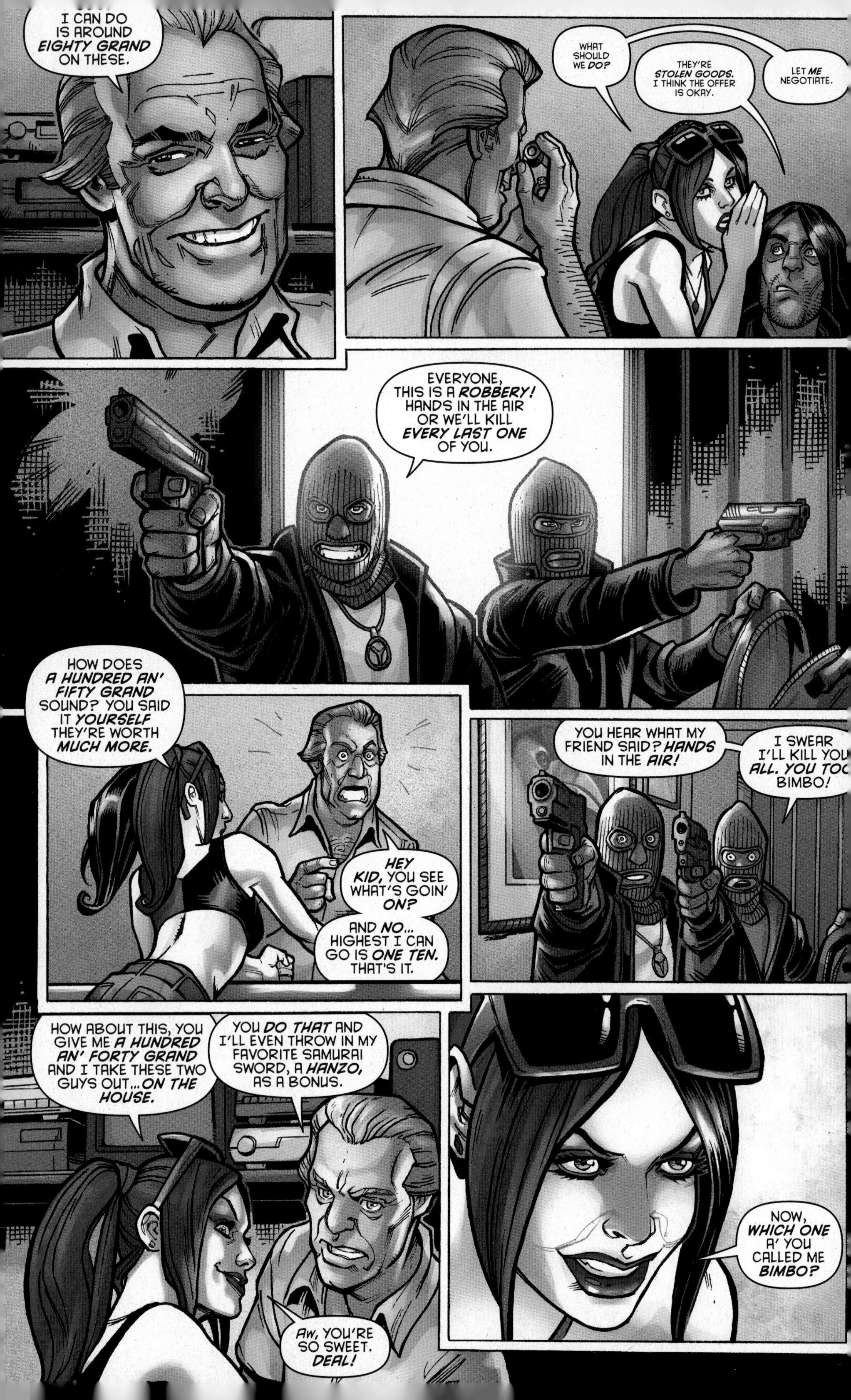

I CAN DO IS AROUND EIGHTY GRAND ON THESE.
WHAT SHOULD WE DO?
THEY'RE STOLEN GOODS. I THINK THE OFFER IS OKAY.
LET ME NEGOTIATE.
EVERYONE, THIS IS A ROBBERY! HANDS IN THE AIR OR WE'LL KILL EVERY LAST ONE OF YOU.
HOW DOES A HUNDRED AN' FIFTY GRAND SOUND? YOU SAID IT YOURSELF THEY'RE WORTH MUCH MORE.
HEY KID, YOU SEE WHAT'S GOIN' ON?
AND NO... HIGHEST I CAN GO IS ONE TEN. THAT'S IT.
YOU HEAR WHAT MY FRIEND SAID? HANDS IN THE AIR!
I SWEAR I'LL KILL YOU ALL. YOU TOO BIMBO!
HOW ABOUT THIS, YOU GIVE ME A HUNDRED AN' FORTY GRAND AND I TAKE THESE TWO GUYS OUT...ON THE HOUSE.
YOU DO THAT AND I'LL EVEN THROW IN MY FAVORITE SAMURAI SWORD, A HANZO, AS A BONUS.
AW, YOU'RE SO SWEET. DEAL!
NOW, WHICH ONE A' YOU CALLED ME BIMBO?

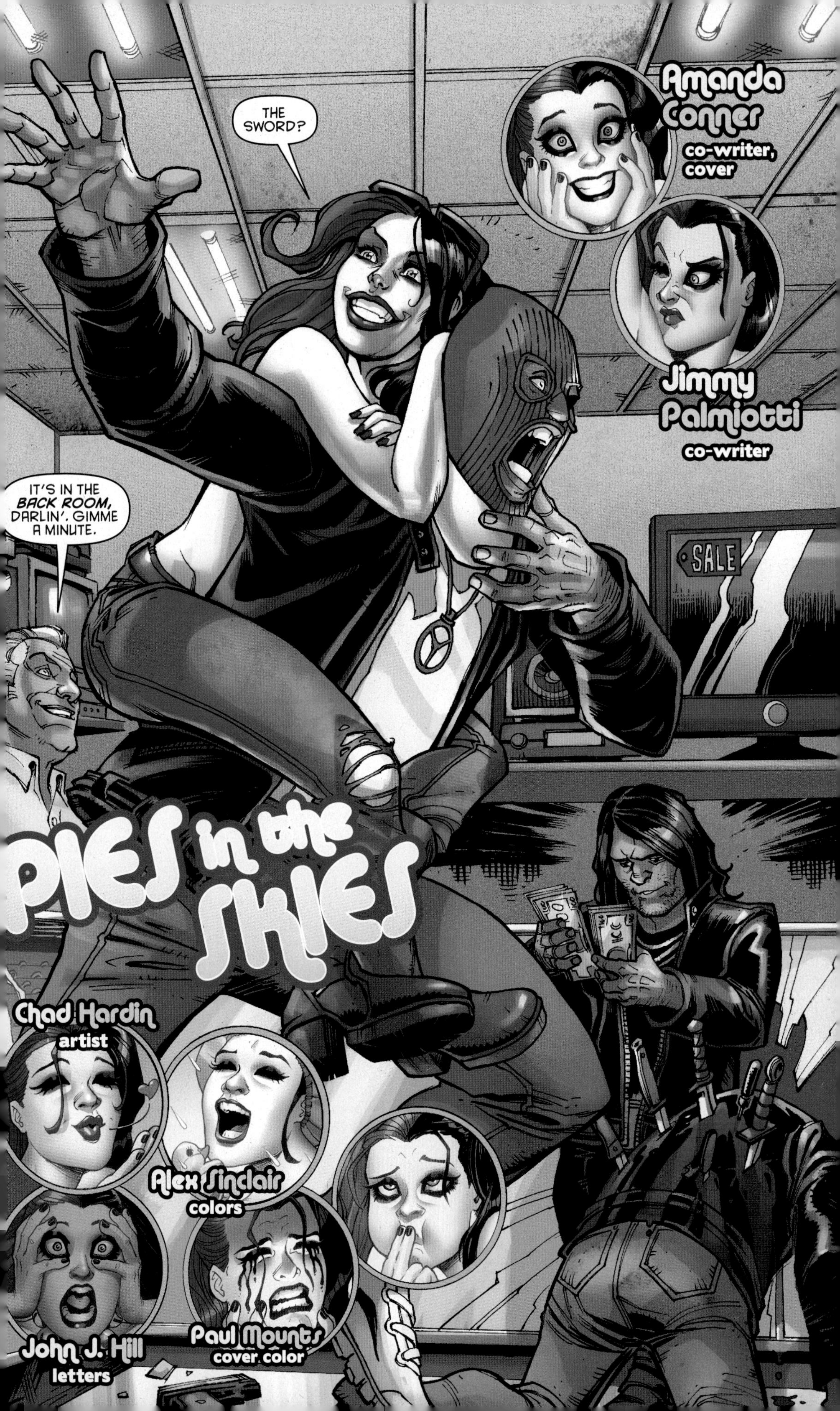
THE SWORD?
IT'S IN THE BACK ROOM, DARLIN'. GIMME A MINUTE.
SALE
Amanda Conner
co-writer, cover
Jimmy Palmiotti
co-writer
PIES in the SKIES
Chad Hardin
artist
Alex Sinclair
colors
John J. Hill
letters
Paul Mounts
cover color

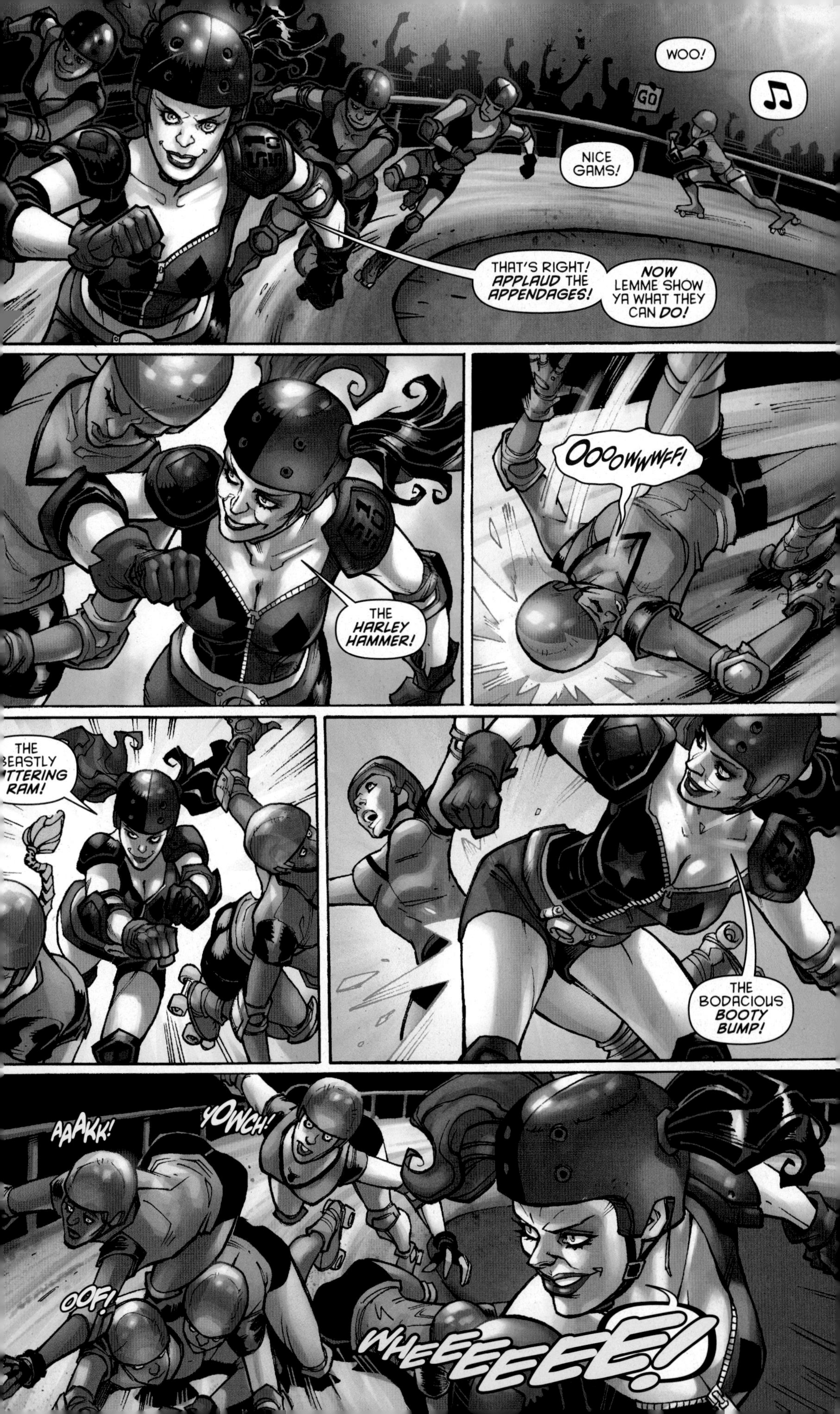
WOO!
♫
GO
NICE GAMS!
THAT'S RIGHT! APPLAUD THE APPENDAGES!
NOW LEMME SHOW YA WHAT THEY CAN DO!
THE HARLEY HAMMER!
OOOOWWWFF!
THE BEASTLY TTERING RAM!
THE BODACIOUS BOOTY BUMP!
AAAKK!
YOWCH!
OOF!
WHEEEEEEE!

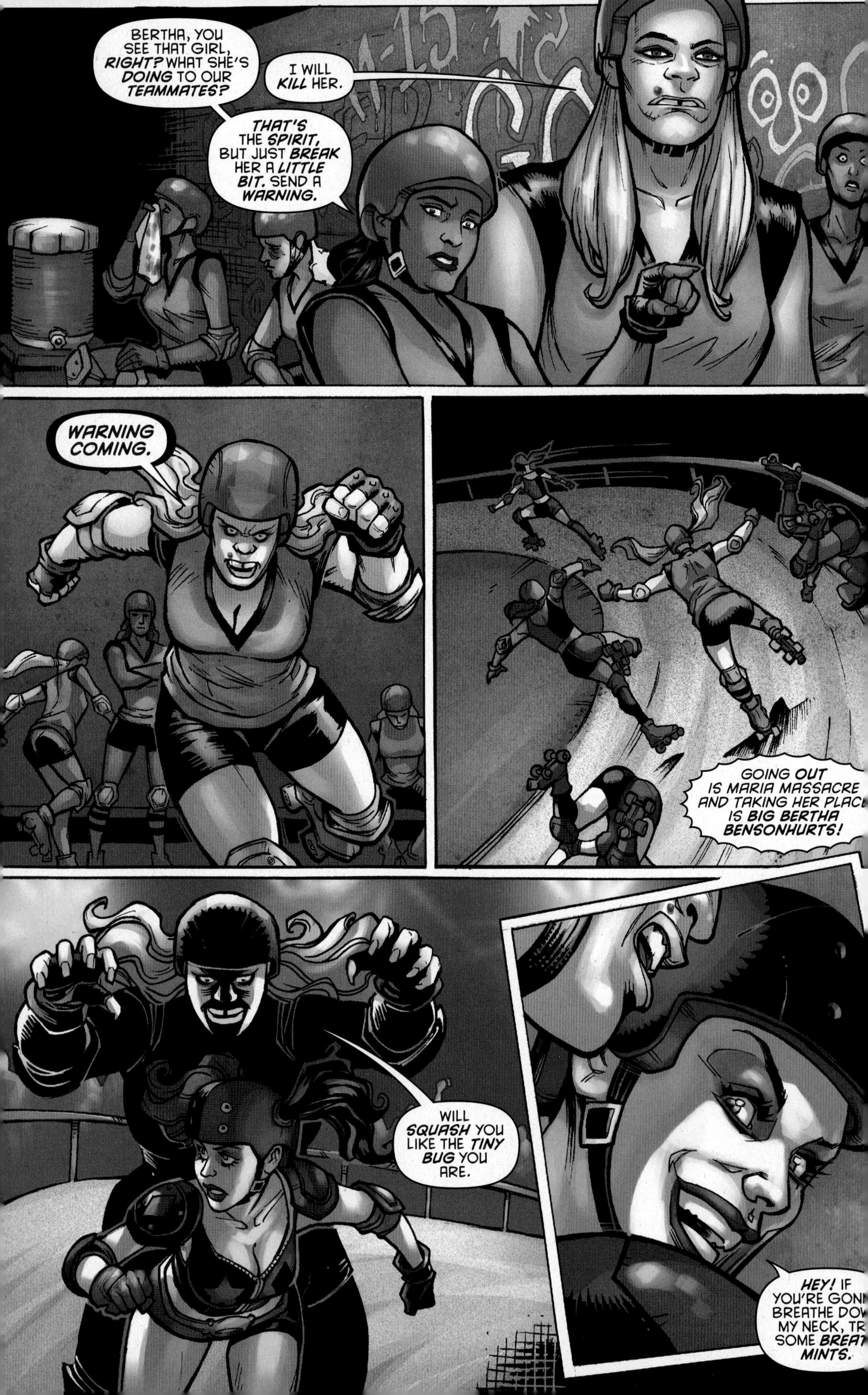
BERTHA, YOU SEE THAT GIRL, RIGHT? WHAT SHE'S DOING TO OUR TEAMMATES?
I WILL KILL HER.
THAT'S THE SPIRIT, BUT JUST BREAK HER A LITTLE BIT. SEND A WARNING.
WARNING COMING.
GOING OUT IS MARIA MASSACRE AND TAKING HER PLAC
IS BIG BERTHA BENSONHURTS!
WILL SQUASH YOU LIKE THE TINY BUG YOU ARE.
HEY! IF YOU'RE GON
BREATHE DO
MY NECK, TR
SOME BREA
MINTS.

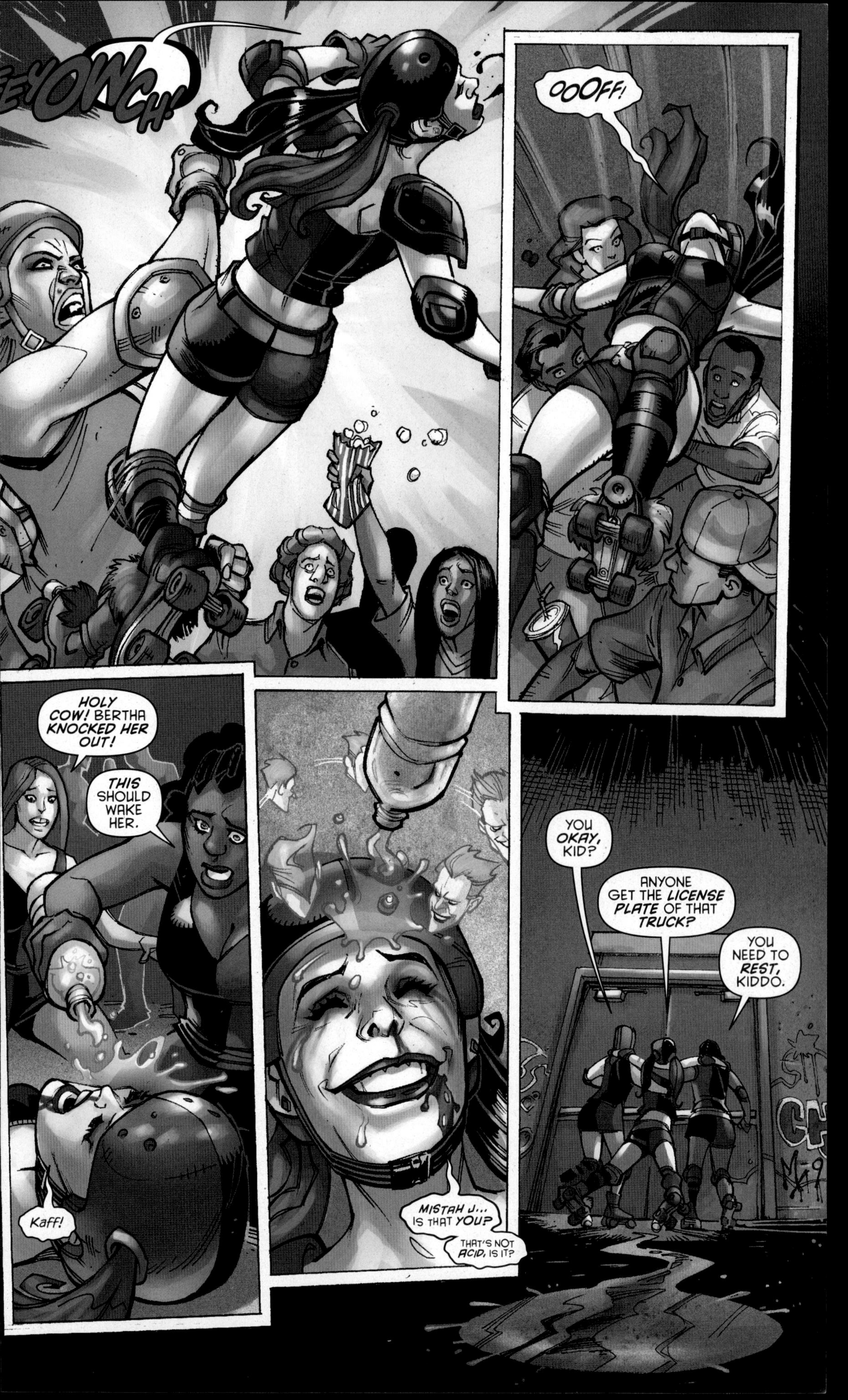
EEYOWCH!
OOOFF!
HOLY COW! BERTHA KNOCKED HER OUT!
THIS SHOULD WAKE HER.
Kaff!
MISTAH J... IS THAT YOU?
THAT'S NOT ACID, IS IT?
YOU OKAY, KID?
ANYONE GET THE LICENSE PLATE OF THAT TRUCK?
YOU NEED TO REST, KIDDO.

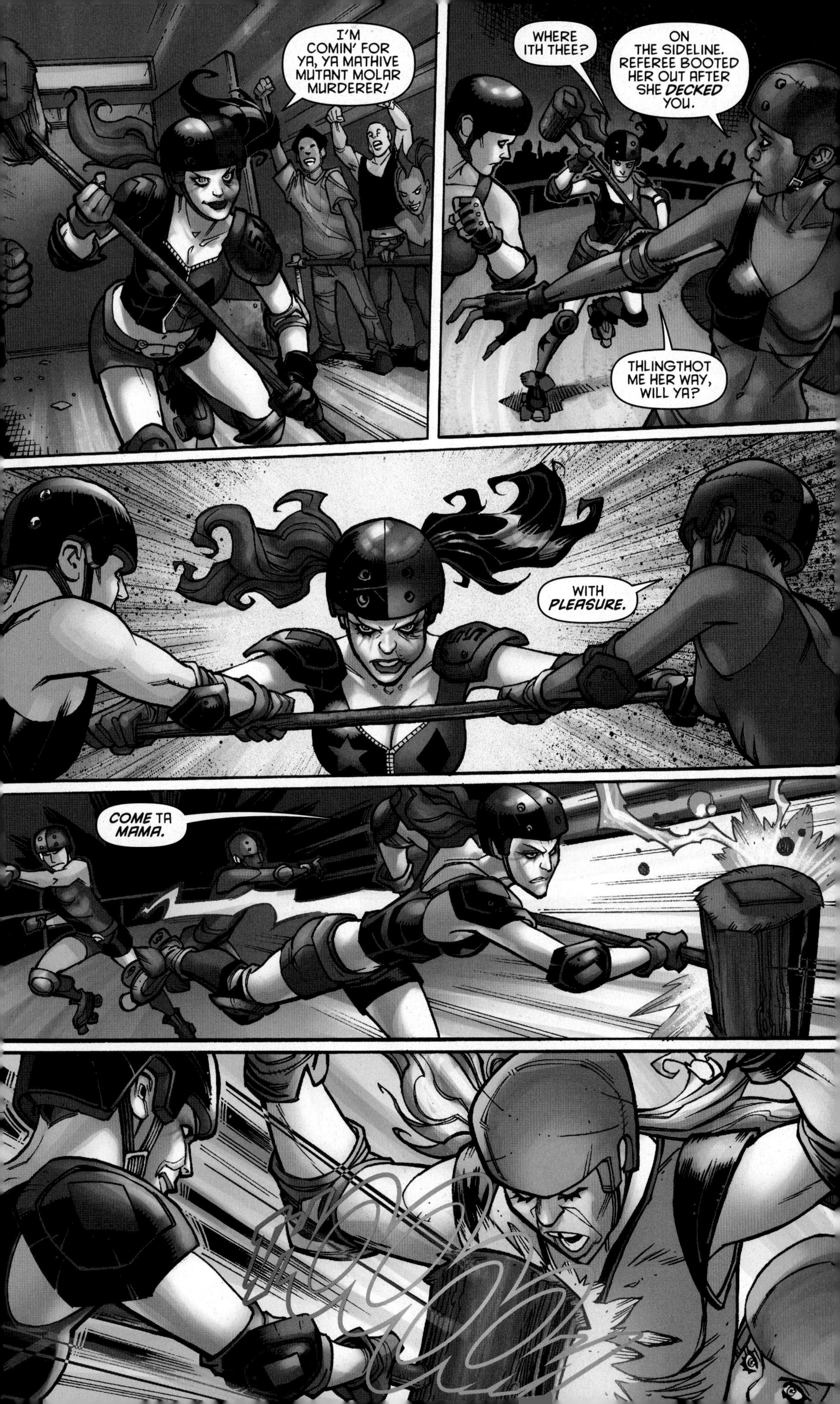
I'M COMIN' FOR YA, YA MATHIVE MUTANT MOLAR MURDERER!
WHERE ITH THEE?
ON THE SIDELINE. REFEREE BOOTED HER OUT AFTER SHE *DECKED* YOU.
THLINGTHOT ME HER WAY, WILL YA?
WITH *PLEASURE.*
*COME* TA *MAMA.*

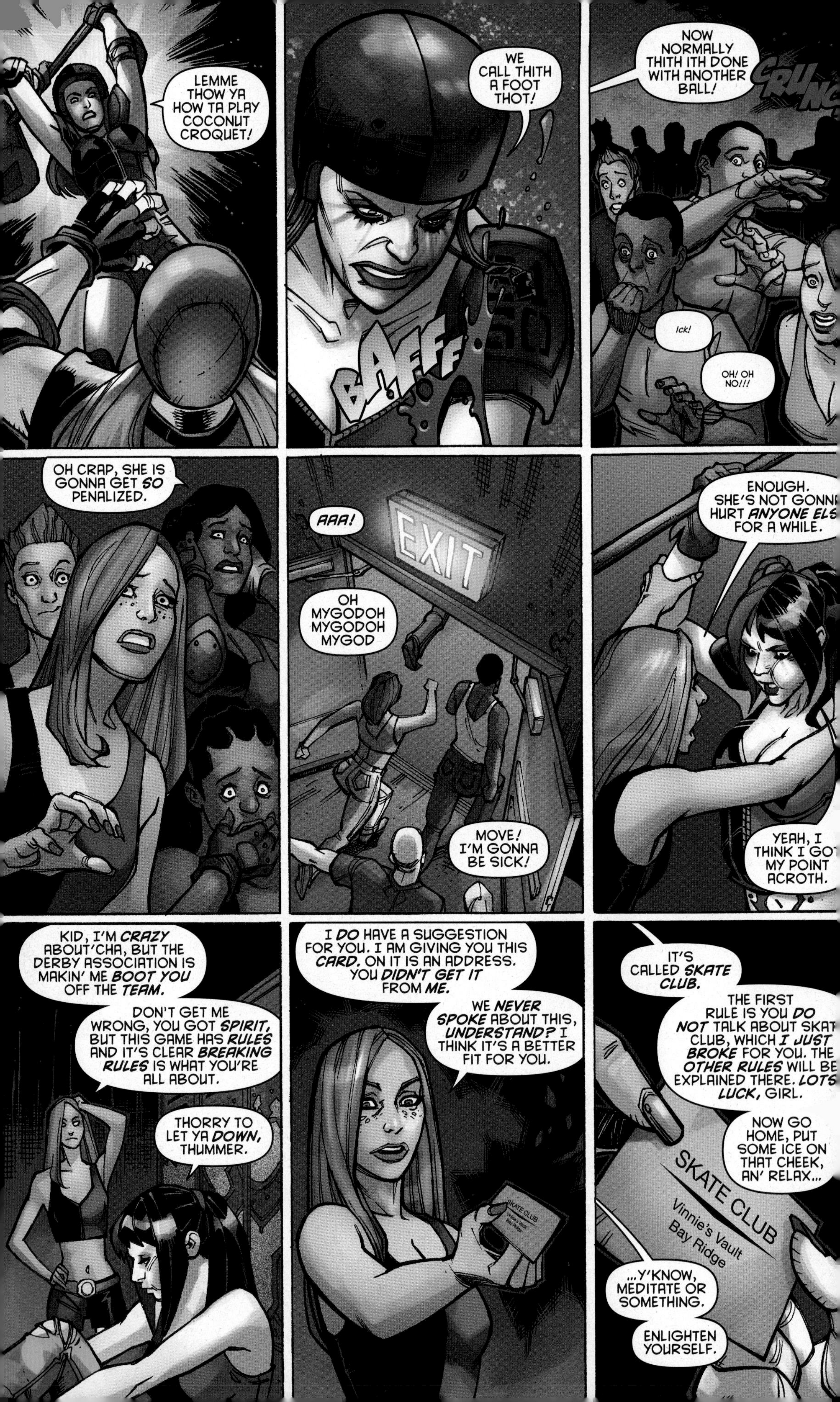

LEMME THOW YA HOW TA PLAY COCONUT CROQUET!
WE CALL THITH A FOOT THOT!
BAFFF
NOW NORMALLY THITH ITH DONE WITH ANOTHER BALL!
CRUNC
Ick!
OH! OH NO!!!
OH CRAP, SHE IS GONNA GET SO PENALIZED.
AAA!
EXIT
OH MYGODOH MYGODOH MYGOD
MOVE! I'M GONNA BE SICK!
ENOUGH. SHE'S NOT GONN HURT ANYONE ELS FOR A WHILE.
YEAH, I THINK I GOT MY POINT ACROTH.
KID, I'M CRAZY ABOUT'CHA, BUT THE DERBY ASSOCIATION IS MAKIN' ME BOOT YOU OFF THE TEAM.
DON'T GET ME WRONG, YOU GOT SPIRIT, BUT THIS GAME HAS RULES AND IT'S CLEAR BREAKING RULES IS WHAT YOU'RE ALL ABOUT.
THORRY TO LET YA DOWN, THUMMER.
I DO HAVE A SUGGESTION FOR YOU. I AM GIVING YOU THIS CARD. ON IT IS AN ADDRESS. YOU DIDN'T GET IT FROM ME.
WE NEVER SPOKE ABOUT THIS, UNDERSTAND? I THINK IT'S A BETTER FIT FOR YOU.
IT'S CALLED SKATE CLUB.
THE FIRST RULE IS YOU DO NOT TALK ABOUT SKAT CLUB, WHICH I JUST BROKE FOR YOU. THE OTHER RULES WILL BE EXPLAINED THERE. LOTS LUCK, GIRL.
NOW GO HOME, PUT SOME ICE ON THAT CHEEK, AN' RELAX...
SKATE CLUB
Vinnie's Vault
Bay Ridge
...Y'KNOW, MEDITATE OR SOMETHING.
ENLIGHTEN YOURSELF.

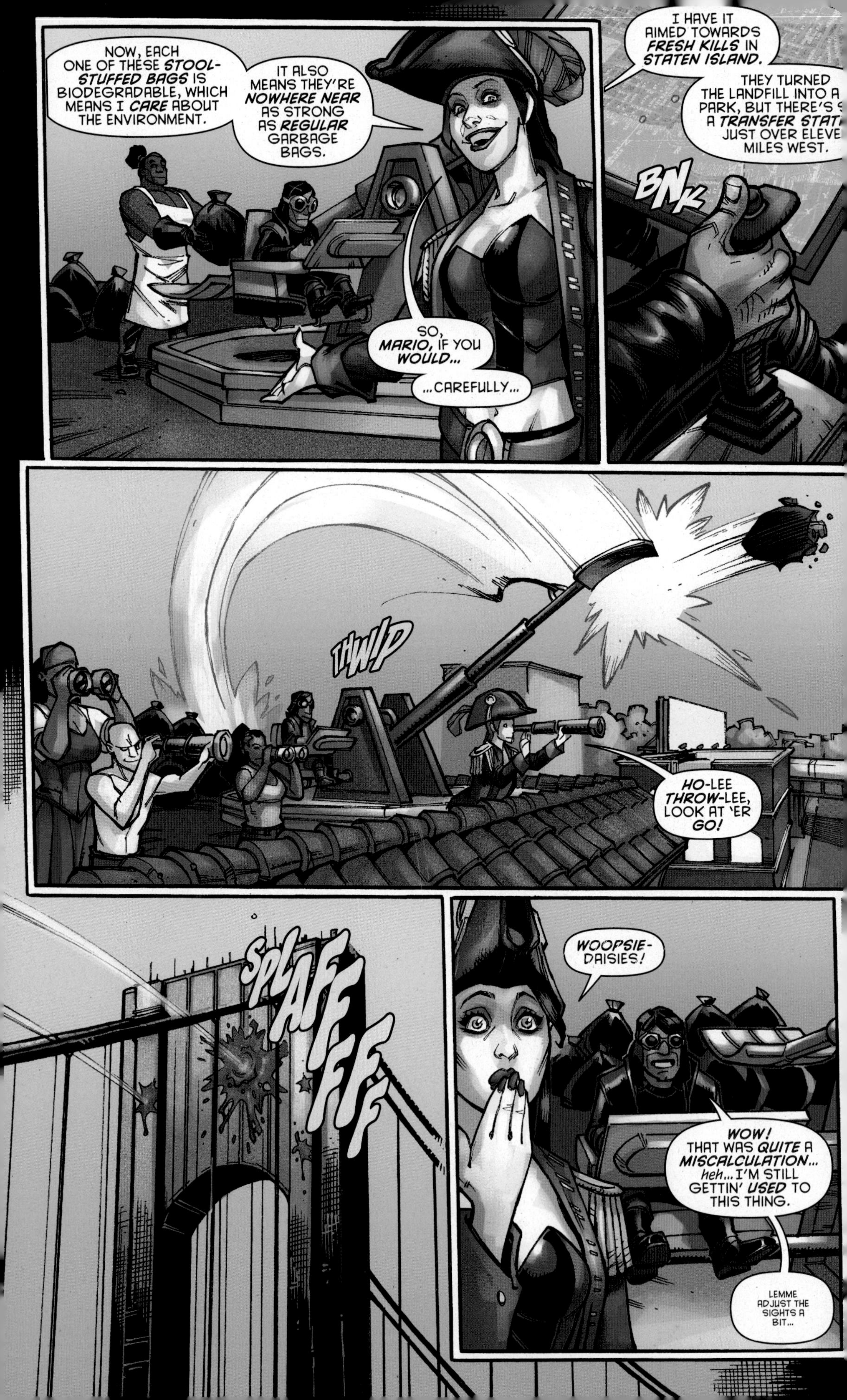

NOW, EACH ONE OF THESE STOOL-STUFFED BAGS IS BIODEGRADABLE, WHICH MEANS I CARE ABOUT THE ENVIRONMENT.
IT ALSO MEANS THEY'RE NOWHERE NEAR AS STRONG AS REGULAR GARBAGE BAGS.
SO, MARIO, IF YOU WOULD...
...CAREFULLY...
I HAVE IT AIMED TOWARDS FRESH KILLS IN STATEN ISLAND.
THEY TURNED THE LANDFILL INTO A PARK, BUT THERE'S
A TRANSFER
JUST OVER
MILES WEST.
BNK
THWIP
HO-LEE THROW-LEE, LOOK AT 'ER GO!
SPLAFFFFF
WOOPSIE-DAISIES!
WOW! THAT WAS QUITE A MISCALCULATION... heh... I'M STILL GETTIN' USED TO THIS THING.
LEMME ADJUST THE SIGHTS A BIT...

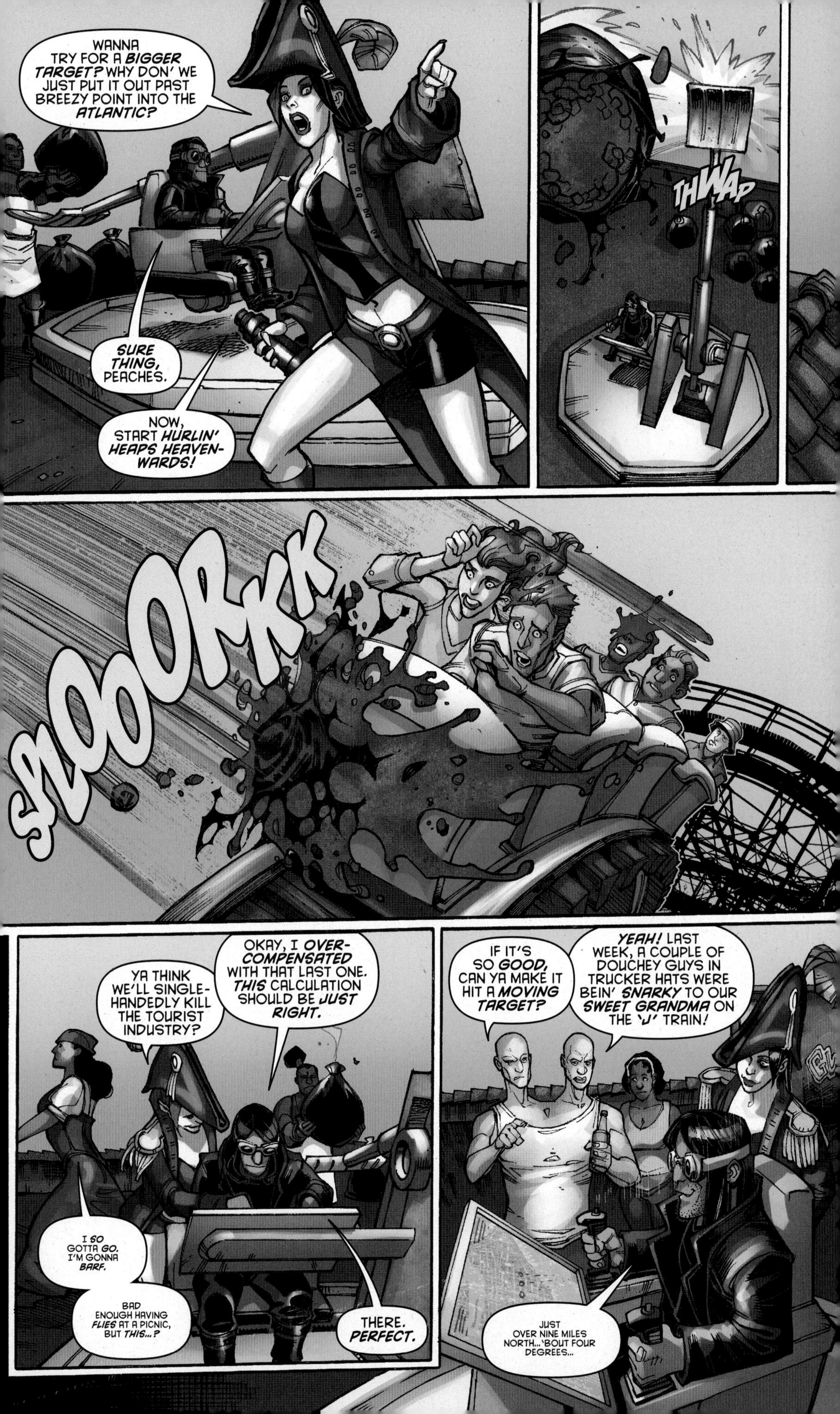
WANNA TRY FOR A BIGGER TARGET? WHY DON' WE JUST PUT IT OUT PAST BREEZY POINT INTO THE ATLANTIC?
SURE THING, PEACHES.
NOW, START HURLIN' HEAPS HEAVEN-WARDS!
THWAP
SLOOORKK
YA THINK WE'LL SINGLE-HANDEDLY KILL THE TOURIST INDUSTRY?
OKAY, I OVER-COMPENSATED WITH THAT LAST ONE. THIS CALCULATION SHOULD BE JUST RIGHT.
I SO GOTTA GO. I'M GONNA BARF.
BAD ENOUGH HAVING FLIES AT A PICNIC, BUT THIS...?
THERE. PERFECT.
IF IT'S SO GOOD, CAN YA MAKE IT HIT A MOVING TARGET?
YEAH! LAST WEEK, A COUPLE OF DOUCHEY GUYS IN TRUCKER HATS WERE BEIN' SNARKY TO OUR SWEET GRANDMA ON THE 'J' TRAIN!
JUST OVER NINE MILES NORTH...'BOUT FOUR DEGREES...

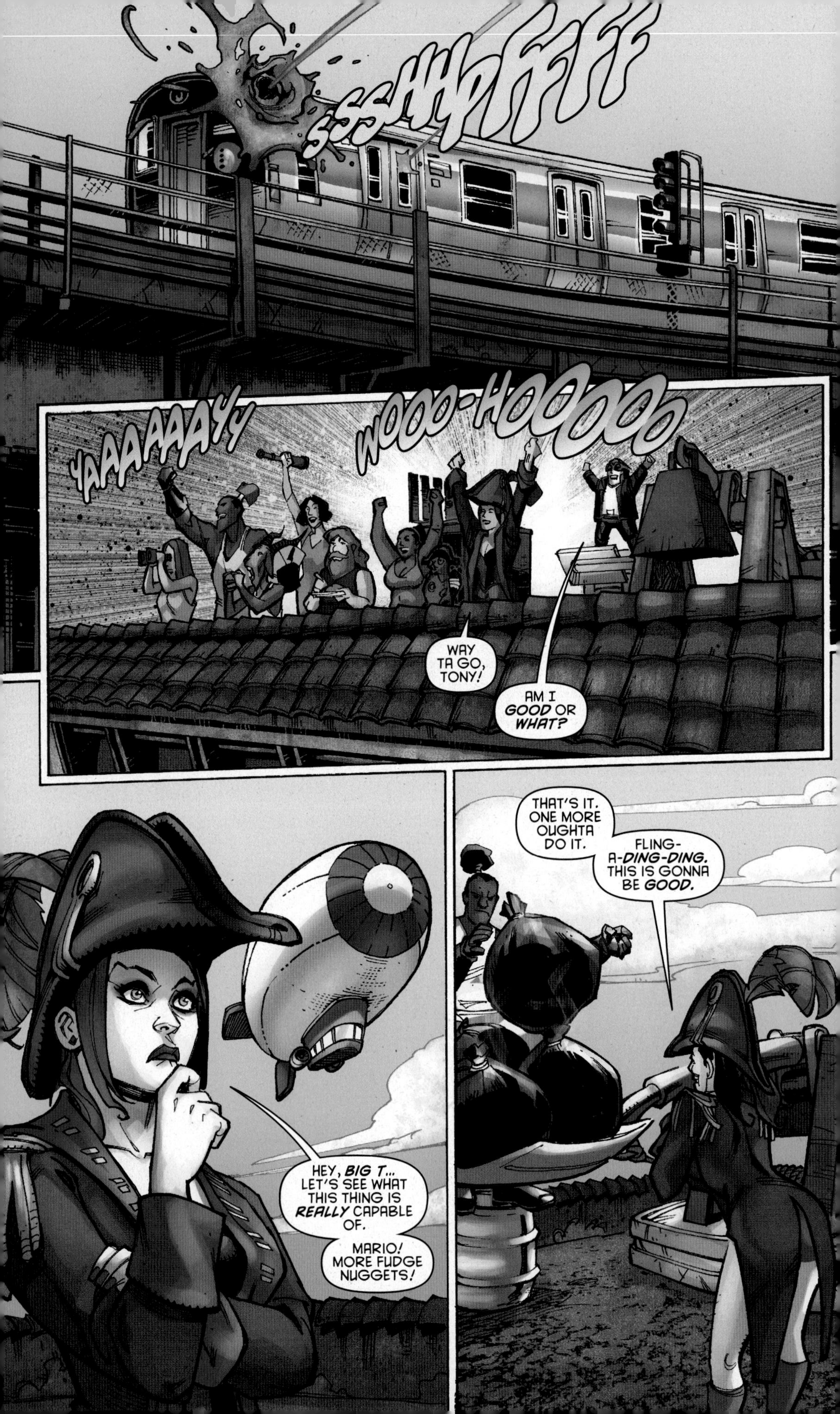
SSSHHPFFFT
YAAAAAAYY
WOOO-HOOOOOO
WAY TA GO, TONY!
AM I GOOD OR WHAT?
HEY, BIG T... LET'S SEE WHAT THIS THING IS REALLY CAPABLE OF.
MARIO! MORE FUDGE NUGGETS!
THAT'S IT. ONE MORE OUGHTA DO IT.
FLING-A-DING-DING. THIS IS GONNA BE GOOD.

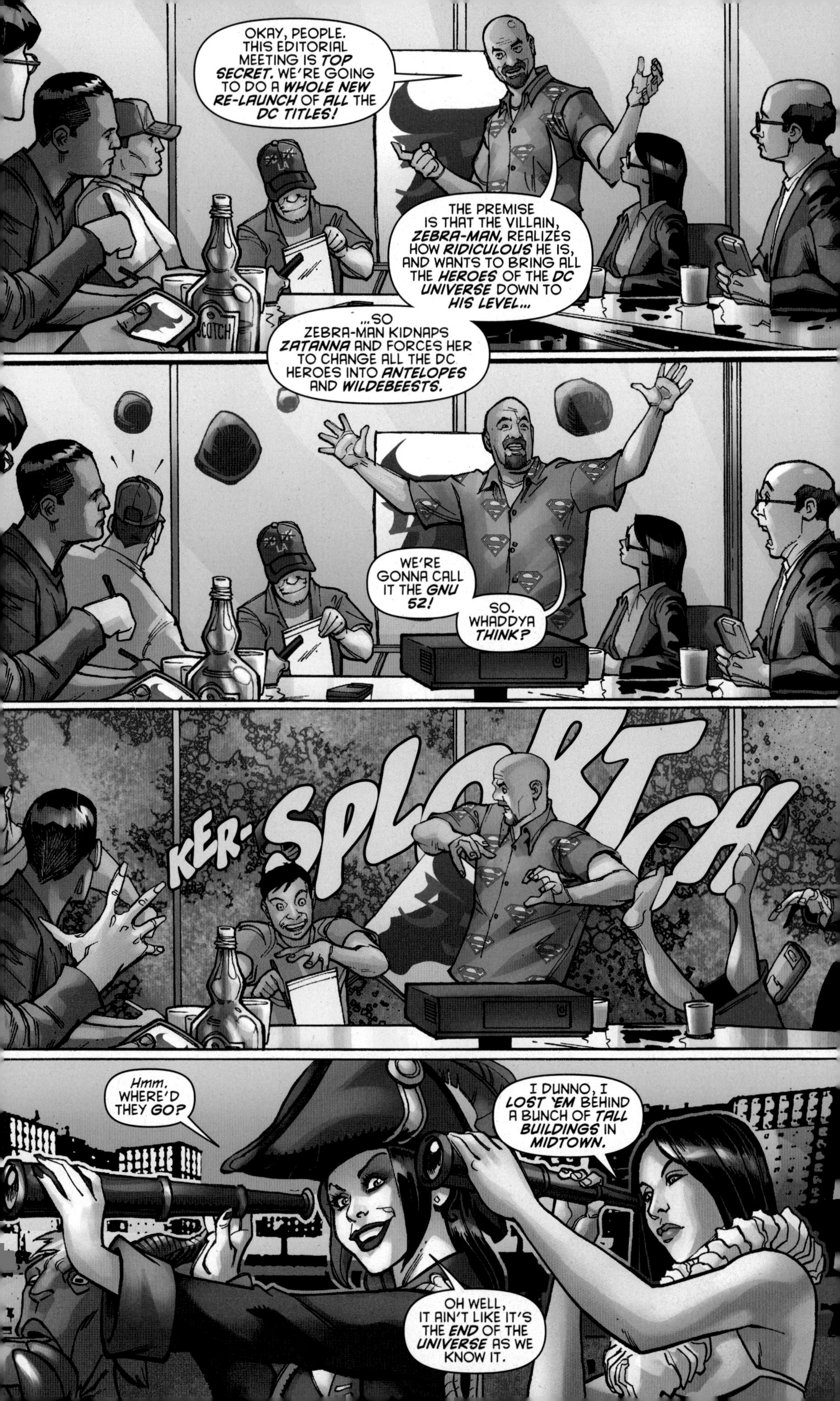
OKAY, PEOPLE. THIS EDITORIAL MEETING IS TOP SECRET. WE'RE GOING TO DO A WHOLE NEW RE-LAUNCH OF ALL THE DC TITLES!
THE PREMISE IS THAT THE VILLAIN, ZEBRA-MAN, REALIZES HOW RIDICULOUS HE IS, AND WANTS TO BRING ALL THE HEROES OF THE DC UNIVERSE DOWN TO HIS LEVEL...
SCOTCH
...SO ZEBRA-MAN KIDNAPS ZATANNA AND FORCES HER TO CHANGE ALL THE DC HEROES INTO ANTELOPES AND WILDEBEESTS.
WE'RE GONNA CALL IT THE GNU 52!
SO. WHADDYA THINK?
KER-SPLORTCH
Hmm. WHERE'D THEY GO?
I DUNNO, I LOST 'EM BEHIND A BUNCH OF TALL BUILDINGS IN MIDTOWN.
OH WELL, IT AIN'T LIKE IT'S THE END OF THE UNIVERSE AS WE KNOW IT.

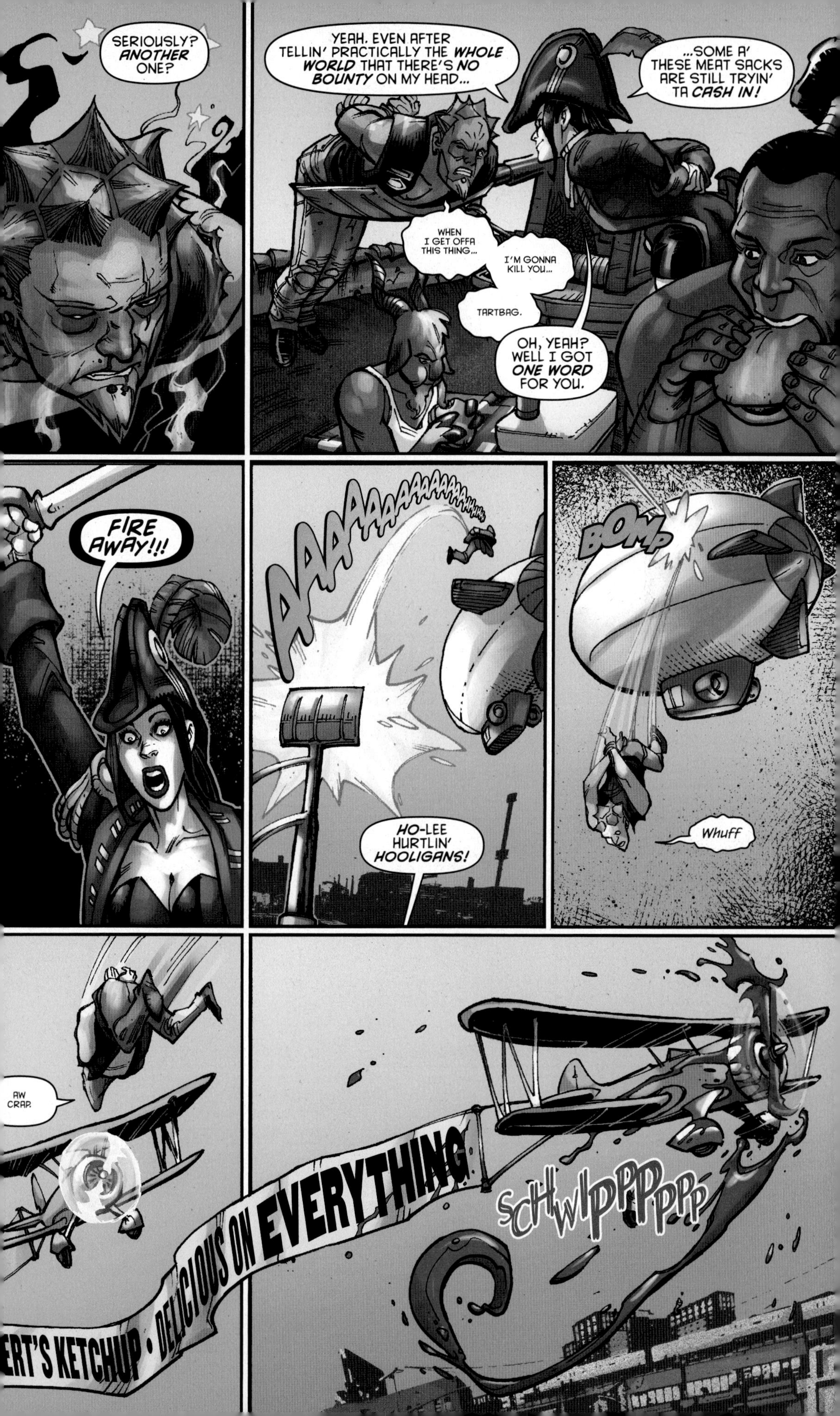
SERIOUSLY? ANOTHER ONE?
YEAH. EVEN AFTER TELLIN' PRACTICALLY THE WHOLE WORLD THAT THERE'S NO BOUNTY ON MY HEAD...
...SOME A' THESE MEAT SACKS ARE STILL TRYIN' TA CASH IN!
WHEN I GET OFFA THIS THING...
I'M GONNA KILL YOU...
TARTBAG.
OH, YEAH? WELL I GOT ONE WORD FOR YOU.
FIRE AWAY!!!
AAAAAAAAAAAAAhhhh
HO-LEE HURTLIN' HOOLIGANS!
BOMP
Whuff
AW CRAP.
ERT'S KETCHUP • DELICIOUS ON EVERYTHING
SCHWIPPPPPP

Harley Quinn #0 Variant Cover by Stephane Roux

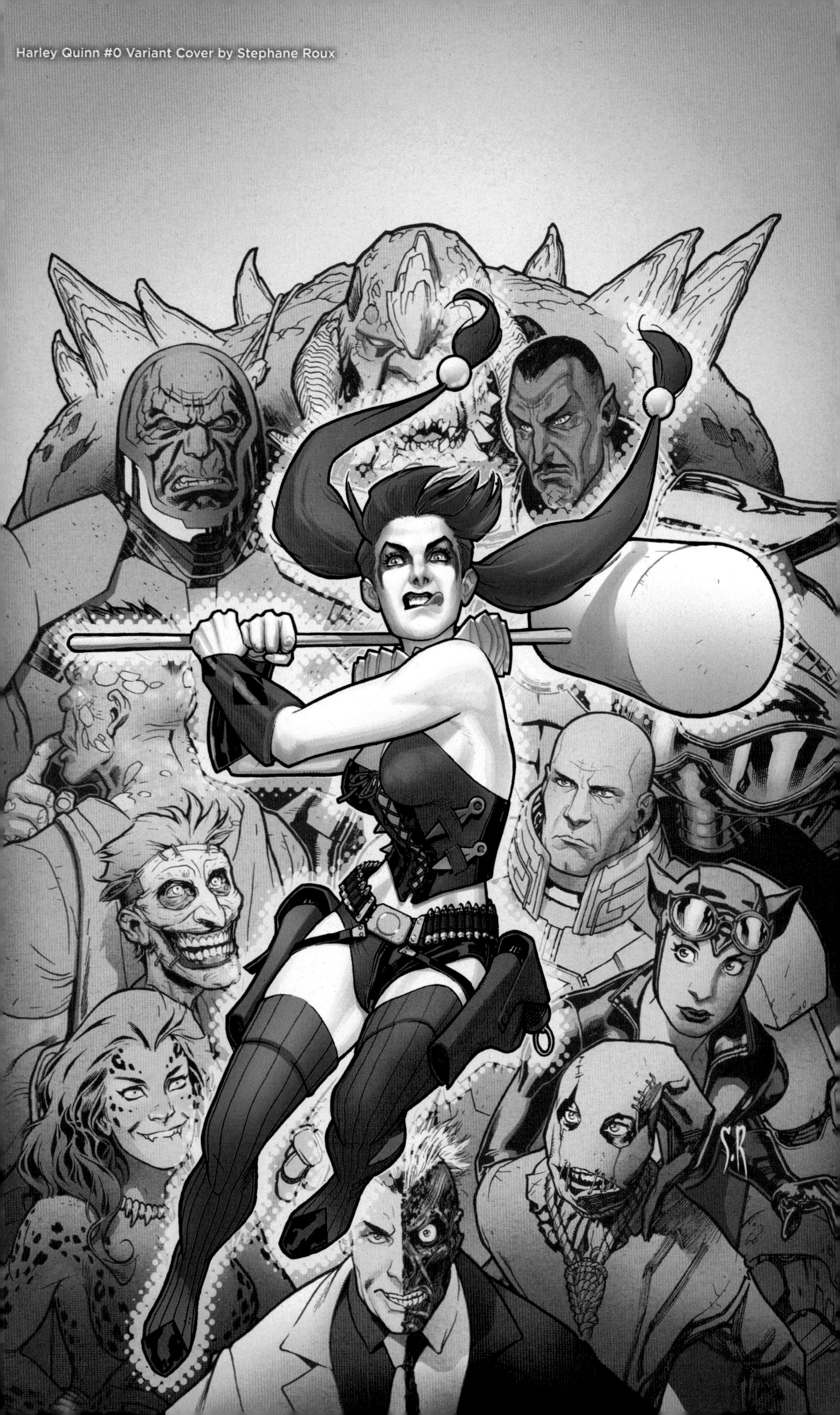

Harley Quinn #1 Variant Cover by Adam Hughes

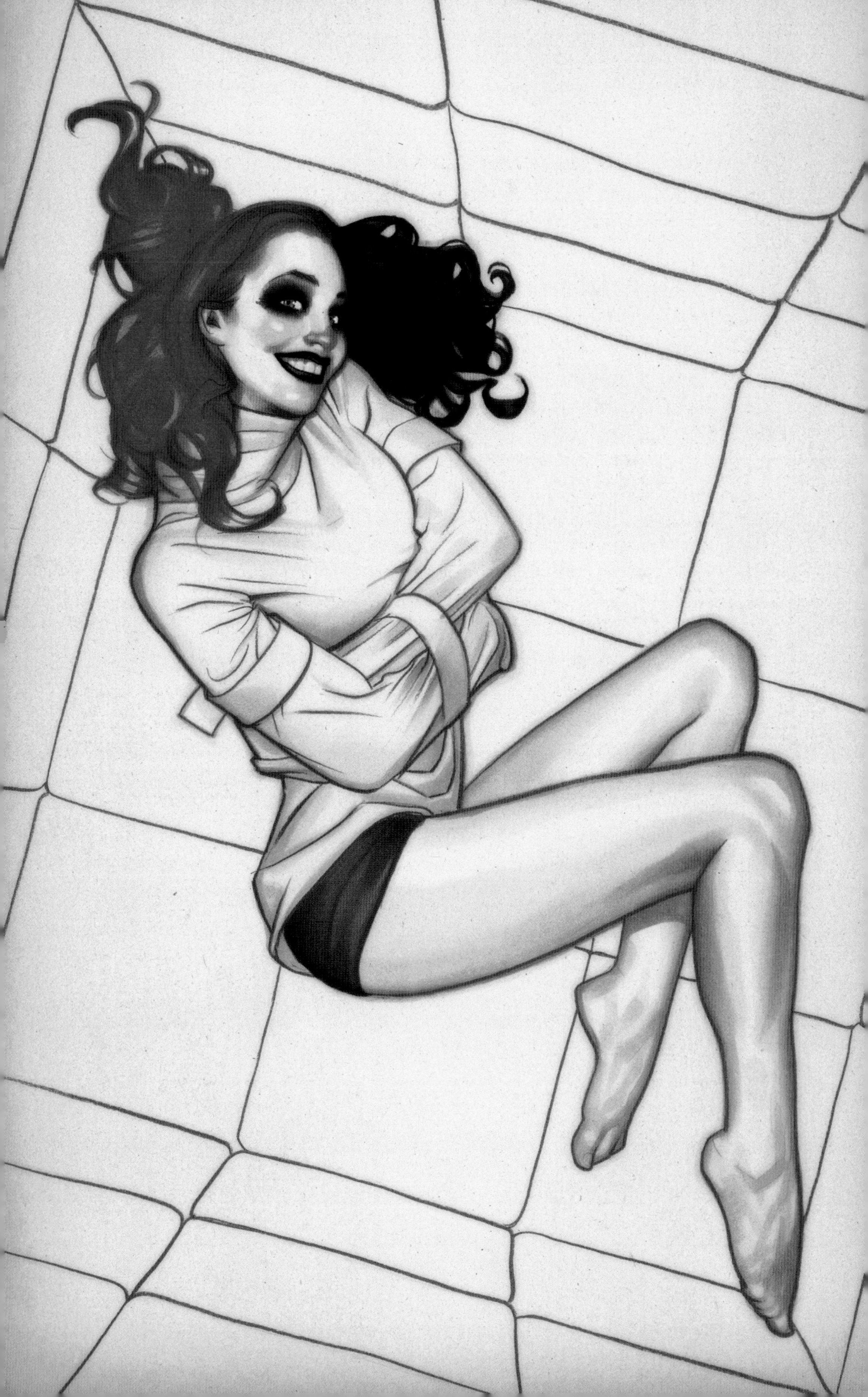

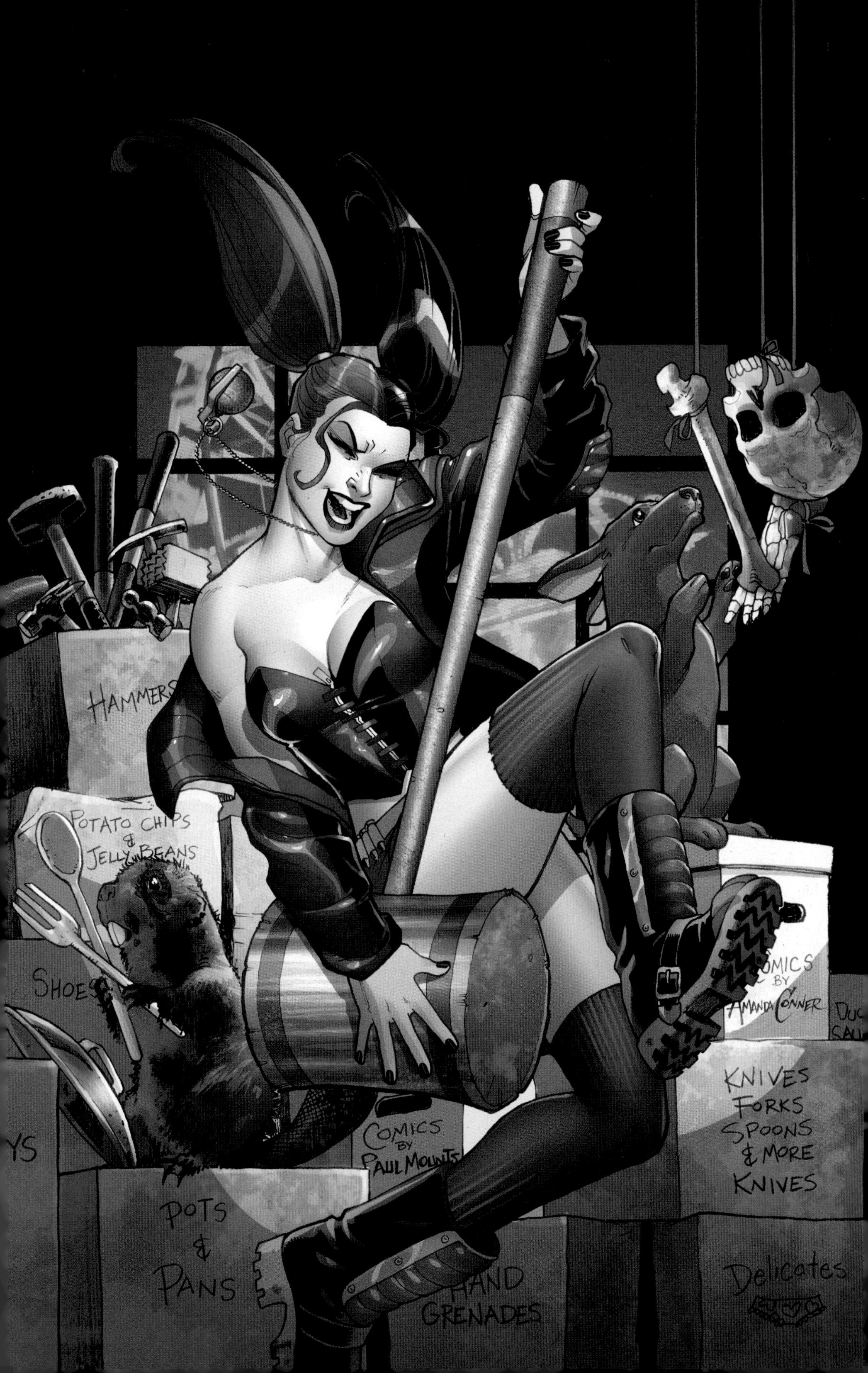
HAMMERS
POTATO CHIPS & JELLY BEANS
SHOES
COMICS BY AMANDA CONNER
KNIVES FORKS SPOONS & MORE KNIVES
COMICS BY PAUL MOUNTS
POTS & PANS
HAND GRENADES
Delicates
Harley Quinn #1 2nd Printing Cover by
Amanda Conner and Paul Mounts

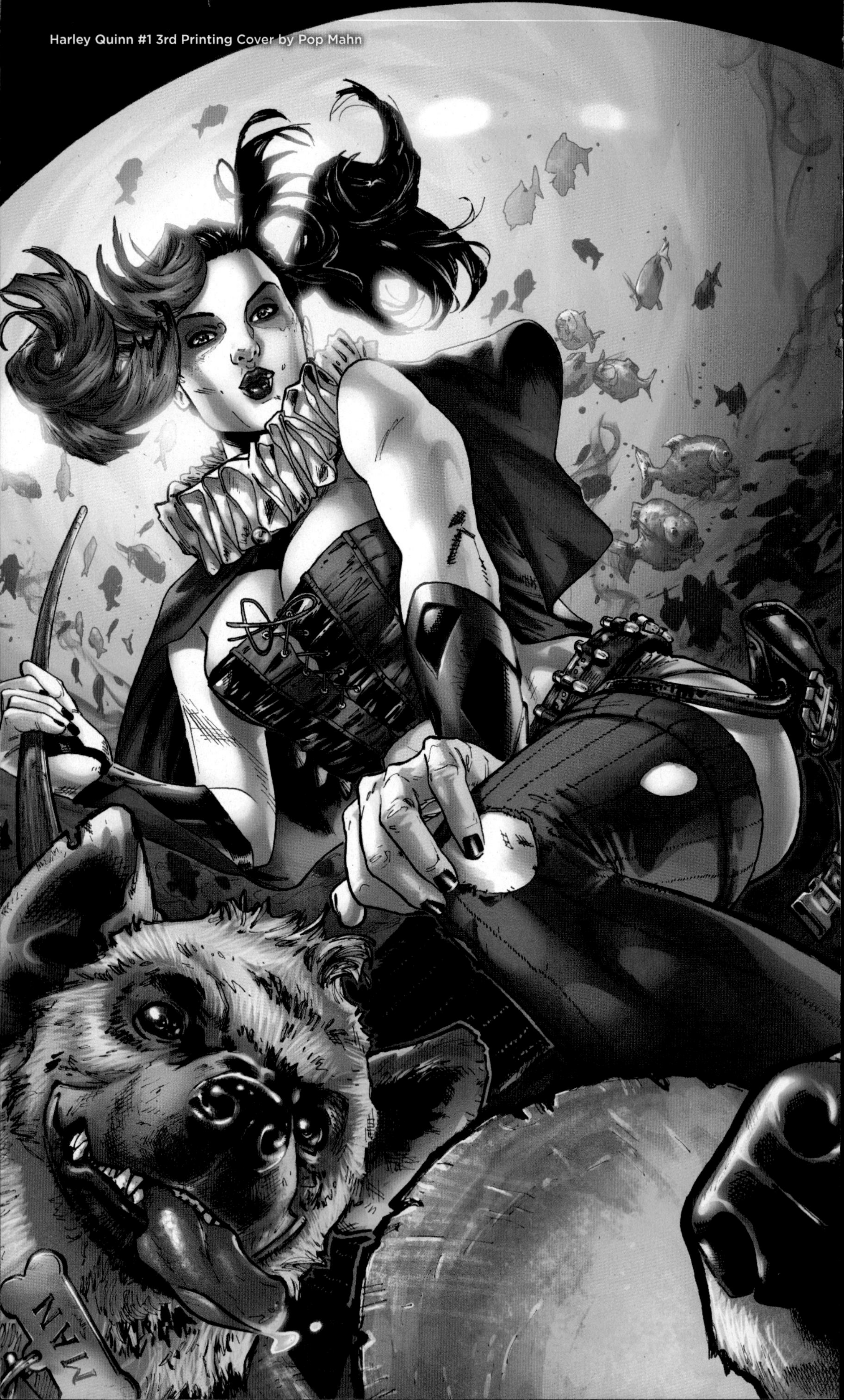
MAHN

Harley Quinn #1 3rd Printing Cover by Pop Mahn

Harley Quinn #2 2nd Printing Cover by
Amanda Conner and Paul Mounts

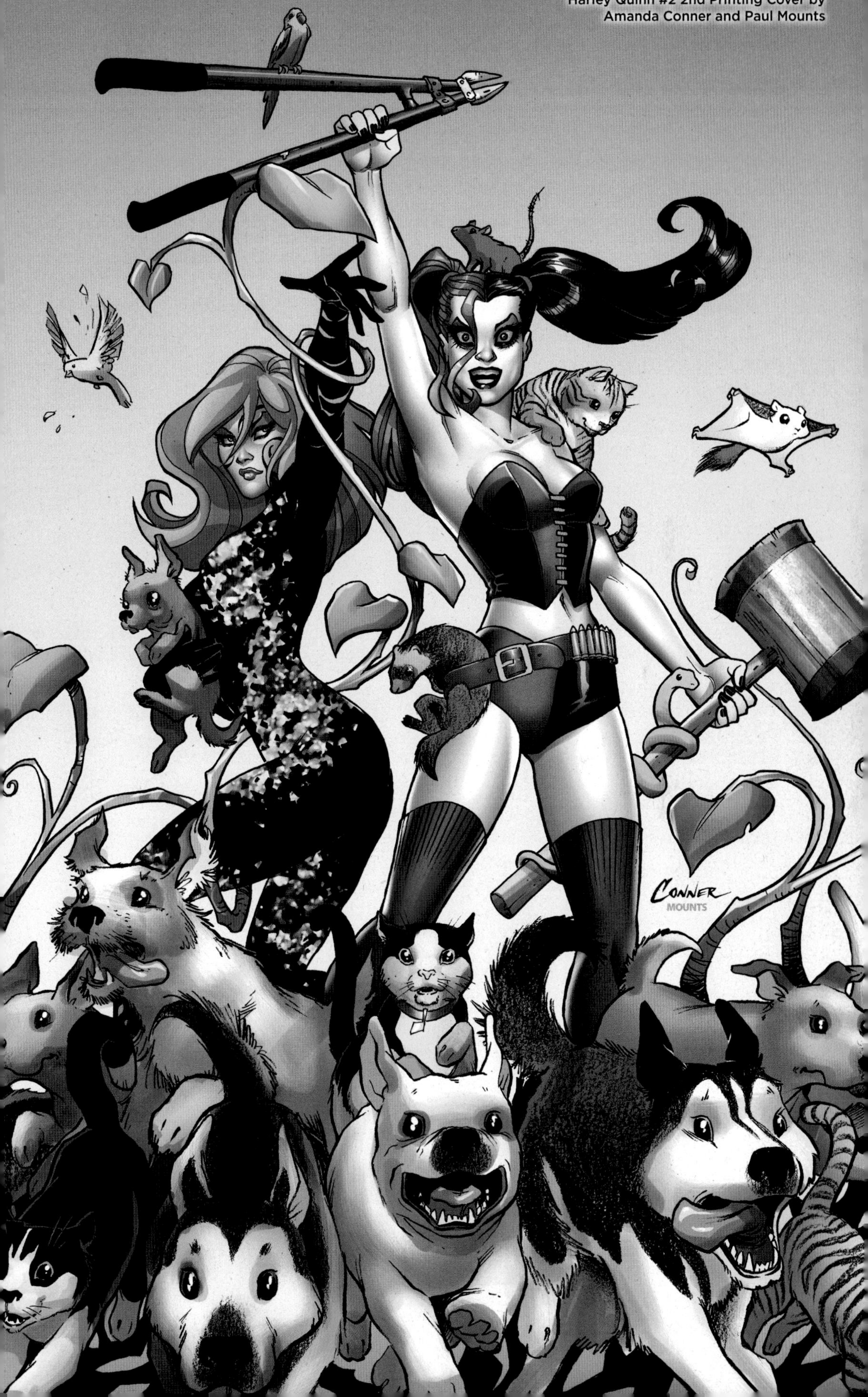
CONNER
MOUNTS

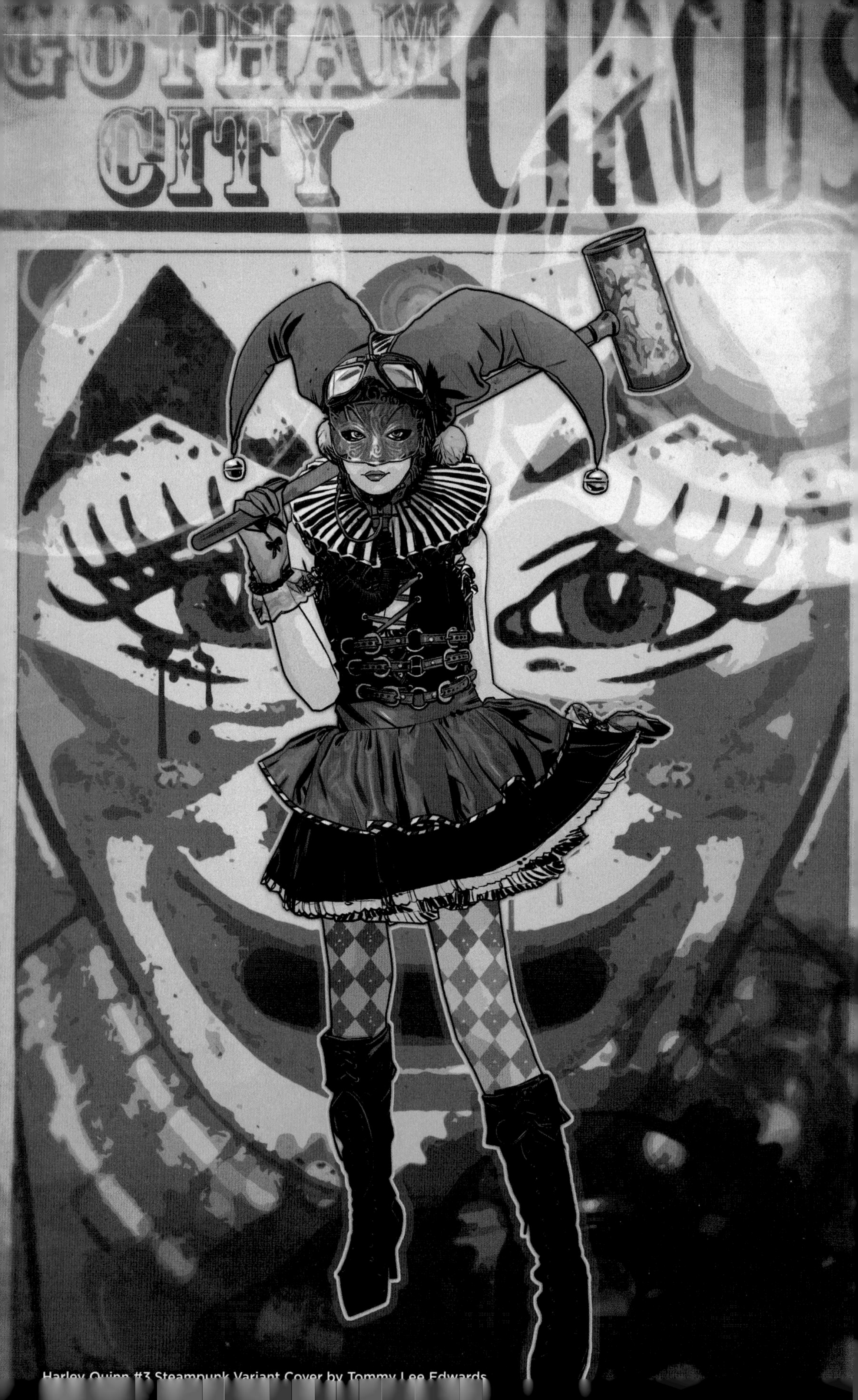
GOTHAM
CITY

Harley Quinn #3 Steampunk Variant Cover by Tommy Lee Edwards

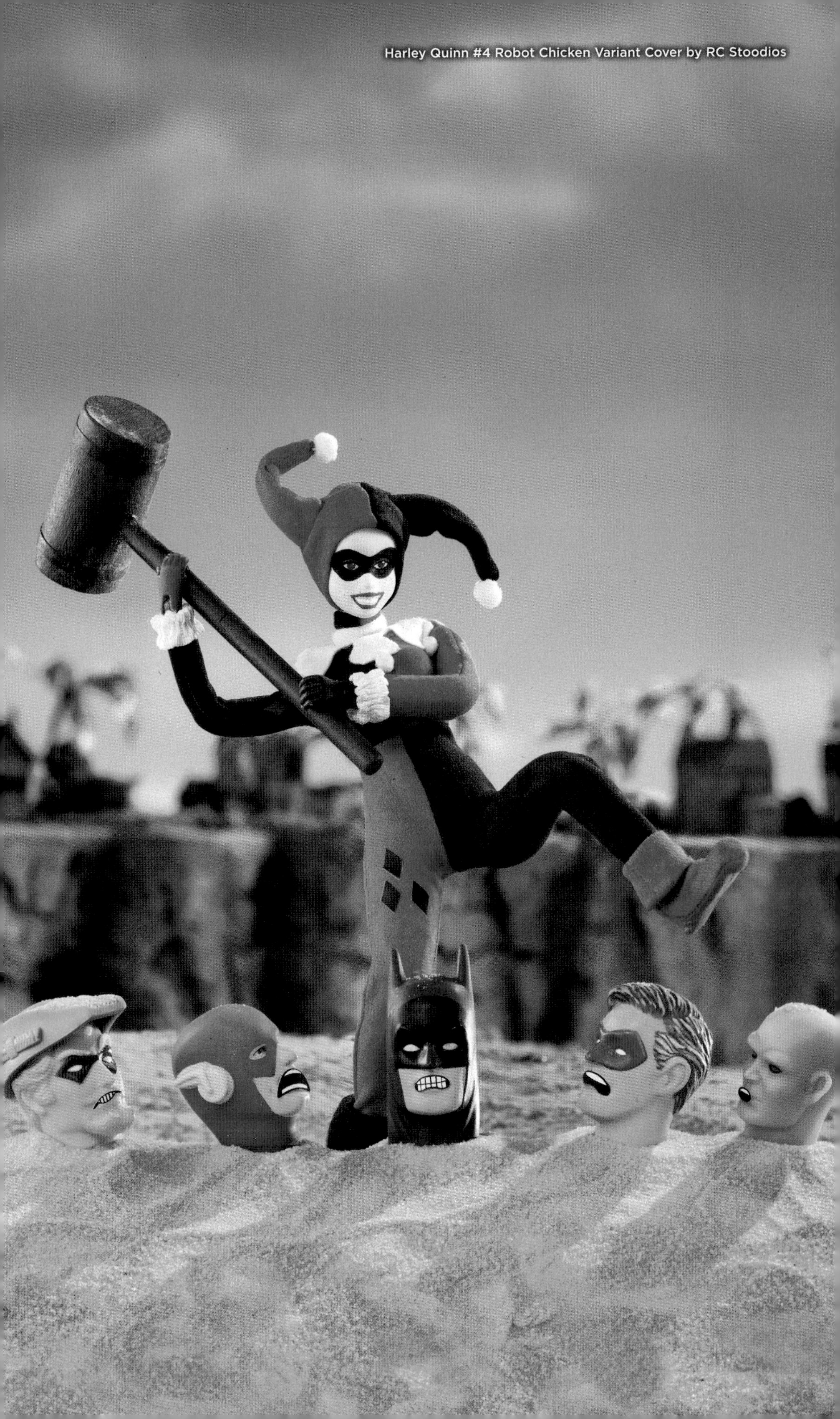

Harley Quinn #4 Robot Chicken Variant Cover by RC Stoodios

Harley Quinn #5 MAD Variant Cover by Sergio Aragones and Tom Luth

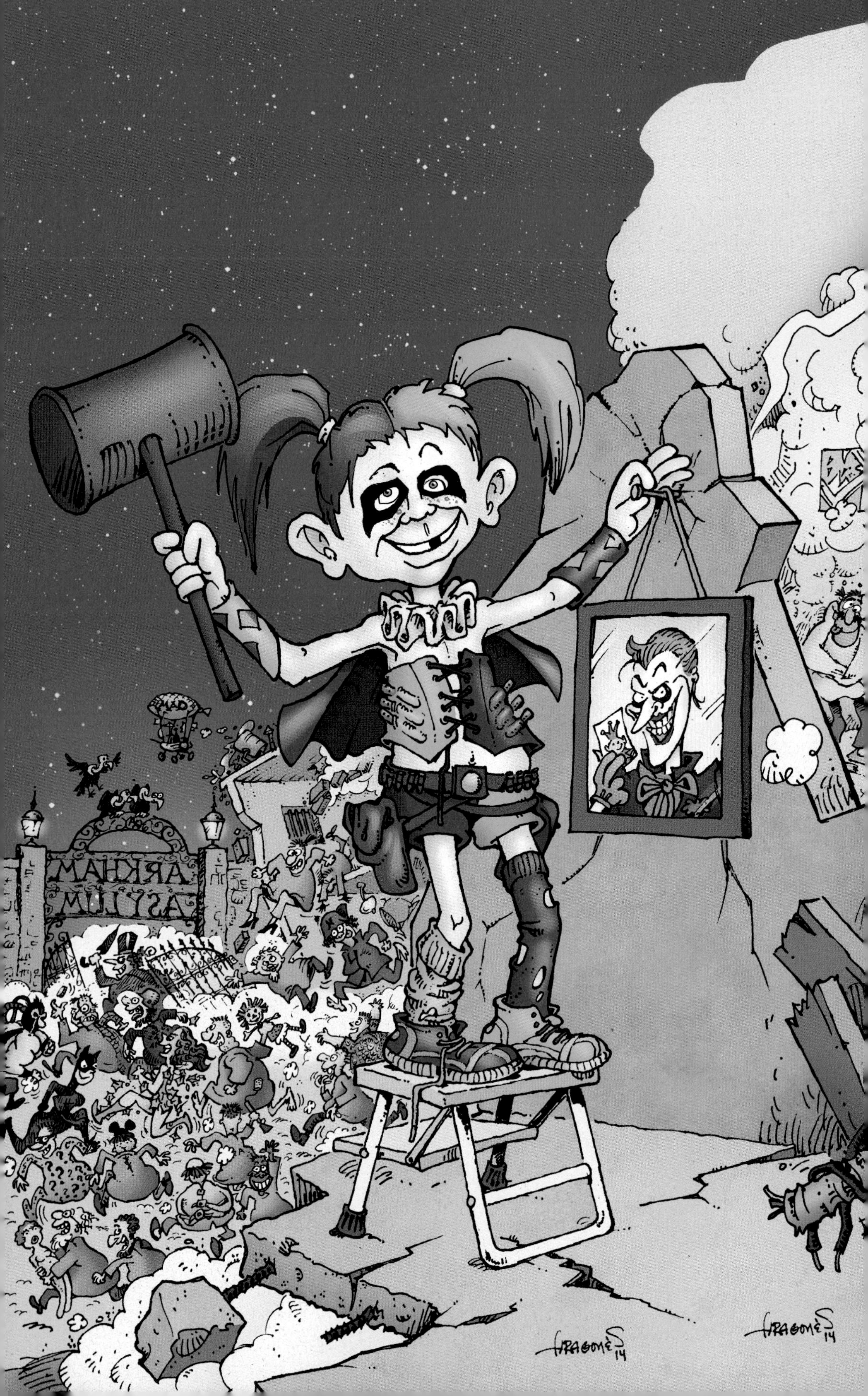

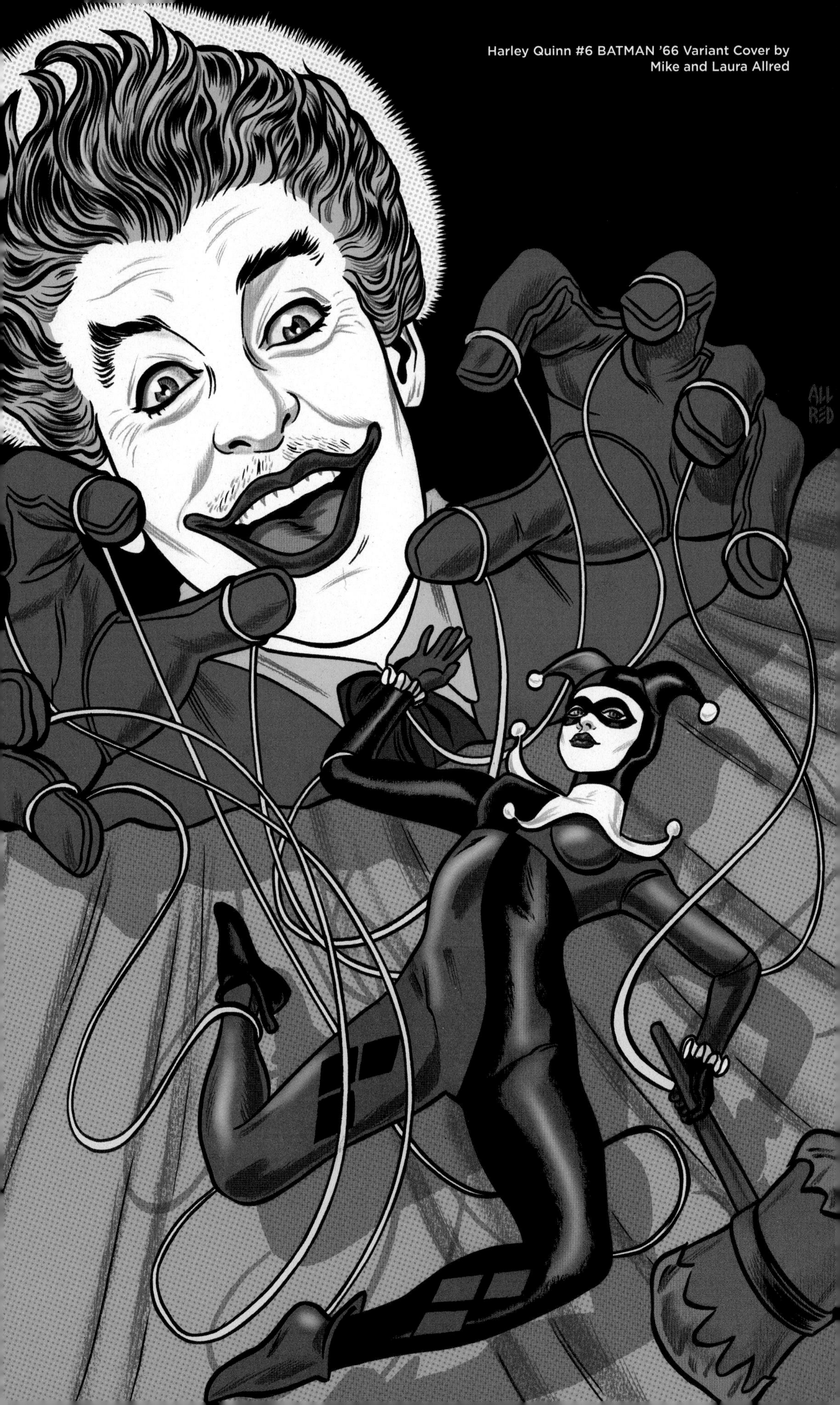
ALL
RED

Harley Quinn #6 BATMAN '66 Variant Cover by
Mike and Laura Allred

Harley Quinn #7 Variant Cover by
Amanda Conner and Paul Mounts

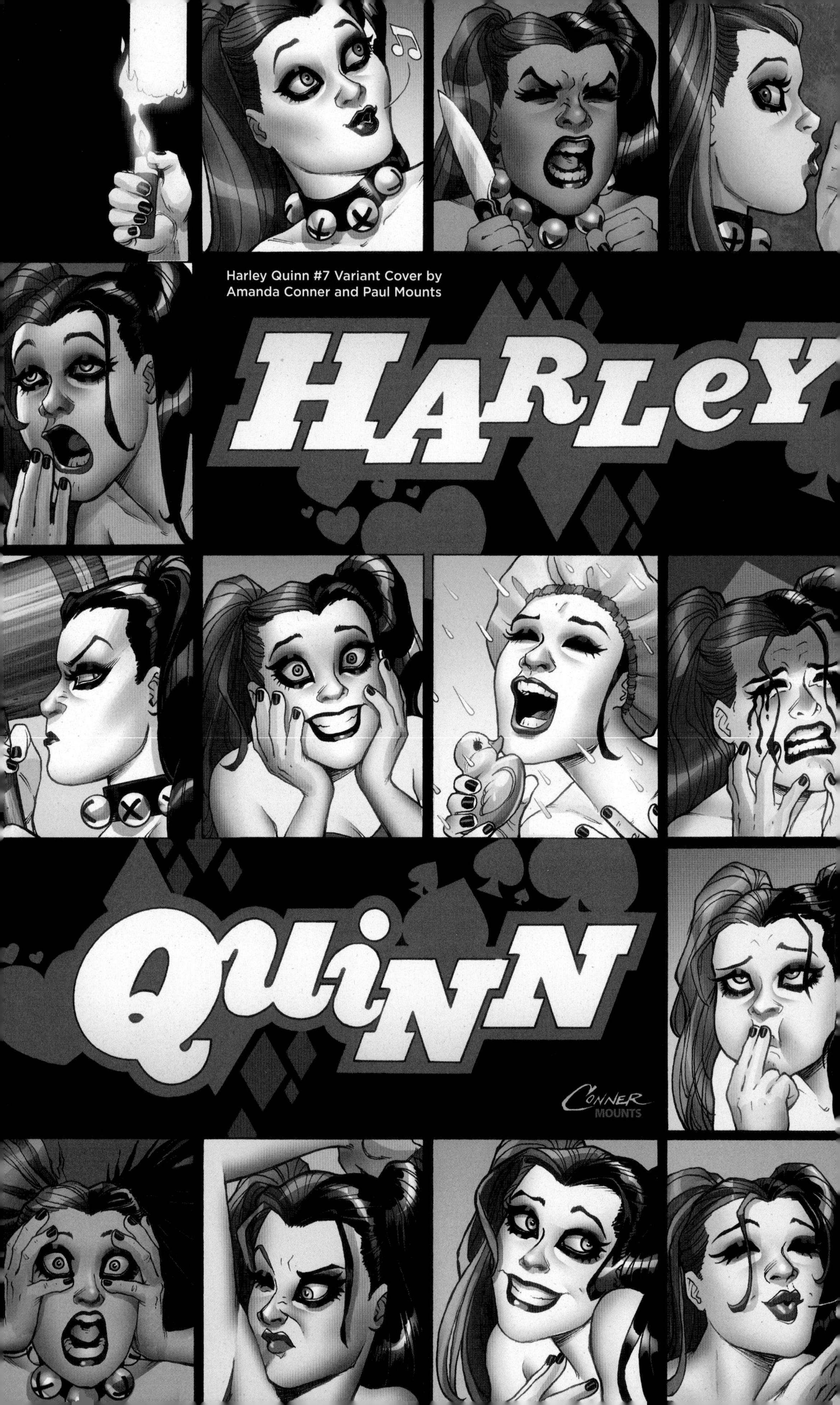
HARLEY
QUINN
CONNER
MOUNTS

Harley Quinn #7 Bombshell Variant Cover by Ant Lucia

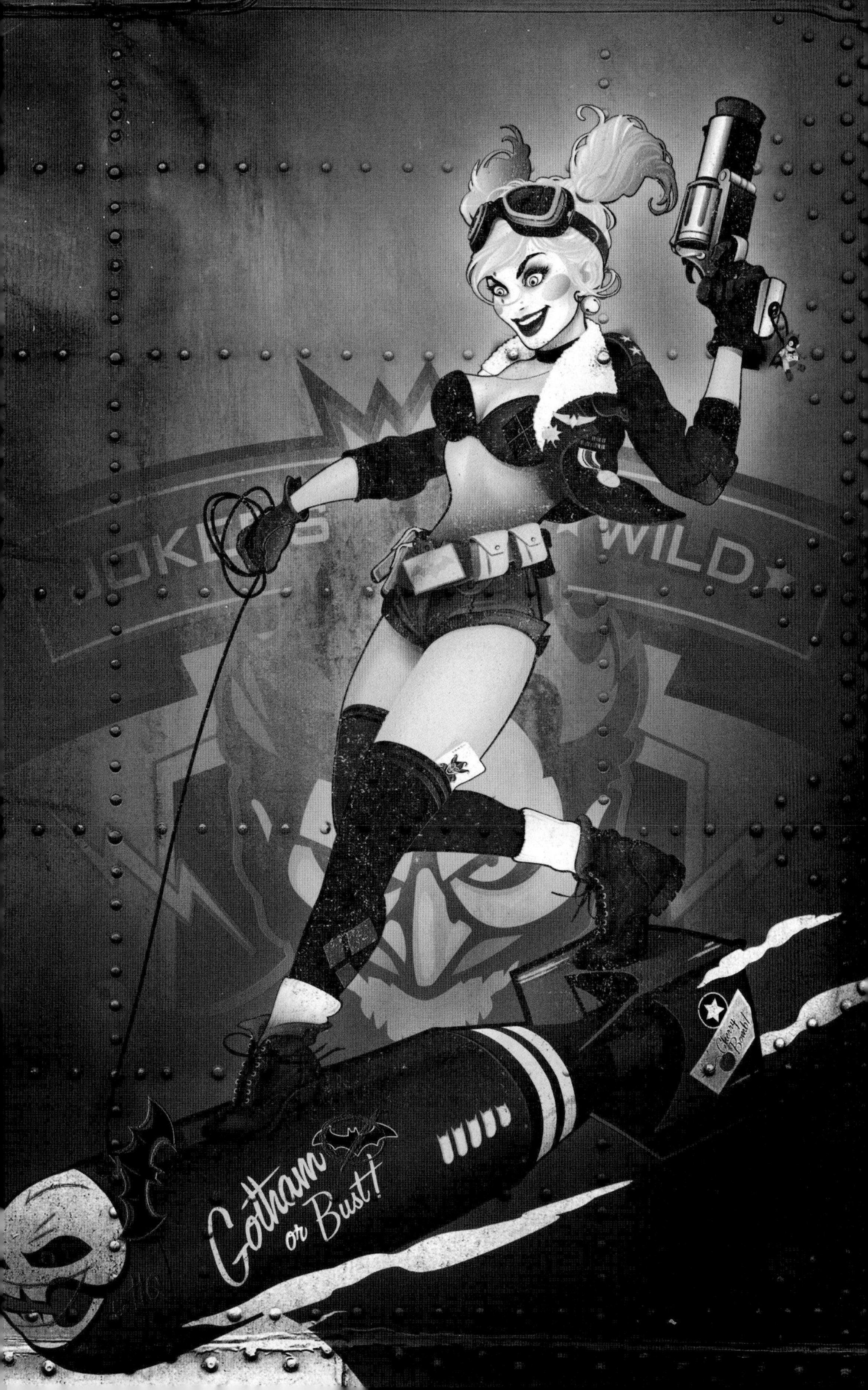
WILD
Gotham or Bust!

Harley Quinn #8 Variant Cover by Dan Panosian

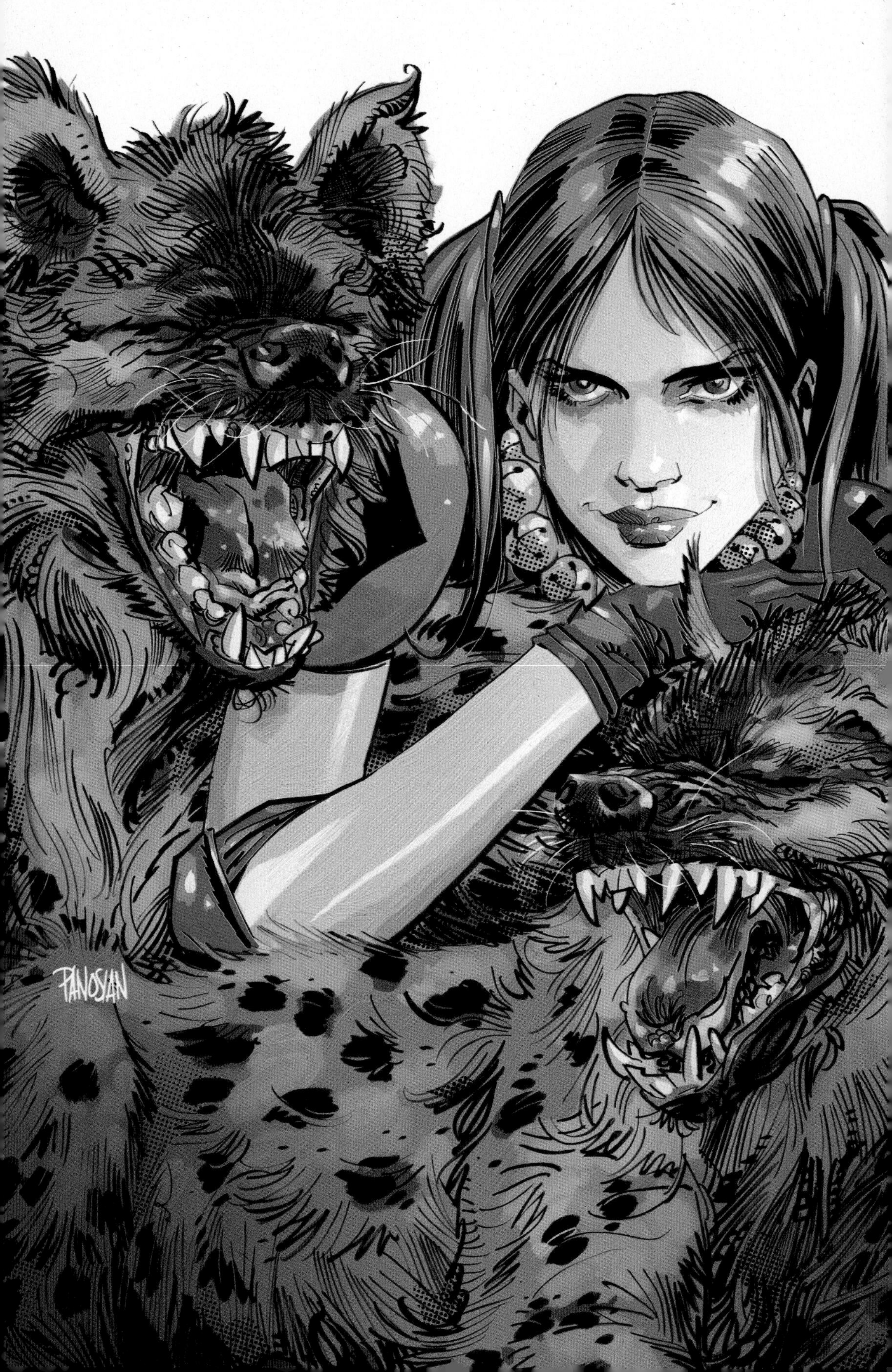
PANOSYAN

Harley Quinn #8 Batman 75th Anniversary
Variant Cover by Dave Johnson

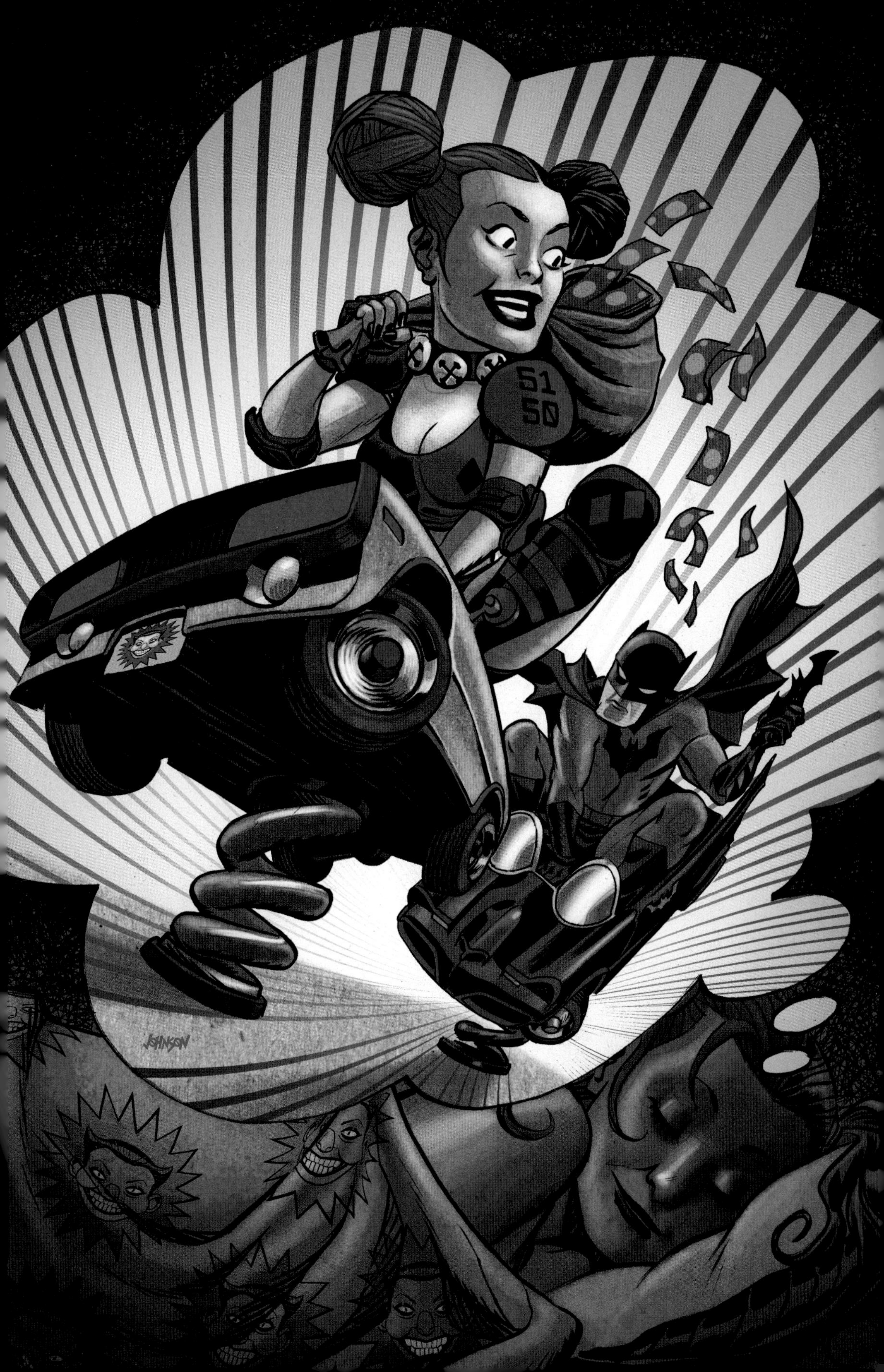
51
50
JOHNSON

Harley Quinn #0 Director's Cut Cover by
Amanda Conner and Paul Mounts

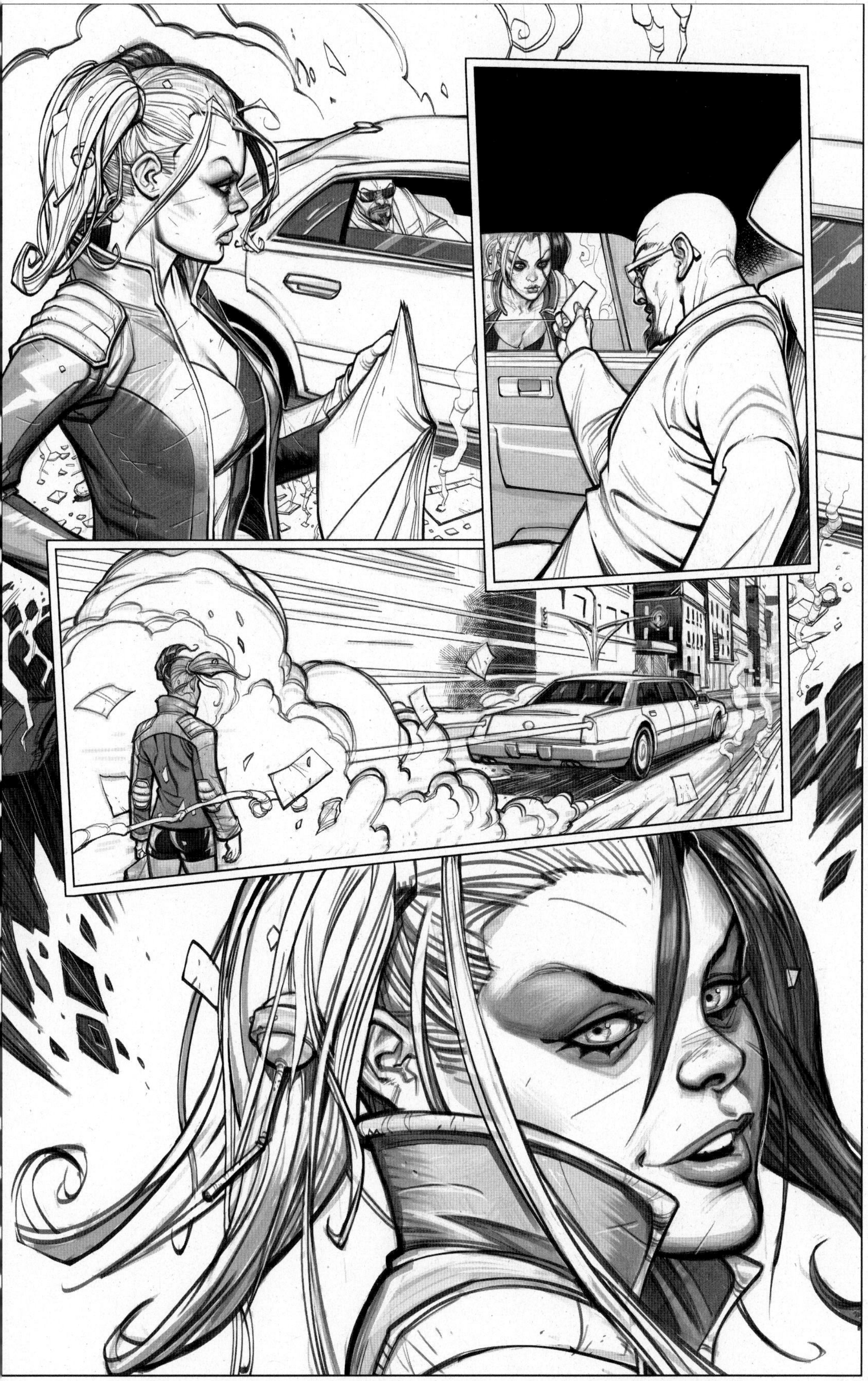

PENCILLER
INKER
PAGE#
INTERIORS
TITLE
ISSUE #
MONTH
DOUBLE PAGE SPREAD: CUT AS SHOWN, ABUT PAGE EDGES, TAPE ON BACK, DO NOT OVERLAP
PENCILLER
INKER
PAGE#
INTERIORS
TITLE
ISSUE #
MONTH
DOUBLE PAGE SPREAD: CUT AS SHOWN, ABUT PAGE EDGES, TAPE ON BACK, DO NOT OVERLAP

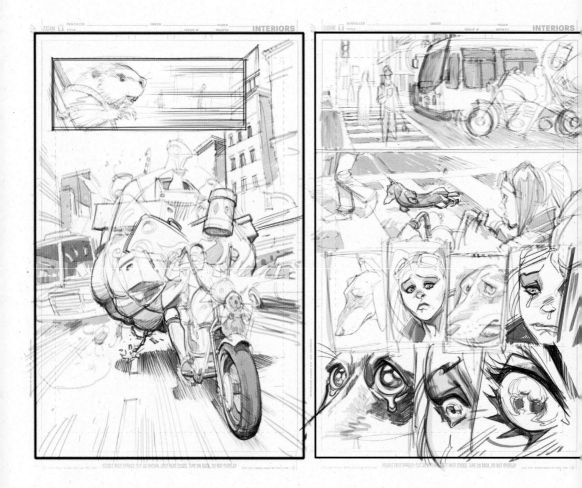

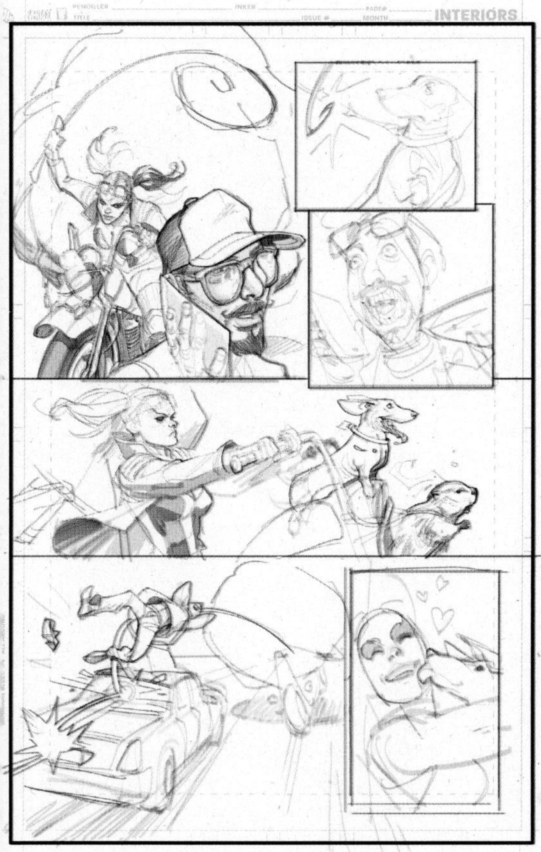
INTERIORS
DOUBLE PAGE SPREAD: CUT AS SHOWN, ABUT PAGE EDGES, TAPE ON BACK. DO NOT OVERLAP

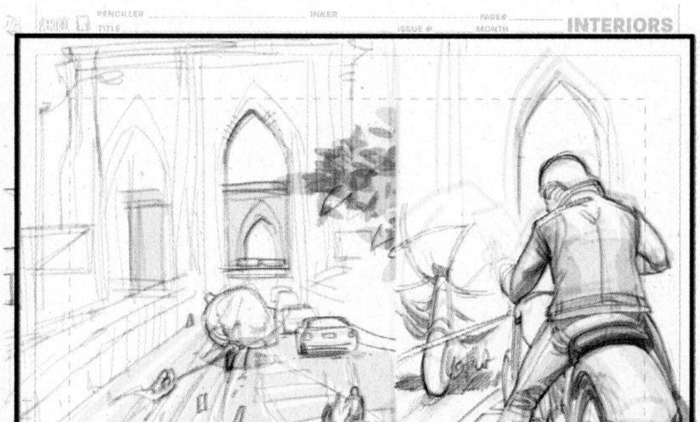
INTERIORS
DOUBLE PAGE SPREAD: CUT AS SHOWN, ABUT PAGE EDGES, TAPE ON BACK. DO NOT OVERLAP

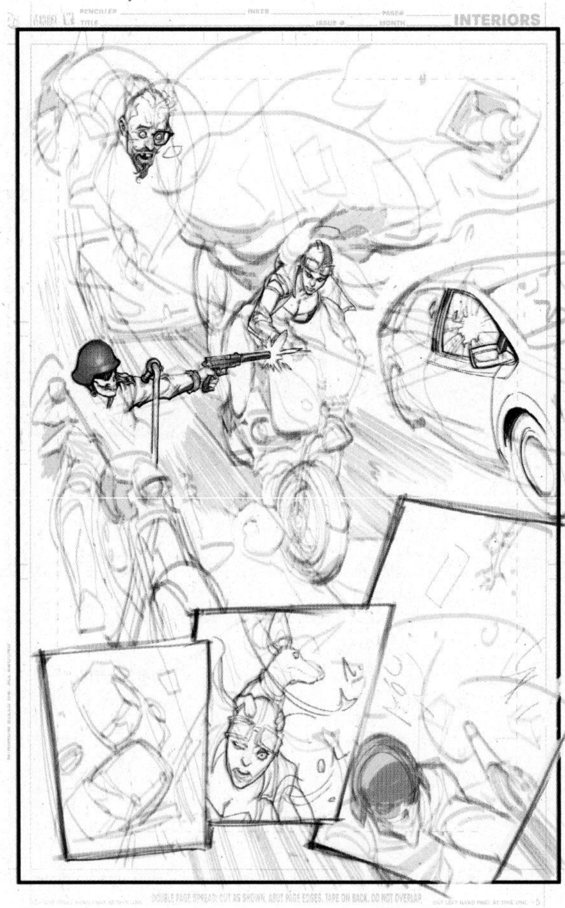
PENCILLER
INKER
PAGE#
TITLE
ISSUE #
MONTH
INTERIORS
DOUBLE PAGE SPREAD: CUT AS SHOWN, ABUT PAGE EDGES, TAPE ON BACK, DO NOT OVERLAP

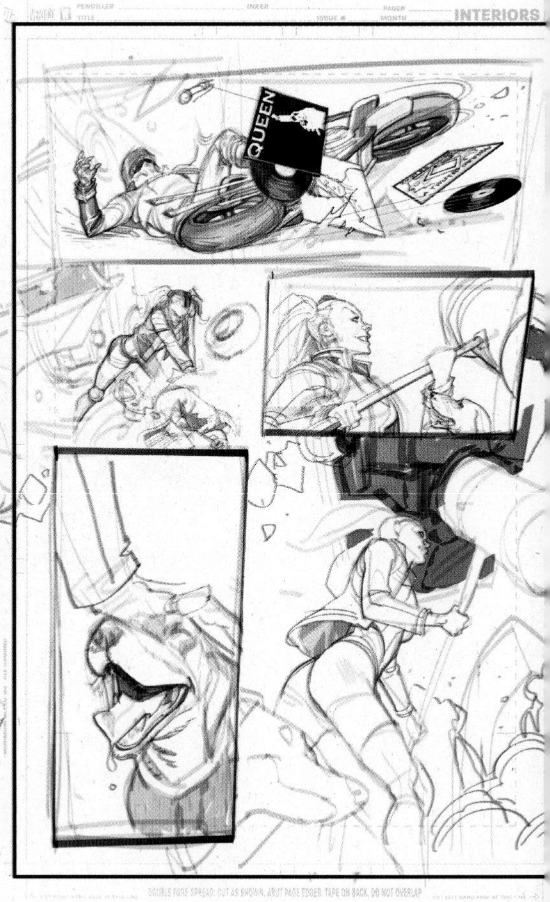
PENCILLER
INKER
PAGE#
TITLE
ISSUE #
MONTH
INTERIORS
QUEEN
DOUBLE PAGE SPREAD: CUT AS SHOWN, ABUT PAGE EDGES, TAPE ON BACK, DO NOT OVERLAP

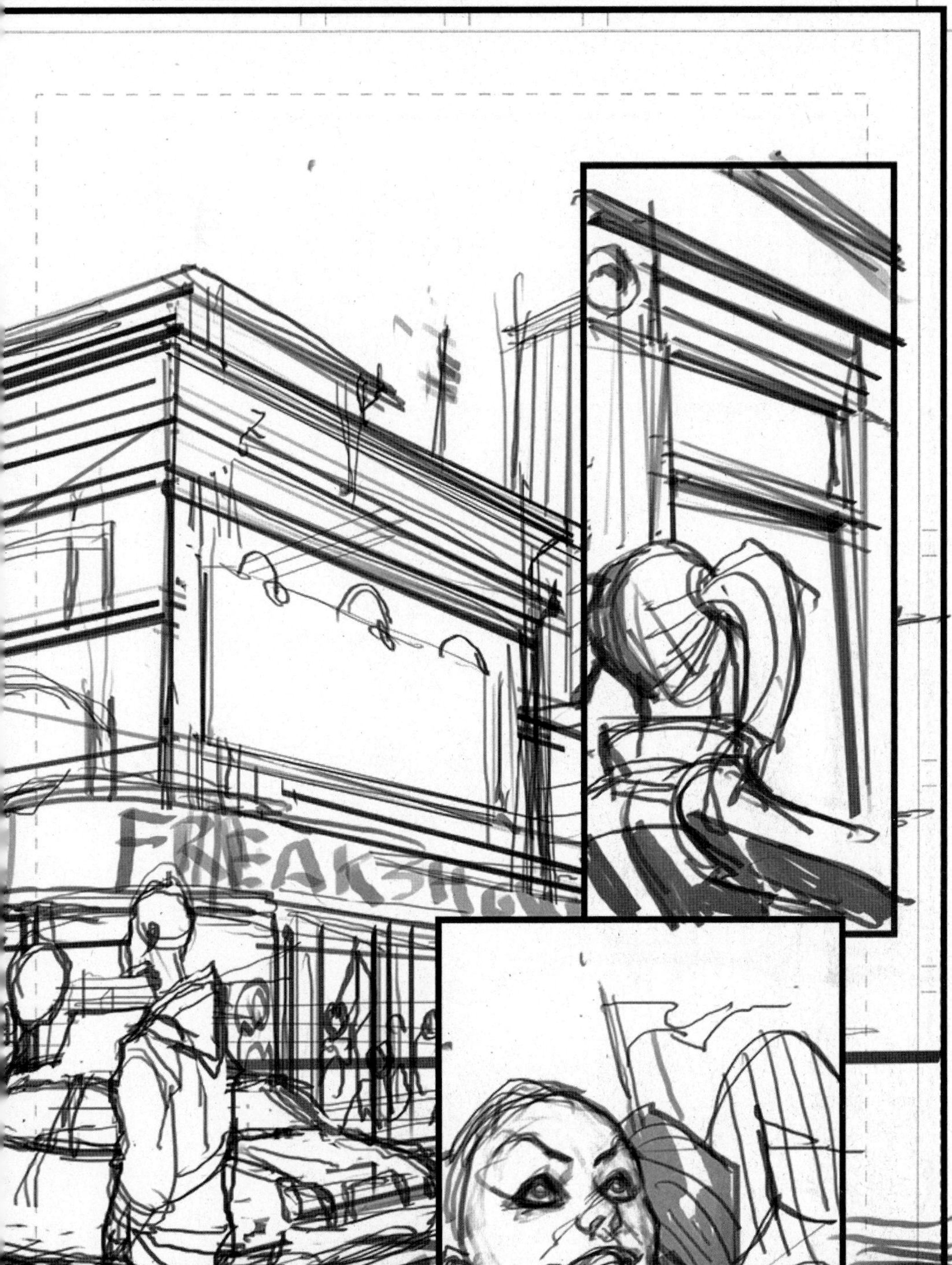
FREAKSH

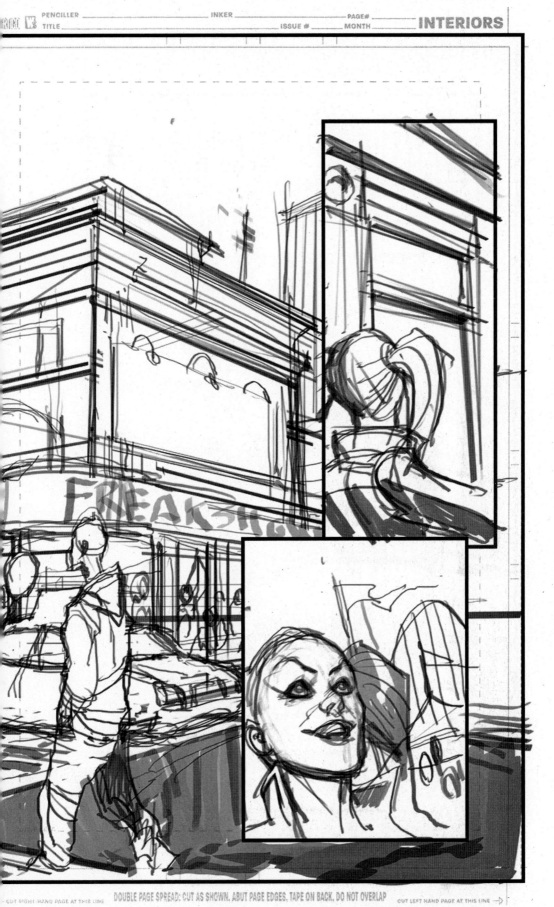

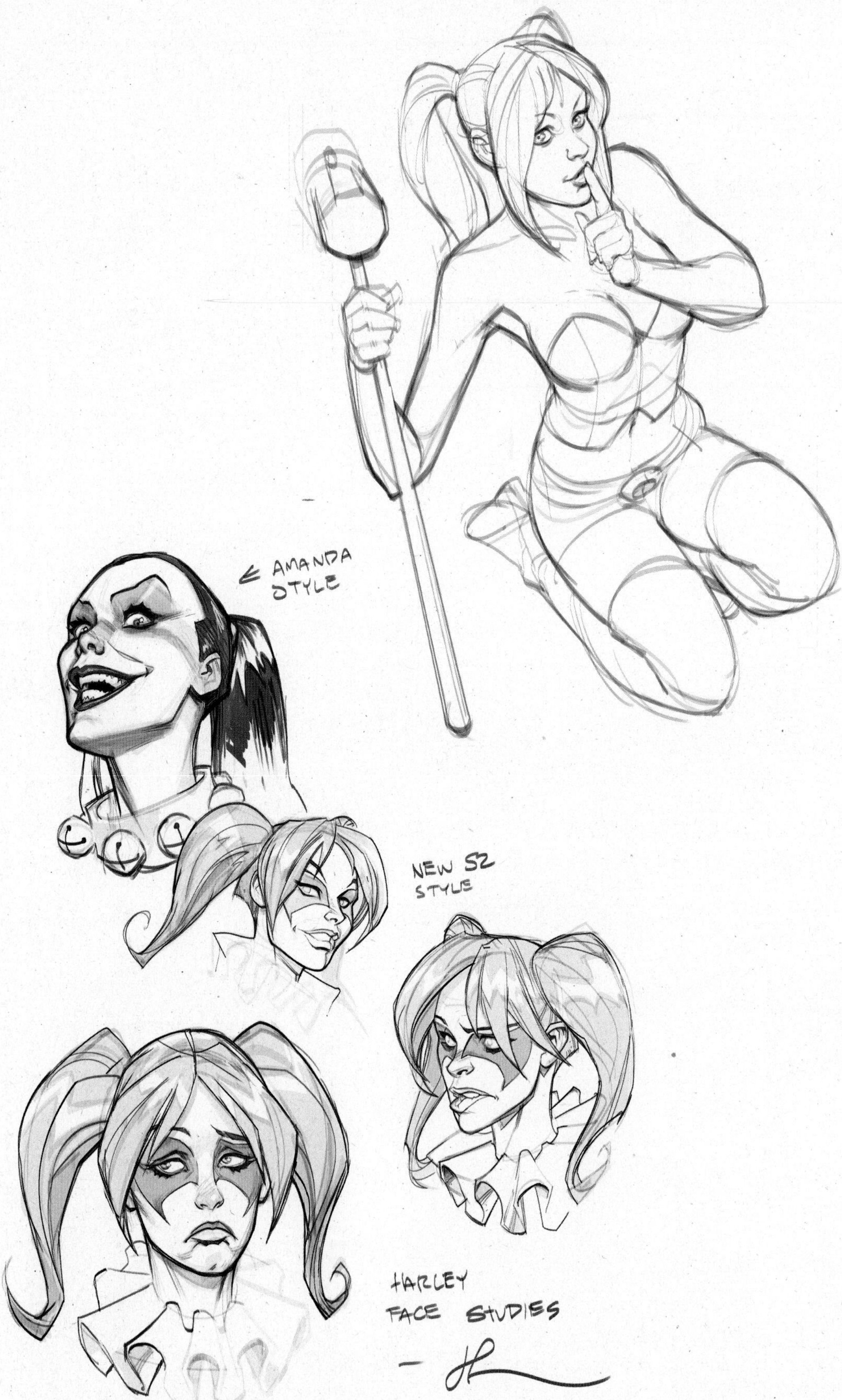

← AMANDA STYLE
NEW 52 STYLE
HARLEY FACE STUDIES